BILL HICKS
AGENT OF EVOLUTION

BILL HICKS
AGENT OF EVOLUTION

KEVIN BOOTH
AND
MICHAEL BERTIN

HarperCollins*Entertainment*
An Imprint of HarperCollins*Publishers*

HarperCollins*Entertainment*
An Imprint of HarperCollins*Publishers*
77–85 Fulham Palace Road,
Hammersmith, London W6 8JB

www.harpercollins.co.uk

Published by HarperCollins*Entertainment* 2005
1

A catalogue record for this book
is available from the British Library

ISBN 0 00 719829 9

Set in Minion

Printed and bound in Great Britain by
Clays Limited, St Ives plc

The authors and publisher are grateful to the following for permission
to use their copyright material:

Plate Section Two: page 8, Bill in Vegas © Estate of Pamela K. Johnson
Plate Section Three: page 2, Bill at the beach © Estate of Pamela K.
Johnson; Bill nurses a swollen knee © Estate of Pamela K. Johnson;
Bill before the Adult Video Awards © Estate of Pamela K. Johnson;
page 6–7, Bill in UK © Chris Saunders

All other photographs are from Kevin Booth's personal collection.

I want to thank my beloved wife Traella for providing constant support throughout this and all our experiences; I believe that Bill helped bring us together. I would also like to thank Cindi Lazzari for introducing me to Michael Bertin; my dad, George Booth, for suffering through my childhood stories; my brother, Curt, for exposing me to real music at age 4 (R.I.P.); and Gary Stamler for being a peacekeeper and a truly fair and balanced person.

Thanks also go to Dave McGurgan for getting me off my ass to work on this book, to Ken Leick for helping to keep this project alive, Robert Smith for dealing with my abrupt Texan-like behaviour, Trevor Dolby for having a cool sounding name, Ben Dunn for having the patience of a saint, to Jane Bennett for being the English schoolteacher I never had and Terence Caven for helping me have better resolution. Also to Larry Stern, Simon Coyle, Mike Wright, Mike Pope, Mary Taylor, Mary Abshier, Amy Sinclair, Spencer Greer, Dave Prewitt & Austin Access, Frederick Troell, Chris Athenas, Travis Marriott, Doug Stanhope, Razor aka Goat Boy the 2nd, KLBJ, Dale Dudley, and Joe Rogan for helping to keep the torch lit. And to all the Hicks fans who have kept his memory alive, I hope this book can leave you with the same feeling I used to get being around Bill.

I would also like to thank Jere Raridon and her sister Lynne (Shotzi) for honouring Bill's memory through the Bill Hicks Foundation for Wildlife.

I would especially like to thank Michael Bertin, who was able to make me sound intelligent and create a book I know would make Bill proud. Capturing a sense of Bill's essence was no easy task.

Thanks to everyone who participated in this book: your love for Bill has kept the circle of hope alive in all of our hearts.

And finally to Bill, teaching me to believe in myself was the greatest gift of all.

I hope we meet again.

Kevin Booth

I happened to be in Sydney, Australia the very day I got the contracts to sign for this book. That night I was having a few drinks with some friends at Circular Quay. At night's end, I took the bus back to where I was staying in Coogee Beach. In the seats in front of me were a three backpackers. Drunk. One of them started talking: "Today a young man on acid realized that all matter is merely energy condensed to a slow vibration, that we are all one consciousness experiencing itself subjectively. There is no such thing as death; life is only a dream, and we are the imagination of ourselves."

He was doing Hicks material and trying to pass it off as his own. Jackie Kennedy and the rifle pendant; a war is when two armies are fighting; and so it went on. I looked at my friend Matt and my jaw dropped. It was verbatim, and it was bizarre.

It kept happening. I was in Chicago, and the first bar I walked into had a little chalkboard hanging up behind the bartender. Scrawled on it were the words: "Every time I think I party too much, I remember that Keith Richards is still alive." Hicks.

Then in Austin, I met a friend for a drink. I went to the bathroom, where the walls were freshly painted to cover a previous generation of urinal wisdom. There was exactly one piece of new graffiti on the wall: "Rush Limbaugh is a scat muncher. Rush Limbaugh munches scat." Hicks again.

The strangest was in Houston, this time at a coffee house. I was sitting down with Bill's friend Andy Huggins. There was a jukebox. It was the kind where if nobody puts any money in after about a half hour, it will just randomly play a song. So I am sitting there with Huggins, and the previously silent machine spits out 'Planet Telex', the lead of track from Radiohead's album *The Bends*. I love that record, so I *know* that it was dedicated to Bill Hicks.

Obscure maybe, but still, there were maybe 100 CDs in the jukebox, each with ten or more tracks. It was a one in 1000 or greater shot. And it was the only song to come out of that thing the entire time Andy and I were talking.

Want more? The final manuscript was submitted on December 16. Bill Hicks' birthday.

Bill Hicks believed in all sort of things that I don't: UFOs, astrology, past-life regression, and just about every religion on the map. He was willing to accept God in any and all forms. As a result of my journey through academia, however, my ontology is far too parsimonious for any of that. But ...

But, the small, romantic part of me really entertained the poetry of it, the notion that someone was watching me and maybe guiding me from beyond. Or if nothing else, just playing with me for his own amusement. For a few moments, some of my most deeply held beliefs were shaken a bit.

It was fun and often comforting to think that maybe Hicks was watching from beyond, but I don't really believe it. Everything that happened can be explained by Hicks' life. That it was so full – full of love, passion, anger, unrest, wisdom, laughter, truth – and that he thought most people were reasonable; and that they thought a lot like him. That's why he spoke to so many people and why he left behind so many traces and souvenirs. People take the ideas Hicks left and keep propagating them throughout the world so that they do keep popping up on a bus, in a bar, a bathroom, or a coffee shop. People will continue perpetuating Hicks, continue populating places with bits of his laughter.

Doing this book was a moving experience for a variety of reasons, but chief among them was meeting the many people that Bill let into his life. I watched people who were strangers minutes and hours previous, sit before me and be moved to laughter and tears as they recalled their friend. And almost every one of them at some point took a moment to themselves, looked out at nothing in particular and muttered to themselves, "God, I miss that guy." You could see how strong a personality Bill was by how alive he still was in his friends. In as much as that's the case, this book is their story. My goal, then, was to stay out of the way.

For that reason the book changes voices. Sections often start or break off into the third person to cover the narrative – just sketch out the basic events in Bill's life – then shift to the words of the people who are still here to tell the story. It's mostly Kevin's voice. He was there from the time Bill started doing comedy until his last days. But the others – Dwight Slade, Laurie Mango, the Houston comics – their words were largely left in their voices. Bill's story is theirs.

People talk about Bill's life and say it was a tragedy that he died so young. Bill's life was *not* a tragedy in any way. Bill's life was a celebration. In 32 years on Planet Earth, Bill Hicks lived more than most of us who are given two or three times that number of years.

That's the lesson of Bill's life. It's for living: for thought, for laughter, for tears. And a person who moves so many other people to think, to laugh, and to cry, that person's life is not a tragedy.

Michael Bertin

PROLOGUE

Kevin Booth

Tripping was very ritualistic for us. It was something we'd prepare for. Meditation. Fasting. Flotation tanks. We even had meals prepared for the comedown, and usually had instruments set up as well so we could play music together to ride out the end of the trip. We weren't just taking psychedelic drugs and running around like crazy people.

It almost always involved us going to my family's ranch near Fredericksburg, Texas. It was 70 sprawling acres of hill country, pocked with enormous live oak trees. There was a 2600-square-foot tract home with a garden and an orchard. Out back was the pond. The reflection of the sun setting over the water made even the monochromatic Texas heat come alive with intense color.

Parts of Bill's routines weren't comedy or jokes: they were directives. When he was talking about mushrooms and he said, "Go to nature. They are sacred," he wasn't kidding. Tripping would allow Bill to commune with nature.

Bill, David Johndrow and I went out to the ranch to trip. We planned and timed everything out. Shrooms were sacred, but they weren't the only thing on the menu. This time we were taking acid. We timed when we dropped so that we would start tripping right as the sun was setting. Once we were tripping, full-on tree-vibrating star-dripping wigging out, we each often had a separate sense of what the others were doing. There would be times when something bad was happening to one of us, and one of the others would just appear. We'd come together and work through it. Then we would have times when we all went out and drifted off on separate paths, only to reconvene at some unspoken spot hours later.

At one point on this particular trip I came across Bill as he was looking pensive and distraught. He was in the yard all by himself, walking in circles. And he was gradually wearing a groove into the grass. I heard him muttering to himself over and over, "What is this thing? Goddammit, what is this thing?" He just kept circling and muttering, circling and muttering. "What is this thing?"

I asked him: "Bill, what are you talking about? What's going on?"

"I don't know, dude. There's just this thing. I don't know what it is, but I've got this thing in me." Bill was pointing to his side, right where his pancreas is, as he was saying this. "I've got this thing inside me," he said. "It needs to come out. It's like an upside-down cross inside of my body. It needs to come out."

Right when he said that – the "upside-down cross" bit – I broke out laughing. Sometimes everything seems funny when you are tripping your nuts off, unless, of course, something is distressing you; and this was obviously distressing Bill.

Fuck. Too late. It sent Bill off.

"Oh, fucking forget it," he fired back, and then, visibly agitated, he stormed off into the woods.

I followed him. "No, I wasn't trying to make fun of you, Bill. What's up? What's wrong?" This was my friend. We were tripping but, shit, he was trying to tell me something important. It got fucked in translation. Drugs can do that.

I tried to assure him I wanted to understand what he was talking about, but he was not going to risk being laughed at again. "Forget it. Nothing," Bill said. I put up a few more weak protests. He brushed them off. And that was that.

That was the summer of 1982, more than a full decade before Bill died of pancreatic cancer.

CHAPTER 1

"I'm not from the States, I'm from Texas."

– Bill Hicks

As a kid in grade school, Bill Hicks was a phenomenal athlete. He was strong, fast, agile. Anyone who ever saw Bill perform stand-up comedy in later years would have a hard time imagining this. With a cigarette dangling off his bottom lip, he'd tell his signature joke about smoking: perusing the front rows of the audience, he'd find someone with a lit cigarette and ask them how much they smoked.

"A pack a day . . . ?" He'd take a drag of his cigarette and inhale like his life depended on that tar-laden cancer stick. "Pussy. I go through two lighters a day."

Bill wasn't exactly a posterboy for athletic prowess. Doubters wouldn't be alone in their skepticism that Bill could ever have run anything but his mouth. A fellow comedian from his Houston hometown who accompanied Bill to New York City for an early Letterman appearance recalls seeing him in the hotel: "He took off his shirt and he didn't have a muscle in his entire upper torso. I've never seen anything like it, it was completely slack. Utter lack of definition. Just zero. It almost had a morgueish quality to it in retrospect."

Dwight Slade, Bill's friend and comedy partner in the formative stage of his career, was in San Francisco in 1991 to perform on the

3

bill with Bill at the Punch Line. The two comedians made an appearance on Alex Bennet's radio show where Bill presented the host with an old 8x10 promo photo of the pair taken when they were just starting out. Bennet looked at the picture and remarked, "Dwight, you look exactly the same. Bill what happened to you?"

Bill replied, "I'd only been drinking for two years then." Bill was 14 in the picture. It was a joke.

Born William Melvin Hicks on 16 December 1961 in Valdosta, Georgia, he was given life and a name he was never ever able to live down. Bill hated his name. "Hate" is a strong word, but Bill *hated* his name. In the early years, he would step on stage and introduce himself, saying, "Good evening, ladies and gentlemen, my name is William Melvin Hicks . . . Thanks, Dad."

He made a short-lived hobby of trying to find successful comedians who had monosyllabic first and last names. He couldn't come up with any besides Bob Hope. Bill even gave serious consideration to legally changing his name. Obviously he stuck with it, but his dissatisfaction never left him.

In late 1991, Bill was at friend Steven Doster's house in Austin. Nirvana had just started to make it big and Bill insisted on taking Doster, a well-respected local guitar player, singer-songwriter, and producer, to local institution Waterloo Records to buy him both the band's albums, *Bleach* and *Nevermind*, then drive around town listening to them.

That was cool with Doster. First, though, he had to take his toddler son, Django, out for a walk. They headed down to the hike-and-bike trail along Town Lake and they walked. Bill says, "So, Steven. You named the kid Django?" Django: named after guitarist Django Reinhardt.

"Yeah, that's his middle name, but it's what everyone calls him," says Doster.

"Of course, you know what's going to happen," Bill baits him.

"What do you mean? Nothing's going to happen to him."

"Surely you, of all people, know what's going to happen," says Bill.

"No, Bill. What do you mean? What are you trying to say?" Doster asks. What, is he destined to suffer a disfigured hand in a fire accident à la his namesake? That's not nice. Bill is just confusing his friend.

"His dad is a songwriter. His mom is a photographer. You named him Django. Surely you know what is going to happen to him?"

"What's going to happen to him?" Doster isn't sure where this is going and is more than a little perplexed. Then Bill grabs Doster around the neck with his hands – friendly, not hostile – and says, "He's going to get sucked and fucked more by the time he's 17 years old than you and I ever did in our goddamn lives."

Bill the reductionist had figured it all out: cool name equals hot ass. His experience was the opposite. Redneck name equals not much ass at all. Jim and Mary Hicks, Bill's parents, should have just called him "Cletus". In addition to the distinctly redneck name, Bill also had the misfortune of being born into a devout Southern Baptist family. With about sixteen million practising patrons, Southern Baptists constitute the largest fundamentalist denomination in the United States. And as fundamentalists they believe the authors of the Bible were inspired by God, making the Bible inerrant. That makes it easy to read: take everything literally.

Convenient for people without any imagination, but it also leads to some bizarre beliefs. Many Southern Baptists really do believe it is a sin to dance. The movie *Footloose* wasn't just pulled from the dregs of a Hollywood executive's brain. Some, not all, but some Baptist theologians maintain that dance is a social form of sexuality. So no go.

When Bill was growing from boy to teen in the Seventies, the Southern Baptists Convention was becoming even more extreme in its beliefs. There was an internal conflict in the church between moderates and fundamentalists, and the liberal factions lost. So, the church then began issuing statements on topics like the submissive role of women and criticizing feminist organizations. It issued a series of prayer guides to help save the non-Christians and lead them to salvation.

Despite his persistent protests and weak attempts to weasel out of it, every Sunday morning Bill was required to go to church. No exceptions. This is the doctrine he was fed; these are the beliefs he was expected to buy into. If every philosophy presupposed a sociology, then it's not hard to see how a reactionary teen looking to get enlightened as much as he was looking to get laid, might have a field day with a religion to which the phrase "figuratively speaking" was meaningless.

Bill's parents claimed they weren't particularly religious; but every Sunday, there the Hicks were in the congregation. According to his mother Mary, "We just knew to go and went."

Unfortunately for Bill, church took place on Sunday morning and Saturday night was the best time to catch late-night comedy. NBC had *Saturday Night Live*. Other networks would program movies late, and later still. Bill was usually up until 2 a.m. watching TV in his room. To him this was the kind of studying that mattered. An 8 a.m. wake-up call for church, though, didn't exactly jive with his preferred sleep schedule.

Like any well-evolved creature Bill had to adapt. He tried resisting entirely, but when that failed, as it invariably did, he would make do. After services Bill would skip Sunday School and go nap in the church library.

Bill's dad, Jim, worked in management for General Motors. He even wore the big GM ring, sporting it like he was a proud graduate of General Motors University. The company odyssey of the South sent Jim to Florida, Alabama, and Georgia, before affording the Hicks family an extended stay in Houston, Texas. The Hicks family bought a two-story hybrid of a colonial and a box in a slice of suburbia called Nottingham Forest, where an olio of shade trees sheltered both sides of the street. It was somewhere between upper-middle and lower upper-class America. The only danger was the boredom.

From the outside it all looked very Norman Rockwell: an immaculately kept house with a pristine lawn (Hicks mythology has it that Jim would measure the cut of the grass with a ruler) in a desirable zip code; 2.3 kids (well, three if you want to get technical – a brother

Steve and a sister Lynn, both older); one dog named Sam, another named Chico. But, the veneer of the happy family wasn't so thick as to be opaque.

As one of Bill's childhood friends recalled, "There were pictures of Bill with Steve and his sister, and I'd ask, 'Bill you've got a sister? You never told me you had a sister.'

"He was curt, responding, 'I don't have a sister.'

"'Well, who is this?'

"'Just some person that was in the house.'" Clearly something was rotten in the state of Denmark. Suburban Houston, too.

As a by-product of this household Bill spent a ridiculous amount of time in his room. It was a sanctuary where he could isolate himself from the foreign world of his parents and inculcate his friends to the virtues of sanity, reason and rock 'n' roll music. Camped in the permanent mess of his bed he listened to everything from Leadbelly to Led Zeppelin while he typed out one-liners.

His brother, Steve, recalls: "He used to write jokes and slide them under my bedroom door. And I would critique them and give them back . . . I didn't even know what it all meant, he just said he was in his room writing all of this stuff."

He was naturally gifted at almost everything. As a junior high football player, Bill's speed and strength made him a natural at running back. He was even more gifted as a baseball player – amazingly so. Little League games are just six innings long; each team needs to get three outs in its half inning. That's eighteen outs. With his wicked curveball and his gangly delivery, Bill regularly accounted for fifteen of those with strike-outs when he was on the mound. That's so unheard of at that level it's gaudy.

It was strange, though, that for all of his natural athleticism, Bill didn't enjoy interacting with direct sunlight, preferring the bright but artificial light of the indoors. Bill and the sun didn't see eye to eye. As a rule, he kept the blinds in his room drawn. The truth is, Bill probably saw as much sun on the small black-and-white TV in his room as in the sky outside. He wasn't a shut-in, latch-key kid, but his room was his refuge from his family. He would stay up and watch *The Tonight Show*. He would read, he would write, and he would listen to records. Everything you needed in order to divine the make-up of a young Bill Hicks, you could get by watching him in his native habitat. Muddy Waters on the stereo, dog-eared copy of *The Hobbit* on the bed, posters of Jimi Hendrix and Woody Allen papering the walls.

That was Bill's yin and yang right there – Jimi and Woody. Bill gave the credit to Allen, more than anyone, for inspiring him to get into comedy. He was 13 or 14 when he first saw Allen in the movie *What's Up, Pussycat?* Later in life Bill himself gave conflicting accounts of that seminal moment. In fact, as Bill got older, the age at which he claimed Allen first infected his life got younger. In an interview Bill gave in the last month of his life, he said that he was 12 and that movie was *Casino Royale*.

Either the next day or the following summer – again, he gave multiple accounts – Bill was in a bookstore and picked up a copy of *Without Feathers*. Years later he confessed to an interviewer he couldn't even explain the affinity. "I'm not Jewish. I'm not short. I'm not a schlemel."

A pre-teen Bill had just seen Allen in *Casino Royale* about the time he met one Dwight Slade. It was in the summer of 1974, when they were both between the 6th and 7th grades at Spring Forest Junior High. They were playing touch football with mutual friends. Dwight recalled simply, "He was odd-looking. Very odd-looking." With jet-black hair, black eyes, and vaguely Asian-looking features, Bill's appearance was not what you would expect for someone with such an authentically Southern genetic make-up.

Bill had become enamored with Woody Allen's character of Dr. Noah in *Casino Royale*. It was the basis for the goofy impersonations he was doing at the time. The physical humor was something that Dwight not only instantly understood, but could match Bill in doing. The two became fast friends and developed a relationship that was part collaborative and part competitive. Recalls Slade: "We would mutually crack each other up, but we also had a sort of sibling rivalry as to who could make our friends laugh more."

"I don't remember the specific moment, but he told me: 'We ought to be comedians. We ought to be a comedy team.' I said, 'I want to be an actor.' That was my dream when I was a kid. But when he said that I thought, 'Well, finally here's a guy that speaks my language.' He goes, 'We should be comics. I've written some jokes.' I went over to his house and he showed me. Here's a guy who thinks like me, I thought. And for Bill I think there was even more of a sense that, 'Oh my God, I'm not the only crazy person here. I'm not the only person that wants to do something out of the norm.'"

Corny as it sounds, the two developed a really sweet friendship. For example, Dwight's Boy Scout meetings took place at St. John Vianney Catholic Church, whose grounds ran right up to the Hicks' backyard fence. During breaks in the Boy Scouting, Dwight would go over to Bill's and throw a rock up at Bill's window to get his attention. Bill would open the window and they would talk.

By the time Bill got to high school, despite his natural physical gifts he had all but left sports behind. He stopped playing football; he stopped playing baseball. He kept running track in the 9th grade, then in the first part of the 10th grade. But that was it. Slade explains, "It wasn't because Bill didn't like athletics, but he hated what it was becoming in high school."

High-school sports were like a religion in Texas. High-school football *was* a religion in Texas. Stadia across the state turned small-town communities into congregations of a sort. Texans from Snook to Shiner easily spent more time on Friday nights in the fall watching the local kids run around the gridiron than they ever spent listening to sermons on Sundays. It was a ratio of about three to one. And Stratford High School didn't just win, it won state championships. Okay, *a* state championship during Bill's junior year ("State in '78" was the rallying cry); but still, for a 17-year-old kid in Texas, being part of a state championship team would endow you with near god-like status. Stratford's football team was fairly exceptional. The star running back, Craig James, later started for the New England Patriot team that played in Super Bowl XX. And Stratford standout Chuck Thomas was the back-up center for the San Francisco 49ers team that won Super Bowls XXIII and XXIV.

This is the environment Bill grew up in. If he had wanted it, Bill could easily have been part of the privileged jockocracy. He had all the physical tools needed to be a star athlete. Coolness, popularity, cheerleaders – if Bill had kept playing football and baseball, he could have had access to all the things that make high school a non-traumatic experience for a teen. But he opted out, and that's where Bill spent the "best years of his life" – a common moniker for that four-year high-school slice of American life.

On the outside. That's where he belonged. Bill was a misfit, both within his family and, with few exceptions, amongst his peers. He didn't drink, and couldn't understand why people did. He wasn't social and he didn't go to high-school parties ("keggers"). He liked to read. He was obsessed with *Huckleberry Finn*, *The Hardy Boys* and *The Hobbit*. Mystery and adventure were clearly his favorites.

Bill wasn't a loser, but high school is pretty binary: either you're cool or you aren't. Bill wasn't in the cool clique. But he had friends and, even though he valued his privacy and being left alone, he wasn't a loner. Most importantly he had Dwight and, once in high-school, Kevin Booth, a neighborhood kid in the class one year ahead of Bill and Dwight.

It was serendipitous that Bill hadn't dropped out of sports completely during his freshman year at Stratford because it was in track that both Bill and Dwight first formed a relationship with co-conspirator-to-be Kevin Booth. They were on the track for practice – well, they were out there in their track clothes, but not doing much practising – when Booth approached the pair to say hi. "What's up? I'm the guy you met yesterday at lunch."

With the two similarly subversive minds of Dwight and Kevin, Bill would begin dabbling in the two activities that would occupy the rest of his life – music and comedy.

That day on the track with Kevin, Bill and Dwight started talking about putting a band together. They had outlandish ideas about what they wanted to do – "We need to have a big stage show with lights and smoke and we want to have bombs going off and lights and big speakers."

"I told them, 'Okay, I know how we can do that,'" Booth remembers. "They were thinking I was full of shit, but I said, 'Why don't you guys come over to my house tonight and we'll get started.'" In Booth they had stumbled across someone with the technical know-how to pull off their oversized designs. They took Booth up on his offer and that night they began their journey to rock stardom. But there was a slight hitch: they didn't have musical instruments; nor did they have the ability to play instruments.

They called themselves Stress. It was perfect. It sounded punk rock. More importantly, it was monosyllabic and ended with two s's. That sounds a bit arbitrary, but it turned out to be an unintentional asset. Every child of the Seventies in America knew the phrase: "You wanted the best, you got the best! The hottest band in the land, Kiss." It was the band's stage introduction on the multi-platinum-selling Kiss *Alive!* Dwight and Bill were big Kiss fans. Huge.

It was hard not to be. In the mid-Seventies Kiss were omnipresent.

One day the guys were talking about making smoke bombs for their stage show. Kevin, of course, chimed in: "I know how to make smoke bombs." He went out and got some dry ice, then they all convened at Dwight's. They sat in his room in a little circle around a bucket. Kevin poured some water on the dry ice in the bucket. The teens watched this tiny stream of smoke frothing up from the bucket while they listened to Kiss records and talked about how they were going to be bigger than Kiss and have a bigger stage show than Kiss. Bill and Dwight held flashlights, pointed them into the smoke and waved them back and forth. They understood the theater of rock, but they weren't even community theater of rock.

But now they were Stress, it was like joining Kiss vicariously. All they had to do was substitute the one word. "You wanted the best, you got the best! The hottest band in the land, Stress." Bill and Dwight would pass each other in the halls of school and greet each other with that rock 'n' roll catchphrase intro. It was plug and play hype. They started taking pictures of themselves in their best rock star poses and circulating the pictures at school. Never mind that they didn't have things like songs or proper instruments. They had pictures. That made it real.

One day Bill was called into the vice principal's office. Bill looked down at the table in the room and saw the word "Stress" carved into it, complete with the Kiss lightning bolt s's. Graffiti was a pretty solid accomplishment for a band that hadn't actually played in front of anybody.

Stress became almost a daily activity for Bill, Dwight, Kevin and miscellaneous other friends who floated in and out of the still-amorphous band. Bruce Salmon, Mike Groner, Steve Fluke, John Terry, all had stints of varying length as members of Stress. Basically, all it took was showing up some afternoon to play at least once. That earned you a place in the lore of Stress genealogy.

Salmon wasn't just a frequent participant early on, but was a co-founder. His older brother had been in bands with Kevin's older brother, and between Kevin and Bruce, they offered an invaluable asset to the fledgling band: Kevin could borrow a bass guitar from his brother; Bruce knew how to play it.

Still, initially it was a band by committee. Who wants to play what? Bill had an acoustic guitar that, depending on how you looked at it, had either a couple of strings missing or had a couple of strings. Sometimes Dwight sang, sometimes he played bass. Kevin played a plastic garbage can for a drum. They miked up everything as best they could to achieve maximum distortion, and proceeded to make noise. Again, their aspirations were way beyond their abilities, but that didn't deter them.

Comedy was something Bill did in parallel to music. The two weren't mutually exclusive: he loved both, and he invested hours of time working on both. Bill and Dwight were already spending much of their after-school time hanging out, but in the 7th grade, joke writing was still a solo activity for Bill. By the time the summer of 1975 rolled around, things began to change. Bill and Dwight were listening to sets by comedians – Johnny Carson, Merv Griffin – taped from the late-night talk shows with a hand-held audio recorder.

They were also developing more characters; better imitations of their goofy parents. Then, a couple of months into 8th grade, Dwight's brother got his hands on a copy of Woody Allen doing stand-up in his nightclub routine. Big deal? In the mid-Seventies it was. This was like finding a copy of the Zapruder film. This was cooler than being made a general in the Kiss Army.

And it's what really brought them together not just as friends with similar interests and tastes, but as a comedy team. "It was our first writing of jokes together," Slade recalls. "Most of them were his, and I mostly just tagged on to them in the beginning. I was writing my own, but Bill was way ahead of me. My jokes were really simplistic and idiotic, to be honest. It wasn't until then – and it's so ridiculous to talk in these terms – but it wasn't until 8th grade that I started to mature in my joke writing."

Bill and Dwight also started working on their own play, *Death*. It was highly derivative of Woody Allen's play *Death Knocks* (not to be confused with the Allen play of the same name, *Death*, that would become the loose basis of his movie *Shadows and Fog*). They tried out for the 8th grade talent show. Woody Allen, however, apparently wasn't good enough for an 8th grade talent show. And as his apostles, Bill and Dwight weren't either. They failed the audition. "Inspired" as it might have been by Allen, the play was not without its own originality and humor. Thirty years later, Slade half-jokes, "I'm still bitter."

There was a silver lining. The Spring Forest Junior High drama teacher asked them to perform their play for the speech class. They happily obliged. In front of the willing audience, Bill and Dwight were stellar. They got real laughs, real applause. They were now as encouraged as they had been dejected after the rejection from the talent show. Their intuition that they were good at this – at writing, at creating, at getting laughs – was correct.

By that time Bill and Dwight (performing under the stage names of Mel and Hal – their middle names) had a fair amount of material: three monologues of about fifteen minutes each, plus the play. They had already put together a half-hour tape of their best stuff and sent it to local agents in hopes of having someone do the legwork of getting them gigs, and also gaining some legitimacy. As it was, they weren't doing so great by themselves.

They still had some hard lessons to learn. Later that month Bill and Dwight saw an ad in the *Houston Chronicle* for open auditions for the Easter Seals Telethon in April. They were still keeping their ambitions clandestine, and couldn't ask their parents for rides. So they took their bikes across town. Drenched from the effort, with the aide of Houston's humidity – like a natural sauna 365 days a year – they arrived at the local school for the deaf where the auditions were being held.

Trying to cool off and stay calm, they did about ten minutes for the judges. Mel and Hal were told they were great writers. They got a "we'll let you know." For artistic teens, this was doubly hellish: in their budding social lives they were getting, "let's just be friends" from the ladies; in their budding careers they were getting the showbiz equivalent. Mel and Hal never heard back from the Easter Seals folks. Neither did Bill and Dwight, for that matter.

On the upside, Bill and Dwight had done their first stand-up gig together.

They soon came across another ad in the paper: an open audition for a restaurant that put on live entertainers. Again, they took their bikes to the restaurant. They ended up in a room in front of five or six adults – restaurant and nightclub owners – who, in Slade's words, "laughed their asses off." Not because two kids showed up, but because of the comedy the kids did. These adults, with no obligations to like them, loved them. Bill and Dwight knew one thing: even

14

if they weren't getting work, they were getting laughs. They had a good solid six minutes of material.

They had also got themselves hooked up with Universal Talent. When Dwight and Bill started looking for agents, they didn't even know what a headshot was. It's not the kind of thing a 14-year-old should know for any particular reason, but it was indicative of the gap between what they were and what they wanted to be. Even the most basic facts about the business of entertainment as a business were beyond them.

Add this ignorance to the fact that they were essentially sneaking around behind their parents' backs, and it's all the more miraculous that they even dared to endeavor this endeavor. They had to call around studios looking for a photographer. When they were able to lowball someone to a price they could afford, they still had to ride their bikes (again) miles across town to the get the shots taken. On top of that, Bill was having to pilfer sweaters from his dad so that he could wear something presentable in the pictures. Finally, when the contact sheets arrived at Bill's house for review, Mary Hicks opened the package before Bill could intercept the mail. That caused another row in the house. One: what the heck were the pictures for? Two: why the heck was Bill wearing his father's sweater in them?

A meeting at Universal Talent? That was another 20-mile bike ride across town. Two hours on two wheels for about two minutes in the offices. Beverly the assistant told the sweat-drenched duo, "We'll give you a call." Nothing was easy. At least they were staying fit.

That summer, 1976, Bill attended camp. Church camp, actually. Somewhere out in West Texas. There he did his first solo stand-up gig. "I was absolutely terrified," he confessed years later. "Not the least reason was that it was a church camp and a lot of the guys who I had been watching were like nightclub comics and Richard Pryor, so obviously I had to edit on my feet a little bit. I felt like I had made a huge mistake and I should have been in the 'Kumbaya' chorus that went up before me." But after the show Hicks was accosted by more than one of his peers wanting to know how he had the courage to get up and do that in front of people.

"I don't remember the exact thing that got the first laugh. I know I had, like, fourteen minutes of material, and, like, seven minutes of it was stolen, or someone else's, like, Woody Allen material which nobody in Baptist West Texas country would ever be able to trace."

Bill didn't tell his parents but it wasn't like he could keep it a secret. He did have the camp, staff and all, as an audience. One of the jokes he told was: "Ladies and gentleman, I had a rough upbringing. I was breast-fed . . . On falsies."

Mary Hicks found out about Bill's stand-up performance from one of the other ladies at Sunday School. Mary then went to the church's assistant pastor to get more details. The pastor told Mary, "You might want to look at how you raised him." Clearly Bill was correct in thinking no one there would ever be able to source his material. (Allen's actual line: "I was in analysis for years because of a traumatic childhood; I was breast-fed through falsies.")

Another faculty member of the Sunday School told Mrs. Hicks that her son thought Bill's comedy was the funniest thing he had ever heard. Bill's first show; Bill's first rave review.

In the fall of 1976, Bill and Dwight were starting as freshmen at Stratford High School. Stratford was a shit-brown brick building with a mod-deco facade. And the near-windowless exterior made it look more like the kind of place where you would have line-up and lock-down than you would take roll. It was somewhere between eyesore and oddity. It hadn't produced any poet laureates. It produced country music star Clint Black.

Right about the time Bill and Dwight were supposed to start high school, they also got a shot at what could have been the biggest gig of their lives . . . or the worst. While, over time, the Jerry Lewis Labor Day Telethon has morphed into a parade of has-beens, back in those days it was a fixture of Americana: Elvis, John Lennon and Sinatra all made appearances. Plus, it was raising money for kids with muscular dystrophy.

The way the telethon works, there is a national show supported by dozens if not hundreds of smaller, regional shows all running concurrently. During the broadcast, the network cuts back and forth from the national to the regional shows. In Houston, this was being held in a restaurant, and the restaurant needed to book acts for the entire forty-eight hours of the telethon.

Frantic to fill the time slots, the telethon's bookers called all of the agencies around town asking, "Who do you have? What can you give us?" Universal Talent called Bill and Dwight asking how much time they could do. They had their normal set of about a half hour, and they had the play. Beverly at Universal told them: "We have three hours we need to fill." Bill replied: "We can fill it all."

"Our idea was that it was going to broadcast on TV," says Slade. "In reality, maybe it was going to be on in the background of the local show." They had no idea even what kind of gig it was. It didn't matter. When they went to their parents to ask permission, they got turned down flat.

Bill spent the bulk of his freshman year working on comedy by using his classmates as his audience. One teacher tried a creative solution to curtail Bill's interrupting of class: she offered him the first five minutes of class. That time was his to get it out of his system. The rest was hers for teaching. Giving Bill the Sudetenland. Bad idea.

Mary recalls, "One of the teachers called me and asked me if I could help her get her class back from Bill. She said, 'I told him he could have five minutes while I was checking the roll,' and she said, 'I can't get it back.' I said, 'That's your problem, you shouldn't have let him get up there.'"

At lunch Bill and Dwight would resume their tag team activities by terrorizing the lunchroom. It was a low-paying gig, but it was a guaranteed booking five days a week. It was proto-guerilla theater. They would perform fake fights, do outrageous character pieces, flip tables and chairs. It was adolescent lunacy. And it was non-stop.

This would continue in track, at the end of the school day. Dwight and Bill would be jogging around the oval. Bill would inch in front of Dwight, slow, then bend over. An oblivious Dwight would unwillingly nail Bill in the ass from behind. Mime sodomy. During the fall, this went on in front of the football team. The team would be practising on the field; Dwight and Bill would be doing their schtick on the track encircling that field. They were performing for their friends on the football team, the people they knew who thought they were funny; but they were also pissing off some of the upperclassmen. It was bad enough that the comedic kids were getting attention in the lunchroom, but carrying it out to the sports arena – that was just showing them up.

"It was almost like doing antics in front of an ape in the zoo. They were initially just confused, then they would want to kill and beat and hit," says Slade. "I remember seeing them once look at each other and nod and take off running after us. It was terrifying because these were very large Texas football players."

Late in their freshman year, Dwight handed Bill a book by Ruth Montgomery called *A World Beyond*. The light went on. Dwight had had a very intense dream about death, and something in the book spoke very specifically to him about what had happened. When Bill read the book, he was similarly blown away. Destiny, fate, choosing your life; the way Montgomery wrote about these things Bill found very comforting. Bill and Dwight spent hours together talking about these concerns. Hours and hours. Southern Baptist tenets, those were his parents' beliefs. Other spiritual avenues were opening up to Bill.

The Beatles had made the Maharishi a hipster-household name in the late Sixties, but by 1975 he had become mainstream, appearing on the 13 October cover of *Time* magazine with the teaser: "Meditation: The Answer to all Your Problems?" Still, it was a bit of a coup when Bill got his parents to allow him to attend a transcendental meditation retreat over the Thanksgiving weekend of his sophomore year. While largely a secular celebration, Thanksgiving is one of the top two family-centric holidays in America. For Bill to be able to leave the Hicks family to hang out with strangers (save

18

Dwight), and do things that his parents not only didn't fully understand but also didn't subscribe to belief-wise, was astounding.

It's no less amazing that Bill and Dwight (this time with Dwight's older brother Kevin) gained permission to attend a second retreat over Christmas break. It was not only longer – a full week instead of a holiday weekend – it was right as families are about to celebrate the birth of Jesus Christ. If the Thanksgiving retreat was a coup, the Christmas one was a minor miracle.

It wasn't the last bit of karmic kismet the pair had in store. During the following semester of school, in April the *Houston Chronicle* ran a feature on a new comedy club in town. This was it. This was the answer. Prior to this, Dwight had been combing the want ads for "Entertainer" under "E", or "C" for Comedians. Obviously there was nothing available for 14-year-old stand-ups. As he describes it, "It was just stupid." Now they had an outlet. About a week after seeing the feature in the *Chronicle*, Dwight and Bill sneaked out of their houses and were standing on the stage of the Comedy Workshop, performing their material in front of a paying adult audience. But it was just a little too late. Dwight had known for months that at the end of the school year his family would be moving to Oregon.

"It was intoxicating," as Slade recalls, "but there was this horror because here we are and we are really clicking, but we knew I have to leave."

They were also found out by their parents and grounded for the rest of their adolescence.

[*   *   *]

Kevin Booth

Who am I? Well, I'll give you an idea. The last few months I've
been doing a one-man show – like a lot of comics these days are
doing one-man shows, and I am no exception . . . The theme of
the one-man show is about my life growing up, as I did, in a
happy, healthy and loving family. And it's called "Let's Spend
Half a Minute with Bill." And uh . . . Well, hell, it's such a short
show I can do it for you right now:

"Good evening, everybody. Mommy never beat me. And
Daddy never fucked me. Goodnight."

I don't know if the show will be able to relate with dysfunctional America, but that's the way I was raised. Sorry. No bone
to pick. Supported me in everything I did.

– Bill Hicks

It's true. Bill's parents supported him. When Bill wanted to be a
musician, his parents dropped $1000 buying him a Fender
Stratocaster guitar and an amplifier to go with it.

When Bill decided he wanted to move to LA after high school
and pursue a career in comedy instead of going to college, his
parents agreed to pay rent on his apartment in the San Fernando
Valley. They even bought him a Chevette so he had a car to get
around in.

Certainly Bill didn't mean the bit about his parents to be taken
literally. The strand of Baptist fundamentalism that wanted to take
everything literally was antithetical to the core of Bill's identity and
everything he ever preached. Still, things were a lot less black-and-
white when it came to the doctrine's notion of the "happy, healthy,
loving" family.

I remember the first time I met Bill's mom. Bill and I were standing in the kitchen of his house, having this hush-hush conversation.
To anyone watching, it must have looked like we were doing a drug

deal. But we were talking about the stage show for our band, Stress, the one that didn't even exist yet. Bill already had arena-sized ideas: "We'll have this one song where we do the explosion thing, and one of the guys will jump out on stage with a fifty-foot papier-maché penis that starts coming over the audience. And the girls . . ."

Right then Bill's mom walked into the kitchen. "Who's your friend, Bill?" Bill's response was less happy, healthy or loving than I ever could have ever expected.

"Godammit, Mom, I fucking hate your guts." He stormed out of the kitchen. I was left standing there. Just me and Mary Hicks. "Uh, hi. I'm Kevin Booth." Thanks, Bill.

His mom's response was as surreal as it was calm, as in her heavy southern drawl she asked, "Do you want some pineapple, Kevin?" Did she not hear what I just heard? I said no thanks to the pineapple.

My lasting image of Bill's dad, Jim Hicks, is a lot more pedestrian but no less ridiculous. The neighborhood association where we lived, Nottingham Forest, would award "Yard of the Month" to the spot with the nicest yard. Bill's dad won the honor frequently enough that Jim could have landscaped in a home for the accompanying sign: it was almost a permanent fixture.

Jim proudly displayed the fuck out of that thing. Tending to the yard – that's how I will always remember Jim. Outside at the break of dawn; Saturday and Sunday mornings; sporting his black socks and sock garters while mowing the lawn or clipping the hedges. Bill made endless fun of his dad for that, and for other aspects of his character Bill found embarrassing; but he also had deep respect for his father's work ethic. Still, when Bill started to set foot on the stage it was open season and many of Bill's characters were just variations on the theme of Jim.

One of my bands wrote a song about Jim years later, called "Yard of the Month." Jim Hicks was like no other father I had ever met. He wasn't just Bill's father. Sometimes it was like he was your father, too.

21

Anytime anyone went to Bill's house, they had to get past Jim, who was always doing that classic "father" pose Bill often mimicked on stage – right arm cocked behind his head, lips pressed forward sternly, eyes squinting and laden with seriousness. Bill would coach you that when you entered the house, go straight to his room. Just go past his dad. Ignore. Just keep going. He could do it. His friends couldn't.

"Where you goin', son?" Jim would start with a heavy southern drawl to match his wife's – the one that almost made "Bill" into a two-syllable word. The question was like gravity: you couldn't ignore it. You were now getting cross-examined by Jim. How you were doing in school, how your parents were, etc.

Bill loved his parents, and they loved him. But they were Baptists. Specifically, Southern Baptists. In Texas we have First Baptists, Second Baptists and Southern Baptists. I know Baptists who don't know the differences between the subsets, but the Hicks were so Baptist that the differences made a difference to them.

My earliest recollections of Bill are in the lunchroom where he used to "perform" on an almost daily basis with his classmate Dwight Slade. For example, they did this one bit in the school cafeteria where Dwight put some raisins into a spoon, and Bill was going to give the raisins to some lucky girl as a gift. Off Bill flew with havoc following. He was running over tables, tripping over chairs, crashing into people. Trays of food and milk were flying into the air. All the while Bill was doing everything necessary to keep the raisins in the spoon. As the commotion grew so did the gathering crowd, as people were trying to see what the big deal was. Well, the "big deal" turned out to be that Bill was presenting a spoonful of raisins to a completely unimpressed young lady. It didn't really win over the audience, either.

But it's a perfect image of who Bill was at that age. It was more important to make a lasting impression than to make a good first impression. He could have said something nice to that girl, and been done with it. Maybe compliment her. But no, there had to be a clumsy production to make sure she didn't forget.

It was also somewhat standard fare of Bill's formative years with Dwight. Here you had these two little punk-ass kids coming in and trying to be funny by acting weird and wacky. In reality, though, everyone thought they were losers. In fact, they were considered more than just losers. The difference between them and the regular losers was that they were also extroverts. Most of the geekier people in junior high and high school tended to withdraw into themselves. Not Bill and Dwight. They seemed actively to enjoy seeing how strange they could behave in front of people to rile them up.

Still, as a personality, I was drawn to Bill. We talked one day during lunch. Then a couple of days later during track practice I went up to say "hi" again. And before I knew it, we were hanging out together seemingly all the time. Lunch, track, after school. In fact, it was track that helped us become rock stars. "Rock stars" is obviously overstating it, given our modest success in high school as musicians. But track certainly wasn't exercise; an exercise in convenience, perhaps.

While it was a year-round sport, track was really just another way for the football team to train together in the spring. In Texas there were rules limiting the amount of time high-school football teams could spend practising. Those limits were usually exhausted during the season in the fall. Across the state, shrewd and smarmy coaches alike would sign the entire football team up for track in the spring, football's off-season. Voilà. They were no longer the "football" team. Rules averted.

So Bill and I were technically running track; however, track was the last class of the school day. And, in the spring, the coaches were generally only concerned with the football players. That meant we were actually doing one of two things. If there was no roll call, Bill and I would leave school, go to my house, and play music. If there was going to be a roll call at the end of class, we would go to sleep on the pole vault mats.

There were advantages to track. Being out there amongst the jocks gave Bill opportunities aplenty to make fun of them. And, of course, when he and Dwight would do these ridiculously stupid things right in people's faces, it only made people want to inflict bodily harm on them that much more.

There were more than a few incidents when Bill got chased. He and I once did an interview with *New Yorker* theater critic John Lahr where I talked about one of these incidents. Bill was sitting right next to me as I finished by saying, "They caught Bill and Dwight and beat the shit out of them."

Bill interrupted me. He was adamant: "No, Kevin, they never caught us. They never caught us and they never beat us." It wasn't nit-picking; it was important to Bill that the truth be known. And the truth is, for a guy who looked so thoroughly unathletic, Bill was a damned fast runner at that time. Damned fast. They chased. They didn't catch.

Bill ran in several track meets before giving it up; and again it wasn't that he wasn't good, he just stopped caring. He got more into music; he stopped caring about sports, stopped running track, stopped playing baseball. Sports had definite objectives – score runs, cross the finish line first, etc. Music gave you more latitude. Here's three minutes of nothing, fill it however you want. Ready? Go! That was clearly more in line with Bill's ethic.

My parents thought Bill was a terrible influence on my life. I'm sure Bill's parents thought the same about me, but Bill was actually one of the best things ever to happen to me; and at that point in my life, Bill kept me out of trouble. I don't think one of our earliest attempts to put a band together, however, would do anything to prove either set of parents wrong. It was born out of misguided anger – inexcusably misguided anger.

We had already been "playing" as Stress when Dwight had a teen crush on a girl, Mila Goldstein, reciprocated. She was, as you might suspect with that name, Jewish. The informal flirtation fell apart and, burned by young love gone wrong, we fought fire with fire by writing a handful of songs. Specifically, songs that made fun of Jews.

We temporarily changed the band name for the occasion, calling ourselves Joe Arab and the Nazis.

In hindsight it was clearly not the brightest of ideas. In fact, maybe it was the dumbest. Despite how much, *prima facie*, it looks to the contrary, it wasn't anti-semitic.

It wasn't anything more than teen angst. Hell, we didn't even know what it meant to be anti-semitic. This was long before the History Channel was pumped into every house in America. There weren't daily documentaries on Hitler and World War II running 24/7 on TV. We weren't very attentive students, either. Plus, think about it: blue, poo, you, shoe, do, dew, screw . . . it rhymes with everything. Given our amateurish creative skills, that only served to help.

We just didn't know – clearly a by-product of our padded suburban upbringing. If Mila had been Italian, we probably would have called ourselves Giuseppe Franco and the Fascists, without knowing what it meant to be fascist. We were kids. Dwight was hurt. We saw our friend suffering. It was a catharsis. That's all.

We may have been stupid (sorry Mila), but we weren't *that* stupid. Only half the reason for putting a band together in the first place was a desire to make music. Less than half: everything always came back around to us trying to find ways to meet girls. Never mind that we were borrowing instruments we couldn't even play from siblings and friends. We had stage props. We had photos. And we had a good line of bullshit ("Yeah, we're in a band"). That was enough to make it real. And being a teenage musician, that was a way to meet girls and impress them before you even had to open your mouth. Even better, write a song for a girl. That would get you in her pants, conditional on meeting her, of course.

Bill was smitten with a girl named Tammy Blue and he came up with this song for her called "Moment of Ecstasy." He told her to come over to my house so we could play a private gig for her. Bill transformed himself into a rock star for the occasion. We might have been standing in the study of my suburban home, but Bill was playing a rock show to a stadium crowd. And there isn't a bridge long enough to link the gap between what was happening in Bill's head and what was happening in my house. My drum? The bottom of a plastic trash can. Dwight had a bass I had borrowed from my brother. Bruce was playing an acoustic guitar that had a couple of strings still intact. We dropped a mic into it and ran it through the same amplifier as the drum.

Then we played Bill's song, which was a really charming number about cuming on a girl's face.

Our moment of ecstasy
I see you laying next to me
And I know it's gonna be right.
Cause I've got it hot, I've got it hot.
And you're not gonna get by
Cause I'll be cummin' in your eye.
Cummin' in your face.
Baby it ain't no disgrace
I'm gonna let it rip all over your lip
Gonna be cum in your face
Cum, cum, cum in your face.

It's funny because Bill was such an innocent guy with no sexual experience. None. Yet here he was, singing ridiculously nasty lyrics.

Everything about Stress was rinky-dink at that point, but it was what we had. It was a doctrine Bill never abandoned. What tools do you have? That was Bill's only question. What do you have? You have a beat-up guitar with just a couple of strings on it? Fine. What can you play on a beat-up guitar with just a couple of strings on it? Pick it up and find out.

It was a very simple choice for Bill: do you want to sit around doing nothing while waiting for someone to give you some better equipment (or money, or whatever resources) so you can do things how you think they are supposed to be done? Or do you want to use what you have and start right now?

To Bill it was an easy choice. Start. Do it now. All you have is a trash can? Then turn the damn thing over and start banging on it. Now it's a drum and you're making music. That spirit and that attitude were infectious. Soon Bill and I were checking out books from the library trying to figure out how to make gunpowder so we could have real smoke bombs to go with our fake band. God, if we weren't a fire hazard we sure looked like one. We made as much (if not more) smoke as noise. I even got my mom involved and she helped make a sign for the band. I cut out the letters S-T-R-E-S-S (yes, they were lightning-bolt s's) from cardboard and wrapped them in tinfoil, while my mom poked holes in the letters and threaded Christmas lights through them.

That's why it was so much fun to be around Bill. He didn't wait for people to give him permission to do what he wanted. He stayed that way through his whole life. When we were older and still struggling, he never waited; he was happy to cobble together whatever resources he could. He never wanted to waste time. It's like he knew he only had a limited amount of it.

The state of Texas allows you to get a driver's license before the legal minimum age of 16 if your family can demonstrate that the child *not* having one would somehow cause a hardship for the family. Because my family had a ranch, somehow this allowed me to get such a "hardship" driver's license. It was complete bullshit, but it meant I had a car, a blue and white LTD station wagon with fake wood paneling.

Bill had an uncanny gift of endowing ordinary things with special qualities simply by giving them catchphrase names. For example, he immediately started calling that station wagon the Stressmobile. He just had a way of making everything seem special. When you were doing things with him, you felt like you were part of some secret club.

From then on, whatever I happened to be driving, it was called the Stressmobile. Along those same lines, in the Stressmobile we used to go on what Bill termed "Nipple Tours." Nipple Tours were just us engaging in harmless teen stalking. It wasn't actually stalking, and it really was harmless, but looking back . . . it could easily have been made to look sketchy if lawyers had ever got involved.

We'd pile into the car with the Stratford school directory, and look up the addresses of girls we had crushes on. Then we'd do a drive-by. We'd just cruise by the house. That's all. We went from house to house with the bizarre hope that we would see the girl or find out something – what, I have no idea, as 99.8 per cent of the time we saw absolutely nothing except the front of a house. Surprise.

On the rare occasion we saw someone, we'd pretend it was coincidence. We just happened to be heading down that street doing, uh, something. It was a form of cruising. The cool kids cruised up and down a central drag; we cruised by girls' houses.

For a while we did our Nipple Tours in my family's thirty-foot-long motorhome. My parents had given it to me to drive to school, like it was a normal car. There was another girl, Tracy Scovell. She was really hot but she had some scars on her face from where she had been bitten by a dog when she was young. The mark was not only a social hindrance but earned her the nickname of Tracy Scar-vell. Bill had a big crush on her. So after Stress got going and we were actually becoming competent musicians, we had all of our equipment – amps, guitars, etc. – in the motorhome, which happened to be outfitted with a generator.

One day we set up our amplifiers and a PA in the motorhome, then pointed everything out the window. When we pulled up in front of Tracy's house Bill took the microphone: "Tracy Scovell . . . this concert is for you." Then he let it rip. Don't know if she was even there to hear it. Surprisingly the cops didn't show up and tell us to stop disturbing the peace.

The band's first big stroke of luck came when a friend of ours, Steve Fluke, broke both of his arms in a rope swing accident. Fluke was a better guitar player than anyone else we were hanging out with, but he just didn't fit in. He was younger, but more importantly he was very "Stairway to Heaven" and we wanted to be "God Save the Queen." However, Steve did have generous parents who had bought him a sweet-ass Les Paul guitar and an expensive amplifier to go with it.

Don't ever let it be said that Bill wasn't opportunistic. The day after Fluke broke both of his arms, Bill and I were over at Fluke's house pretending we felt bad about his accident. After expressing our supposed sympathies, we turned to our more concrete interests. "Hey, man, since you can't play guitar for a while, can we just borrow this for a couple of days?" Bill asked. "We feel really bad. We'll come back and visit you tomorrow."

We ended up leaving with his guitar and his amplifier (this was before Bill's parents had bought him his rig); and not coming back to visit the following day. Nine months later Fluke turns up at my place raising a stink: "Dude, I want my guitar back." Bill is going, "Oh shit, this isn't mine. Is it?"

I don't think Steve Fluke was unique in being involuntarily generous to us. Looking back, we would use people. We would act like we liked people just so we could use their equipment. We would beg and borrow just to get what we wanted.

It wasn't long before we started to get a little more serious. Stress was never a joke, but it was just something to do that we enjoyed until Bill forced the issue by getting his parents to buy him a guitar and amp. Suddenly he was asking, "Well, Kevin, what are *you* going to do?" There was that bass of my brother's we had been using. My brother Curt had schizophrenia, and at this point he was in and out of mental hospitals and halfway houses, so I was often using his equipment without even asking him. It was there. He wasn't. I became a bass player.

It's funny how Bill's different worlds collided, but it's when he and I were headed downtown to shop for guitars that we passed the Comedy Workshop for the first time. Bill stared at it as we drove by, his head careening to hold as long a glimpse of it as possible. "That must be the place I read about in the paper," he muttered to himself. "People get up on stage and do comedy."

A high-school kid in Texas in the Seventies? I didn't even really know what a comedian was outside of Bob Hope or maybe Johnny Carson. Weren't comedians old guys who stood on a stage in leisure suits making "Take my wife . . . please" jokes? It was something we equated with our parents.

But suddenly it was a budding sport in Houston where people were getting up on stage in front of a room full of strangers and expressing their thoughts; hopefully getting some laughs in the process. Comedy wasn't really on the radar back then. There just weren't many comedy clubs around – probably LA and New York, maybe Chicago – and the fact that one popped up in Houston in 1978 was pretty incredible.

For Bill, opportunity was meeting preparation. The Comedy Workshop had an open mic night every Monday. You show up, put your name on a list and you can perform.

When Bill and Dwight heard that, they said to each other: "Okay, we gotta go try this." Their friends, myself included, were right there encouraging them because people thought they were hilarious. They were too young to know they were too young to sign up for an open mic night at a comedy club. Bill and Dwight knew they could get laughs in front of their friends; and their friends in turn would tell them, "Man, you guys are really funny. You should do this in front of other people." There comes a time when you have to jump that chasm.

I told my mom we were going to a music store. Bill told his mom we were going to the library. We went to the Comedy Workshop.

It was the middle of a school day. I can't even remember why we weren't in school. We weren't skipping, but there we were at a comedy club. We knocked on the door. A comic by the name of Steve Epstein answered. Bill asked some basic questions: Can anyone do it? How do you sign up? Does it matter that I'm only 16?

Yes. You put your name on the list. Maybe, we'll have to check.

Epstein gave Bill a "What It Takes to Be a Comedian"-type speech. Dedication to the art. Hard work. Sacrifices that, with a bowl haircut, it doesn't look like you are ready to make. Blah blah blah. The irony is that for all Bill didn't know, he probably knew almost as much as Epstein at that point, if not about the practice of comedy at least the theory. Bill was already well versed in Woody Allen, Richard Pryor, Charlie Chaplin – people he had studied intensely and was already borrowing from.

But Epstein didn't take Bill seriously at all. Why would he? He was just a kid of 16.

Monday, 10 April 1978: Dwight and Bill performed together at the Comedy Workshop in Houston, Texas. Bill again told his parents he was going to the library; Dwight told his an organ recital. I picked them up that night at the end of Bill's street and off we went.

Oddly enough, Steve Epstein was the first comic to stand up that first night Bill and Dwight went to perform. They got themselves moved up as early as they could so as not to jeopardize their chances of lying to their parents and getting away with it in the future.

Bill and Dwight did about seven or eight minutes. They got laughs. Legitimate laughs. Some illegitimate or, more accurately, laughs that were a function of the novelty of it all. Here were kids who, legally, were too young even to be in the club (legal drinking age in Texas was 18 at the time), yet there they were. That these boys even had the balls to get up there and do this, wow! But certainly the audience had to be thinking, "Well, this is the first and last time we'll see these kids."

It wasn't. Bill and Dwight had both been grounded after their first foray into the world of adult nightlife. So the next time and the next time, they sneaked out of their houses. Dwight did the classic pillows piled under the sheets to look like a body in bed, then left a note as to his whereabouts in case his parents checked.

It has become one of the more famous bits of Bill Hicks lore, that he used to sneak out of his house as a teen to go perform stand-up comedy in nightclubs. It's true. I ran the getaway car. Aiding and abetting.

The side parking lot for the Catholic church my family attended, St. John Vianney, ran adjacent to the backyard fence of Bill's house. I would drive over to the church, park behind Bill's house, he would climb out his second-story window, scale down the back side of the house and off we would go. I had the hardship driver's license, of course.

Even after Bill died, his parents were in denial about it. I remember getting into a fight with Jim about it when he said, "That window was double-bolted shut. It's just not possible." The lengths people will go to believe what they want.

Bill and Dwight performed together three times that spring. That summer, Dwight and his family moved to Oregon. It was something both teens had known about. Dwight's dad told him the previous October – before either Mel or Hal had even heard of the Comedy Workshop – that they would be moving at the end of the school year.

Bill did his first set at the Comedy Workshop sans Dwight before Dwight and his family left for Oregon. He didn't tell Dwight about it, and he didn't let me go to the show, either. Bill was very sensitive to the fact that I thought Dwight was funnier than he was. I did, and I thought Bill doing comedy depended entirely on Dwight.

When Dwight announced the previous fall that he was moving away it was a really depressing moment. We were going to lose him from the band, and it was the end of the whole comedy team. I could see Dwight doing comedy without Bill, but I could never envision Bill doing comedy without Dwight because I had seen Dwight do things that were side-split funny.

In speech class, Dwight would do this routine where he would make a cone out of a piece of paper and he would go, "Okay, is everyone ready for some fun . . . nel?" Then he would hold the funnel over his head and say, "A clown," then he would hold it over his nose and say, "A Jew," then he would hold it over his knee and say, "Gout." Looking back it might not hold up, but for a bunch of teens in the mid-Seventies, Dwight was a cut above his peers. He was already a performer.

I still feel like it's my job and my mission to tell people, "Look, Dwight was doing this stuff from day one with Bill. Dwight's not doing a Bill Hicks impersonation. They came up with those bits together." I still get defensive whenever anyone puts Dwight down.

But Bill took it a step further. He started talking about his parents, started talking about his (still hypothetical) girlfriend. He started talking about personal stuff. Bill also dissected bits that belonged jointly to the two of them. There were certain jokes that you thought, "Okay, this one they wrote together." Bill went on to take the parts of those jokes he felt were his, and he really made them his own – particularly the stuff about his parents.

When the two of them were together it was the wacky, straight-man/funny-man, classic back-and-forth thing. When Bill got up there without a partner as a net, he tried to lose the innocent kid routine. He tried to be tougher. But at the same time, he became more sensitive to his looks. He hated the kid with the gap teeth, the bad bowl haircut, and the goofy mom-dressed clothes. Bill always was a well-spring of incongruities.

But it wasn't like something monumental had happened. Sure, it was significant that Bill was now doing stand-up, but it wasn't a genesis; it was just another point in the evolution. Bill still very much loved rock 'n' roll. It's something often misunderstood about him. It was never a case of "Are you gonna be a comedian?" or "Are we gonna be in a band?"

Stress never died completely. In fact throughout Bill's life the idea of revitalizing Stress at some point stayed with both of us. But Bill (and Dwight, for that matter) was just a kid doing whatever he was doing. He was on a mission that didn't really have a specific objective. He was creative and he loved expression. This was part of the early exploration.

The night after Bill and Dwight first did stand-up at the Comedy Workshop, we went to the Zipper Lounge to celebrate. We had known about the Zipper Lounge for a while, but we didn't know the first thing about what went on inside. We just knew the name and the location, and we knew we had to go there at some point.

There was something intrinsically funny about the name itself. The Zipper Lounge. There was also the mystery of what was behind the door. Was it a strip club? A whorehouse? What the hell was going on in there? The rest of the appeal was its lack of appeal. From the outside the place was pathetically unassuming. In an area where most of the surrounding titty bars had flashing neon "Live Nude Girls" signs or something similarly ostentatious, the Zipper Lounge had the most ordinary of signs. There was no fancy facade. It just sat unobtrusively by a restaurant and a convenience store. In fact, that's the only reason we found the Zipper Lounge in the first place. It shared the parking lot with its neighbors and we had gone to that convenience store.

So it was something we had wanted to do for a while. We just needed the proper excuse. Bill and Dwight performing stand-up comedy together at the Workshop proved sufficient. We had already spent the first part of the night in the adult nightclub world. We now had the cockiness to match our curiosity. Dwight, Bill and I were under-age, but it was a case of us just walking up "as if." As if we were old enough. As if this was something we did all the time. As if it was no big deal. Plus, the sex industry, as we would find out time and again in our lives, isn't particularly picky about whose money it is taking.

We walked in to see a popcorn machine and an unappealing, unkempt older man behind a glass window in the lobby. We quickly figured out this was some kind of adult movie theater. We were kids, but we weren't stupid.

There was a nominal cover charge and a two-drink minimum. We pay the cover and go into the main room. Great. We're in. It was dark. Unusually dark even for a movie theater. A grainy porno movie is playing on an undersized screen. There it is: people fucking. Moving pictures of people fucking. It was definitely my first exposure to pornographic movies. And Bill's. And Dwight's. And anyone who ever came with us after that.

The Zipper Lounge was a huge revelation. This was long before the ubiquity of porn in any format. The home-video market barely even existed. This was a real education, both in sex and business.

34

The place only sold soft drinks – no liquor license – and the Cokes were $10 apiece. They were served in a glass without ice. This was going to be a warm and expensive proposition, especially for a bunch of suburban teens on a limited allowance.

Of course, there was another feature of the Zipper Lounge designed to separate you from your money. It wasn't just an adult movie theater; there was also live entertainment. This wasn't the kind of place where men in raincoats went in to masturbate. It had women – scantily clad women – who would come to your table and sit on your lap. It wasn't lap dancing. It was just lap-sitting company.

"Hi, what's your name? What do you do?" We'd lie. I don't remember how old we said we were, and we worked in the oil industry. God, could we have been more unbelievably ridiculous? Teen oil tycoons. We were 15, maybe 16 years old. And Bill would have had a hard time passing for 15. He was baby-faced. Even into his twenties, Bill still looked like a teenager. But this place was dark, so the employees probably had as hard a time seeing us as we did them. Thank God: any time the scene in the movie was bright enough to catch a glimpse of the women working there, it wasn't exactly a pretty sight.

There were about a dozen tables in the place and roughly the same number of women working the room. So usually only one woman would come to the table and she'd pick one guy's lap to sit on. So, for example, Bill would be sitting there with a girl on his lap trying to flirt with him, while Dwight and I would just be sitting there.

Once on your lap, the woman was pressing you to buy her a drink. Champagnette, it was called: alcohol-free champagne. The stuff cost maybe $2 a bottle; you were getting hit for another $10 a glass. Then there's the, "Would you like to go back to the party room with me?" That was another $50 for some time in the "party room" where, well, we weren't really sure what happened at this point. We just didn't have $50 to blow. "Uh, no thanks. I'm just going to watch the movie."

After the first time we went, all of us had intense dreams that night.

I had insanely weird sexual dreams. Bill had insanely weird sexual dreams. Dwight dreamed he was gay. At school that Monday all of us were just reeling: "God, I dreamed I was . . ." etc. It was all clearly precipitated by our first exposure to hardcore pornographic films.

The Zipper Lounge soon became just another one of the things we did. We were going regularly but not frequently; bi-weekly or monthly. The summer after Bill's senior year of high school, it was even more regular than that. Bill treated the whole experience like it was the most normal thing. He would call down to the theater and ask what movie was showing. He didn't just want to know the title, he wanted to know what the movie was about, the plot. Jesus cornflakes, this was porn. But he would call down there and the poor bastard running the theatre would have to explain the film like it was the latest blockbuster.

And if Bill hadn't called ahead of time, he'd ask when we got down to the theater, like the decision of whether or not we walked in was based on the plot of the movie. So, we'd pay and go in, and Bill would always get popcorn. The rest of us were worried about picking up hepatitis or some orally transmitted sexual disease from the glasses they served our drinks in; but here's Bill diving right in. There was a movie, I guess he felt he needed popcorn.

Once we sat down, he was in a different world, just completely at ease, blissfully watching the movie. I'm sitting there half-ashamed even to be in there, thinking either the cops are going to raid the place or someone is going to blow a load that hits me in the back of the head. Something awful. Not Bill. He was in his happy place. Seeing a pornographic film was a hyper leap ahead of anything we had experienced before. Hardcore action was something entirely different than airbrushed shots in a *Playboy* magazine. It's what Bill wanted. "Show me the pussy." It could have been Bill's epitaph.

But the Zipper also started this delusional pseudo-fantasy that we were somehow better than the other patrons; that we would rescue these girls. We were spiritual. We were artists. We were different and we could take them away. In reality we were teenagers living at home and entirely dependent on our parents for survival. We were full of shit and we were kidding ourselves. We just didn't know it yet.

One night, Bill spent over $100 at the Zipper. Half of that was to go to the party room. He came back and was so disappointed because, for all of the money he spent, he didn't get to have sex. He didn't get to do anything. On the other hand I think he put himself on some higher ethical or spiritual because he didn't try to force the girl to do anything.

Girls were the big mystery to both Bill and Dwight in high school. One of the earliest conversations I recall having with both of them – it was right after one of the first times I was fortunate enough to have a girl agree to sleep with me – was my trying to explain sex to them. We sat there for what seemed like hours as they asked me endless questions, trying to get me to describe to their satisfaction the sensation of being inside a girl.

"So, let me get this straight, you actually touched her pussy?" "Well, yeah." "No way. What's it like?" How many iterations of "What's it like" are there? Answer: about ninety minutes worth, because that's how long this went on.

The thing that made Bill and Dwight different was that they weren't afraid to admit it. Most guys who were virgins would just keep their mouths shut and act like they knew what was going on. Bill and Dwight were really open about how not laid they were getting. They didn't want to be virgins, but at the same time they wanted their first experience to be more than something cheap.

Especially Bill. He had really bought into the white picket fence fantasy. Maybe the Zipper Lounge skewed that a bit, but not so much that it ever stopped fitting into the picture of how he wanted things to be. He certainly didn't do anything to make it easier on himself. He didn't drink, wouldn't drink. Yet it was such a part of ritual high-school mating. The two were so inextricably intertwined that it almost makes you wonder: how do teenage Mormons ever hook up?

Bill used to make fun of me for drinking. I used to sneak six-packs of beer into his room. I'd sit there drinking as we were hanging out. He'd watch me and make snarky comments like, "Hey, are you a better person now?" I wasn't special. He used to make fun of anyone and everyone for drinking.

Drinking, that's simply not who Bill was. Not at that time, anyway. He was too sensitive, too romantic. This is a guy who in high school told me his goal in life was to become enlightened. Shit, most teen dreams fall into one of two categories. One: "I'm gonna score a touchdown at the game on Friday, then go out and drink twelve beers before I have sex with one of the cheerleaders." Two: "I can't wait to go to college, graduate, make a million dollars, marry a *Playboy* bunny, then make all of these assholes who pick on me every day jealous." Certainly Bill wanted to get laid, and he probably wanted some combination of fame and revenge-cum-envy. But shit, he was serious: he wanted to be enlightened.

Bill. What misfit teen didn't fancy himself as Holden Caulfield. Bill loved *Catcher in the Rye*. He also loved the Beatles. Thankfully he didn't like guns, and was generally mentally stable. But as an archetypal misfit, Bill was a closer fit with Conrad Jarrett, Timothy Hutton's character in *Ordinary People*. There's a scene when Jarrett is sitting in a McDonald's or something like that, and he goes into this deep, dark moment describing his attempt at suicide. All of a sudden, these jocks come walking in, singing a song, and they grab his hat off his head. It's the moment he's trying to pour his heart out, and yet the girl starts laughing at him, and he goes cold and gets mad at her. Moreover, Jarrett is growing apart from his old friends. They are all on the swim team, but as Jarrett starts coming of age, he realizes he has nothing in common with those guys.

That was very Bill.

[*   *   *]

Dwight Slade

There were two things Bill and I talked about throughout our whole lives.

One of those was spirituality. He was always very interested in it. For him, I think it started to get serious in high school when we got into transcendental meditation. Of course, it helped that Bill hated church, hated everything about it. What he hated most was that he had to go. But with TM he was exploring different spiritual issues. It was huge at the time. We had long late-night conversations about this knowledge that was dawning in our lives. I think many young people have these experiences, but at 14 and 15 in Houston, Texas, most kids are sitting around talking about women and pot or going out and getting beer. Bill and I were talking about metaphysics.

The other, and maybe bigger, overriding theme we talked about throughout our lives was characters. I think Bill was surprised by it, too: "Why are we always talking about these things?" he would ask. It was characters. Characters, characters, characters. Constantly. In fact, that's how I met Bill. It was because I was imitating a mutual friend of ours and Bill thought it was really funny. So that became something we did. We had two notebook pages listing people in school and parents and whatever we used to imitate.

Later, when we were living together in Burbank, again: characters. Because we were working on a screenplay, we'd invent new characters and do them back and forth to each other.

We went to New York in 1991, and we did a lot of walking. That's what's great about New York. Bill loved to walk. It's an odd thing, but I never met anyone who liked to walk so much. So we would walk and we started to do more characters. It was odd because his career was really starting to go well, and I remember him sensing it and being surprised: "Wow, why are these little characters that I thought were just childhood fun things to do, why do they keep recurring, and why are they so fucking funny?"

A lot of our early stuff – the father characters – that stuff goes deep. It was the first thing Bill and I talked about. One of the most valuable things about my relationship with him is that I was there when the first aspects of his humor started to emerge. I think it's telling because in stand-up you get out, you exorcize, those things that are most incongruous in yourself; things that cause emotion in you. The first characters we had were the characters of our fathers.

You look at his early stuff and his father character is there all of the fucking time. And it became more and more elaborate and further and further over the edge until it became corrupt. The relationship between the character of the father and the son was corrupt beyond redemption, but maintained that southern civility. That's why it entertained Bill and me no end.

It was this hopelessly incestual, horribly corrupt relationship, but the affection, odd as it seems, was there. It still makes me laugh. It's so fucking funny. Bill would call me up – and this was repeated a million times; we never got sick of it, we just loved this character – but he would call me up:

BILL
This is your father.

DWIGHT
Hello, Daddy.

BILL
I have some special news for you.

DWIGHT
What is it, Daddy?

BILL
I'm actually your mother.

DWIGHT
Why's that, Daddy?

BILL

I have a vagina. You were born from me.

DWIGHT

Are you sure of that?

BILL

Yes, you piece of shit.

DWIGHT

Well, you're an old fucking coot is what you are, Daddy.

To us it was, well, it was telling. To me, Bill's humor was about violation. Violation of common sense; violation of personal space. The idea of violation came up in his humor over and over. And certainly in the characters we had and the relationships I saw, there was violation and Bill would stab back with humor.

Bill had a lot of anger towards his parents. Why? I guess the better question would be "why not?" If you met them, you would know in a second; you could see the friction that existed. I've thought about them because, like every family, they are dysfunctional; but their dysfunction is phenomenal. It's deep. There is some secret in that family. And the secret erodes it from the inside. I don't know what it is; it's a very odd family.

But I'd heard something, and Bill had heard the same thing, that metaphysically you are made up of three things: 50 per cent is your soul; 25 per cent is your parents; and 25 per cent is what your mom was encountering when she was pregnant. Those aspects are put into you when you are born. He heard that and it seemed to resonate with him; he tried to analyze it.

Later in life – in the late Eighties – I found a channeler. He was a psychic, and he would channel different entities, then he would give you a reading of these different entities. It was really good, so I recommended him to Bill and he had a reading done. In that channeling – and this is something that struck a chord with Bill – something that

41

emerged was that, when Bill came into this life, he chose his parents primarily because of physical attributes.

When Bill heard that it helped to explain the friction in his family, because he felt like he was the odd man out. If you look at the Hicks family their fucking shoulders are just massive. Mr. Hicks is this big barrel of a guy. Bill and Steve – I had never seen guys that were just this barrel of power. I've tried to get Mrs. Hicks to talk about the rather odd genetic make-up in the Hicks family. It's unusual for a southern family to have jet-black hair, a slightly Asian appearance and black eyes. And I said to her, "Where's that come from? What side of the family?" And she would not talk about it.

Bill was really fast; really powerful. He was a great pitcher. Strong. He took karate early, so his balance and coordination were great. He was also a little ahead in terms of physical development. He was born in 1961; everyone else in the grade was born in 1962. So he had the advantage of great physical prowess and ability, and that gave him a certain confidence throughout life.

He unquestionably had an inner confidence, but when I think about it, it didn't relate to women. When it came to athletics or stand-up or comedy or spirituality or intellectual conversations, he had that fucking fire in his eyes that said, "You're not going to win this. So whatever you want to do, go ahead and bring it on." But the one thing about his relationship with women, especially early on, was that he was over-swinging.

As we were the same age – we went through high school and middle school at the same time – we talked about women at lot. At the time "girls." But Bill would just try too hard. He was an artist and a romantic; but teenage girls don't like guys who are overly romantic. The last thing you want is a love letter when you are 16 years old. I know Bill wrote love letters. I know he was writing a lot about women in his journal: that's one of the reasons he started a journal.

I think he later threw out all of his journals because they included some very, very harsh things about his parents that he didn't want them to find out. I do know that most of what he talked about in his journal was his anger towards his parents, and girls. Also, early on, his career. Those three subjects were always there.

With regard to women he was extremely romantic. "Why do girls always talk about wanting romance and commitment? They hate guys who just want them for sex. I would never do that. I would always be respectful." Then you see these turds, these jocks, walk off with your princess even though they are just blind idiots. Of course girls want that because they don't want a commitment. They just want fun. They don't want anything heavy at 16. They can't handle it.

Bill was always confused by the double standard. I think he was always attracted to romance because it draws out the heart. A lot of artistic creative people are drawn to romance and passion. That was how he approached it; that was how he approached women: "What I want to do is be a romantic."

He must have told me the story of Robin McCullough a million times because there was a lot of romance in it. He really liked that. He really liked going to Toys R Us, or lying in a field, or telling her that she smelled like his dog Chico. He would say: "Don't take this wrong, but you smell like my dog, Chico, because Chico used to have to be shampooed." He really liked the smell of that shampoo.

But nothing about his family really connected to him, except for the fact that his mother was very dedicated as a mom, even though it was in a psychotic way. Bill did love his parents, but you wouldn't know it. That's what was always so mysterious about Bill. When I was in Houston, I witnessed first-hand these horrible fights Bill would have with his mother and father, saying things to them that I was completely taken aback by. It was traumatic to listen to. Screaming, "I hate you. I hate you. I HATE YOU. I wish you were dead." Saying that out loud. Yelling that.

And then his parents: "Well, I'd wish I was dead, too, if I had grades like . . ." Completely unfazed. His parents would not allow him to get to them at all. He wanted to hurt them, but they wouldn't be hurt.

It was a little nutty in that house. They were a very normal family in appearances, but the crazy part is that there was all of this shit going on that no one ever talked about. I saw his journals. Horrible. Raging hatred. All capital letters. Every teenager has problems with their parents, every teenager has a separation from their parents; but maybe it's a matter of degree. Maybe we just look at Bill's personality, and he had that obsessive personality, so when it came time to separate from his parents, he dove in with a frickin' vengeance. Capital 'R' in Rebellion. He took it to the extreme. Fury. Fury. Fury.

But despite all this he really loved his parents. I remember when we were together in New York he would call his mom every single day. It was always in the afternoon. But here's the thing: what man in his twenties calls his mom every day? I would listen to him. He would be in the chair and he would be slung over, hunched. And it was the same monotone response: "No . . . No! Nooooo." He was obviously miserable talking to her. It was strained, teeth-clenched anger. When they started the phone conversation it was friendly . . .

I don't know how to define Bill politically, but it would certainly be close to libertarian, social-anarchist, whatever. So to him the fact you had to register your car was: "Why? Tell me why?" He wouldn't do it. He would rebel against things like that. "Bill, you have to have a driver's license." So his mom took care of that. His mom was a bit like his personal manager. And that was a lot of the relationship: she handled his taxes; everything about everyday life she would handle.

In his stand-up and his life Bill really saw things as black and white. He wanted that. That is where the comedy came from: the incongruity, making distinctions. He was also a wise enough soul, when you got down to it; he saw the gray area. He not only saw it, but he could feel it and live it.

For example, I disagreed with a lot of the things he said about children. Yet when I looked at Bill, I realized he would be an outstanding father, because children love people who play, people who are passionate; they love interesting people; they love romance and mystery and adventure. The thing is that Bill was really in tune with his childhood self, so he would have been a great father. What he hated was what society made of children. But once he was around kids, he would see the grey areas. He certainly loved his nieces and nephews.

The thing is, Bill could have done or been almost anything. Here is a guy who could have had an enormous career in athletics. He was already great in 8th grade – a phenomenal athlete. He could have evolved through high school and won a college scholarship. Who knows where he could have gone. In track he was always the anchor leg of the relays. The 200, the 400 metres. It is weird even to talk about Bill running because he was such a pie-faced smoker. It's not how people think about him, but he was phenomenal.

Then he turns to music. Gifted guitarist; definitely had song-writing talent. Easily could have focused on that, especially because he started young in high school. Clearly could have had a career at it. Where does it end with this fucker?

Not to detour, but what Bill really wanted was to be a rock 'n' roll star. He loved the showmanship of Kiss, the charisma of them. He just loved the personality that was in rock 'n' roll. It's what attracted him. You look at the *Revelations* special, it starts out like a rock concert. A lot of critics made the observation: this is a guy who took comedy and made it rock 'n' roll. That's valid. He wanted to be a rock 'n' roll star, and became more and more attracted to it.

But when you are that good at so many things, you spend a lot of time in the grey areas. Bill understood what he wanted, and he knew it long before you or I or anyone else would. And you can imagine the impatience he would have had at being treated as a 16-year-old high-school student when he knew inside that he was going to be a great artist. How frustrating that must be.

To move to LA when you are 18, what does that take? It takes a bug inside that drives you. And I think that bug was never dormant in his life; it was always burrowing.

I didn't realize until now, when I look back on it, how rare a relationship it was that I had with Bill. We knew what we were doing, the life we were living, the position we were in. Being 14 and having headshots and going to auditions – we knew something was going on that was special. We just figured we must be guided by some greater force.

What I realize now is that I was caught up in Bill's destiny. I was fortunate enough to be right in the midst of the inferno. When you were with him, you just felt this momentum. Even though he had ups and downs, there was always this great charge of energy and purpose about him. Anything was possible.

Bill was also a serial monogamist, which meant he had these very intense personal relationships, one after another. Me, Laurie Mango, Kevin, David Johndrow. There were periods of time when there was just one person he focused on. It was an amazing experience to be that person because he was such an intense guy.

The thing you recognized about Bill is that he had an addictive, obsessive personality. Whether it was drugs or video games or food or a subject matter or pornography; he picked at it until there was nothing left. Then he moved on. Relationships were the same thing. He'd call you and, fuck, you'd be the person. Constantly. Then he'd move on.

I eventually realized that he got something different from each person. It didn't matter, he was so generous about his friends. He had something he wrote in Dr. Donovan's office when he was going through chemo. I think he was reading *The One Minute Manager* and he was making a list of priorities. Number one was his friends.

He wasn't married, he didn't have a lot of relationships with women, but he really enjoyed his friends. He got so much from them. He did have a lot of best friends: you don't meet people like Bill very often, so people would want to hang out with him.

I learned a lot from being Bill's friend. The influence is obviously in me. I'm not going to try to analyze it. You don't spend that much time with another human being and not come away influenced.

I try to avoid talking about him as much as possible. I just enjoy my memories of him, which didn't have that much to do with comedy. We didn't talk about comedy a lot. We never talked about work or anything.

[*   *   *]

CHAPTER 2

On the last day of school, 10th grade, Bill went up to Laurie Mango and asked her out on a date. Tall and dark, striking features: she was Bill's type. His weakness was Italian women; they didn't necessarily have to be Italian; just looking it was sufficient. The Mangos had come to Texas from California and, like a disproportionate number of families whose kids lived in the area, her dad (a geologist) worked for an oil company.

Although she hardly knew Bill at the time, Laurie agreed to go out with him. "He was unlike anyone our age I had ever met and I was immediately attracted to him," recalls Mango. Bill opened up to Laurie, and shared all of his passions with her: books, movies, music. Bill also showed Laurie the *Sane Man* comic he had created. Sane Man was a superhero of sorts, a character Bill created that could defeat all of the injustices of the world with the twin powers of reason and logic.

Bill unleashed the full force of his personality on Laurie. He wrote her long, ten-and fifteen-page love letters. Bill wasn't just smitten: this was the be-all and end-all. At times it was a little too much for Laurie. This was high school. Laurie would get embarrassed about public displays of affection, holding hands, and kissing. Still, even if a little lopsided, they had a true teen romance.

For the next year-plus of high school, Bill's primary occupations – Laurie, Stress, etc. – were anything but school. School was just something he used to facilitate participation in his other interests, including comedy.

Bill also started taking guitar lessons. He was a natural, of sorts. Despite the fact he was lacking in musicianship, he was fast and had the coordination to run his finger up and down the fretboard quickly enough to sound cool. But Stress had pimped itself into a corner. They had told so many stories and passed around so many action shots of themselves, that everyone at Stratford thought they were not only legit but fully functional as a rock 'n' roll outfit.

The reality was they had parts of songs – chord progressions, melodies, lyrics – but nothing to get from "One, two, three, four . . ." to "Thank you, goodnight." It was far too freeform, if you can even use such a word to describe their proto-punk.

Still, everyone at school assumed the band would play the Stratford Senior Follies, one of the school's annual talent shows, so Stress now had to put up and perform or look like complete morons. Dwight had long since escaped to Oregon. The floating in and out of Bruce Salmon, and other guys wasn't conducive to being able to put together consistent performances.

So Bill and Kevin took on honor student Charles Lloyd as a drummer and later added Dave DeBesse as a singer and as a ringer. DeBesse was everything Bill wasn't: he was good-looking and popular. Having Dave as the frontman was a way to ensure the girls in high school would take a greater interest in Stress, if only for the eye-candy aspect of it.

For, as punk rock as they wanted to be in attitude, they were really just a rock band. After opening the Senior Follies set with an original instrumental called "Globe," they played covers of Alvin Lee's "Help Me" and the Beatles' "Slow Down." Not exactly the choices of someone wanting to be anarchic. Stress played some-where in the middle of the Follies line-up and, after the remaining acts had performed, also got to close the show. They opted for classic rock staples, first with Zeppelin's "Rock and Roll," then Hendrix's "Hey Joe."

The joke was that Bill would play a guitar solo out of "Hey Joe" until they shut the band down. He did around twenty minutes of high-speed noodling until finally the principal got someone to go around the side of the stage and literally unplug them. It sounded like a broken record with the same bass riff over and over while Bill maniacally ran his fingers up and down the guitar neck.

But it legitimized Stress. They were a band in myth alone no longer. They played several more gigs during Bill's junior year. There was a courtyard near the Stratford where people would hang out on weekends; on a few occasions the band set up there and played for anyone who cared to listen, and even those who probably didn't care to, for that matter. They had amplification, after all. They also played a few keg parties, putting Bill squarely in the drunken teen environment he dreaded.

Stratford had an unofficial student group called the Stratford Senior Party Team, the function of which was to throw parties. They would rent houses, clubhouses, or even apartments for a night, then buy kegs and sell tickets to friends at school. Anybody who wanted to could get drunk, a few people made a bit of cash, and everyone went home happy. Because Booth was a member of the Team, he had the "in" to arrange Stress as the live entertainment. They scored a few more gigs that way, but Bill was ambivalent. The upside: he was playing live music in front of people. The downside: he was surrounded by the party people he ruthlessly ridiculed.

The summer before Bill's senior year started, Comedy Workshop owner Paul Menzel opened the Comedy Annex, a ninety-seat club converted from a strip bar right around the corner from the Workshop.

Live comedy suddenly became one of the hip things to do and Houston, Texas, had the only live comedy venue in the South. It started drawing people from around the region: Sam Kinison came from Oklahoma, Jimmy Pineapple (real name James Ladmirault) came from neighboring Louisiana. These people moved to Houston to pursue comedy as a career.

The scene was exploding, and with it the crowds. With the larger crowds there was more opportunity for the comedians. When Bill first started coming to the Workshop, the open mic nights were just Mondays, then it progressed to Mondays and Tuesdays. It built and built. Originally there was no cover, but as the crowds got larger, they also got rowdier. So the comics eventually insisted the club not only start charging cover but also start paying the performers a cut.

Steve Epstein recalls: "Even though we didn't have much material, other than borrowed – I was borrowing a lot – the energy was really cool and the audiences were great, very supportive." Many of the comedians had been pushing Menzel to expand, but he was happy with the status quo. Epstein and Mike Vance decided that, if Menzel wasn't going to open up another room, then they were just going to open up their own club.

They went out and got backing from renowned Houston sports-writer Mickey Herskowitz, whose son had been performing; and from a prominent lawyer whose daughter was also at the club. Once this was in play, Menzel approached Epstein and Vance and said, "Listen if you'll drop your plans to open a club, I'll open one." He converted the strip joint around the corner and the Annex was born. And now the comedians were really starting to get good because they could go at it every day.

Before the start of Bill's senior year, his dad was getting sent to Little Rock by General Motors. The original plan was for Jim and Mary to go to Arkansas, have Bill stay behind in Houston for the first half of his school year, then move up at Christmas to join his parents. Logistically things ended up not being that simple; the end result was that Bill got to stay the year. In Houston. By himself.

A better scenario young Bill could not have designed for himself. The biggest source of tension in his life – his family – would have a much more difficult time annoying him from 500 miles away. And with the Annex open, there were slots to fill. Bill was free to perform whenever he wanted. There was no parental guidance to hinder his development as a comedian. He was also making a few bucks.

He was still a teen, barely old enough to drive, but Bill was a wunderkind in an adult world. He was already as good as the guys twice his age playing the same stage. And they knew it.

One weekend home from college, Steve got an invite from baby brother Bill. "I knew [Bill] was writing these jokes," says Steve, "but I did not know what that meant, and one time . . . he said, 'Come down to the Comedy Workshop.' And I said, 'Well, why?' I'd never been to a comedy club, it just wasn't a big thing. And he said, 'Just come down there tonight.' So I went down that night, and I couldn't believe it, he was a superstar already. There was a sold-out show, lines waiting to get in, and that was my brother, I couldn't believe it."

Bill wasn't just the pet apprentice at the Annex and he wasn't the socially awkward kid at school any more. During his senior year, he scheduled himself to a lunchtime performance at one of the athletic fields adjacent to the school. About 200 students showed for the impromptu set. When a member of the audience told Hicks, "You have the sense of humor of a third grader," Bill replied, "Then you must have the comprehension of a second grader."

The son of a Pentecostal preacher, Sam Kinison survived being hit by a truck at the age of three. After leaving a broken home, he and his brother started off following in their father's footsteps, as they headed up religious revivals across the Bible Belt of the south.

Failing first at the ministry, then at marriage, Kinison traded one pulpit for another and stepped into stand-up. He was ruthless. "It's not what you say, it's how you say it." Sam took that to a level comedy hadn't seen before. With Sam the key to comedy wasn't timing but screaming. Kinison would get his break on a Rodney Dangerfield special where he explained why people starve in Africa: "See this? See this? It's SAND. YOU LIVE IN A FUCKING DESERT . . . GO TO WHERE THE FOOD IS. ARGHHH. ARGHHH."

To say Sam lived fast is a mild understatement. His brother once found him snorting cocaine off the back cover of John Belushi's biography, *Wired*.

Even though Bill had started (i.e. done his first gig) before Kinison, Sam was able to spend more time on stage; to make a commitment to comedy as a career. So he quickly established a reputation not just in Houston but in the whole state, being named Funniest Man in Texas by the *Dallas Morning News* in both 1979 and 1980.

One night, as Sam was beginning to take off, and Bill was still starting and showing when he could, Sam gave Bill his initiation. He did a bit where he was "Mr. Lonely," using the Bobby Vinton song. Sam would get up on a barstool and start singing, "I'm lonely. I'm Mr. Lonely. I have nobody . . ." and he'd be taking off his clothes as he sang. "I'm a soldier. A lonely soldier." As he got near the end of the song he'd be taking down his pants. Then he'd drop his voice from that of a romantic crooner to a mischievous screamer. "But I see my boy now, and I ain't lonely no more." Then he'd jump off the stool, into the audience, wrestle someone to the ground and pretend to anally rape him or her with his clothes on. "I've got my boy. I've got my boy. Ugh. Ugh. Ugh."

One night Bill just happened to be sitting there at the corner of the stage when Sam made Bill his catamite. Welcome to the family. Bill liked to hang around the guys as much as possible, and the guys liked him. Moreover, pretty much everyone recognized that Bill was supremely talented, even as a teen; but age and lifestyle kept him at arm's length. When the other comics went out late after the club closed to take the party somewhere else, or even just to go eat, Bill often went home. He had school the next day.

Plus, despite the general camaraderie, not everybody at this point was a Musketeer. According to fellow Houston comic Jimmy Pineapple, "I don't think Kinison was ever Bill's favorite person. They had a connection in that they were the two most famous people to come out of the Houston comics, but Sam wasn't going to do anything for anybody except Sam. He always used to set people against each other. He used to pull one of us aside: 'It's you and I, Pineapple. You and I are the best ones here. Everybody else sucks. So and so is a piece of shit. You and I are the only ones . . .' Then he'd pull Bill aside,

'Bill, it's you and I. You and I are the best ones here . . .' Then he would do it with someone else."

In April of 1980, Sam first got banned from the Workshop. He had a self-explanatory bit he called "Barstool Rodeo," where he once broke the barstool while riding it. So when they repaired the stool, Menzel had the bar manager write, "If you break this, you owe $20" on the bottom of the seat. A few nights later, Sam, who tipped the scales at about 250 pounds, is on stage when he simply sits on the stool and it breaks. He is a little upset by this, but more upset by how much the other comics are laughing at him. Naturally he wants to know what the deal is, and they tell him to look at the bottom of the stool. He reads it. Ha, ha. "Oh, twenty dollars? That's no problem." He takes twenty dollars and tosses it onto the stage.

Then he went off. "And here's what I think of your fucking rules. So cheap you can't pay for a stool. You can't pay for the props." Kinison started smashing the remnants of the barstool. Another one of the comics, incited by Kinison's display of insolence, picked up a chair and, thinking he was going to break it on a beam, ended up putting it through a wall. They were both tossed out and banned from the club for a couple of weeks.

Sam's second excommunication from the Houston comedy community came from doing "Baby Jesus and His Pal Nigger Dog." He would just ad-lib: "I'm Baby Jesus, I can do anything I want. What you gonna do? I'll turn you into a leper. I'm Baby Jesus, I'll drink your drink. You can't stop me." One night this mutated into the Adventures of Baby Jesus and His Pal Nigger Dog. Management would let comics get away with most things. Apparently, though, that was too inappropriate. Sam was gone. Steve Moore, the club art director (and a comic himself), was given the job of breaking the news to Sam.

The next day, according to Epstein: "I came to the club and there were a few guys sitting at the store across from the club. They were talking about going to LA and we were like, 'Yeah, that sounds like a good idea. It's time to move on.' Sam goes, 'Let's go.' And I thought he meant, 'Let's go right now.' I'm saying, 'Great. I love sponteneity. Shit yeah. Let's do it right now.'

"What I had missed before I got there was them talking about beating the shit out of Steve Moore, who had fired Sam. That's what he meant by 'Let's go.'"

Sam led the vigilantes, who proceeded to start a fight in which Moore broke his leg. That was it for Kinison. He put together a fundraiser for his favorite cause – himself. He headed up the movement to go west, borrowed money, promised favors, and put together a show with Bill, Carl LaBove and Riley Barber. Sam also recruited Argus Hamilton to come out from LA and be the headlining draw. They rented out the Tower Theater for a mid-September gig, and promoted the show as "The Outlaw Comics on the Lam."

The point of the show for the comics was to make money to finance their relocation to LA, but with Hicks' parents agreeing to finance his move to Hollywood, and Epstein having already left for California, the point of the show was really for Sam to make enough money to finance *his* relocation. Financially it was a disaster. Sam lost in the thousands of dollars, much of which he had borrowed.

Despite the fact that Argus Hamilton had been on *The Tonight Show*, hardly anybody in Houston knew who he was. So he wasn't much of a draw. Plus, nobody wanted to pay a premium ticket price to see the comics they could see any night of the week at the Annex for pennies on the dollar.

The show worked out great for Hicks, though. Hamilton took a liking to Bill, and since Hamilton was dating Mitzi Shore, the owner of the Comedy Store in LA, Bill now had an "in" at the Store. Located right on the Sunset Strip, at that time the Store was Mecca, the Taj Mahal and Angkor Wat all rolled into one. And Hamilton was not only going to help get Bill fast-tracked at the Store, but he was Bill's line on getting an audition for an HBO *Young Comedians Special*.

[* * *]

Kevin Booth

During Bill's second year of high school, one of our friends – probably Brent Ballard – "discovered" Eric Johnson. There was this skinny kid who was a fucking wizard guitar player that we had to see. A few weeks later, he was playing at a place called Fitzgerald's. We piled into the Stressmobile. We had to see him.

This was another nightclub. I have no idea how we were even getting into these clubs: Houston, Texas, in the late Seventies was just a different place. The drinking age was only 18 and to say there was lax enforcement was an overstatement. We didn't have fake IDs or anything. Probably because we *thought* we could get in, we got in.

Mindblowing? It was like the second coming. This wasn't a guitar player, this guy was a fucking messiah; he was like nothing we had ever seen or heard before. He was technical as all hell but he had melody. And he was fast. Blazing fast.

Bill used to call Johnson's playing "whittling." He was describing the sound you made when trying to use your mouth to duplicate the sound of Eric playing super-fast: "Whittle -ittle -ittle -ittle," etc. On a more subversive level it was Bill having a fun stab at his redneck heritage. Whittling was stereotypical southern. A knife. Some wood. The banjo player on the porch in *Deliverance*, he was probably also a good whittler. Bill was trying to endow the term with a bit more sophistication.

From that first night on, we would see Eric Johnson any time we could. Bill, Dave DeBesse, Brent Ballard and I, that was the core group. If Eric was playing five nights a week, we would go see him five nights a week. It also became a Maginot Line, with Johnsons Eric and Robert on either side. David Johndrow, he was with the latter. We were in the camp that worshipped the skinny white kid with the skinny tie.

Even though Bill was the only one who sat comfortably on both sides of the barrier, he was also the one in the Eric Johnson race – who could turn themselves into Eric Johnson the most and the fastest – with Brent Ballard. It affected the way they got their hair cut, the shirts they wore, the shoes they wore, the skinny tie, the vest. Everything.

One night we went early to try to talk to Eric before a show at Fitzgerald's. We had this image of Johnson as a major rock star. We thought, "He must have an army of roadies. He's such a good musician, he must be famous and rich." We just didn't understand. But we went behind the club to the parking lot where we saw this waifish pixie of a man get out of a van, then we watched him have to carry his own amplifier up the long stairway at the back of the stage. Lesson number one.

Still, we approached him; we were super-excited and Bill was leading the charge. "We come to every one of your shows." We came on fast and hard. It freaked him out. He was a very private person. What were we thinking? Actually, I know exactly what we were thinking. We thought he would be warm and appreciative: "You're at all my shows? Oh wow. Thanks." Maybe he would ask us if we wanted to go eat and we would have this connection. No. Lesson number two.

After that incident we would still sit right up in the front at his shows, looking up at him. Rapt. Especially Bill; his slack-jawed awe was a few orders of magnitude more intense than the rest of ours. Johnson would look down and occasionally catch sight of us. Often you could see a slightly nervous look break out across his face. I think he was amazed we could sit through it over and over again.

Eric Johnson wasn't just a guitarist, he was influential to Bill for another important reason; specifically, he was also heavily into meditation and mysticism. He didn't just dabble either – veggie diet, drug-free lifestyle, everything. Like Bill, he didn't touch a drop of drink. So in Johnson, Bill thought he had a kindred spirit. And if non-western approaches to spiritual enlightenment also meant Bill might become equally as bad-ass a guitar player, all the better.

Plus, Johnson was this super-scrawny guy but he always had the super-hot women around him. Always. So it was confirmation of the equation: good musician = hot babes.

Even cooler was the fact that he wasn't fawning over girls in return. It was our first glimpse into the "proper" way of handling physically attractive girls; specifically not acting like you're too into them. When you're young you tend to think girls want guys that pay tons of attention to them. Then you see the weird, skinny artist guy surrounded by hot chicks and he's not doing that. "Oh man. He's indifferent towards her. And for some reason she wants him even more. Wow. How weird? I don't get it."

Bill was also a bit of a prodigy on guitar. He had the hand-eye coordination so, once he got serious, it wasn't long before he could also play blazingly fast. But speed was just speed. Bill lacked musicianship at that point. To most people it sounded cool, cramming dozens of notes into a couple of seconds. But to someone who really understood music, it just sounded like dozens of notes crammed into a couple of seconds.

For a birthday party, Laurie Mango actually arranged to have Eric Johnson play at her house. Bill was super-excited because *Eric Johnson* was going to play at his *girlfriend's* house. It was like a double dose of "fuck yes" with a side of "yippee" sauce. Until Bill and Laurie broke up. After that, Bill just assumed that the whole thing would be called off. Laurie was just doing it because Bill wanted it. Or so he thought. When she went through with it, to Bill it was obvious she was just doing it as a dig at him.

He was probably still welcome to go, but that's not who Bill was. Out of principle, even if that principle was just spite, no way, no day he was going to go. It was the love of his young life and his favorite musician in the world, but Bill was too stubborn. We boycotted.

Then he had to hear all of his friends talking about it. Even the guys who were, like, "Eric Johnson is crappy. I'm into the Grateful Dead" talked about how great it was. If Laurie wanted a dig at Bill, it had worked.

Years later, when Bill started drinking, he lost some – not all, but some – of his taste for the antiseptic. Suddenly Bill was way more into the Rolling Stones. Mick and Keith in, Eric out. Bill gets fucked up, he likes music of people who get fucked up, and not the elfin magic of a clean-living mystic. But at some point during his heavy drinking days, Bill (doing comedy, obviously) actually opened a show for Eric. Bill got fucked up and told Eric that if he would just eat meat, maybe a hamburger, and drink a beer, then he could write a hit.

Bill never opened for Eric again.

Well before Laurie, I tried hard to help Bill score, or even just meet girls. But he refused to take part in the juvenile ploys we cooked up. The origins of this go back to before I was ever a friend of Bill, but we used to have dinner parties, the whole point of which was to get girls to come over to my house. Not just any girls, but girls we thought might have sex at the end of the night. It sounds a little sleazy, but it wasn't like these girls were ridiculously easy lays. They couldn't have been: we didn't get laid that much.

My parents were always out of town; and we had a great house for entertaining. All we needed were the guests. So we were constantly hitting on girls who didn't go to our school. With girls from a different high school, you could make yourself out to be whoever you wanted. Put differently: it made it much easier to lie.

Later, when Bill and I started hanging out and he was continually asking, "God, how can I get pussy? How can I meet women?" I was telling him: "Dude, you have got to come to one of these dinner parties." His response was always the same: "No, I'm not interested in meeting these girls and getting them drunk. I'm not interested in your other friends. The whole concept of trying to get a girl drunk to have sex with her is wrong." Bill saw it as tricking a girl into having sex.

Then, of course when I ran into Bill the next Monday at school the first word out of his mouth was always: "So?" And, provided I'd got laid, I'd tell him.

Bill's later periods of overindulgence in alcohol (and drugs, for that matter) might make it hard to believe, but during this time Bill made fun of teenage drinking. Drinking in general. And smoking. He and Dwight had their own private code phrase –"WDPS," short for "Why do people smoke" – to confirm to each other how superior they were in the way they lived. We were just trying to point out to him that, well, if you wanted to get some pussy, it really helped your cause to get girls drunk. It was part of the recipe, and that's just the way it was.

Of course, with so much peer pressure, eventually he caved. Sweet Jesus, it's a miracle. He wasn't going to start drinking, not yet anyway, but he would come to a dinner party.

Originally, it was just, "Hey, show up." He wouldn't have it, saying, "No, it's too weird. I don't drink and I don't want to get sucked into this big, long evening with your friends." So, he was never a normal dinner guest, but he found a way to participate. We had to make a joke out of it. For me, it was funny. "Ha-ha" funny. For my other, "cooler" friends, it was less humorous and more: "Why is Kevin dicking around with this goofy guy?" But Bill created a character named "Happy." Happy was somewhere between Jerry Lewis and Charlie – *Flowers for Algernon* Charlie. Mix that with a few hundred gallons of caffeine, and that'll put you in Happy's head.

Bill, or Happy, couldn't just be there, hanging out when the guests arrived. There had to be an entrance and a show. Bill needed to perform. It was all in the timing. We would actually sit there and chart out everything. At precisely 19:30, I call Bill's house. I let the phone ring exactly once and hang up. At precisely 19:42 Bill arrives at my house, and waits in the bushes at the north-east corner of the lot.

While Bill was bicycling across the neighborhood to my house, we were setting the table. "Yeah, we have this friend. He goes by the name 'Happy.' He's kind of, oh, 'special.' He's kind of 'different.'" The girls would be asking, "What? Is he retarded? What do you mean?" "No, you'll see."

At some point in the charade, when the girls seemed sufficiently intrigued, I would usually go up to my bedroom and open the window to signal Bill, then I'd go back downstairs and, after just a long enough pause for it to seem that the two events might be unrelated, "Bing-bong-bing-bong-bing-bong." The doorbell. Right on cue. "Uhp, there's Happy." We open the door and this super-manic teen 'tard comes bouncing into the house. "Hi, I'm Happy. Hi. Hi. Hi."

The character was so hopeful, but also tragic. And at its core, it was just another ploy. We were scheming to make the girls think that there was this other level of depth to us because we were caring for this person with special needs, trying to paint it so it looked like we were more interested in making sure this person had a place to spend his Saturday nights than we were in getting laid. The exact opposite was true. And, of course, this was supposed to get us laid.

Sometimes Bill, as Happy, would come and eat, but he never stayed the whole night. Right before it got to the heavy drinking portion of the evening he would usually disappear. About that time the character of Happy would start to wear thin. Bill knew it, too. "Yeah, I gotta go." And he'd go. The girls would make their false protests. "No, Happy. Stay." Then the next day they'd ask: "How's Happy? Is he okay?" You'd like to think that we got our comeuppance for this. In fact, the whole thing only turned Bill on even more.

But "Happy" kind of ran its course. It was putting Bill in social situations, but its questionable aphrodisiac effects certainly weren't getting him any closer to getting laid. It might even have been hindering the efforts of everyone else.

For us to go out and act cool –"Look how muscular we are" or "Look how cool our car is" – that was never going to work for us. I was driving a station wagon. Bill had no car. Bill was emulating Woody Allen in his comedy, why not emulate him in his social life as well? Allen was not just Bill's role model; we all adopted him as our anti-hero. He gave us our instruction manual for how to pick up women. The goal, quite simply, was to be the biggest nerd, the biggest dweeb you could be, yet still interact with other people. The right woman, the one who also thought jocks were losers and being arty was cool: she would get it.

There was even this one girl, who hooked up with both Bill and, later, David Johndrow. She was a complete knock-off of Diane Keaton. Straight out of *Annie Hall*. Coincidence? Maybe. We watched a lot of Woody Allen movies. This girl actually ended up being David's girlfriend. I remember David saying on multiple occasions, "Well, I'm just glad Bill and her never slept together." He'd always say that. I'd go, "Uh, yeah. Right, David." Bite my tongue. Apparently she had told David that she never slept with Bill. Bill told me different.

Guys will believe things because they want to, and being a sucker can make you cynical in a hurry. There's a balance between being a cold and callous womanizer who uses girls like a commodity and someone who can be genuine. Despite what his stage persona intimated, and for all of our clumsy attempts at teenage mating, Bill almost always tried to tip the scales in favor of being the latter. But he was not someone who was opposed to a one-night stand either.

Watching Bill interact with women in his mid to late teens really was like watching a Woody Allen movie as he would try to impress girls who were way out of his league. I don't think it was any consolation to Bill for him to know how well he was emulating one of his comedic idols. Except it wasn't funny. Sure, at the time it was a little funny, in the way that any teen misfortune of a friend is funny because it happened to them and not to you. But Bill was just clumsy with girls.

I don't think he had any, *any*, luck with girls until his junior year of high school. God knows we tried to get the boy laid. He tried, too. He would talk to girls, but he'd be doing these goofy routines that were long and involved and predicated on the girls playing along. The bowl haircut, pale skin and gawky figure didn't do anything to help.

As uncomfortable as Bill was in a nightclub, he was totally comfortable in the comedy club. He belonged, despite the fact that his choice of lifestyle was 180 degrees from the rest of the comics doing sets at the Comedy Workshop. During his senior year he was doing a couple of shows a week at the club. Sometimes fewer, usually more. One or two weekends a month I was coming back to Houston from The University of Texas in Austin. It's about three hours west of Houston down Highway 290. Piece of cake. We would get together and play as Stress. And he'd have a gig. Just about every time I came back, Bill was doing a show. And every time the crowd was just a little bit bigger.

Bill got along with the other comics. He might have been a kid by age but not by his comedy. For that they respected him. But he couldn't hang out. He was still in high school, and even if he hadn't been they were just at a different speed than Bill.

At 18, Bill went to LA to be a comedian. Novel? No. It's a cliché. The busloads of teenagers who turn up in Hollywood to "make it." Bill was now one of those. But, given where he came from, Bill was being incredibly daring and bold. The Midwesterners, those people were desperate. What were their other options? Stay in Dubuque, Iowa, and serve Blizzards at the local Dairy Queen. Bill came from a background where he had everything to lose.

For the middle-to-upper-class kids at Stratford, it wasn't a question of "if" you were going to college. The question was "where" you were going to college. It was just what you did. It was why we lived in Nottingham Forest in the first place. Our fathers went to college. Got a job. Worked for the company. Bought a house. Birth. School. Work. Death. It was the sure bet. Low risk. High reward. Bill set off without a net.

When most of his classmates went to college, Bill went to Los Angeles to be a comedian. It still amazes me to say that, and not just for the courage it took. The point can't be made clear enough: Bill wanted to be a rock star. It wasn't like he ever wanted to make a choice between comedy and music. He never saw himself as having made that choice. Throughout his life – Stress, Marble Head Johnson, Arizona Bay – Bill loved making music as much as he loved doing comedy.

Rock stars were his idols. For a while he fancied himself a Sinatra of sorts. And when he did material about drugs, he didn't build jokes around Timothy Leary but instead glorified Keith Richards. When Bill was doing his last series of shows, he came out on stage playing air guitar and lip-synching to Bob Dylan's "Subterranean Homesick Blues." He was not long for this world and he was still using a rock 'n' roll pantomime to introduce himself to the audience. Bill fucking loved rock 'n' roll.

But the world forces people to be practical and out of necessity Bill had to move something to the forefront. Two, maybe three, things pushed Bill in the direction of comedy.

First, during his junior year of high school, Bill brought a booking agent over to my house to see Stress play. It was an uncomfortable scene, trying to explain to my parents what a middle-aged man was doing in our house. He booked bands into the Whiskey River, a local rock club in Houston. With his mustache and oversized Seventies hair he looked the part. If he hadn't been standing in the Booth family living room, he could have been up for the lead in the sequel to *Behind the Green Door*.

We gave some vague explanation of what was going on. It was lost on my parents: "Well, Kevin is going to college next year."

We played our set for him. He was less than impressed. We were a novelty because we were young. Hanson twenty years too soon. Bill and I were both quite baby-faced. We could have passed for 12. Combined. That was also the appeal. "Hey this guy is only 15. Listen to how fast he can play guitar." That was going to be the gist of it, but Bill and I had already had a brief conversation about the wisdom of being pigeonholed as kid rockers.

Me: "Man, that's not going to last long." Bill: "Yeah, that'll work for about two years."

The booking agent told us we needed to play more popular songs, suggesting we learn "My Sharona" and some other hits that were popular that month. It's all anyone ever said: "You gotta do covers before you can be in an original band." That used to bum Bill out. "No, we want to be original right off the bat."

It was a defeat for Bill. He was hanging a lot more on Stress than Charles and I were at this point. Charles was going to college. I was going to college. Without anything to keep us in Houston and keep us in Stress, those two things weren't going to change.

In addition to this lesson, Bill really was an exceptional comedian. Even at the age of 17. No doubt about it. And, as much as I loved making music with my friend, the truth is Bill was fifty times the comedian that he was musician. He belonged on stage, but he was better off telling jokes.

I went to college. Bill stayed in Houston for his senior year. I returned to Houston regularly so we could still jam together. We were still Stress if only in name. When we weren't playing music, we were working on film ideas. We had a super-8 camera and we used to concoct scenes. It was very Steve McQueen. We'd block out the shot – usually doing an action scene where we would line the stairwell with mattresses and have some sort of fall or body slam – then "shoot" it. Point the camera and . . . "Action!"

Oh, there was no film in the camera. We couldn't afford it.

We also watched the TV show *Soap* religiously. Bill loved *Soap*. It was appointment television.

That summer, Bill stayed indoors at all costs. It's like he was a space alien – like direct sunlight wasn't good for him. He could only survive in dark, air-conditioned environments. The whole summer consisted of a handful of activities: eat, sleep, play guitar, watch movies, watch *Soap*. The only difference was that now the episodes of *Soap* were reruns. It didn't matter to Bill. He was still parked in front of the TV every Tuesday night. In reality, though, he was just biding his time until he headed out west.

The thinking was: Kevin goes back to college, Bill goes to LA, and in a year or so, when we both get things going, we'll get the band back together. Exactly how and where that would happen was never addressed.

Bill's parents agreed to finance his comedy career as long as he would also go to college. So he signed up at LA Community College for a martial arts class. The first day – and Bill was going in there with some experience of the basic moves from previous instruction – the instructor lines them up and has them facing off. The whole class is filled with kids wanting to be in gangs: tatted-up kids with shaved heads in the days before every kid had a shaved head and a tattoo. And it was a lot more scary and dangerous than it is today where half the kids are copping to some gangsta-rap fantasy lifestyle they saw on an MTV video. These kids were the real shit.

So Bill had to face off with one of these kids. The first thing, the first day, the guy punches Bill right in the nose. Didn't break it, but gave him a nice bloody face. It was all too perfectly Bill. There would be something that he was going to get into, and he was excited about the class. He had his hopes up about how good this was going to be, put a lot of energy into it, then the very second he shows up to get started something goes horribly wrong and he bails out immediately.

It's rare for kids to be like this, and I didn't know anyone else at that age who could be so self-deprecating. "I'm goofy-looking." "I don't fit in." He called me up to tell me about it. "Oh my God, Kevin, I got my ass kicked by this guy." And he was laughing at himself.

Bill had that kind of vulnerability, and it allowed him to capture people's hearts. It wasn't contrived or synthetic. Even towards his later days, you still had the feeling when he was on stage that if you yelled something from the audience, even though he might have the perfect comeback and put you in your place, or even explode and start screaming expletives at you, it really would hurt his feelings, because he was always trying to open up his heart to people. It takes a lot more of a man and a lot more of a warrior to stand before people in that way – have an open heart, and put yourself at risk.

[*   *   *]

When Bill arrived in Los Angeles, September 1980, he took a cab from the airport straight to the Comedy Store. Since he was a naive hick, he might as well play the part. He walked in with his suitcase still in hand and asked Andy Huggins, the comedian minding the store during the day, "When do I go on?" He played the part all the way through his audition for HBO that evening, bringing his suitcase on stage.

Bill didn't get the HBO special, but he got the attention of Mitzi, who instantly liked him and started giving him regular spots.

His parents paid for the one-bedroom apartment, he rented in the Valley. He had a bed, a TV, a tape-deck, and not much else. He had a small support group with Steve Epstein and Riley Barber, but Bill spent a lot of time by himself: reading, going for long walks in Griffith Park and along Mulholland Drive. He also wrote tons of letters to friends. He didn't even have a phone.

Sam Kinison finally turned up in LA about four months after Bill. When he got to town, he didn't get stage time from Mitzi, he got a door job. He had debts from the "Lam" show and he was staying on Epstein's floor. He asked to borrow $1000 from Bill. Sam thought he'd be flush. Bill balked. Sam went off on him.

A couple of nights later, as Bill was walking down the street, Sam pulled up alongside him in his car and went off. "You're out here because I put you on that show I lost eight thousand bucks on." He berated Bill because Mitzi liked Bill more, then he accused Bill of stealing his schtick. "You're doing me. I brought you out here and you do my act." Sam threw a can of pop at Bill, then drove off. Bill lent him the money.

The truth of the matter is that despite the fact that Sam might have been the face of Houston comedy when he left for LA, and would go on commercially to be the most successful of the Outlaws, Sam wasn't nobody's favorite person, except Sam's.

Bill had been asking around town and everyone told him the same thing: if you have a good comedy script, you can own LA.

Bill was going to write a comedy. A teen comedy at that. He was 19. He was funny. Never mind that the bulk of his writing to this point had been relegated to private and semi-private papers – letters, love letters and his journal. Because of his age and his chronological proximity to high school, Bill felt he would be writing the first legitimate teen comedy ever. He began hounding Dwight to move to LA and join him. Bill was now the property of the William Morris Agency. He was a client of theirs, and that meant he had a real opportunity to get the script into the hands of people who could make things happen. It wasn't just getting read; Bill's agent would certainly read it. If it was good, then William Morris would put it out to people who could turn the words into pictures moving at twenty-four frames per second.

In July of 1981 Dwight moved down to Burbank to join Bill in his tiny studio apartment in the Valley. Bill's friends were sitting through chemistry classes and studying for midterms, but he was living the dream. Now, best of all, Dwight was in on the script for *The Suburbs*.

"We worked on it non-stop in July – eight to ten hours a day to get it done," says Slade. They woke up, started working, broke for lunch, then worked some more.

Shore offered to help Bill and Dwight get the script typed by a professional. They delivered their stack of handwritten pages. About a third of the way through the typist told Bill he was on target for about a 300-page script. The rule of thumb in Hollywood is that a page of script equals about a minute of film. A five-hour teen epic? No agent, no development executive, no development executive's assistant would do anything but laugh at a 300-page anything. The brief was teen, not Tolstoy.

They began editing, paring down their adolescence to something shorter and more readable.

The pitch: *Fast Times* meets *Catcher in the Rye*. Their timing was right: they were actually submitting their script right as *Fast Times at Ridgemont High* was going into pre-production. But the material was nowhere near as funny as the former nor as poignant as the latter.

The adage is that your first work is autobiographical. And *The Suburbs* was pulled straight from their Nottingham Forest upbringing. The main character was even named Kevin.

They were trading off the memories of how horrible it was to grow up in the suburbs. The truth is, the suburbs of Houston were actually a pleasant place to be a kid. Nobody was trying to kill you and there was plenty of parking. The only crime against humanity was that it might have been a little prosaic and sterile. The Hicks had a nice house and money. Bill had his own room and never had to go to bed hungry. They were trying to play up the lost childhood – what Bill thought his life had been to that point. The main character realizes he can survive this thing and just be himself.

As real as Bill and Dwight thought *The Suburbs* was going to be, just because they were teens writing about teens didn't make it exceptional or even novel. Half of everyone in LA fancied themselves a screenwriter, and half of those people had a quasi-autobiographical script in which they also fancied themselves to be Holden Caulfield. Even those past their teen years were still scarred enough by the experience of high school that it appeared in their writing.

While agent John Levine was impressed with the writing, the script never made it past his desk. A great comedy script was gold. But before you could convert that gold into actual dollars, agents wanted to know you could replicate the feat; that you hadn't just fluked your way into something brilliant. They wanted you to have not just one, but two, maybe even three scripts. Then they would take you seriously.

According to Slade: "We didn't know that yet, and when we did finally put it into someone's lap, which was not until February of the next year, that's what happened. He said, 'I want to see another. And I want to see another. Then we're going to talk.' It was encouraging because he really did like us, but we had shot our wad and Bill was just not into writing another script, even though we had more ideas."

[*   *   *]

Kevin Booth

It seems almost incomprehensible now. Either it really was that long ago or things have changed so much it's almost ridiculous to entertain the notion, but in LA Bill didn't even have a telephone in his apartment. There was a payphone downstairs. He would call me at college in Austin frequently – not quite daily, but close to it. On top of that he wrote letters, honest-to-God pen-to-paper handwritten letters. Each began with the same sentence, or a rough equivalent thereof:

> Capon,
> Maybe Dave is getting mad because he's having goil problems.
> Maybe it's possible to have too many goils . . . of course only
> Dave would know.

> Kev-sters,
> Howdy! Is Dave still getting the girls? I thought so.

> Karbon,
> Dave still getting the goils? Ha, I realize that's a stupid
> question . . .

> Carbon Both,
> Howz things?! Dave still getting' the goils? Ha – I thought
> so . . . some guys gots all the luck.

> Krotkin,
> Dave still getting the goils?. . . some things never change . . .
> One time he tricked it up a bit:

> Kevvy,
> Has Dave made any addition to his love harem?

Bill was obsessed by David DeBesse's ability to meet, pick up, and hook up with "goils," probably because he was such a failure at it, Laurie notwithstanding. All but one or two of the letters he wrote me start with Bill wondering about the status of Dave's sex life. It was

71

partially Bill's ability to take an idea and bludgeon it into submission; it was partly that Bill was lonely.

He had to be. Otherwise he wouldn't have been constantly hounding me to get Dave to line up some dinner party dates for the next time he came back to Texas. LA was crawling with hot young ass, and Bill was fixated on what his friend two time zones away from him could do to help him get laid. One time he even asked if Dave knew any girls in LA that he could fix Bill up with. Clearly he wasn't getting any.

There was good irony in this, too. We had got Dave to be the singer in Stress in high school because he was everything that Bill and I weren't; specifically, super-good-looking, total football player, had chicks.

When Bill went to LA, a sizeable chunk of the Stratford student body went to Austin to attend the University of Texas. It's an enormous place. Enrollment floats upwards of 40,000 students. In Austin, DeBesse and I got an apartment together our sophomore year. Dave was on *the* path. He was a business major, and still good-looking; and, while he wasn't playing football at Texas, he was still very much a jock. He would have been a yuppie by 25, his parents by 30, retired by 50 with some wise investing. Then Dave inexplicably started trying to convince himself that he was as big a loser as Bill and I were. We wanted to be everything he was; or if not, at least we wanted to get the chicks he had. He wanted to be us. Dumbass.

Anyway, Dave and I had this contest in which whoever got the most mail was more popular. To be "mail" it had to be a letter or something personal. Bills and solicitations didn't count. The object, of course, was to lose, to get the least mail and thereby prove you truly were less popular. Again, Bill and I just wanted to get pussy. And here was Dave, who could get pussy, playing this game because he thought it was somehow leading him down the road to being an artist.

Dave would get the *Wall Street Journal*. It was my contention that this was mail, and since I was tall enough to reach the tote board we kept score on and he wasn't, I would mark it as such. It was just this stupid thing to do, but Bill would call almost every day and ask me, "Did Dave get mail today?" Then he would get on the phone with Dave, "Dude, the *Wall Street Journal* counts."

Bill wanted to be Dave; Dave wanted to be Bill.

Bill still hadn't figured out that the best way to make yourself attractive to women was just to be yourself. None of us really had. Bill was funny and he knew it. Or at least he had an inkling that he was funny enough for people to take notice and that he was only going to get better at comedy. That was complemented by sheer bravado. That's why he was in LA when most of his friends were slacking it in college. Sure, Hollywood was littered with delusional kids certain that they, too, were going to "make it," or whatever. What distinguished Bill was that he was genuinely talented.

Bill never even made mention of interacting with any females, aside from Mitzi Shore, the owner of the Comedy Store in LA. He once wrote me that he was spending a lot of time at the library because he had a crush on a librarian and was "checking her out." He may even have fabricated that for the sake of a pun, bad as it was.

If Bill had just been his own mostly charming self, he would have been fine. Instead of charm, however, he had schemes, very bizarre schemes. Gags. Bits. Whatever. They didn't work in high school. They still weren't going to work because the degree to which they were weird for the sake of being weird was rivaled only by the degree to which they were lame:

> I've got a great new idea. We go up to the girls, right? And we ask the ketchup question. Whatever the answer is, I'll go, "Ha ha. I knew it! Pay up, Mister!" And I'll turn to you and you'll look all discouraged and start counting out the money to me – five hundred dollars! After you've given me the five hundred bucks, I go, "Come on. All of it." You sigh, shrug your shoulders, and reach in your pocket and hand me three pennies, a nickel, a peso, and a rattlesnake rattle. Then you go,

"Wait a minute, I've got a chance to get even . . . Have you
girls ever ridden in the back seat of a bike made for two?"
Whatever their answer is, you go, "All right!" I go, "Shoot!"
and you stick out your hand and I give you back the peso,
the rattlesnake rattle, and the button off my shirt. Pretty
weird, huh?

The question was rhetorical, I know, but, yeah, it was pretty weird, as
well as creepy, strange and absurd.

In addition to asking Dave to hook him up somehow, Bill was also
pleading for stories. He bagged on me for living in a "city where half
of the population of Stratford moved to", yet not digging up enough
gossip to satisfy his curiosity. "Stories. I want stories." Despite physically being in La-La land, mentally he was still half in a Lone Star
State of mind. These were mostly people Bill had spent a good chunk
of time and energy either a) making fun of or b) trying to get away
from. Now, Bill wanted to know what they were up to.

He couldn't cut the umbilical cord. On top of it, Bill was probably
trying to experience college vicariously. The luxury of doing trivial
things was something he didn't have. But for someone who actually
knew what he wanted to do with his life, and didn't drink, college
was really a poor fit. Plus, he was having trouble masking his home-
sickness and his general misery, having second, maybe third and
even fourth thoughts about his LA plans.

Guess who was at the Comedy Store last week? Richard Pryor!
He didn't go up but he was hanging around. I, of course,
wasn't there that night. DAMBO! Oh well – I guess I'll be
spending a couple of nights at the Comedy Workshop when
I'm [in Houston]. Boy, I hope I can stay longer. Not enough
time to try out all the new goil gags. I was really going to use
this Houston trip as a determiner of my next move, but now
it'll be kind of hard to do in only four days. It's really tough
out here. You have to understand what I'm talking about when
I say I want out of here. The Comedy Store is filled with guys

74

that just ain't superstars. I want to be great, and believe me, that doesn't happen in just one year. Look at Richard Pryor or Rodney Dangerfield – years and years and years! You see what I mean? There is no hurry for me now. I must think in terms of longevity. Think of the ups and downs those two have been through. Yikerbooes! The Comedy Store is a comic factory for producing these LA modsters. It's *very* scary. I don't know what to do, ya know? Stay out here and take a chance of not becoming jaded and bored with everything, or leave – give up my position out here, and go to college for a few years and work in a club with a more productive atmosphere. See what I mean? I think I'm gonna take off now. Hang loose. Keep cool. Check you later. Gotcha on the rebound. Shoot me in the face.

Your buddy,
Bill

Bill's letters were like children's books. They were as much about pictures as words, and almost every letter he sent me from LA had some pictorial history of Stress. It was something he hadn't given up on and, inasmuch as that was the case, Bill was still half in Houston. The novelty of LA was wearing off.

The thing is, Bill was doing exceptionally well, by any measure. He had been in Los Angeles less than a year and he was getting regular stage time at the Comedy Store and the second location in Westwood by UCLA. That in itself was no mean feat. On top of that, Bill was living the "someone is going to see me on stage and put me in their TV show" dream.

That's almost how it happened. Bill got a part in *Bulba*, the pilot for a network sitcom cast in a mold similar to that of *Fantasy Island*. Starring was Lyle Waggoner of *Wonder Woman* fame. Bill played the part of Marine Sergeant Phil Repulski, a guard at the Madcap American Embassy Office.

This was still in the days when TV in America was dominated by the three major networks: ABC, NBC and CBS. It's the kind of break people have probably literally killed for at some point. Bill just kind of backed into it. He always did that. Throughout the early part of his career I heard other comedians marvel about how Hicks got work without ever picking up the phone. Even during the times when Bill was getting his phone cut off for not paying the bill, work was still finding him.

When *Bulba* happened Bill was totally stoked. His part wasn't even a stretch for him. Basically he got hired on his impersonation of his father. Do that for twenty-two minutes, and everything else would be cream cheese.

He had some stupid catchphrase like, "Ba-loop baba loop-bop." Just a nonsense word. And one of his sight gags was raising the flag up the flagpole while his pants were falling down. This was very broad, not heady, comedy. He called me, bragging about that scene in particular. The area around the flagpole was fenced off but there were four or five hundred girls from the local Catholic school gathered nearby watching the shoot. They kept cheering Bill on during his scene.

Bill was going to like TV. I remember thinking: "Wow, that's it. Bill is going to be a star."

On one hand, I was happy because, shit, my friend was going to be a fucking star. On the other, I was upset because I thought, "This is the end of Stress." We had both been operating under the assumption that Bill was going to go out there for a little while and that I was going to get a few things in order, then we would get the band back together. Every conversation we had, every letter he wrote: girls and Stress. Bill acted like Stress was something that was going to happen in the future.

In hindsight, Bill was simply keeping all avenues open. I want to be a musician; I want to be a comedian; I want to be a writer; I want to make films; I want to do television.

Only the pilot was an unfunny piece of crap. The network and the rest of America agreed. The pilot aired once, and that was it. No series. No nothing. The end. And it's not like any of the schoolgirls went home with him. He got a decent check out of the deal. He said it was somewhere in the neighborhood of $9000 for a week's work. Not bad.

Bill knew a network sitcom was a completely retarded thing to be doing, but he had just got to LA. To get a sitcom that quickly had been a total coup; he didn't have the luxury of turning it down. And he had been genuinely excited about it. Moreover, it got him a fucking high-power talent agency. By doing this one stupid thing, he advanced a thousand steps.

It's strange. Bill was worried about getting jaded and bored. He was homesick, yet if he had left after his first year in LA, Bill could have counted himself a bigger success than 99 per cent of the people that ever cross the Mojave Desert. Considering the amount of human wreckage LA causes on a daily basis, Bill was kicking ass.

But he had something bigger in mind. "As seen on TV" wasn't who he was. And he wasn't digging it.

Maybe if Bill knew that the vast majority of the world's pornography was produced in his backyard, he might have bucked up.

[* * *]

David DeBesse

When we graduated high school, I didn't really think much of it because it was just this thing that happened. But Bill was so honestly happy for us; it was striking. I remember seeing him right after the ceremony; he was really thrilled. It was just a real honest enjoyment that we were done. It was the stepping-off point for this huge life he envisioned for himself.

It didn't really occur to me at the time, but maybe it's because when he graduated, he packed up and started something. For the rest of us, we were sticking to the script. This is what you do: you graduate high school, you go to college. It was a continuation of something that was very much more the norm. Maybe Bill's excitement was because he had a different sense of what was going to happen, or what could happen.

I don't know if he had any use for high school other than, if he did well enough to stay in, then he could continue living by himself and work at the Comedy Workshop. It was a means to a much greater end for him. He knew if he graduated, he could then go on and do all of the things he wanted. I think he saw it in a much wider scope than we did.

It was an interesting time for me; it was almost like reading *Catcher in the Rye*. I had been surrounded to a large extent by people who were like me. And being around Kevin and Bill and Charles made me aware for the first time of how much else there was. Looking at my own life from a different context, I had this strange, bland set-up for myself; a not-very-interesting plan of going to school. I tried to play football in college at Southwest Texas State but I had discovered I wasn't very good. But I actually approached college very differently because of Bill. It's hard to give one person credit for that but because of the whole thing that happened – getting in the band, meeting Bill, expanding my outlook – I started doing things I wouldn't have done otherwise. I said to myself, "I'm just not going to be on this narrow path."

I took classes in music theory, and ultimately I ended up taking a non-majors acting class for fun. And that hooked me. What had been my plan of economics as pre-law changed to my being an acting major, and going on to having this pathetic career for all of these years.

The whole reason I took the non-majors acting course, was because of Bill. I got interested in acting because at his urging I decided to sign up with a local talent agency. I ended up not getting involved with them when they wanted money and it was clearly a scam, but they later called me to let me know about auditions for the movie *Taps*. The producers were trying to find the leads from unknowns, and were casting in Houston. I ended up getting down to the final eight, not overall but in Houston, and that was all because of Bill saying, "Do this. Go do this." He was way more confident about it than I was. "You can do this." So, I really do have him to blame, now that I think about it.

Anyway, I had transferred from Southwest Texas State to the University of Texas, and changed my major. I was taking a summer course in comedy by a professor, Lee Abraham, and it was a silly class in that the teacher knew in advance he wasn't sure where it was going to take him. By and large the course dealt with physical comedy, using material from Buster Keaton and Charlie Chaplin films. We talked about the elements of comedy in taking a normal situation and turning it into something funny. For example, you are having lunch in the cafeteria, how can you make that funny?

I talked to the teacher and told him my friend was a stand-up and maybe he could come in. Bill did. There was this whole discussion about what you could do – everything leading up to something – then it reached this point where Bill would say, "Then you're funny." You do something funny or you say something funny. He couldn't break it down any more than that. Ultimately you have to have this skill. You can talk about it, but you need actually to be able to do it.

Either you are funny or you aren't. Bill was funny but there was nothing he could tell people to teach them how to do it. And that could frustrate him. He really didn't understand that he was special and that things were easier for him than for other people.

He experienced that with the audience as well. He wanted the audience to go from A to Z in one show. People show up to get a laugh and maybe they are going to leave at C. And maybe when they are at home they are going to think about it later and perhaps find their way to H over a few months. It was going to take time. But it was hard for Bill to not have them be Jim Jones converts by the end of the night. He got it. But people weren't as sharp as he was.

To say that Bill was confident and knew what he was trying to say, and felt the fact that he was right – well, he really did believe the stuff he was talking about – that doesn't mean he had no concern about the feelings of others. Knowing him well, I also saw the person who was affected by things. On some level you have to think that was one of his best qualities because it is also the genesis of wanting to change the world; wishing to make it better because you really want life to be good for people, not just to show somebody they are wrong. Sometimes that is hard to do with Bill because so much of what we saw of him was his public life.

When somebody is the class clown, as Bill was, it is hard to know when he's being himself and when he isn't. People talk about how he was trying to change the world, but he also just loved to laugh. He really enjoyed laughing at things. You get the right people together – and one of the things I remember most about Stress is how much we laughed – and you can laugh yourself silly doing the most ridiculous things.

But I know things did bother him sometimes because there seemed to be something incomprehensible to him on a simple level. For example, when I saw Bill for the last time, he and Kevin had just had a fight about playing music together. It was about playing the blues. Kevin didn't want to and Bill was really upset about that. He was just bothered by it because he couldn't understand what the deal was. "Why couldn't he just play the blues with me?" It wasn't like he was angry at Kevin. That was never the impression I got. But he just couldn't understand, and it really mattered to him.

It gets kind of easy to talk about Bill and forget he did things that were black-and-white and things that were controversial. Or to be more accurate about it, for the purposes of his act he saw the world in very black-and-white ways.

Bill as a messenger is not necessarily the same as the message. There are people who espouse the notion that Bill was very spiritual, and in his own mind he was a preacher – he said as much to his mother – and he was really trying to make the world a better place through his belief system. That's all true, but at the same time he was talking about pornography and drug use and things that were a lot more controversial. Some people want to sweep the vehicle of the message under the rug. It's: let's see Bill as this person with really wonderful goals to change society and make the world a better place, but let's not talk about the *way* he did it because that's kind of uncomfortable. I'm not into drug use in any way, shape or form, but so what? That doesn't mean I couldn't listen to his stuff and laugh and think about the hypocrisy in his comedy. You don't have to agree with everything he talked about specifically to agree with the overall message.

Just look at the world in a broader context, even if you are talking about drug use. It's a horrible thing, then you get the same people going, "Well, we've done our job today. We worked on our campaign for 'Just Say "No" to Drugs.' Let's get to the bar because there's still half an hour of Happy Hour left." They're doing the same thing. It's just a different vehicle.

I find it odd when someone can't stand back and look at the whole picture. I think people get so close to something in a weird way that they get hooked into an idea that Bill was this way and he was perfect, or he was this way and he was horrible. He was just a human being like everybody else. Albeit one with an amazing energy and gifted in so many ways.

CHAPTER 3

After it was clear that the *The Suburbs* wasn't going to get made, wasn't going to get bought, wasn't going to get anything, Hicks was battling a bout of geographical fatigue. It was compounded by a string of gigs back home in the summer of 1982. He used the shows to take the thought of going back home to Texas for a test drive.

In Houston, Bill tracked down Laurie. They went out on a few dates. In Austin, Bill hung out with Kevin and David Johndrowh, who along with Brent Ballard had moved into a house together near the University of Texas. Laurie, whom he had never got over, was in Texas. His best friends were in Texas. There were good comics in Texas. Everything Bill liked in the world was in Texas. What was in LA? Everything else?

During the trip to Texas Bill got into astrology and numerology and any "-ology" he could get his hands on. With numerology, Bill found his number. In numerology, numbers are assigned to letters, and you can derive a number from your name. For "William Melvin Hicks" Pythagorean numerology produces a number of six; the characteristics of a six are to be generally responsible but anxious and guilt-ridden. He worked this out for all of his friends as well.

Bill had a favorite astrologer working out of a bookstore in Austin, and took Laurie to get her chart done. Then he got his chart done. Then he got their chart *together* done. Bill became unglued because his and Laurie's compatibility was off the chart. Sagittarius and Aries generally have a great deal of compatibility in their signs, but theirs was exceptional. Bill also decided he was going to have his and Dwight's chart together done. He called Dwight up, very excited because Bill and Dwight were an even better match than Bill and Laurie. "He said basically that if I had been born with a pussy we'd be perfect together," said Slade.

Bill's hiatus from Hollywood lasted a couple of months. When he got back to LA uncertainty – where to live, how to approach his career, should he reconnect with Laurie – was permeating every aspect of his life. He and Dwight got it into their heads that the way to make a breakthrough, to get guidance, was to open up to the universe, to allow for any spiritual force to enter their lives.

Slade describes it: "We got up on a Sunday, and we were silent the whole day. Lit candles, did prayers back and forth. The idea was to offer up ourselves to God's will, or the will of whatever the Universe's power was."

They started out with meditation. Dwight doing a TM and Bill doing a TM that morphed into a thing of his own design. They listened to a tape Bill had picked up in Austin of an Indian chanter named Kuthoumi. Then, according to Slade, "The next step was to invite in all the masters to help us, to surround the area with white light and protect us as we went through this prayer."

They exchanged prayers about what they wanted. "Bill's prayers were surprisingly Christian in their nature," Dwight recalls. "Mine were kind of generic in terms of 'higher power,' 'universe,' 'nature.' His were 'God, the father,' 'Jesus.' They were very Christian-oriented, which was odd because he felt so betrayed by Christianity. Creative people, especially greatly creative people like Bill, can't ignore their spirituality because it is so essential to their work and their being. It comes up whether they like it or not. And Bill was raised in an environment where you have this – the only way you get to express it is with this two-dimensional dogma that is more about the process than it is the goal. He was so betrayed by that.

"I remember him saying what he wanted most was to do God's comedy. He wanted to do stand-up, and he wanted to do it like it had never been done before. He wanted God to speak through him.

"Later on we went and had doughnuts. It's like we were exhausted so, 'Let's go have some fucking sugar, Jesus.'"

A couple of weeks later Bill left LA. And even though he left some of his belongings behind, it was clear he wasn't coming back any time soon.

When he left, he wrote a note and adorned it with a drawing, a self-portrait of Bill playing the guitar, cigarette dangling from his mouth. WDPS.

Calling the comedy biz in LA "*Sybil* in reverse," Bill was happy to be back home. "There are 10,000 bodies out there with one personality," he said. But LA had taught Bill that he didn't even truly have his own voice yet. Yet. He was about to take a big step towards finding out how to let that voice scream. The dirty clothes in Bill's suitcase had barely had time to air out when he decided he was going to try taking mushrooms.

Bill rang the bell. It's a user's term. He had that seminal experience. On stage that night he claimed he could read the audience's thoughts. Mushrooms did things meditation clearly couldn't. All it took was a few caps and about a half hour and Bill transformed himself into a clairvoyant with dick jokes.

This was the answer. How could he bomb if he could tap into what the audience was thinking? Easily. Bill started taking mushrooms and going on stage every single night. It got less and less effective, and he got less and less funny.

One night he exhausted the mushroom magic completely. He went up on stage after dosing and soon ended up lying in the fetal position on the corner of the stage. The audience took their coasters, their wadded-up napkins, and started playing target practice with Bill's inert body.

Then he turned around. He said to his friends, "You know what? I'm never going to take drugs and go on stage again."

Bill quit doing mushrooms and immediately turned to alcohol. He was at the Workshop in Austin when, having never drunk a drop in his life, Bill started downing tequila shots before going on stage. Here was a kid who had never had those formative experiences where you learn about losing control. Part of teen drinking is learning what you can and cannot handle. Bill missed out on that in his priggish crusades.

When he got on stage, he unloaded, and started berating the audience in general.

Then he got into it with individuals in the audience. That set the blueprint for the mythos of Bill. It wasn't every night. It wasn't even most nights. But it could happen any night. First Bill would get drunk, then he would get really drunk. He'd go on stage and someone in the audience might say something to set him off. And that was it. He'd tear into anything. Says Pineapple, "You know, people were kind of wary about hiring us, because you never knew what was going to happen."

There was one certainty with Bill: the party had started.

Once Bill started drinking, he completely transformed his lifestyle. He wore all black – black shirt, black leather jacket, black sunglasses. The diet was changed. He was off tofu and rice. Smokes? If he couldn't get a Marlboro Red, he'd tear the filter off a Marlboro Light.

His material was changing as well – less pilfering and emulation of his idols – but it still wasn't that hard-hitting. There wasn't any politics, there wasn't any religion. He was angrier, but there was no mission, no message. The anger wasn't focused on anything, it was just stand-up. "Those army commercials, they're inspiring. Aren't they? 'The Army: we do more before 9 a.m. than most people do in a whole day.' Is that supposed to get me to join? I got to bed at eight." Or, "You turn the air conditioner on in a Chevette while driving it, it's like hitting the car in the nuts. Erh. Erh. Erh. Errrr. It goes to five miles an hour. It's like the Flintstones are driving this thing. I hit a moth the other day and did $400 worth of damage."

He did have jokes the joys that accompanied his new-found appreciation for alcohol: "Regularity is more important than lust to me now. You drinkers know what I'm talking about? If I have a solid shit, that pretty much makes my day." And he still did the goober dad.

Bill got an apartment in the Montrose area of Houston, not far from the Annex. The club and the Outlaw Comics became his life. Kinison was gone, but there was still a solid group of comics dedicated to speaking their minds. Epstein had also come back from the aborted assault on LA. They all had the same comedic ethos and generally the same affinity for drinking and drugs.

Was it really that bad? It's a matter of perspective. To a guy like Ron Shock, who had both been a CEO and spent time in jail, the drinking was pronounced but not excessive. Says Shock: "My memories of that time do not include a bunch of drunks. There would be times when they would get plastered, but it wasn't out of hand."

But to someone with a little more white-bread background, like Laurie Mango, who also had the perspective of being more to the edge and not quite in the thick of it, it really was that bad. "You can pretty much summarize the whole thing by the fact that they're now all in AA. It was all about drinking. Going from one drinking thing to another, one bar to another." Pineapple, Jack Mark Wilks, even Hicks himself, they all ended up getting with the program, literally.

On 16 December 1982, Bill turned 21. He celebrated with a set at the Annex in Houston. It wasn't like he and the Outlaws needed an excuse to party, but give them one and they'd take it and run with it.

Bill's 21st was supposed to be a monumental event. When Dwight moved to Klamath Falls, Oregon, his address was 2021 Lakeshore Drive. When he moved to Burbank with Bill, their address was 2021 West Olive. That was enough to convince Bill the universe was orchestrating a scheme with the numbers 20 and 21 involved. Bill had concluded that when he was 21 and Dwight was 20, that's when they were going to make it.

So Dwight called Bill at the Annex on his birthday. Bill was with Laurie, and he was absolutely shitfaced. He was slurring. Dwight was disenchanted. He hung up and thought, "Bill's gone."

Two months later, in February of 1983, Jay Leno came to Austin for six shows. Bill drew the opening slot.

For Bill, it wasn't so much of a break as he was already a known quantity in Austin, but it was six nights in front of locals who might not otherwise make it out to the Workshop. More importantly the friendly relationship the two comedians would forge that week would last Bill's entire life, both for good and bad.

Leno's visibility had increased in the previous year thanks to David Letterman. Letterman's fledging NBC talk show, *Late Night with David Letterman*, had become the hip channel destination for college kids and insomniacs. Leno had already made appearances on *Late Night* since the show hit the air in 1982. Letterman would have Leno on and ask him what his current "beef" was, then Leno would tee off. He wasn't political, it was middleweight ranting. But it was funny and it brought Leno fans.

To wit: Jay packed the house at the Workshop for the week.

Leno hung out backstage with Bill's friends all week: Bill and Laurie, who had come to town for the week; Kevin and his girlfriend Jere; Mavis, Leno's wife, talked astrology and gave the couples personal readings.

From his earliest interactions with Bill, Leno knew he was good, recalling: "I was playing in Austin, and he would come and listen. You know, when you're a comedian, you've been on TV, inevitably, the comedy club owner always says, 'Oh, there's a group of people in the city, would you talk to them about comedy?' Okay, so, one of the afternoons, you go down, you talk to them about comedy . . . I always find when you're teaching comedy, the one who sort of gets up in disgust and leaves and thinks you're a jerk is usually the best comedian in the room."

That was Bill. With Bill opening for him that week, Leno gave him a nickel's worth of free advice. He had to clean it up if he wanted to do television. That was the best way to make it to the next level, to be seen by millions of people at once. "Fuck" wasn't going to get it done with Standards and Practices on any network.

In March of 1983, Bill headed back out to LA to collect his things. He brought his new pet ferret, Neil, with him. When he got to the California border he made the mistake of disclosing the identity of his traveling companion to the authorities. The State of California is fairly protective and restrictive on plants and animals entering the state. No ferret for Bill. Bill turned around, drove back up Interstate 10 a few miles to the rest stop inside the Arizona border. He proceeded to nap and loiter for eight hours. Long enough to assure a shift change at the agricultural inspection station on the California side of the border. Bill stashed Neil in a dirty sock, buried it in his dirty laundry, and said nothing as he drove through the checkpoint station.

The guy who arrived in LA four hours later to see Dwight was completely different from the one who had left LA several months before. The tip-off might have been the all-black wardrobe, but the change was one of more than just clothes. According to Slade, "It was almost as if you were watching your big brother come back from college. He left the varsity athlete star and he came back hippie who's smoking grass."

It was an accurate description, if a bit off in the details, as marijuana was the one drug Bill didn't care for. "Well, this person has taken a giant leap in his own evolution and it certainly doesn't include me. It kind of hurt my feelings but at the same time I had enough respect for him to know it was a step he needed to take. He seemed to communicate that too," says Slade.

Dwight knew Bill was coming back to move out, but he had established his own life in Bill's absence. He was going to school, and was taking a playwriting class. The class instructor was so impressed with Dwight's work that he decided to produce a one-act play Dwight had written. That was occupying most of his spring.

Bill spent the next two months in LA not doing much. LA was the best place in the world to be busy all day doing nothing. He read, smoked, slept, hung out at the Store with his roommate (Dwight, not the ferret). He had a couple of showcases to hang around for. He saw Richard Pryor perform on the Strip, the one "true master" of stand-up, as Bill thought of him.

Bill was also putting together a personal catalogue of his work with Dwight, his past partner to that point. He was collecting and curating himself. Bill wanted to chronicle all of the characters he and Dwight had ever created and preserve them in a less ephemeral format than just mutual recollection. Dwight had an 8mm camera they had played with before. They sat down with pen and paper and brainstormed all the people they had ever invented in the name of comedy.

Although Dwight had continued to build his own life in his friend's absence, still Bill's departure affected him, as he concedes: "The reason I moved down there was to finish a project with Bill, so once he left, I was only there for another three or four months."

In mid-May of 1983, Bill packed up the Chevette and made the 1400-mile journey back to Houston where he promptly made a stab at starting a more practical life. He moved in with Laurie . . . at her parents' house.

Moving back to live with your own parents after leaving to go to school or start a career was usually a sign of failure and humiliation; either that or it made you the ultimate mama's boy. Moving in with someone *else's* parents, especially your girlfriend's, was so unusual that there were no social stereotypes even to attach to it. It was just strange, but Bill got along well with Laurie's parents.

That summer, Bill enrolled in classes at the University of Houston. Also known affectionately by the locals as "Cougar High," U of H was not the most academically rigorous institution. Bill had a couple of standard jokes he told about his foray into college life: "I just couldn't make it up for that eight o'clock class . . . And I was in night school." He studied philosophy: "I found out it all meant nothing and I left."

Bill and academia just didn't make a good couple. But he had his comedy career.

Until he quit, that is. In 1983, at the ripe old age of 21, Bill retired from stand-up.

Bill's first Last Show Ever was at the Comedy Workshop in Austin. By showtime, he was exceptionally drunk. Even by his standards. He got up on stage and started to rant. He was talking about how he wasn't going to end up like Lenny Bruce. He wasn't going to end up in a bathtub dead from a drug overdose. He was screaming at the audience. It stopped being comedy about thirty seconds into it.

One woman in the audience kept calling out to the stage, "We love you, Bill. We love you. Don't go." He yelled back at her to get her own life.

Mercifully some of Bill's friends got up and spared the audience. Spared Bill. Dave DeBesse was among the mercy killers. "I'm fairly certain I wasn't alone in doing it, because it wasn't anything quite that heroic, but I know along with some other people I went up and took him offstage."

On stage Bill was enraged and outraged. He was angry at the audience for needing him to tell them what to think. He was fed up with trying to enlighten them, yelling at them for being lemmings, for not thinking for themselves. Offstage Bill was contrite. "I remember taking him back to the green room. He kept saying, 'I'm sorry, Dave. I'm sorry.' He was apologizing for the set, which wasn't even a set. It feels like he was on stage a really long time, but I'm sure he wasn't."

The retirement didn't last long. More than a month, less than two. Considering that Bill would "quit" comedy dozens of times over the course of his career, it was actually fairly impressive. His other attempts to get out of stand-up usually lasted just a day or two.

[*   *   *]

Kevin Booth

Bill called me up, "Dude, I'm back in Houston." I wasn't surprised to hear Bill's voice on the other end of my phone, but I was surprised by what he was saying. "Oh yeah. Cool," I said. Bill had taken a break from LA once before. It wasn't for very long, maybe a couple of weeks. But he spent so much time talking about it in advance that it seemed longer. This one was unexpected. The first time, in every phone call and every letter he made mention of how he was taking a brief hiatus from LA. This time he had barely said anything until he was already back.

"Dude, I'm here to stay." Again a surprise. And a much bigger one at that. "What about Los Angeles?" Never let it be said I didn't have a flair for the obvious.

"Nope. I'm done. I think Texas is going to be the Third Coast," he opined. That was a term that had been bandied about regionally in recent years. There was New York and LA, but Texas was teeming with creative types as well who didn't much care for the arrogance and narcissism offered in either main option. So with the Gulf of Mexico to the right, locals proclaimed themselves the Third Coast.

"We can make it happen here. The Outlaw Comics are as good as anything going on in LA. And they just don't like me out there. I'm just not getting anywhere." Bill was certainly selling himself short again – they adored him at the Store and he had already done network TV – but he wasn't the first Texan to go west, get bummed out and bored, and come home. Hell, Riley Barber and Steve Epstein had both done it within the last year, give or take. Still, his coming back to Houston was kind of like his admitting defeat in Hollywood. On one hand, Bill felt that's what he was doing. But deep down, he also really did feel that he could do more in Houston. It had a real comedy scene. He had a whole base of friends there. It was a real city (the 4th largest in the US). He could still tour all over the place.

So here he was, back in Texas. Bill wasn't done dropping surprises on me though, and the next was Hiroshima. "Dude, hear me out.

I know you are going to freak when I say this, but tomorrow night you and I are going to take psilocybic mushrooms together."

"Yeah, right."

"No, dude. Seriously."

All I had ever heard about mushrooms was that they caused people to go insane. My parents had convinced me that tripping had triggered my brother Curt's schizophrenia. Even all my pot-smoking friends had bizarre stories about hallucinations. I drew a line and became categorical. "I'll drink. I'll smoke pot, but I'm never going to trip. I'm never going to take acid and I'm never going to take mushrooms."

Bill was telling me: "No, it's not like that. It totally depends on who you do it with. Nothing can harm us because we are so close. We will keep this positive ball of light around us."

"No, I can't, Bill. I can't."

"Kevin. You're going to do it. You're going to do it."

I've always said it: only Bill Hicks could have gotten me to try hallucinogenic drugs. Why? Because he was so against it. He was more against it than my parents – shit, my parents watched what they believed was the destruction of their son at the hands of hallucinogens – than I was, than anybody I had ever met outside of the priesthood! He was against any chemical. He and Dwight, they were like the self-righteous brothers. After getting over the I-can't-believe-it aspect of it, I started to think about reconsidering my stance.

Even my girlfriend, Jere, who had an extensive drug background before we met, was telling me: "No Kevin, you don't want to do that. I can't believe, after all the things you've said, putting down people for doing drugs, now you are actually going to go out and do it."

Bill: "You're going to try this, Kevin. Trust me." Bill was Obi-Wan Kenobi: "These aren't the droids you are looking for." And this was his Jedi mind trick.

I drove down to Houston from Austin. Late that afternoon Bill came and picked me up, and we took mushrooms. One of the other comics, Steve Epstein, I think, had procured them for Bill. He had been going out to a field by the airport to pick them. A little cowshit. A little rain. A little East Texas warmth. Boom. It really was like magic. These suckers were fresh from the field.

We drove down to the Montrose area where Bill was performing that night. We had dinner in the gay area of Houston at a vegetarian restaurant called The Hobbit. "Gay" couldn't have been more appropriate because we sat there and laughed our asses off.

Bill went on stage that night and described it afterwards by saying he thought he could read the entire audience's mind. Collectively. Individually. He had established some kind of connection.

Even before drugs, Bill was trying to push the envelope. He was always saying to me, "There's gotta be something else out there. There has to be more meaning." Bill felt like there was something he was missing, some secret psychological passage or some track to try to take things to another level. Suddenly, he thought he had found it.

That night he had an incredible mind melt with the audience, and I was right there with him. Totally in sync.

That launched the next incarnation of Bill. After that night on stage he told me, "This is it. This is the trick. I've got to start taking mushrooms every night before I go on stage." He did. Again Bill wasn't an 85 per cent kind of guy. Once he made the decision, he was committed. Full on.

Bill spent every night after that chasing the same experience. He was textbook in his failure. The same dosage came up a bit short on night two. "Maybe if I just take more mushrooms." So night three he took more mushrooms. Same result? Still can't read the audience's mind? Night four he took even more. Ad infinitum.

It didn't work. It never works. That's the thing about drugs: you can never recapture that virgin moment where you get that rush and that new part of the world just opens up.

His frustration was compounded by the fact he was sharing it with an audience who was watching him bomb more spectacularly each time out. Bill was speeding down a dead-end alley; and the closer he was getting to the wall, the faster he was going, the more fuel he was trying to pump into his body. He was going full tilt when he hit the wall.

Bill lay on stage curled up in a fetal position. Do not pass go. Do not collect $200.

Throughout his life, Bill made comments about how he felt like an alien on this planet. Like there was something about him that was different. He didn't know how to have a pleasant but inane conversation, didn't know how to watch football with the guys; didn't know how to play golf and would not talk about it like it was a fucking spiritual journey – all of the things that allow you to pass through this world undetected, Bill was no good at. So he felt.

Then you watched him, or you were around him, and he would say and do things that made you think, "God he really is like an alien." And the way he put it was so funny, because he sounded like someone who had just landed on this planet. He turned to me and asked: "What's alcohol?"

This was after ages of hanging out in clubs watching people get inebriated and ruthlessly making fun of them; after years of him and Dwight doing impersonations, imitating drunks and the dumb things they say and do. But Bill was looking for what might be next. "What's alcohol. What does it do?"

I told him: "Well, it kills your inhibitions. It makes it so you don't give a fuck about anything or what you do in front of other people." Shit, wrong answer. I mean, it was the right answer but it was the wrong thing to say to Bill.

"That sounds perfect. What's a drink? What's a drink people drink?"

"I don't know?" I was caught offguard and still processing the flip Bill had just flopped. "Tequila. Maybe margaritas. That's a drink people drink." This is Texas. It's hot. margaritas are a dietary staple and tequila is what makes a margarita a "drink."

"Okay, I'll have seven," Bill announced. He had no patron saint of moderation. Bill knocked back seven shots of tequila before going up to do his set. Bill had his first train wreck to accompany his first drink. The disaster started while Bill was putting back the tequila, when he had the unfortunate pleasure of hearing the paying customers fawning over the mediocre comics performing before him. Bill had brewed contempt for the audience before he even got up there. When he got on stage, it was blind rage.

It wasn't just being drunk; tequila is a harsh drink, it puts an edge on everything. So if you're predisposed to anger and hatred, Bill couldn't have chosen a better (read: worse) way to lubricate his rage. Bill was combustible and the tequila had lit his fire – it was only a matter of time. He tore into the audience, berating them and letting them know how much he hated them, how much they were responsible for the fact that everything in the world sucked.

"You people, you're the ones responsible for Gary Coleman! You're the reason why *Diff'rent Strokes* is the number-one show on TV!" Bill had never had a drop of alcohol in his life. Not. One. Single. Drop. He went straight from that to seven shots of tequila straight. Belligerent. Fuck You. All of that.

He was ranting about how the flag didn't represent anything and he started talking about America's Bullshit Wars. Vietnam was a Bullshit War. Korea was a Bullshit War. To all rational observers and armchair pundits, we were on the eve of getting ourselves into another Bullshit War.

There was a couple sitting near the stage who were none too pleased with Bill's views on foreign affairs. At some point Mrs. Patriot Missile had heard enough: "My husband fought in Korea for your freedom." She tore into Bill. The husband, a big, older guy with anchor tatts on his arms, sat there as the fireworks started going off. He and the missus were Americans, for sure, right down to their colors: blue collar, redneck and white trash. "He fought in that war so you could have the freedom and the right to stand up there and say what you're saying."

Bill fired back: "Your husband didn't do shit for me. I didn't ask him to fight for me. I didn't ask him for shit."

They exchanged a few "did not" "did too" blows. Then the vet stood up. He was also super-drunk. He flared out his chest and verbally beat on it like a simian: "You don't know what you are talking about. My friends laid down their lives for your freedom."

Bill. "No they didn't. No they didn't. No they didn't." Bill wasn't backing off. "The price of freedom is high? Bullshit." Bill didn't buy into it. "Freedom is free. Freedom is fucking free!"

It's amazing that episode didn't end in violence. For all of the inflammatory shit he said on stage, for all of the staunchly political views he took, and for all the antagonizing of audience members he did, it's somewhere between statistical anomaly and miracle that Bill didn't get the shit beaten out of him on a regular basis.

When people got up to leave Bill's shows, Bill didn't just let them go. He encouraged them to go with epithets: "Go. Go ahead, you fuckers, leave. Go home to your American Gladiators. Go. Get the fuck out."

It's not to say that Bill's shows weren't without incident, it's just that the incidents seldom ended up with Bill being on the receiving end of a fist or chair. Not that he didn't deserve it every now and then.

LA had caused Bill to re-examine some of his deepest-held beliefs. His comedy had been stagnating. And before, when he got into a rut in Houston, he could always blame it on being in Houston: you were only going to go so far when you were a thousand plus miles from the epicenter of showbiz. That excuse was off the table. In LA he had been performing at the same club where Richard Pryor got his start, and that was deeply symbolic to Bill.

Drugs were seeping out of the walls at the Comedy Store in LA. Legend has it that Pryor himself used to have a bodyguard who would escort him from the stage to his car after the show because there were so many drug dealers and hangers-on waiting around who wanted to give him free blow. He needed a bodyguard just to get out of there or it was a three-day coke binge waiting to happen.

People wanted to hand the really good comedians free drugs. That's just the way it was. It was the Eighties. This wasn't like a high-school keg party, this was Bill's workplace. And it was one of the few places in LA that he liked to hang out. So Bill was surrounded by it.

Bill also wanted to take the spirituality and the TM and do something with it. He was sick of *talking* about levitating, he wanted to levitate. He didn't want to imagine his third eye, he wanted to see through it. He was ready for all of it. All of the things he had read about and learned about with Dwight, he was ready for them to manifest themselves in some way. Bill wanted it to be something more than a concept. He wanted to open his eyes and see trees talking to him. He wanted to split across time. Static to kinetic.

So, comedy-wise he was feeling stagnant; drugs were all around him, and drugs might help facilitate advancing his spiritual quest. And maybe his deeply held beliefs weren't that deeply held. For a person of such great conviction, he was hopeless at making radical changes.

Plus, he was getting reassurance from his peers. Guys like Steve Epstein were able to say, "Bill, it's totally normal. Nothing bad is going to happen. It will only last a few hours. There is no physical damage." So Bill tried it. And it was, "Oh my God. This is the answer to everything."

So in just a few weeks Bill had gone from teetotaler to drinker and drug user. Given Bill's personality, it wasn't difficult to see where this would eventually wind up.

Bill had spent so much time and energy putting down people who used drugs it was practically a second career. So when he turned up in Austin after the mushroom experience wanting to drop acid, it put me in the awkward position of having to look like a total hypocrite. Among the users Bill had made fun of were my girlfriend Jere and her friends. Now I had to ask Jere, the object of Bill's ridicule, to get drugs for him and me.

"We're doing this for spiritual reasons," I excused myself.

We really did want it for spiritual reasons. We were trying to break barriers. Which ones, we didn't know, but we were experimenting for the same reasons people turned on in the Sixties. We were pioneers, we wanted to go there, too, wherever it was the acid would take us.

We ended up scoring, from the cousin of Jere's friend. He came riding up on rollerskates to sell us some blotter acid. He had four little postage-stamp-size hits in a dime bag. One each for me, Bill, Jere and David Johndrow. Blue cheers. Pink panthers. Purple hearts. Yellow sunshine. We never even knew what it was, but we dropped it.

We wanted some kind of breakthrough, but the acid trip was fundamentally different from that first mushroom trip. Everything seemed so harsh. When someone would knock on the door it was a bummer. When the phone would ring it was a bummer. When we had to get something to eat it was a bummer. This wasn't what we wanted.

Bill had read Carlos Casteneda's *The Teachings of Don Juan, A Yaqui Way of Knowledge* and some of John Lilly's work. He was also more interested in naturally occurring hallucinogens than anything concocted in a bathtub laboratory. So the budding psychonaut made a reasonable inference from what he was absorbing: this is a communion with nature you are trying to achieve, ergo, go to nature.

That's when we first decided to go to the ranch. And that's where everything changed.

We took this seriously. We prepared for our trips. We fasted for a day and a half before. We did yoga and meditation. It wasn't just us getting fucked up. Others thought differently, but we behaved differently. They were taking pills and going to titty bars. We were taking mushrooms and sitting by the pond on my family's ranch until we were transported to the Last Supper and talking to Jesus.

Going to the ranch totally changed the experience of acid. The first times we did it in Austin, all the noises of the city – the sounds of cars and sirens and even the buzz of the fridge and the lightbulbs, all of the man-made things surrounding us – would turn into anchors and walls. You don't realize it because you are so used to living in it, but when you are tripping in it, first it seems artificial, second it stops making sense.

One time Bill, David and I were tripping and we went to a McDonald's drive-thru to get something to drink. And it was just bizarre and confusing, the colors, the sound of the voiceover speakers. Those people who take acid for the first time and go to a Black Sabbath concert, they probably think they have died and gone to hell.

When you take acid in the city, "Wow, everything is weird." When we took acid and went out the middle of the woods, "Wow, I'm following my spirit guide." In nature, it became more a journey of the mind; more an experience of being one with the world. Once Bill not only discovered tripping but also discovered the doors that tripping in nature opened up, you couldn't keep him off the ranch.

It was another one of the astounding reversals Bill made in his life.

During Bill's senior year at Stratford I dragged him out to Fredericksburg. Charles Lloyd was going to come out and we were going to have a Stress mini-reunion. Bill missed Stress so much that I figured he would be excited about playing together again. Instead he spent the whole time complaining about how he was stuck. He was pacing the floor, worrying about what he was missing.

BILL
The Tonight Show is going on in LA right now and I'm not a part of it.

KEVIN
Bill, can't you just enjoy nature? Take a break.

BILL
No, this place is backwards. It reminds me of places I would go as a child.

KEVIN
Bill, there are plenty of things to do for fun out here.

BILL

We are never going to get a big showbiz break out here in the
middle of nowhere, Kevin.

KEVIN

But look, isn't the bright red dirt pretty?

BILL

No, it reminds me of Mississippi. I hate it. I hate it.

KEVIN

Jesus, Bill. You are here. Just enjoy it.

BILL

I can't. Life is short. It's short.

He was being irrational. And he was being a baby. But he felt that
without the carbon monoxide to feed his city-starved lungs he was
withering away. God, it was a couple of days with his friends. Chill.
Please.

He tried to get into it. He once had a pet raccoon as a child, so he
decided he was going to build a raccoon trap. With a stick propping
up a box, it looked like something out of a *Road Runner* cartoon.
That had to be the design inspiration. Beep fucking beep. Bill also
rode my Suzuki dirt bike around. He went over a jump and had a
horrible wipe-out. I rushed to check the condition of the bike.

BILL

Holy shit. I just had a wreck. I could be laying here with
broken arms and all you care about is that stupid motorcycle.

KEVIN

You're fine. Quit being a baby.

Charles finally showed. We set up on the patio. Once we started
playing, Bill's demeanor improved. He had a good time being Stress
again, but he was still visibly detached and worrying about what he

was missing. Turned out to be nothing. Bill took a bus back to Houston and had us send his amplifiers back.

When Bill came back to Texas, he and Laurie also got back together, but Bill was still tortured by bits of her past. After they had broken up in high school, Laurie started dating this guy named Mike Warthan. Mike wasn't from Bill's circle of friends. Maybe their circles overlapped at some point on the perimeter, but they weren't friends. So Laurie's dating Mike tortured Bill for a couple of reasons. First, as much as jocks, Bill hated pseudo-intellectuals, guys who thought they were smarter than they were; guys who stood in front of Van Gogh paintings and said things like, "The way the pigmentation is presented reflects an imagery that is so astonishing."

That was Mike: a homely, poorly dressed, socially awkward high-schooler, but he was up at the top of the class academically, where Laurie was, and he smoked pot. That didn't make him cool, but it kept him from being a total loser in the eyes of others. But not Bill, because while Mike acted like he was friends with Bill and cared about Bill, Bill hated his guts.

When Bill found out they'd had sex without using a condom, it drove him nuts. Now he and Laurie were back together he had to deal with her having been with someone he detested. Bill became obsessed with the question of when a guy comes in a girl, does it all ever really come out?

"There's no way. All of those folds. All those compartments down there. All of those weird places. It just goes on for ever. When a guy comes in a girl there's no way it ever all comes out. So in essence when-ever I am going down on her, I am eating Mike Warthan." What a fucking nightmare it used to be. It was one of the things when he was drunk and angry that he would not let go of. It's like Bill was carrying her baggage. It was chivalrous, if you took it literally. Taking it figura-tively, Bill was just torturing himself and everyone else in his life.

As well as living with Laurie at her parents' house in Houston, Bill was also spending a lot of time in Austin. David Johndrow and I had moved into a house in Hyde Park a few blocks north of the University campus. 609 41st Street. It was next to the Hancock Golf Course. We called it the Biggs House because our landlord was named Mr. Biggs. The house actually stayed rented in our circle of friends for years. Mr. Biggs didn't know we all knew each other and just kept passing the house down.

Next door to the Biggs House was this Christian cult. It wasn't a cult per se, but it was definitely cultish. There was a mid-thirties, happy born-again running the house. He was like a proto-Koresh, right down to the mullet. And he looked at us as a bunch of people who needed to be saved. I think on some level we wanted the same for him.

He had shiny happy followers, though. We did not. We didn't even have groupies. The whole downstairs of the neighbor's house was set up like a classroom/church where they had Bible studies every day.

When we were playing music late at night he would come over sometimes and tell us we were horrible. He didn't tell us we were horrible because the music was bad, he told us we were horrible because we didn't play Christian rock. Of course, he was never hostile to us. Instead he was constantly suggesting: "Hey, why don't you come over and let's talk?"

And Bill would. He wanted to know: "Show me God. Show me Jesus." We were openly exploring all the religion we could get our hands on. One day we would take acid and meditate and read Buddhist texts, then the next day we would go to a Bible study class. The next day a Baptist church. And a Catholic church the following day.

If we had Jehovah's witnesses knocking at the door, Bill would let them in and sit there and have a debate about Jesus and God. He wouldn't debate by going: "No, you're wrong. You're wrong." He would sit there and listen to them and try to understand them.

It was zetetic: "Look, if Christianity really is the only way, and having a relationship with Jesus really is the only way, then come on, show it to me. I want to know. But I need to see it for real." As far as I know he never saw it.

Thing was with Bill, at the end of the day, he could have a debate and after it was over, even if he still disagreed with everything, he could say: "Well, I accept you as you are. Let's go break bread as brothers."

When Bill started doing drugs and alcohol, it would just give the fundamentalists an extra edge of condemnation: "Look where your beliefs have brought you." But they just didn't get it. Bill's whole trip was: "I have my own communication with God. We are all the son of God. No middleman required." And initially, the drugs were part of that communion and that communication. That's how it started, anyway.

Just a few blocks from the Biggs House was a place called Float to Relax. They had flotation tanks to help you, well, relax. Yeah, they weren't trying to trick anyone with that name. Flotation was actually more about sensory deprivation. And nearly every time Bill came to Austin, he would want to go at some point during the visit. Over a period from some time in 1982 until some time in 1985, Bill, David and I (and any other number of friends from the circle) went somewhere together between fifty or sixty times.

It was something that usually involved drugs and again something with which we were impossibly ritualistic in our approach. Before we'd go into the tank, we'd each take the same drug in the same amount at the same time. We tried just about everything. One day it was Valium, the next mushrooms, the next Percodan, the next Mandrax. We were trying to synchronize the experience. For example, Bill, David Johndrow, Steve Epstein and I would all take whatever hallucinogen we had selected for that particular day, then we'd agree all to focus on the same thing. "Okay, concentrate on some cake ingredient," or letter of the alphabet or color, etc.

We would each crawl into a separate tank. We'd come out an hour later. "You were thinking about flour, right?" No. Bill: Eggs. David: Vanilla. Steve: Icing. Is icing even a fucking ingredient? It never worked. We did have some pretty intense visions, but we never achieved clairvoyance. We couldn't read minds when we were sober and sitting on the couch watching TV. We weren't going to read minds floating in heavily salinated water. It did make our skin itch, though.

At some point a video arcade moved into the space adjacent to Float to Relax. Good walls make good neighbors, but these walls weren't quite good enough. Bill was lying in the tank and he could hear Pac Man coming through the walls. He's trying to meditate, and this wakka – wakka – wakka – wakka is rippling through the tank. That was the last time Bill ever went to Float to Relax.

It wasn't the end of Bill's fascination with sensory deprivation, however. Bill once developed a personal and portable sensory deprivation device. It consisted of a pillow and a belt. You wrap the pillow around your head and strap it secure with the belt. Voilà, you are now in the neurological netherworld. He was serious. He even talked to a lawyer about patenting the idea.

Aside from such ridiculous ideas, we were almost artful in our approach, and obsessively so. We were trying to break boundaries. What those boundaries were, we weren't even sure. Everyday life just seemed so everyday, so let's try anything and everything we can to get beyond feeling ordinary and average. Basically we were just getting high, but we truly were aiming for something more.

I guess we never thought we were using it as a crutch. Looking back, I'm sure a lot of people would think it was, but we had this really analytical, exacting approach to it. For all the acid and later mushroom and ecstasy trips at the ranch, first we all had to meditate for two hours, and we had to fast for twenty-four to thirty-six hours. Those were the basics. It got ridiculously specific. We were all going to eat two carrots before taking acid and drink three glasses of water. We had to drop at precisely 17:15, because the sun would be setting at 18:00. All these things were really important to us.

[*   *   *]

105

Laurie Mango

All of this traveling, all this moving from town to town, living out
of a suitcase, you know, it's a hard life for anyone to comprehend.
It's going to take one very special woman . . . or a lot of average
ones.

– Bill Hicks

I remember sort of "officially" meeting Bill, if you want to put it that
way. He was in a few of my classes, and I had gone through the Wendy's
drive-thru where he was working. That's how he noticed me. The funniest thing is how we finally met. It was the very last day of school,
I think our sophomore year of high school – 1978.

I was going down the stairs, and he comes up from behind me,
and says, "Laurie Mango, how would you like to go out on a big high
school date?" There was a very sarcastic tone to it, so of course I
laughed. I turned around and it was him. I think I said, "Sure!" or
something dopey like that. I had seen his face around – we were in
Biology class together or something, too – but that was our first
introduction, as I recall, anyway. I said "Sure" or "When?" or whatever. I don't remember the rest. I gave him my phone number.

Our first date was just wonderful. We bonded immediately. He
had the exile-from-the-rest-of-society thing going already. And, high
school being a great thing to feel cynical and exiled from, he had this
dark soul; or not "dark soul" so much as "Isn't this all a bunch of
bullshit?"attitude. He was this misanthrope.

He started in on his perspective of the life we were living, and,
although I can't say I shared that perspective at that time, he had
enough of something I identified with, resonated with, that we
clicked. We really clicked at an intellectual and philosophical level.

I definitely felt like I wasn't sure where I fitted in, either. If anything, I was one of the nerdy types, but I didn't fit in with any clique.

I had an antisocial bent as well, but we also both had this very kid-like side to us. On that first date before dinner we decided, "Let's go to Toys R Us." We're running around Toys R Us, just laughing at the absurdity of it all, buying rubber giraffes, which I still have to this day. For some reason, I kept the giraffe. That's how it started, and the whole summer we had this classic, wild, young summer romance, including drive-in movie theaters. It was the Seventies. We were in his father's car. It's just too funny.

But that element of the social misfit was genuine. It wasn't that Bill was miserable. That's not who he was. He was, in fact, living and loving as much as anybody else, but there was an intellectual side of having a greater perspective, almost like someone with a lot of wisdom coming back and laughing at how wrapped up in stupid little things people get in high school; how trivialities can become so amplified.

He was right. I can think back on myself – the make-up, what you're wearing, all the superficial stuff, especially for girls in Texas. Oh my God. In a different way, it was true for boys as well. So that perspective was real for him, and it was the source of his comedy. I think that way of looking at high school and suburbia is where his comedy came from.

But the tortured part of it – not to get too deep here – even though it allowed him to make fun of things, to turn it into comedy, I think there was something painful to him about the fact he didn't completely feel he was part of something. He felt isolated at some level. I really believe that was real. It's impossible for me to say with complete certainty what he was like at 15. I'm sure I'm retro-applying some of this now that I know what he turned into, but to the extent that I can be objective in talking about what he was like then, I would say the isolation was real.

By senior year we weren't together. I was kind of nasty and broke up with him. What it came down to was: it wasn't just me, it was the way Bill did everything. Bill fell deeply in love, or so he thought. How in love can you be at the age of 16? After the summer with me, and into the next year, it scared me. I wasn't ready. Not that he was asking me to marry him, but he was writing me love letters every day – long love and sex letters – gushing stuff about how much he loved me.

A lot of it was hormones. Part of it was just how Bill did everything; he was an extreme person. Just like he got into drugs and alcohol in a very extreme way. If he was going to do something, he did it to the 89th degree. So that's how he was with me. The other part was that he was more mature than me, in the sense that I was very caught up in appearances. I was too into that crap that I didn't want to make out in the halls or hold his hand. Stupid things like that. I was too embarrassed. Not embarrassed because it was him, but maybe because of how it looked to other people.

Anyway, it ended with me saying: "I can't take this, goodbye." Then I also developed a crush on somebody that was in his circle of friends. I think he really hated me for a while because I started dating this other guy, Mike Warthan.

We got back together when I was in college and he was wandering around, becoming a stand-up comic. When we got back together, he was drinking. It was a real contrast. I had been out with him once during my freshman year. He was doing the veggie thing and meditating. He kept claiming he was levitating. I didn't believe it, but I believed that he believed it. He was ultra-healthy – legumes, veggie, the whole thing.

The next time I went out with him was about a year later – and I love this about Bill, this is such classic Bill – the very next time, he was smoking Marlboro reds and drinking straight scotch.

It fitted beautifully with me, because I had just broken up with my first love in college. He was a mountain climber, and he had rejected me because I had gained some weight in college, so I was now anti-everything about healthy people. I was completely ready. I picked up cigarettes and booze right along with Bill.

When Bill moved back to Houston from LA, we lived at my parents' house. It really wasn't as weird as it sounds. You want to hear weird? Weird is how he used to talk about my mother being really attractive.

I know it now, but back then I had never heard the thing about teenage boys being into good-looking mothers. Even more so – and I think this is pretty weird – he used to talk about, and I think seriously, that he really wished I would get little gray hairs put into my head. Dyed gray. No stripes, but a little dusting of gray.

Bill and my mother had an odd relationship, not sexual, never physical, but they had something really interesting going on. He definitely bonded with her. For instance, he would go into the study with her – and I'm around, but doing something else, obviously – and have a couple of bottles of wine, and just sit and talk to each other and drink wine for maybe three hours. That's a little weird, especially when your girlfriend is in the same house. But my mom, she really resonated with him.

Bill loved women, not just physically. I think he had a side of his persona that found everything about women, including how they think and act, unbelievably fascinating and attractive. He had a real deep attraction to women in all ways – almost in a spiritual, mystical way. Some of his love letters to me in high school even had that side to them. It was coming from somewhere deep inside, a place that was way beyond what you would expect to find in a 16-year-old. It was almost an obsession.

Bill's relationship with my parents was absolutely a surrogate for that with his own. And they played surrogates for more than just Bill. I have another friend who also developed cancer but recovered from it. His parents were just monstrosities, so my parents played surrogates to him too. I wasn't in a relationship with him, he was just a friend.

Bill ran all sorts of things by my parents. That summer he lived with us we had a big discussion about whether or not he should change his name. He really wanted to change his name. I don't think we got as far as coming up with alternatives. The discussion really just kept revolving around should he or should he not. My father especially, was arguing vehemently that he should not, that "Bill Hicks" was a great name. It was a great stage name, a great name in every way. Bill, however, hated "Hicks," he wanted to distance himself from his family; this was something commonly done by other comics. We also had long discussions about whether he should stay in comedy at all. That was the summer he went to the University of Houston, summer school. And he even retired from comedy.

I think, frankly, one of the things that drew him to me was that I was going to all these schools – to university and med-school, getting degrees. Bill was kind of mad at himself for not having gone that route. I would talk to him about that too. "It's just a different route, it doesn't make me smarter or any better than anyone." But he would get on himself about that.

It really did bother him that he didn't go to university. I think there, too, is where you're seeing his parents come through – their voice of what makes you legitimate and what doesn't. He couldn't ignore it. We heard all about it the summer he stayed with us. The theory was that he was going to the University of Houston to become an actor, but the other thing was that he just wanted to go to university. He thought he was missing something.

I think he found out he wasn't missing anything. He found university as absurd as high school and just couldn't take it. It was a philosophy class – and that was the wrong thing for him to take – that really finally did him in. He said, "All of this is just absurd." And it helped in some ways. It once and for all gave him the answer he needed: "You're not missing anything, and these people aren't any smarter than you, definitely aren't smarter than you, and your true calling is to be a comic."

It wasn't just a period, it was for a good number of years I was with him. Every night he was questioning what he was doing. After every show. It was like self-doubt, "Am I funny?" God, how many times did I hear that question from him?

I use the word "torture" when I talk about what he was dealing with in himself. It was like an obsessive torture. Constantly. I'm sure a lot of comics question themselves, but he really meant it. "Oh my

God, I'm not funny." And he had done so well, people were laughing so much, it was like, "What is he not seeing?"

So for a long time I was playing the role of: "No, you're so funny," but that got old. I began to try to get to a different level by asking him, "Where's this coming from? What is this inability to see what's happening around you?" Of course, that answer was given on stage, too. It was his family, I guess. Or who knows? I actually gave up trying to understand Bill.

But it was genuine insecurity. A mixture of insecurity and having unbelievably high standards for himself. It wasn't manufactured to drive himself. I think Woody Allen was one of the few comics Bill respected, but there weren't many others. It was that level he was thinking he had to be at, or he wasn't good.

Certainly he needed the laughs from the audience. That satisfied his ego. He might even have been hard on himself because he needed that. It was a bit of an addiction. Sure, all comics have that kind of addiction, or else they won't drive themselves to make people laugh. But Bill had a weird love-hate relationship with the audience too. It was almost like somebody looking for a drug they needed. They loved it, but they hated it. It made them feel good, but they hated that it made them feel good.

He used to tell me that after shows, too. "Oh what a stupid audience." And this also is classic Bill. If the audience laughed at someone that came up before him, someone he considered not funny – which was most people, right? – then their laughter for him meant nothing. He would tell me, "No, no, no. They laughed at that guy. What do they know?" It's like judging their humor. And he did absolutely contemplate not going on stage because of that. I witnessed that. I don't know if he ever pointed it out to the audience, that they had laughed at a complete idiot who wasn't funny. Probably in one of his drunken rants, he pointed that out. He did everything during his drunken rants.

Bill had this unbelievably serious side to him. One of the ways we really connected, in high school and even in college, what he really loved about being around me, was he didn't feel like he had to be "on." He didn't have to make jokes; and he felt that, with a lot of his friends, or in general, he had to be funny around them. That was why they liked him.

Somehow our connection was different. It wasn't like he never made jokes or was never funny, because he did do that, too. But there was this other side – it had an element of philosophy to it: about matters of life and death, about "What does it all mean?," a side of him used drugs to try and get at those things, and that side of Bill was unhappy about being a comedian because he wasn't getting close enough to it. And he identified with the Baptist in his blood as if, "My calling really is to be spreading the word." The problem was that he didn't know what the word was! And it certainly was not organized religion. His version of the word always ended up being something that was delivered in his stand-up.

But I think what really pissed him off the whole time was, "Yeah, but this is comedy. This is just people laughing. I want to be sharing knowledge with them." That's what Bill really did want to do – discover truth, understand the world and share that enlightenment with other people. He felt a bit like it cheapened it to be delivered in a way where people laughed. That's really more him than anything else: this desire to learn and understand, ask the big questions, and then pass that on to us. You can see that in some of his comedy. The whole thing about how life is just a ride.

We had our most intense bonding times when I was in my early twenties. He hadn't really "made it" yet. He was still struggling. We lived together in this little apartment on Richmond and he was going to the comedy club there.

The apartment we had was really slummy. We shared it with our two ferrets. It was pretty run-down and had a pawn shop, a liquor store, and something else, maybe a convenience store, or maybe it was even an adult books store right across the street. We used to joke: "One stop shopping for comics." I never realized how bad it was until the little brother of a very close friend came to visit us there and he was just horrified. But we were very happy together and very much in love; I have very sweet memories of that time. We were friends and lovers, intellectual mates, and all the rest that went with it. I felt like it was a pretty healthy relationship in that sense; it was multifaceted.

I didn't party with the comics as much as some, but when Bill and I were together we did coke a lot. Bill's drug of choice was LSD; well, actually he much preferred mushrooms to acid, but with Bill it was definitely, "Let's have an experience together." I did acid with Bill a couple of times; we definitely did chemical engineering together – mixing and matching. But most of the times I was hanging out with them, it was drinking.

It wasn't like he was just getting fucked up like everybody else, because Bill wasn't like everybody else. He really did things differently. Even though, from a behavioral perspective, it's doing the same things, Bill managed to make it a different experience. There was a party side to him for sure, but there was also an I-need-to-do-this-to-get-away-from-things escapist aspect to it, too.

I had a really strange trip with him once. This is odd because it points to his spiritual, mystical side, whatever you want to call it. Yet looking back as a physician, it really makes me wonder if it wasn't also a prelude to his pancreatic cancer. He would describe it for me – the pain in his left side, his left abdomen – and it really came out in this one trip. What he would always tell me was that it was a remnant of a bad prior life, and he removed it.

When we had this acid trip together, he went through what he later claimed was a rebirth experience, with me being his mother. How Freudian is that? That's when he put it together, that this pain in his left side was related to the fact that his birth didn't go well.

I don't remember all the details about how he was given birth to. It just made me wonder. A lot of people with pancreatic cancer have pancreatitis, which is the inflammation of the pancreas. And especially with his drinking, it wouldn't be inconceivable that it could have been causing a pain on the left side of his abdomen.

I remember him talking about that pain a lot, not just during trips. Obviously it was something that was deep down in his memory and consciousness for it to come out during all these trips. Who knows if it was medically related or not; I just thought it was strange and another classic Bill story, because it's just high drama. You're going to go through a trip and it's not just going to be watching the trees move, it's going to be having a birth experience with your girlfriend as your mother.

But the drinking, it really was that bad. They could all drink unbelievable amounts of alcohol. Bill would put down thirty scotches in a night, over the period of five or six hours at a club. That's not an exaggeration; he was downing five an hour easily. Hard liquor, too. Bottles of it. At Birraporreti's, I remember they had racked up like a $5000 bar bill. I couldn't believe the sum. They had to do a show just to pay the bar bill.

Bill wasn't fun to be with then. He was slurring his words, he couldn't walk. There were lots of nights like that. But he was a person of extremes, and I tended to be, too. He often blacked out. He wouldn't remember anything the next day. He was asking, "What did I do?" He wouldn't remember that he hadn't been nice to me.

Was it the worst drinking I had ever seen in my life? Certainly not. Was it extreme drinking? Yes.

I think it's right to say that the only reason Bill did coke was so he could keep drinking. Alcohol was the thing he loved most.

We did one road trip driving around Texas together. I remember we were doing coke in the car. We'd stay up all night with some of his friends and do coke. The coke made you able to drink more, so it was drinking, playing poker, and doing more coke. And even while we were doing it, we had the idea, "You know, this is going to get old." It was okay while we were in our twenties, but there was the sense that this was going nowhere fast. There was a slight desperation to it for both of us.

But he was definitely a real alcoholic. Later, he told me that I was an alcoholic. That was in Houston House. He got sober and we got together at his place and he was telling me that I needed to get sober as well. Then he left for New York.

[*　　*　　*]

CHAPTER 4

I don't have any luck in school. One time in first grade our teacher left the room; we started playing keep away from this guy with his pencil. Everyone is laughing. It came to me, I threw it. It went in this guy's eye. Everyone in class is going, "Jesus, Hicks it's a game, chill out! What are you, a psycho?" And suddenly I'm Henry Lee Hicks here because this guy can't catch a number two pencil like a normal human being. "I got it UHH." Good move, you dork, I'm an assassin now.

One day I was late to class. This guy who sits next to me pulls my chair, I hit the floor, everyone laughs. Even the teacher, "He, he, he, he. That's what you get for being tardy."

"Great, I can sleep better down here anyway."

Later on that same guy was late running into class.

I pull his chair, he hits the floor in the middle of class, breaks his back.

"Get up."

"Try."

He is in my classes for the next five years.

[Bill mimics a guy in a wheelchair.]

"You're real funny, Hicks."

Guy with one eye pushing him around.

[Bill mimics a one-eyed guy pushing the wheelchair.]

What are you supposed to say to these guys?

"Well, you all can park closer to the school now. No more tardies!"

– Bill Hicks

117

Jay Leno made good on a promise to Bill, and on his recommendation, Letterman's people decided to bring Bill in to audition for the show. Bill couldn't have designed a better way to sabotage the deal if he had wanted to. First, he didn't have a working phone-line as the one in his apartment had been cut off. A leitmotif of his lifestyle: large bills and non-payment, that'll happen. *Late Night* producer Robert Morton had to call the Comedy Workshop in Houston, then someone from the Workshop had to go over to Bill's place to alert him to the fact that Letterman was looking for him.

Getting into the *Late Night* rotation wasn't actually that daunting. Although hip, the show was still relatively young, so if you had a solid six minutes on tape, gave it time to fall into the right hands, and the show's producers liked what they saw, you could be on TV. A recommendation from a show favorite (such as Leno) was a shortcut to the front of the line.

The show wanted Bill to call Morton ("Morty" as he was known) later that afternoon. That was fine, except Bill already had a date that afternoon: to do mushrooms with a friend. Bill didn't want to let a little thing like perhaps the biggest break of his career interfere with his day tripping.

The friend arrived and they chewed their caps and stems and walked down to Rice University. With heavy hanging trees lining the residential streets, Rice sits like a neighborhood oasis inside the less than picturesque city of Houston. It's a good place for a walk, maybe better when you are on mushrooms. At three o'clock, the friend reminded Bill that it was time to call. "From where?" Bill asked. His friend offered the novel suggestion of a pay-phone. "I don't even know the area code," Bill protested.

A couple of hours later Bill finally got the courage to approach a pay-phone. He called the *Late Night* offices and asked for Morton. It was now well after 5 p.m. on the east coast. By the time Bill called, Morty was gone. Morton's secretary informed Bill that Morty had left for Connecticut for the weekend and would be back in the office on Monday.

Above Bill's house in Nottingham Forest; (*inset*) Bill's bedroom window.

Left From top: Kevin Booth, Dwight Slade, Bill Hicks, 1976.

Left Stratford High, deep in the heart of suburbia, where football rules.

Above Laurie Mango, 1979.

Bill Hicks, 1980.

$TRE$$

Above Bill playing with his teeth *a la* Jimi Hendrix at a private party for football player Craig James.

Right The birth of Joe Arab.

Above Keg party at Kensington.

Right From left to right: Charles Lloyd, Bill Hicks, Kevin Booth, David DeBess, sit on stacks of speakers in front of Kevin's house.

Above Bill's promotion shot for William Morris Agency, 1981.

Right Bill Hicks and Eric Johnson, 1980.

With a face like rubber, Bill displays the multiple characters of the singles bar scene.

Bill outside the Laff Stop, 1989. Billboard in the background reads "Bill Hicks, Jimmy Pineapple, Jimmy Bicus".

Villa Capri Hotel, 2nd day of a 3 day party, 1985. *Front Row*: Steve Epstien, David Cotton, Mark Wilks. *Middle Row*: Jere Raridon, Sam Kinison, Bill Hicks, Reily Barber. *Back Row*: Steve Doster, Kevin Booth, Brent Ballard.

Bill performing at the Austin Comedy Workshop, 1984.

Above Sam Kinison, Villa Capri Hotel, 1985.

Right Bill as The King, Rockerfellers, 1987.

Left Bill and Ron Shock, New York, 1990.

Left Rockerfellers, Houston, 1987.

Below Michael Horan confronts Bill Hicks and Jimmy Pineapple with the bar tab for Birrporetti's.

Bottom Ticket from "A Special Night of Comedy: The Outlaws Pay Their Bar Tab".

BIRRA
PORETTIS   and   **KKHT 96.5**
                        HOUSTON

presents

"A SPECIAL NIGHT OF COMEDY"
Tuesday, April 19, 1988
at 8:00 p.m,
When

THE OUTLAW COMICS PAY THEIR BAR TAB

featuring

Bill Hicks and **Jimmy Pineapple**
With Special Surprise Guests

Birraporetti's   No Cover
1997 West Gray   •   River Oaks Center   •   529-9191

Bill had fucked up, and he knew it. All he needed was the confirmation from his friend. "Did I just fuck up?" Bill asked over and over and over again for the next couple of miles of their walk. Every half dozen steps: "Did I just fuck up?"

As the two sat in Greenway Plaza, a plane dragging a banner behind it passed over their heads. They looked up but the plane was too high for either of them to read what the banner said. Still, Bill watched the plane traverse a little patch of sky above, then, slowly and deliberately, with pauses between words he started "reading" the message from on high. "You fucked up, pal. You know who I'm talking to."

Bill's self-destruction was actually serendipitous. He probably would have been worse off had he got hold of Morty that Friday afternoon. Bill called on Monday, the producers on the show hadn't the slightest clue as to Bill's recent state of mind, and everything worked out hunky dory. Only Bill could fuck up like that and not have it count against him.

The last week of November, Bill and Laurie traveled to New York for Bill to make his first appearance on *Late Night with David Letterman*. He never made it on stage. Phil Donahue ran long. Bill got bumped. He was disappointed. Still, the experience also yielded Bill's first lesson in working on network TV. Prior to arriving in New York, Letterman's people had had the opportunity to review Bill's set, but, just before he was scheduled to step under the lights, the show's producers told him he couldn't do a joke about handicapped kids, specifically one about a kid getting hit in the eye with a pencil and the other who ends up in a wheelchair.

"I was with him in the green room," Laurie recalls, "and he was sort of freaking out about that, bitching about how they could not only do it at all, but do it right before he was going to go on, too. I think they did it maybe twenty minutes before. They had a previous opportunity to review it, but they didn't make the decision until right before. He was very mad about that, and legitimately so."

On Wednesday 5 December 1984, Bill was back in New York. He

stood nervously backstage sucking every last gram of tar out of a Kool menthol as he heard David Letterman's voice: "He will be working this weekend at the Comedy Workshop in Houston, Texas. Please give a warm welcome to Bill Hicks."

Warm was the last thing Bill needed. He was already sweating so badly he had visibly pitted through his black shirt when he walked out to face the audience, the cameras, and a viewing audience of fifteen million Americans. He did five minutes. Five minutes he later described to the *Houston Chronicle* as "harrowing." He explained that he was just "tying one-liners together," lines that the show's producers "almost literally picked for me."

It was standard early material – parents, school, him wanting a go-kart but getting a dictionary (Dad: "Well, 'go-kart' is in the dictionary." Bill: "Yeah, Dad, so is 'tightwad.'"). Bill had tried again to get the set he had wanted to do a couple of weeks previously approved, only to be told again he could not do the joke about the kid in the wheelchair or the kid getting hit in the eye.

Still the impact was undeniable, and undeniably good. Bill had a standing offer for a return booking on Letterman, and off the buzz of the initial appearance Bill was now getting booked to do gigs nationally at a scale of $1000 a week.

Then things started to unravel, and quickly. When he was out on the road, Bill was hardly a model citizen or prize performer. Sandy DiPerna, a club owner from Virginia who was working as Bill's booking agent, was watching her own reputation suffer because of the client she was putting into clubs. Bill would drink, a lot; and he was doing more and more material about religion and politics, and often doing it in front of tiny southern crowds. Insulting small-minded small-towners: that was a surefire way to make your life nasty, brutish and short.

If Bill drank a lot, he would cut out the prolonged alienation and go straight to berating the audience. They were idiots for laughing at the opening comic who wasn't funny and, more generally, they were responsible for everything wrong with the world. Bill had no problem telling them that. Several shows were simply bombs; on a couple of occasions there were fights. For every person who got it, there were more who didn't. Some would get upset and leave. That would justify Bill's contempt for his own audience. And the vicious circle would continue spiraling.

Another variable in the equation was that Bill was simply fearless on stage. The show was his and not to be fucked with. Even if it wasn't a drunken disaster, things still might end in a mêleé. Bill was doing a show. Sitting at a table upfront were "Arab Mafia" (his description), an oil-rich Middle Eastern and his entire entourage. They were there with a girl. Her birthday. They were acting like they owned the place, talking loudly but tipping huge. Twenty bucks a drink, stripping the bills off a huge wad.

The house was packed. Great crowd. Bill got on-stage and the place started going berserk. He's doing his show and everyone loves him, everyone except the Arab guys up front who will not shut up. Bill does anything he can to quiet them, knocking them down verbally and calling them assholes in clever ways. Nothing worked. Finally, Bill stopped his set and says to them: "Look, I've heard this material. These other people can't hear. So why don't you shut up?"

The Arab guys shoot back, "It's her birthday, man. Fuck you and do your act."

Bill doesn't give a fuck and tells them, "I don't give a fuck if it's her birthday."

So the Arab peels off another $20 bill, throws it at Bill and says, "Do your fucking act."

This sets Bill off. And now he has to make the point. "I don't want your fucking money. You're fucking up the show. I don't need your fucking money. Look, I shit $20 bills." So Bill took the $20, wiped his ass with it, then threw it back in the guy's face. The crowd starts giving Bill an ovation. And the Arab assholes actually laughed at this. They liked Bill's uppitiness. Still, they were making it impossible for anyone else to enjoy the show. "No one can hear," said Bill.

The Arab tried to blow him off, "They can hear."

Then a woman sitting next to them joined in on the side of Bill and the rest of the crowd: "No, we cannot hear."

The Arab with the wad of money looks at her and goes, "Shut up, cunt."

So this lady's Texas linebacker-sized boyfriend immediately gets up. "I'll be right back. I need to go talk to this little foreigner." And the mêleé is on. Bill jumps off the stage and starts doing a play by play. Meanwhile, Laurie is trying to drag Bill out of there by his hair. He sees tables and chairs flying. "The last thing I saw," said Bill, "was the waitress jumping up on the stage saying, 'Well, that's our show. Thanks for coming out.'"

Bill's relationship with Laurie also fell apart again. Medical School was no longer a good complement to babysitting Bill. Paid bookings rapidly fell to two or three a month, and soon Bill was unable to cover his rent. One day Bill came home to find himself padlocked out of his place. By the first week of June 1985, less than six months after *Letterman*, Bill was sleeping on the floor of fellow comic Jack Mark Wilks and had $15 to his name. He acknowledged to an interviewer that he had "hit the skids." Master of the obvious. Master of the understatement.

While college graduates entering the workforce were maturing and entering the adult world, Bill was prolonging his adolescence. His life revolved around comedy, the comedy club, and the other comedians. The common element was alcohol, and, to a lesser extent, drugs. Bill used hallucinogens to synthesize spiritual epiphanies or augment spiritual experiences, but he also used recreational drugs for the fun of it. Even that had a lot to do with drinking. As David Cotton, Bill's former coke dealer and friend in Austin explains, "It wasn't about doing the blow as much as it was that you do the blow to keep you awake, so you can drink more. It was a social thing."

His job and his friends only facilitated things. Most nights Bill would have a few drinks before heading out, either to a bar for a few more before moving on to the Annex, or go straight to the comedy club for a few more. If he was performing, he would have several drinks while he performed, then have a few more because the bar was still open and serving. Even after the club had shut down, it was still open for the comedians. After the patrons were cleared out, the comedians would sit around for hours longer telling stories, ribbing each other and drinking more.

It was steady and it was almost every night. His only responsibility was if he had a set at the club. That usually meant being on stage some time around nine or ten at night. Bill would set his alarm clock if he had to be up before four in the afternoon.

The Houston comics were a tight-knit group; insular and a bit arrogant, but they drew patrons to the club night after night, so to the degree that comedy was happening in Houston, they *were* the comedy. That made them the stars in the movies of their lives. Half of the original "Outlaws" had returned to Houston, and the same spirit was permeating through the other comics working in Houston. Steve Espstein would even revive the Outlaw moniker and some of the Houston comics would start performing theme shows using the name.

In 1987 Epstein *et al.* booked shows in Houston, Austin and Chicago called "Outlaw Comics Get Religion." A loose roll call of who constituted the second iteration of the Outlaw Comics could be considered the guys on that show: Andy Huggins, Ron Shock, Steve Epstein, John Farnetti, Riley Barber, Jimmy Pineapple and Bill.

Riley Barber was a big, lumbering, red-haired, red-skinned Irishman. His friends used to call him a hapless dupe to his face because he was such a klutz. Bill used to joke about Riley that he would break everything he touched. If Riley touched your refrigerator, the door would fall off; if he got in your car, the stereo stopped working. He was a lovable buffoon. He and Andy Huggins used to work together doing straight-man/funny routines with Riley playing the part of the redneck foil.

123

Of all of those guys, Huggins was the least likely to be an "Outlaw." He was not the kind of guy to lose his temper. He was calm and level-headed, and he was dear to Bill. Maybe more so than any of the other Houston comics – Bill really had a special affection for him. But Andy seemed more cut out as a writer than a stand-up.

If Huggins was the least likely to be an Outlaw, Farnetti was the least likely to be a comedian. First off, he had a real job; second off, that real job was as a lawyer. He had money, more than anyone around him (he actually built a comedy club, called Rimshots, in his house). He also had somewhat normal hours so didn't do most of the nightly ritual partying; still, he was a bit of a pot smoker. Farnetti's schtick was that he was the man from the Planet Jazz. He sported the Village Vanguard beard and dark shades on stage. With a piano (Mr. Dave) and sax player backing him, he was a hipster who landed on planet earth and was now pointing out its humorous nature (e.g. there's "A plague upon your land, [being] passed from one homosexual to the next . . . it's the new George Michael album.").

Ron Shock, one of the last to join the party in Houston, ended up being maybe the best comic of the group after Bill, evidenced by the fact that while many of the other Outlaws ended up in rehab, Ron ended up on *The Tonight Show*. He always performed high, even when he appeared on Carson, he went out in the NBC parking lot, stood next to Johnny's Corvette, and smoked a joint before going on. Shock was a tough, scrawny guy, a little reminiscent of Yosemite Sam. He'd been to prison before; he'd also been a CEO.

The gamut of Ron's experiences maybe gave him a perspective the other Houston comics lacked. While they'd be drowning in their own ennui, and torturing themselves over women who had cheated on them, Ron had the line: "Pussy don't wear out. Why would you care if she fucked a hundred guys? Pussy's just as good after it's been used, it don't wear out."

Jimmy Pineapple, along with Huggins, was the other guy Bill had a special affection for. A dark-haired Cajun, Pineapple was a really endearing, lovable guy. Smart. Very sincere. He was a guy with the talent to be a headlining comic and make it big. It never happened for him.

The core of the clique – including maybe Tracy Wright, of course Epstein, and a couple of others – might have been cozy, but the Houston circle was much larger, literally a couple of softball teams large – for a brief period, after one of them discovered that the lights at the baseball fields in Memorial Park were being left on until 2 a.m., late-night softball became a frequent post-performance activity. And there were usually enough comics to field two teams for a game.

Sometimes the games would get heated, arguments would flare up, and border on fights. James and Bill were always the cool heads, amused at the fights that would break out. They would also be amused by the fights that broke out at Birraporetti's, if they weren't the ones instigating them. Birraporetti's was a yuppie hangout near to the Comedy Workshop. But Jimmy and Bill and some of the other comics would go into Birraporetti's and start fake fights.

It would actually take a minimum of four people. There had to be two people to pretend wanting to throw down and two people to pretend wanting to restrain them. They'd fake an argument and fake its escalation. Then stools would be toppling and fists flying. It was a put-on, but they would be loud and obnoxious and piss off customers and generally act low-class boorish. And they'd get away with it. The owner, Michael Horan, a Mickey Gilley doppelgänger, took a liking to the comics, so they had free rein to go into this bar that was classier than they were and raise small hell.

They took full advantage. They were (generally) young, brash, fearless, drunk. The drunk probably aided the fearless, but the Houston comics played the part. They wanted to be the pets of the city. Act "as if," that was the strategy.

Bill was different. Anyone could be a drunk. As a comedian, he was just better. And everyone knew it. Bill and Shock were out walking one day: going for a walk was one of Bill's favorite things to do. The two were talking about money and the economy. Shock was giving Bill an education; about the money supply, about the Federal Reserve system, about the gold standard. Says Shock, "They were just things Bill didn't know anything about. I told him about how Nixon took us off the gold standard, and that money isn't backed by anything. It only works because everyone agrees it works."

Bill took it all in. The next time Shock saw Bill on stage he did ten minutes on money and the Federal Reserve. Not only was it ten minutes, but it was ten minutes of jokes. "I had known about that stuff for twenty years," recalls Shock, "and hadn't ever thought of a single funny thing to say about it." Still, nobody was jealous or envious of him when Bill did *Letterman*, the other comics were happy for him.

[*   *   *]

Kevin Booth

There were only two kinds of nights: the good and the bad. Both were ugly.

Bill would get offstage. Everybody was already kind of fucked up. The comedians and the hangers on would coagulate in the parking lot in back of the club and shoot the shit. "My girlfriend cheated on me." "Man, you were great." "We're all going to be famous." From that point the night would turn one of two ways.

A good night meant that, from the parking lot, there might be more hanging out and drinking in the comedy club after they cleared the patrons out. It was like a second home for the comics.

Once it got to around 2 a.m., bar time in Texas, we would all caravan over to a Mexican restaurant in the Hispanic neighborhood of Houston. The authenticity was important; it had to be a place where the Mexicans ate. Two reasons. First, you knew it would be good. Second, it would be cheap. You could feed yourself and a friend for $5 and have change. Important when you are poor.

It wasn't always Mexican. There was an all-night Chinese place next to Kinison's old apartment that was also a favorite. We'd eat, let our buzz subside, and end up back at Bill's Houston House apartment asleep by four or five in the morning. That was a good night.

A bad night – and these happened, oh, about half of the time – meant we landed the big coke deal. The truth is that eating at two in the morning only meant we'd failed to score coke. Otherwise, the dealer showed, and everyone burrowed into their wallets and cobbled together all the cash they could scrounge to buy all the coke they could afford.

Those nights ended up in someone's apartment or a shitty hotel and lasted until eight, nine, maybe ten the next morning. On odd occasions momentum would prolong the party until it became a two- or three-day bender. It was fueled by testosterone almost as much as by drugs. You were a pussy if you dropped out. Eventually you realized that, if you wanted to live, you needed to drop out at some point. That point, for me anyway, was usually when Bill and Jimmy and whoever else broke into Sinatra. That's when things started to resemble an insurance sales convention male-bonding activity. Who wants to party with people acting like their fathers?

Of course, nobody's father put it away like Bill. On a multi-day bender Bill would put down two or three or more bottles of straight liquor, a case of beer, maybe a few shots, and definitely several 8-balls of coke.

No matter how long the bender, eventually the drugs ran out and suddenly everyone was suffering from the desperate craving sensation. You were no longer a super-hero. You were no longer walking on water. You were no longer going to change the world with jokes. Not even close. The sun was up and it was time to sleep. It seemed so normal. Morning would come twice a day or not at all.

Seven nights a week Bill was out with me, the other Outlaws, Laurie, everyone, anyone, whoever. All seven nights involved drinking. Most of those it was heavy. Half the week involved drugs. Go home. Get up and do it again. Lather. Rinse. Repeat.

It was a miracle Bill or any of the Outlaws didn't end up in jail, or didn't seriously hurt someone. I've never seen so many people driving so fucked up, so often, and suffer zero consequences.

On the occasions Bill got pulled over he would just say, "Hey, I'm one of the comedians." It was their get-out-of-jail-free card. They had a special status that kept them from getting in trouble with the law. It was incredible.

There was another force at work during that time beside some low-level regional immunity with the local law enforcement authorities. Bill had a guardian angel. There is no other explanation. The way he mixed chemicals and cars, Bill cheated death. That sounds like the shittiest, most insensitive thing to say about someone so talented who was victimized by cancer at such an appallingly young age – Bill didn't get to live long enough as it was – but save for a guardian angel

128

or some force that can't be explained by probability, Bill could have, maybe should have, been a traffic statistic at a young age. Something was watching out for that guy.

Maybe the scariest escape – or at least the scariest I can actually remember from not being as fucked up as Bill – was when we were on the 610 loop near the Astrodome. I was driving one car, Bill was driving another. We both had passengers and were moving side by side, doing close to 90 mph, weaving through traffic. We were on our way to the next bar.

Bill rolled down his window, looked over to us, and started shouting something. What he was saying I have no idea. It wasn't important. What was important were the things Bill was paying no attention to: the road and what was ahead of him. In his lane was a car going maybe 40 mph. Less than half his speed. Bill was closing fast.

We started screaming frantically and signaling him. "Look, Bill! Oh my God! Look up!" He had milliseconds to react – I felt for sure he was a dead man – and missed what was likely a fatal or severely debilitating accident by millimeters. He swerved and slammed on the breaks and it was so fucking close. Literally days before, a mutual friend's wife was involved in the same kind of accident on the same stretch of freeway. She was paralyzed.

There was a myriad of times when I know I was fucked, but I could still look at Bill and see he was clearly more blotto. There were somewhere in the number of, oh, about fifty occasions in my life where I suggested, "Bill, maybe I should drive."

The one response I'll never forget: "I got it under control. Dude, I'm a professional comedian." Comedy and driving? There is absolutely no causal connection between the two things. For someone who prided himself on being such a whiz with logic and reason, he could be kind of a retard when he was loaded.

He also just enjoyed scaring people. He was a crazy driver, even after he went sober. If I tightened my seatbelt or gripped the sides of the seat, that was Bill's cue to accelerate a little more into the blind corner. He knew he was scaring me; now he would see if he could get me to stain my shorts. If I suggested he back off a bit, he'd call me a whiner and tell me I worried too much.

Bill was aware that coke was the drug that made you feel an endless void. You were constantly chasing. After that initial rush you were beset with the feeling of: God, I need something. That's so much of what Bill was like when he was an alcoholic and a drug addict. He was a black hole, trying desperately to fill some huge void in his life. He would suck anything in if he thought it might help.

When he was all coked out, he would sometimes talk to me about this. He would try to figure out what the void was. Did it have something to do with his parents? With his inability to find love? Was it because his girlfriends all cheated on him?

On multiple occasions Bill told me he felt like he had had some kind of psychic injury during his birth. He was endlessly infatuated with his own birth. When he took acid, sometimes he would describe the experience as having gone through a rebirthing process. When you're young and you cut yourself, you scar your skin. That scar grows in size as your body grows and you become an adult. With Bill, the same thing had happened with his psychological scars. The emotional scars cut into his psyche when he was young, they just grew in size as he did.

During those days the drugs really did control everything, take precedence over everything. Bill had incredible talent and ability. He was the same Bill that later in his career could hold an audience of 2000 in his hand for an hour plus. He was already that guy, but he gave up the control to drugs and alcohol. He detoured.

All that time practising transcendental meditation, studying non-western religion and spirituality: that taught him that all of the powers he needed in the world were already inside him. But there was something that caused him to have to go *outside* of himself, to keep searching for answers to questions that, quite honestly, he never fully shared. Again, it was like a vacuum, and for a period it sucked down a lot of Jack Daniels and sucked up a lot of blow.

It's hard to tell if the drinking and drugging was dragging his career down or if his stagnant career was pushing him to a pusher. At some point they reinforced each other. Since returning from LA to make a go of it in Houston, his career certainly hadn't been anything to phone home about.

Except for about five minutes in December of 1984.

That's when Bill got his first shot on *Late Night with David Letterman*. He called me right after the taping. It was still light outside. "Well, I just did the Letterman thing," he said. I couldn't believe it. I called my dad, my whole family, because everyone in my family thought Bill was a fucking loser – a drug addict and an alcoholic. I told my dad to watch Bill; my dad told me he didn't stay up that late and wanted to know if I could tape it.

It wasn't just family, it was a lot of friends and acquaintances from high school and since. All the same people that used to diss Bill and talk about what a loser he was, they couldn't be fagged to stay up another hour and turn on their TVs. Almost everybody I asked who I knew had known about the show said they missed it. The sad fact is that "I'll show those bastards" was part of Bill's motivation, but the bastards he wanted to show, most of them didn't even care.

In all honesty, I was disappointed, not in the former friends, but the performance itself. It didn't have much to do with Bill, either. He did his best. It was an on-the-job hazard. He would put in weeks and weeks of preparation, then go do a five-minute spot on Letterman. It's like paying $5000 for a hooker and blowing your load after fifteen seconds. He really had to bring the noise in that five minutes, but he was always starting out with one joke tied behind his back. It was network TV. Bill was never able to be Bill.

His best material was not rated PG. On top of that, even eliminating the F-words, he just had too many subjects that were simply off-limits.

The lines the show specifically objected to were the bits about the kid in the wheelchair, and throwing a pencil and having it hit the other kid in the eye ("Jesus, Hicks, it's just a game."). The joke was really about Bill, and his rotten luck, his knack of bring unintentionally inappropriate. But for the network censors to get that was going to require thought. It was easier for them to act like a flowchart: if-then. If your joke has wheelchair in it, then you cannot do it on TV.

There's just so much competition out there. You slug it out in shitty clubs night on month on year, then you finally get on TV, your "big break," but you can't even do your own routine. Fuck, man, what's the point? You also start realizing that maybe some of those fucking horrible people on TV really were talented, but they weren't allowed to be themselves.

I was proud of him that he was doing it. The simple fact that he was on Letterman to me was amazing. It really was special, but I always thought of him doing TV as a vehicle to get people to see him in his proper environment: whet their interest, get them to the club, then once they were in Bill's territory he could work on converting them. But the first time, he was genuinely excited about it. Extremely so. Who wouldn't be? He said he thought it went pretty well. He second-guessed himself on some of the material – what he thought he should have done instead. We talked for a couple of minutes, then he said he wanted to call his mom. That night, I turned on the TV and there was Bill Hicks on David Letterman. Fucking cool.

Then Bill went from being somebody for about five minutes back to being nobody. It was back to Houston and back to the road. He was regularly doing short regional tours – a night in Austin, San Antonio, Lubbock, Oklahoma City – broken up by long stretches in Houston. But he was amassing miles on the odometer, driving from gig to gig, playing for audiences that often had no idea who he was, making next to nothing.

It was brutal. I asked Bill how he could put himself through it. "Well, we're comedians. What else are you gonna do?" If he could get booked in Baton Rouge, he had to go to Baton Rouge. That was one thing about being a comedian – you could be a total broke-ass guy and tour around and try to help your own cause. All you needed was

132

a shitty car – the white Chevette Bill had taken to calling "Toad" – and enough money to put some gas in it and buy a hamburger. Usually the club you were playing would set you up with a $20 hotel room. I'm sure there were times when Bill slept in his car.

Those nights on the road were also when the phone calls started. The notion that a headlining act could go on stage and berate the audience – you people are the reason for Tony Danza having another sitcom, the reason Debbie Gibson has the number one album – was funny in itself, but the show would end and Bill's anger wouldn't. He was drunk. There were no more patrons to berate. The club would shut down, the club owner would tell Bill to head back to his hotel and sleep it off.

Call it a night? He rarely did. He called his friends instead. The hotel-minibar and a phone. Not a good combination. All the rage, it came from drinking. Bill was an angry drunk. And the phone calls became as regular as breakfast. For six years – six fucking years – the clock struck 3 a.m. and my phone started ringing.

If I wasn't there, Bill would just go down the list of friends. Kevin's not home? Try David. David's not there, call Doster. He called a lot of people. It didn't matter who was on one end, it was always Bill on the other.

The topics never changed. He was screaming about his girlfriend cheating on him, about the government, about the dumbasses in the crowd that night who didn't get it, about all these shitty people coming out of Hollywood becoming famous yet he wasn't getting anywhere. There were times when I literally put the phone down, fixed myself a cup of coffee, came back to the phone and Bill was still blithering without even having broken stride. One time I even managed to make myself a sandwich. He was doing a monologue. Nobody had to be on the other end of the phone.

Basically, he was telling me, or whoever else was dumb enough to pick up their phone in the middle of the night, about how much the world sucked. He always had hope for the world and for mankind, but it was an honest hope. His hope for mankind didn't always include the happy ending everybody wanted. There wasn't really a happily ever after. His hope for mankind was that, after all of the assholes were wiped off the planet, then the rest of the people left could actually forge a world worth living in. Like he said from the stage, "We're a virus with shoes." Bill was even comfortable with the thought he might have to be one of the people to go, if that's what it took.

"Hitler had the right idea. He was just an underachiever." It's something Bill said during one of his more infamous shows. You can try to explain it away, but maybe that's disingenuous and superfluous. Here was Bill, this really honest, naive, pure person, and he was plopped down like a Martian in the middle of this corrupt, bizarre planet filled with hypocrisy and lies. He had enough time to comprehend all of the dishonesty and deceit, then liquored himself up to the point of being belligerent. That's what you had in Bill. "Sometimes I feel like an alien on this planet." It's something he said to me and probably every one of his friends. And if he didn't spell it out for them, most were intelligent enough to make the same observation.

In high school and when he first went to LA, Bill was the most pure kind of guy. He was so innocent. Then he found alcohol and drugs and he just drove off the cliff. But it was fitting of his personality. Moderation wasn't in Bill's credo. Unfortunately, drugs and alcohol lead you to places you would never otherwise go and make you do things you would never otherwise do.

Once a month, maybe once every six weeks, Bill would announce "I'm not drinking." The hard living would wear thin, he'd be feeling like shit and he would want to stop. It might have even run deeper into wanting to change his lifestyle, change his life. "Dude, I can't do this any more. I gotta start taking care of myself. What am I doing? This isn't me. I'm not like this." Okay, great. Let's clean up.

Bill and I would go out and eat a healthy meal somewhere. Something veggie: sprouts and tofu. We'd work out in the gym: lift weights, maybe swim laps. Then spend the rest of the night trying not to do anything self-destructive. The makeover was thorough – wash the dishes, vacuum the floors, do the laundry – unfortunately the makeover was also merely cosmetic. It would last one night, maybe two.

The sporadic desires to right his life were usually precipitated by some epic bender. One morning he woke up with a bloody nose and had no idea how he had got it. Another time in the pre-Houston House days, he woke up and realized he couldn't pay his rent because he had given all of his money to a coke dealer. And that would spawn Bill's latest renaissance. "I'm done. I'm not drinking any more. I'm not doing coke any more."

Bill was always quitting two things. He was quitting drinking and he was quitting comedy. He sobered up and retired from stand-up so many times that it had become its own self-referential meta-joke. Only Bill wasn't kidding. And he wasn't just quitting, he was making a production out of quitting. There had to be an announcement where he'd tell anyone and everyone, "Hey, did you hear that I'm not drinking any more?" or "Hey, did you hear that I'm not doing stand-up any more."

Of course they had. If not on this particular occasion then on the previous twelve or fifteen times he had retired in the past year. It happened often enough that friends had a hard time feigning interest. That only made it worse. Dissing Bill made him that much more indignant. His friends are telling him: yeah, sure, right, whatever. And he's telling us: no, I'm serious, I'm done.

Even if he meant it, or wanted to mean it, everyone who knew Bill knew that his will had a half life of about forty-eight hours. That's how long he stayed sober and that's how long he stayed retired. Maybe he made three days. Four was exceptional. Bill was a stand-up comedian, and, for this period of his life, an avid drinker. It's who he was.

And who were his friends? Other comedians, musicians, artists. Where did they hang out? Clubs and bars. If he was back at the Comedy Annex, even just hanging with some of the other comics, he was going to do a set even if it was just five minutes; and if he was doing a set he was going to have some drinks, even it was just five drinks. That's who the Outlaws were; they were the people Bill got fucked up with. And the parties were sometimes epic.

It was more than a clique or a club. Bill loved those guys like brothers, respected most of them as comedians, but once the lines were cut it was the Great Mutual Admiration Society. We were all constantly congratulating ourselves, telling each other how great we were and how much greater we were going to be. My band, their comedy; we were all going to change the world. Fame. We're going to live for ever.

Funny that the two truly talented, the two genuinely special people in that room – Bill and Sam Kinison– they were the first two to go. That's "funny" as in "not funny at all."

I heard Bill say, on numerous occasions, that you ended up hanging out with the most vile people, the most disgusting people, the biggest losers, people you would never hang out with under any other circumstances, when you were doing cocaine. That drug somehow pulled you down to the lowest rungs of humankind.

I knew another musician in Austin who was a big ecstasy dealer but was also usually holding coke. Bill and I went over to his house to buy from him. When we got there he hit us with what seemed like bad news: "God, the doctors found a hole in my nostril like the size of a quarter." Our reaction was basically: "Dude!"

He responded, "Yeah, I'm not going to be snorting coke any more."

"Good for you, that's great."

We didn't anticipate what he told us next. No rational person could have done. "Because I found a whole new way of doing it!" Then he takes out a pipe and shows it off.

We were thinking this guy was turning his life around. Instead he was so happy that the hole in his nose wasn't going to keep him from doing the drugs he loved. He was actually taking the time to explain to us all of the ways that smoking cocaine was going to be better for him.

Think that's fucked up? Here we are handing him our last bit of money to buy from him the same shit that was perforating his nose. How dumb are we?

Our involvement with drugs was beyond recreational. For a time, it was serious. And it got us involved with Duke. Duke wasn't a lowlife scum, but he was one of those people who never would have got as deep into our lives if it wasn't for cocaine. His real name was Lewallen Duplantis. Who wouldn't go by Duke if their real name was Lewallen? It was analogous to what Bill later quipped about David Koresh. "The guy's real name is Vernon. Let him be Jesus for a little while."

I was taking Tae Kwon Do classes and he was one of my instructors. The spitting image of David Carradine. Yes, Grasshoppah. Completely "Kung Fu." Probably about 48 years old. He had been a pilot in Vietnam – and a mercenary. This was all common knowledge amongst the people that knew him. One side of Duke's family was French Mafia, the other Native American. He spoke about seven languages fluently. He was a black belt. He claimed to have been a bullfighter. It sounds unbelievable, but if you ever met Duke, you'd know there was no reason to doubt him.

Duke's story isn't Bill's, it's mine. But it is important because he's the reason we were even able to start work on the ten-year odyssey that was *Ninja Bachelor Party*. And Duke's philosophy of women did leave an indelible impression on almost all of us. Especially Bill. More than that, the story of Duke is just fucking insane. It's the reason I had so much cocaine to share with my friends for about a nine-month stretch starting in 1984.

Through a friend of a friend, I knew – or more accurately "knew of" – people who were bringing coke into central Texas, to a farm about a half hour outside of Austin.

For some reason Duke took me under his wing. One day we were driving around – his car, Lincoln Continental, Duke in his gi, CIA sunglasses, guns in the trunk – when he sparked up a joint. Not surprisingly, the conversation quickly turned to the subject of drugs. Duke says something about cocaine. "I know this Columbian who's got some coke," I say. I think I'm being cool. My life is about to change.

"Really? You serious?" I was. "Well, I'll buy some," he says.

I'm thinking he wants a gram or two. Duke asks, "How much can you get?" I told him I could get however much he wanted. He says he wants a couple of keys. Keys? He wasn't fucking around. But I don't take him seriously. "Yeah, right," I said.

I should have taken him seriously. He reiterated straight-faced, "Kevin, I'm not joking. I'll take a couple of keys." Now I'm thinking, "Shit, this guy has got to be a narcotics officer. I am going to jail." I backed off a little and stalled while I asked around. But everyone vouched for Duke, told me he's totally cool and totally for real.

So on one hand I know people who know people with piles of cocaine, and on the other my new friend John Rambo wants piles of cocaine. I came back to Duke and said that I wasn't sure about a kilo, and suggested we start with a smaller amount. He was okay with that.

I had become a drug dealer. That's only the half of it. When I ran a deal I had also brought some resources of my own. I had inositol, a white powdery crystalline B-vitamin supplement that looked exactly like cocaine. I also had scales. I would take a few grams out of Duke's lot, put it on the scale, weigh it out, then dump that into a baggie. That was now mine. Then I would weigh out the exact same amount of the inositol and dump that into Duke's bag of coke. Mix it up. Shaken not stirred. I did all of this in the car while driving back to Austin, and on Duke's stopwatch. Ridiculous.

I was buying cocaine for $1100 a ounce and charging Duke $1700. On any given transaction, this usually meant I was walking away with a couple of thousand dollars and about a dozen grams of really good coke. I was doing this to a man who could kill me seven different ways with his bare hands.

But it was really fucking good coke.

Or so I was told. In the beginning, I used to watch *Scarface* religiously just to remind myself that if I ever touched my own shit, that is what would happen to me. So I never did, in the beginning anyway.

But just like Tony Montana, eventually I got into my own stash. And Bill knew that I wasn't paying for it, so of course I was letting him slide. There were times when Bill and Laurie would be staying at my house, and they would be begging me for coke. It always put me in the awkward position of, "Well, here's a little bit more." It wasn't just Bill, it was every one of my "friends." I'd break out the coke, but nobody broke out their wallet.

"Don't worry, I get paid tomorrow." Yeah, the check is in the mail, and I'll respect you in the morning. Whatever. How often do you think I got paid? Still, just by profit taking and skimming off of Duke's deals I was flush with cash. So, after making my first scores, I turned around and bought a video camera system. In 1984, to tell people you were buying a portable color video camera, they didn't even know what you were talking about.

It was a two-piece set-up. The camcorder wasn't on the market yet. The camera and the deck were separate pieces, Panasonic and Hitachi respectively. All of a sudden here we were, and we were able to shoot endless video. The very first thing we started doing was to shoot karate sketches. We even used Duke.

My relationship with Duke got closer. One night he told me, "I gotta run some errands. I need you to drive for me." I wasn't sure what this meant. I met him and he gave me the keys to his car. I drive him to a liquor store. He gets out of the car and goes to the trunk where he pulls out a briefcase. He comes back to the driver's seat, hands me a loaded shotgun, and tells me: "If I'm not back in two minutes, I need you to come in for me." No way. No fucking way.

That was the start. It actually started getting more intense and more fucked up. He was telling me I was already involved. I was telling him that I was a bass player in a rock band.

Bill had met Duke several times, but he wasn't in the loop. Duke and I would have private meetings at the Biggs House when Bill was there. Once Duke left, Bill was like a 6th Grade schoolgirl after the dance. "What happened? What'd he say?" I'd tell him. "Holy fuck, Kevin. You shouldn't be doing this. This is crazy." He was totally trying to keep me from getting more involved. Of course, he was also asking, "You got any coke?"

About the same time all of this was going on, I found out that my girlfriend Jere was cheating on me. A friend tipped me off. He had seen her in public – specifically, at Steamboat, the bar where I spent most of my time – with another guy. I took a loaded gun and knives and strapped them to my body. Then I drove over to her house. I was the picture of clichéd rage. I put my fist through the window and unlocked the door. Then I stormed into the bedroom. She was asleep next to this guy. I beat the shit out of him, then I got out of there before the police got there.

I called Houston and got on the phone with Bill around 11 p.m. I stayed there until seven the next morning. During the conversation I downed an entire bottle of whiskey. He knew what to say. He had been through it when he had caught Laurie cheating on him. "Kevin, this is not who you are. You are not a killer. Don't throw your life away over this." It sounds like dialogue for a Lifetime movie now, but at the time it kept me from killing someone. That phone call, and that friend, are the reason I'm not in jail for murder.

It wasn't completely over, though. I was calm, but I still wanted that guy dead. A couple of days later, I talked to Duke and actually had the conversation where I asked him how much I had to pay him to get someone to take care of this guy. Duke said to me, "Kevin, Jere is the one who cheated on you. It's not this guy's fault. No woman is worth hurting another brother over. All men are your brothers. Don't hurt a brother over a whore." I was initially indignant. "Don't call her a whore."

"What do you mean? You caught her cheating on you. Kevin, all women are whores." Duke said that over and over again. All women are whores. This exchange happened in the presence of Bill. And it was like a light went on over Bill's head. "All women are whores." "All men are your brothers." I don't think Bill stopped being a sensitive guy that day, in fact I don't think he ever stopped being sensitive, but around this time is when he stopped being a milquetoast when it came to women. Is Duke responsible? Maybe. That phrase really resonated with Bill.

But Duke believed to his core that all women were whores. Right down to his saying: "My mother was a whore." He kind of became a demigod for us. All women are just looking for money, all women want someone to take care of them, etc. They were all things that we didn't want to hear, but the evidence to the contrary – what we were experiencing at the time – kept staring us in the face. It was the harsh reality. "All women are whores" summed up the mentality of all the Houston comics for those drinking and drugging years of the early Eighties. When you hung out with any one of those comedians they had all come to that place. Duke represented the iconoclastic progenitor of that philosophy. Those stories of Duke became legendary and he was the inspiration for the character of Dr. Death in *Ninja Bachelor Party*.

Bill and I used to watch Kung Fu Theater religiously. Every Saturday morning low budget martial arts films were on TV. This was before the days of the parody, but these were unintentional parodies. They were actual martial arts films; they were bad. Hysterically so. Bad acting, bad lighting, bad camera tricks. One film inspired us more than any other. It was called *Buddharama*. The plot was roughly that of a young white outcast going to Asia to find a master. Of course, he gets involved with a hot Asian girl and has to rescue her.

The one scene that made us puke with laughter was a scene where the American guy fights the ancient master. It's ridiculous. In the scene, the whole house gets smashed. But for the *fromage de resistance*, one guy punches his arm through the sheetrock into the wall and pulls out a piece of lead piping, and starts beating the other guy with it.

That was it. That scene inspired us like no other. We had to do our own piece of Kung Fu Theater. In the beginning, it was nothing more than David Johndrow filming me in short scenes. Shot one would be me hurling a throwing star. Shot two would be me against a wall with the same throwing star flying into the wall right next to my head. After doing dozens of these single camera sketches, we finally decided to make a real karate movie. Or rather a "real" karate movie.

It seemed like everybody in Austin and Houston was locked into the mentality of: "Maybe some people from Hollywood will discover this and make a movie out of it." Both cities were littered with struggling artists thinking some outside person was going to come rescue them through their career. Again, Bill had the mentality of just getting things done. I was saying, "You can't make a movie with a video camera." To which Bill responded: "Why not?"

Well, it's cheesy and it'll look like home video.

"What does it matter?" Bill asked. "Just make it." He always had the sense that our time on earth was limited, and this had nothing to do with his dying young. From our earliest days working together Bill understood that time waiting for someone to give you permission and a check was time wasted. Even if it meant making less money and reaching fewer people. Half of the pleasure was taking the trip. That was it: it's more fun to take the trip when no one is telling you where to go or what to do.

So we started making *Ninja Bachelor Party*.

The night we shot the first scene, Bill had performed at the Workshop in Austin. We were all doing line after line of blow and constructing our own synthetic celluloid coke-fueled fantasy. After Bill's show we all went back to the Biggs House. We were playing Hollywood. "We're going to the shoot." "The party is on set."

The first scene we shot that night was one where Bill and I are sitting in the lotus position and meditating after a workout. So there are two people in front of the camera and thirty people behind it all drinking and snorting cocaine.

David had a lot of the ideas for the things we were doing in the early shots. And we had to be creative. This was the Mesozoic era of video. There was no digital anything. Fix it in post? What the hell was post? For example, to get the dreamy look, David smeared Vaseline over a piece of glass then held the glass in front of the lens.

Ninja was a project that took the better part of about eight years, off and on.

As for Duke, it went downhill fast for him. David Johndrow and one of his classmates decided they wanted to make Duke the subject of a short film for class at UT. I got Duke to agree to it, but the night David and I went over to Duke's place, he went on a mad rampage. He came out and put a machine gun right up to my face and stood there with the barrel of the gun right at my mouth.

A coke deal I did for Duke went sideways and only compounded his problems. The regular connection no-showed me at the farm. Instead, I got another guy with different coke. And it was shit. About twelve hours after the transaction Duke called me up and accosted me: "What's the story? You think I'm stupid? I need my money back."

"I don't have your money." I was confused. All deals are final, but that wasn't acceptable to him. He gave me a couple of hours to get his money back. Shit, what was I going to do? It was gone.

"Well, Kevin, you've got problems," Duke told me. It was the moment in the movie where everything changed. This was the plot twist I wasn't expecting.

Again. Bill saved me. He was right there. We were talking to Duke from a pay-phone and Bill helped me reason through this. It was Sane Man meets Cyrano. He fed me the lines I fed to Duke to get Duke to realize that this wasn't something I was pulling over on him. I was just the courier taking it from point A to point B. That was it.

Duke and I were done doing business; and it was right after that deal he starting losing it. He kept all of that crappy coke and did it all for himself. I remember going over there a few days later and he had a mirror out. Twenty lines on the mirror. Every single line was about a half a gram. Bottle of gin. Snorting and guzzling. It was fucking insanity.

The next time Duke taught a class – and he began class with a meditation or an invocation – he walked in and said, "Tired of living, afraid of dying." He clapped his hands. Class started. After that I never saw Duke again and I was out of the coke business.

One of the big misconceptions people have about Bill and his pro-drug stance is that he was a pot smoker. First off, "pro-drug" is a loaded phrase. Bill was for choice, and if you want to do something to yourself (say, mushrooms) that had absolutely no impact on another person, then that shouldn't be illegal. Your body is your own.

It was the kind of thing Bill wanted to be so clear on that he would spell it out explicitly on stage: "As long as you don't harm another human being, what business is it of yours what I do?"

Bill just didn't like marijuana. One night he was backstage at the Annex and someone handed him a large joint of some super-kine bud. Bill took some massive hits off of it. I remember finding him several minutes later, standing in a dark hallway near the bathrooms with his face buried in a corner like a psychotic person. He was muttering to himself: "Oh my God, I'm in fucking Hell, I'm in Hell right now, I'm never going to smoke pot again. Oh my God, don't ever hand me pot again."

When Bill did an interview with *High Times* in 1993, the interviewer asked him, "Back in the days, when you were still smoking pot, what's the most fun you ever had?" Bill immediately let him know, "I was never a big pot fan.' Bill was for the legalization of pot because he was for the legalization of all drugs. Law enforcement didn't stop people from using, it only made users criminals.

Plus, Bill couldn't stand the hypocrisy. Alcohol is a drug, but the media, specifically advertisers, are allowed to glorify alcohol consumption. Yet things that grow naturally on the earth – marijuana, mushrooms, etc. – are demonized. And that attitude wasn't something Bill picked up when he became a drug user; it wasn't something he adopted to justify his own drug consumption: it dates back to when he was a teen teetotaler.

Back at Stratford, for the Talent Show one year Bill was told he couldn't play "Cocaine." But Clint Black's band got to cover "Whiskey River." So Bill can't do a song about the negative effects of cocaine, but someone else can do a song about wanting to get so drunk that you lose your memory? Wasn't that the exact wrong message a school should be sending out? It pissed him off.

We were out at a cemetery near the ranch in Fredericksburg with David Johndrow taking promo pictures for my band Year Zero. One of the guys in the band started teasing the rest of us, saying he had a "special treat," something that would totally dissolve your ego. So we went back to the ranch and took these little pills. David and I soon had this experience where we were living through the Last Supper. Results may vary.

The first person I called was Bill. "Dude, stop the presses. Get rid of your mushrooms and your acid. Dump the coke. There is this new thing called ecstasy and you are not going to fucking believe it. It is everything. It's a trip. It's a body high. It is pure euphoria. And when it's over, you're not scrounging for more. Dude, you have to try this."

And Bill is like, "Sign me up."

We got three hits – for me, Bill and David – and went out to the ranch. One hit would give you maybe six hours to play. Bill was like a horny teenager: "Let's do it. Let's do it." We managed to stick to our plan. We wanted to be peaking right as the sun was going down.

That first X trip was amazing. We were walking through the woods and we found a spot where we saw these patterns of power emerge – how power and energy were flowing through the woods, how it affected our bodies, and how our bodies were all connected to each other. I started walking in well-defined circles and David started walking in another pattern, while Bill sat in a lotus position. He came out of the lotus and said, "Dude, do you realize that the patterns you just walked describe how our horoscopes interrelate with each other?" Then he explained the whole thing in detail.

It sounds goofy now, but it was so intense and vivid at the time. It was everything you wished acid could have been. The first trip we took together, it was unifying. It unified the three of us together: me, David and Bill. And unified us with the land and the ground and the trees. It was perfect.

Ecstasy was the answer. It allowed you to control your thoughts and direct your trip. I remember one time Bill sat there thinking aloud: "Jesus dying on the cross, what did that really mean? He put himself through a crucifixion and wanted to be born again." There was another time when we were again at the ranch. Bill looked up at everyone there – me, David Johndrow, Brent Ballard and Bob Reilly – and said, "Gentlemen, we are about to be cleansed." It was like a stage cue. The skies opened up on us, and it began pouring down with rain.

Usually you would be screaming, "Shit, let's get out of the rain," or you would run to get an umbrella. Instead, because Bill had put us in the right frame of mind with his comment, we drank it in. It was a beautiful thing. We were being cleansed. We loved every drop that hit us.

After finding ecstasy, we would still take mushrooms, but when MDMA first hit the market, when it was pure, it fucking ruled. Why would you ever want to take acid any more? Why would you want to buy coke any more? And for a time, it was legal.

[*   *   *]

The Outlaw Comics

> People who hate people, come together.
>
> – Bill Hicks

JOHN FARNETTI

The first time I saw him was the first time he went on stage on the Workshop in '78. I saw him with Dwight. The place had been open about three weeks, and on my way out I clearly remember thinking – and I had no thought about Dwight but about Bill – "That kid is like Woody Allen." He was just that good.

He was not borrowing material from Allen, not even paraphrasing. Not dissimilar, but not parallel. Again, they were juniors then. The line I remember was: "Cheerleaders papered my house last night . . . It was used paper." That's not Woody Allen. I had sought out comedy since the age of 6, at that time I was 31. I was clearly and totally taken.

But as a thirty-something-year-old lawyer who went to court four days a week, I didn't drink, had a wife and kid, so I didn't go to any of those parties. Those nights were after the club closed. I always went home. Staying up all night drinking was not an element of the group or the show. It was part of their behavior. Also, despite doing a great deal of acid in the Sixties, I never did ecstasy with any of them either. I had a life going on in addition to what they did.

They were young and had absolutely no responsibility.

Bill would mostly call me at 10 a.m. after he had been up all night. He would call people and start talking non-stop, but I don't think he had any idea what day or time it was. He would not be calling me at lawyer sleep hours.

It was a drag and it was a burden. And you kept holding the phone

147

and kept grunting and so on. He was going on and on, like you read about raving alcoholics. And he was also fueled by coke and sometimes by speed and it wasn't interesting, it wasn't amusing.

One time he called me right after Tiananmen Square and raved sophomorically about liberty. You put up with it, without a doubt, to be his friend. The rose is surrounded by thorns. It was no fun at all but it wasn't a problem. You didn't have to humor him much, you didn't have to look at him, you didn't have to have any positive expression on your face. It was telephonic.

This is what I did, and you only had to do it once in a while: "Yeah . . .?" That's all. That wasn't taxing.

I first talked to his parents in person in 1988 or 1989. I've had some correspondence since. Sometimes I send Mary Hicks flowers on Mother's Day from the Outlaw Comics. And Mary always sends a wonderful handwritten thank you. Her generation of college graduates has impeccable grammar and handwriting. Bill's dad was almost a non-entity in all of this. It was always his mother talking and his dad didn't seem to have a hell of a lot to say.

I only saw Bill's sister once in my life and that was at the kitchen table the night before the funeral; and his brother I first met at an Outlaw show in Austin. I did not ever hang out with him. He was totally different and completely straight in every regard.

Pineapple came across Pamela just going in to get a haircut. I think he invited her around. Then Wilks was involved with her. She came to the Annex. She wasn't particularly attractive, but she was nice. She'd cut everybody's hair for free up at the Houston House. Suddenly, she was hooked up with Bill – to my surprise, because I didn't think Bill would be interested in her.

She was there to serve him. She was there as his valet, his sex partner. She had two kids. They were never around. Never seen. They were with her mother.

He could put up with her, but for the most part Bill was utterly self-absorbed. He could be nice to her and romantic and chivalrous and so on and so forth, but he always wanted her to be available at any given moment around the clock. So she couldn't go out and have a career or anything, she had to be by the phone or with him.

She wanted to have a kid with him. He said, "You've already got two kids back in Houston." She said that she wanted one with him. He told her: "I am my child." It wouldn't be confused with maturity. One girl would-be comic in Houston wanted so much to have a child by Bill, and I don't think I was rude enough to say to her, "But if he just acts like Bill and is as funny as you, it'd be the world's worst child."

ANDY HUGGINS

I don't remember the first time I saw Bill, so I don't even have a first impression. It was a cumulative effect. Anybody can have one good set or a good twenty minutes, but the cumulative effect of watching him night after night, I think I came to the realization that he was special. I certainly don't remember sitting there the first time going, "Holy mackerel, this guy is a genius." It was over the course of three, four, five months.

But at some point it was like when we used to talk baseball in the Seventies. You would have a discussion about who was the best catcher. Well, you were really having a discussion about who was the second best catcher because everyone knew Johnny Bench was so much better than everyone else, that you didn't bother making him part of the conversation. It was the same way with Bill.

We just all knew he was that much better. Bill certainly didn't big-time it, either. As valued and protected as he was, he didn't take advantage of it. He wasn't temperamental, he wasn't bratty. He was quiet. He was just one of the guys on stage. It was kind of unspoken, though. No one ever said, "Make way, here comes the genius."

Before I got there in September of 1982, the comics did have a certain status. They would get invited to parties at mansions, and they really did have the run of the city. In terms of the popularity of stand-up it had just peaked when I got there. It didn't plunge downward, but it was starting on a long slide.

But I'm told that, when it was really hot, it would be one continuous show on the weekdays. There was no break. People would stand in line and wait for somebody to leave and then they would go in. You didn't know when people would leave, but people were willing to stand in line in order to see at least a part of the show. So that little room at the Annex, which held ninety to ninety-five people, it was full for a couple of years there, and it slowly tapered off. Weekends were still great. Weeknights were okay. Then my memory is that attendance fell off entirely during the week.

Still, for a while when I was there, you were either performing every night or you wanted to. There would be ten or twelve comics a night on weekdays, then they would usually have about three comics doing two shows on the weekends. We were there all the time.

I always thought I wasn't an Outlaw. There was Kinison, Bill, Riley Barber and Carl LaBove. They did a show in the early Eighties called *Outlaw Comics on the Lam*; Steve Epstein financed it. I always thought the word Outlaw was attached to that. So Epstein decided to revive the name, and put together another group, and this was probably '84 or '85, somewhere around there. The show was the *Outlaw Comics Get Religion* – I know there were six of us on the poster to promote the show. I was part of that, so I always thought of myself as a part of that second group.

That particular six wasn't a group per se, it was just who would make a good show. I was part of it because I made a good emcee. At parties, with Riley, I would feed him straight lines and we did a great two-man act. Well, you can do that in the show and you make an emcee. Nobody ever wants to emcee and open anyway. That's why I was there. But we were all friends and we shared some things, emotionally and psychologically. People would come and go. It was a very fluid and constantly expanding group. There was nothing significant about the six of us other than that would make a good show. I couldn't even tell you who the six were. Riley, Epstein, Me, Farnetti, Bill and Shock?

I mean, Eppy, who was more or less running it, would let anybody on stage, so I didn't take it at all seriously as something significant. Jimmy Pineapple was so well-respected and liked that he was an Outlaw even if he didn't want to be. And Wilks wasn't even, though he wanted to be. Wilks, he was Bill's friend. Wilks wanted to be Jimmy. That was the problem.

But there was actually a group of us, twelve to fifteen of us, some nights, twenty. After the Workshop had closed up we'd sit around telling stories and riffing off of each other or something that had happened. We loved the stories. That's what I remember, laughing. Just laughing. I can't imagine anyone having laughed as much as we did. I'll maintain that until I die.

We also used to go to Birraporreti's. Michael Horan owned it at the time. It was a real yuppie hangout. It clearly wasn't our kind of a joint, but we went up there because it was convenient to the Workshop and Horan took a shine to us. He used to buy us drinks and send us over pizzas. We used to go in there and insult the customers, paying customers, people that were actually spending money. Our behavior at Birraporetti's wasn't very good. I don't have a memory of causing real problems, but we were not particularly well-behaved in any way.

Bill and Jimmy eventually ran up a bill so huge they couldn't pay it. Horan never got mad. I guess his accountant insisted he do something about it. So that's the famous incident where they had to do the show to pay the tab. They did a great picture when they were advertising, a publicity shot. They had Horan in the middle and Jimmy and Bill on either side holding the sheet, the actual tab, Jimmy looking like "So what?" and Bill looking chagrined like "Oops."

I did get the phone calls from him. We talked a couple of times a day on the phone. When I got sober my hours changed. I can't recall him calling past midnight. I don't recall one conversation like that with Bill. That's not to say it didn't happen, but I don't recall it.

It was interesting, though, Bill kept his friends compartmentalized; and he kept certain topics compartmentalized. He talked to me about certain things, and he knew there was no point in talking to me or Jimmy about other-worldly matters that might have taken place out in Sedona with spaceships. I know that whole story about the spaceship and the Harmonic Convergence only because I read about it. It was something he knew was pointless to bring up with me.

We had other things to talk about. We talked politics a lot. We talked about other cultural matters. Once every three or four months, Bill would call up and he would say, "Look, I know we love Elizabeth Taylor, but I forget why." And I would run through the various reasons why. "Oh, okay. I knew we did. I just couldn't remember why."

About four months later: "I know we love Elizabeth Taylor, but why is it again that we do?" It was a running joke. Every time he saw her in something he would call me up and get reacquainted with her history.

We also talked a lot about comedy – the approach one should take and different comics. Except for on stage, I never saw Bill work on his comedy. I think, and all comics do this, but sometimes when Bill and I would be having a conversation and he would be telling me a story, he was kind of working it out in his mind how this would play on stage. But all comics – when I say all, I mean most of us – if we happen upon a story we'll try it out on a friend. In that sense, I would listen to him and be an audience for him.

I think he probably did a lot of writing. The genius in the performance was in seeming like he just walked up there. He also did a lot of improv – if he was watching the news a half hour earlier and something caught his attention, he wouldn't hesitate to take the idea on stage and see where it went. But I have no doubt – I couldn't document this – but I have no doubt Bill spent a lot of time writing.

Bill's superior craftsmanship gets overlooked because of his performance and his passion and the funniness of it. But Bill was a very good writer. I don't think well-crafted sentences come out of your mouth with any regularity. You have to sit down and write it, rework it, and rewrite it again until it's perfect.

For a time we were both in LA. My memory is that Bill had signed on with management that convinced him that, since he had these ideas for TV shows, he could pitch them more easily if he were living in LA. He never warmed to LA. Never. He went out there with a pain in his gut. It was another career move.

He had a small circle of friends in Los Angeles, but I don't think he socialized that much. He went on the road a lot. We talked a bit. We'd go out to lunch or dinner. He went to movies. He loved movies. He spent a lot of time reading and writing and playing his guitar. And talking on the phone. He worked the phone. I can only imagine if Bill were still around, emails would just be flying all around the world. The information superhighway, the Internet. He would have loved it.

RON SHOCK

I'd gone home and told my wife I'd seen a genius. It was a stunning thing. I'd never seen anything like this. I had started in late November 1982, so this must have been January, February 1983. I hadn't seen Kinison, I'd seen the other guys. They were very, very funny. Then I see Bill and it's a different level.

It's like seeing a real-good high-school basketball team and seeing a couple of really good guys. If you don't know anything about basketball you think those guys are pretty good. Then you see Michael Jordan.

They were all funny, the Outlaws. They are still the funniest guys – I've seen every goddamn comic out there and there are maybe three or four that are as funny as those guys were. Day in and day out they were brilliantly funny. But Bill was so much better that there wasn't even any kind of envy. Jealousy wasn't part of their makeup. You didn't even mind him being so much better because you knew what he did, you were never going to be able to do anyway. You just sit back and watch and go, "Wow."

I've had this conversation with everybody else that knew him, and they've expressed the same thing. He was so good, he almost made you want to quit. You'd think there was no sense in being a stand-up because anything you could say, Bill was going to find a way to say much better. He'll eventually get around to it if it has any importance. He was that good. He was a genius. And there was no other word for it. He was a genius and we weren't. We were just real good.

The Annex, which was our home, was an asylum run by the inmates. They would open up the bar. We just stayed there. The audience was gone and we weren't. It was nightly.

I never was much of a drinker. Alcohol doesn't sit well with me. I don't have anything against it and every now and then I'll have a drink on stage, but a lot of the guys at that time consumed vast amounts of alcohol. But it wasn't like it was drunken orgies. It was a bunch of highly intelligent people, sitting around talking and, as they were talking, having a drink.

Bill was a genius and knew he was, without putting those words in his mouth. He was 21, 22, 23 years old? Jesus Christ, what were you like when you were 22 and 23? You were pretty wild. We all were. And they were giving him free drinks. It was just a phase. I don't think it hurt his career at all.

It wasn't that long a period that there was that heavy drinking. A year, year and a half at the most. Bill did do a couple of shows in Austin where I remember reading a review that said he was drunk as a skunk, but the thing is Bill Hicks drunk as a skunk is funnier than anybody else is stone-cold sober. It was just a phase. And he was young, real young. Bill and I had some wonderful mushroom and LSD trips together. Bill and I drove to Atlanta – this must have been '83 – his name was already getting out and the Punch Line was open.

They wanted Bill to come over and do a set because they thought they wanted to book him, but they wanted to see him first. Bill's car wouldn't make it and I had a brand new Mazda truck. He told them: "Okay, but you've got to give [Ron] Shock a guest spot, too." They didn't know who I was but I got to go because I had the car.

So we go over there and do the spots and I end up getting a booking from them, too. On the way back, right at Montgomery, Alabama, we decide to take some LSD. And what a trip. Oh my goodness gracious, that was great fun. You know acid trips, and it's been a long time . . . I only remember two things. I remember having to stop the truck and both of us having to get out because we were laughing so hard that we couldn't continue. We're sitting on the side of the road with tears pouring down our faces we're laughing so hard. Over what I have no idea.

Then when we get to Jackson, Mississippi, we decide we're hungry. And we're really fucked up. We know we can't go into a regular restaurant so we decide to go to a KFC and get some chicken. We get in line and these people behind the counter – I don't know if they really were as ugly and bizarre-looking as they seemed to be to us, but I wanted to pee real bad. I tell Bill, "Here's some money. Get us some chicken. I've got to go to the bathroom."

And Bill said, "I don't know if I can do this."

"Yeah, you can do it, Bill."

So I come back and Bill is standing out in the rain and he's holding the boxes of chicken. He's got so many of them that he has to have both of his hands clasped together down around his waist, and the chicken piled up on top of them up to his chin. And he's laughing and tears are running down his face.

He's sopping wet, standing out in the rain. And I go, "What are you doing out here and how come you have so much chicken?"

"I couldn't decide, so I just started pointing at stuff and this is what we got." And he said, "I couldn't stay in there and you locked the truck. I didn't want them to think I was weird so I came out here."

And I said, 'Oh, that'll work, Bill, they won't think you are weird now."

That's the final bonding we did. That's when we knew we were meant for each other.

It wasn't about us being a bunch of drunks, though. You know, it was just a magical time. A magical time. I can't speak for everybody else, but it inspired me to be a much better human being in all kinds of ways – honesty and caring about other people. Up to that point in my life I had either dealt with crooks or the corporate world. Both of which – and I said this on *The Johnny Carson Show* – made me realize that I met more honest people in prison than I ever did in the corporate world.

When I got into comedy and met these guys, they didn't lie, they didn't cheat, they didn't steal. They cared about other people. They cared about their country. They knew what was going on in the world. They could hold an intelligent, compassionate conversation about almost anything. To this day, they are still the best people I ever met. Bar none. Unequivocally. Across the board. Patterson, Riley Barber, Jimmy Pineapple, Andy Huggins, Bill Hicks, John Farnetti. These are good people.

STEVE EPSTEIN

He and Dwight came in, then kind of rushed out. We would see them just on occasion, until he started coming to the Annex, and once Bill started developing material it took no time at all. Even though he wasn't necessarily the best guy at the club, we could all tell this kid was going somewhere and if anyone was going to make it, it was going to be Bill.

In the early days, I just remember him being so innocent and so brilliant. Until we went out to LA. He was so not broad-minded, at first: he couldn't understand why we ate anything besides peanut butter and jelly sandwiches. He was a hamburger, meat and potatoes kind of guy. I remember him asking questions: "What's the appeal of

Asian food or of Greek food? Why do you need all of these other foods? What's wrong with a hamburger?" He was just not very broad-minded when he first came out here.

I went out to LA before the guys. I had money, so I just went. I was six months ahead of them. They were all sleeping on my floor. Kinison and LaBove and Barber stayed for a while. Barber stuck around for too long. Bill, I think, could only take it the first night, then he got a place in Burbank, but he didn't have a job.

I was on probation when I was in LA. The police from West U – this is in Houston – had come and woken me up early at like 8 o'clock in the morning, knocking on my door, yelling, "Epstein, Epstein." I thought it was Kinison pulling an all-nighter. I'm naked except for a Snoopy bedsheet when I come to the door, and there are a couple of police officers. One was in the bedroom with a gun and me and my Snoopy bedsheet, the other one looked and saw my stash box was open. There was a little baggie of speed. It was only there because it was offered to me, but it was so terrible that I never used it. It really stung the nose.

The lady goes: "What's this?'

And I said, "That's the worst speed you've ever had."

She said, "I've never had speed."

And I told her, "Well, don't start with that. Sanka is stronger."

I could have got off, but my lawyer sucked. So as part of my probation I had to have a job. I found a place in LA right at Hollywood and Vine called Preview House. They had a bank of phones and what you would do is call people and get them to come out to see what were allegedly previews of new TV shows or movies. It sounded good, but mostly what they had were people wanting you to check out and judge commercials.

I helped Bill get a job there. He was the only person they ever had work for two weeks who never got one person to come to see a preview. Not one. He got fired for that. But that was never Bill's thing. He never had to sell. He never had to pick up the phone to get work. It's almost magic. I think that's one of the reasons he was so against advertising, because he never needed it. It just came to him. People wanted to do it for him to help themselves.

Anyway, Preview House was bullshit because most of them weren't real previews, they were mostly commercials. But I'm trying to be fairly diligent there. I go to the bathroom, I come back and Bill has taken the mouthpiece out of the handset of my phone. He unscrewed it and took it out. So I'm calling people and they are not hearing me, and it's getting me pissed off. I'm talking away and nobody is hearing me. And I have no clue. Finally, I see Bill laughing and figure out what the hell is going on.

So, a day or two later I do the same thing to him, but he just plays it. He keeps it going for, like, a half hour. Part of it was Bill's genius, that he could pull it off, part of it was my idiocy, but for a half hour Bill was talking into the phone: "Tickets . . . Hello, I said, 'tickets . . . free tickets.' Bill Hicks. My name is Bill Hicks . . . Doesn't anybody in this town speak English?" And he'd hit the phone on the desk. It killed me. He had me going for easily fifteen or twenty minutes. He actually had me for years. Of course he was fucking with me, and he eventually told me that. But he came up with these great conversations. It was such a great visual thing. And the way he played me.

Ron Robertson, he came out to LA and rented a room in the hotel next to the Comedy Store. Me, Robertson, Hicks and maybe Barber, we were talking about getting Bill laid, because there were all of these hookers out on Sunset Boulevard all the time.

Bill was a handsome kid, but he had that terrible kind of crew cut. He had this bit where he talked about his mom giving him this bad haircut, but I think he figured it was helpful for him not to look handsome, so he gave himself this terrible haircut. Anyway, we were going to get Hicks laid because there were gorgeous women out there. These were Sunset Boulevard hookers, there really were some that were in the league of Julia Roberts, from the movie where she played the hooker. Some really were that good. They ran the gamut but some were that good.

We were up in the room, next to the Store, and some girls saw us leaning out the window. We started shouting back and forth at each other. We were telling them to come up and they wanted us to come down, so we agreed and went down But we had talked Bill into letting us buy him a hooker. And he was into it. So we go downstairs and we were negotiating. We are talking to the girls with Bill standing off to the side. Me and Ron are negotiating a price and we come to an agreement, and they say, "Okay, we'll do anyone . . . but him."

And they point over to Bill.

And he's not hearing anything.

We say, "No, no, no. You don't understand. This is for him. He's a kid and we want to get him laid."

"No, I won't do him." I don't know why the girl said it. He was standing there looking kind of goofy with the bad hair and all, but it was ridiculous that she said that. I don't understand where she was coming from, she was a hooker. But she said she wouldn't do him.

Then she turns to one of the two other girls there and says, "Well, I won't do him, will you?" And of course they are not going to, because they don't want to imply that she is any better than them. So they all say they wouldn't do him.

"No, you don't understand. He is the one we are trying to get laid." No. No. And no.

We let them go and went back over to Bill. "So what's the story?" he asked.

"Well, Bill, you don't want to hear."

"Hey, if it's more money, I'll put in, it's not a problem."

"Bill, that's not the problem."

"What is it?" We didn't want to hurt his feelings and that really doesn't sound good. The guy didn't need to be knocked down like that, to hear that a hooker didn't want him. So even though we were not the sweetest of guys, we didn't want to tell him this. But he wouldn't shut up about it.

Finally we said, "Bill, they won't do you."

"Fuck you. They've got to do me, they are hookers."

159

"No, they won't."

"Ah, come on. Fuck you guys. Fuck you guys."

It was probably the lowest point in Bill's life, in a sense. After this we had gone into this place on Sunset where they used to have this biorhythm machine. I had used it a few times. So me and the guys went in there and tried it. It told you how much energy you had in, like, six or seven different categories: intelligence, sex, another one said money, a couple of others. Then they had levels for each category, starting at zero, then it went up. It also had a little area below zero. We all did this, and we were at various places. Then Bill does it, and he didn't get anything. Every level was below zero. The rest of us were fine, but even the machine was telling Bill he was a loser.

It's funny because later in life Bill had no problem. He would have all of these women – of course, some of them were complete loons, but he had a charm about him. I remember we were hosting a benefit – I can't remember for what but this is back in Houston – but sometimes people would come to comedy clubs to do it; we would get the bar and they would get the door. That's just the way most benefits work. We were having one of those where a River Oaks society girl who inherited all of her money was kind of running the show. She was really upper crust. You could tell by the way she looked, by the way she moved. She had not spent much time out of the mansion or the presence of multi-millionaires.

She was kind of the emcee of the charity portion of the show. So Bill went up there, and he was as fucked up as ever, I mean really fucked up, and he was ragging on all of these people, particularly this one chick. He was doing a Mick Jagger: "Aoh, strut your stuff baybee. Show us wot you got." It could have been taken pretty offensively, but she liked the edginess.

After he talked to her for a while, she goes, "Gee, you are really drunk. Do you think you should be drinking like that?' That isn't really good for you. You shouldn't be driving. I should drive you home." She drove him home; and he ended up going back and fucking her. He fucked her pretty good. That's about the last I remember of that. But it was pretty impressive to me that Bill at his most fucked up could pull it off, because this chick, she was a real society princess.

Bill told me he wanted to do it, that he wanted to do a hallucinogenic. So we went picking mushrooms. We went to Katy, Texas. You used to be able to get them right off the farmland. Now I think they put something in the cow feed, in the grain, that kills the spores, but back then it was not difficult just to find them growing.

We were on this one piece of land picking mushrooms, and this farmer and his son show up behind us and the guy goes, "What are you boys doing on my land?"

Bill goes: "Oh, we're just picking some fauna for one of our science classes, our biology class."

So he tell us, "Well, get the hell off." And he's got a shotgun.

"Well, okay sir." So we start leaving and we get to a certain distance when I ask, "Shotguns can't shoot that far, can they?"

And Riley says: "No, I think it's pretty much a close-up kind of gun." All right. So when we were about 100 yards away I started picking mushrooms again, and we hear, "BAM!" Then we just took off.

We were behind the Annex. There was this little area, a little porch and we were sitting there. Bill had taken the mushrooms and kept asking me – and this is how I know for sure it was the first time – "Eppy, how do I know when I'm high?" because he had never been high before. "Eppy, how can I tell? What's it like?"

I told him, "Bill, you really can't describe it to someone who has never been high before."

"Is it kind of like when you hold your breath and you hyperventilate?"

"Well, there is a small aspect of that, I guess."

"Well, how do you know?"

"Bill, it can encompass a whole range of feelings. There's no saying." It's like asking, 'How do you know if you're straight?' So he keeps trying to ply me for information on how he will know. And finally I tell him: "Bill, you are just going to know."

So after about forty-five minutes he goes, "Uh oh. Oh yeah. Okay. Okay. All right, I think I know. I think I'm high."

Just then, the emcee comes out and goes, "Bill, you're on."

"Eppy, you think I should go up?'

Then I said – and it's the word I am most famous for – "Sure" because that's what I want to see. I want to see Bill go onstage right after he came on to mushrooms. It's just so perfect and hysterical. The guy had never been on anything in his life, including alcohol. This is the very first time; and he's going on stage.

Bill was big into studying Chaplin and Keaton. And he was noticing the subtlety that could bring a laugh, like, just the raising of an eyebrow could bring a laugh, and how funny that could be. "And really if you take it to the farthest extremes, the ultimate to me," he said, "would be where you just basically communicated by thought." I don't think he really meant that people were reading your mind, but in a sense, yeah, he thought he was really practising to see how little he could do and to get the best response. He was really studying this stuff.

So he goes on stage the very first time on mushrooms and he's doing quite well. He started telling the story of the Jim Bowie museum and talking about what could be in the Jim Bowie museum, "A knife?" And it's too funny to him, that particular concept. He falls down on the stage and he's holding up his hands to show the size of the knife. That would be the whole museum. And he's in hysterics laughing at his own stuff. It was contagious, because it was so real – and the audience has no idea he was fucked up. They were already laughing, but now watching him laugh and roll around on the stage, pounding the floor and coming up with his two hands showing the size of the knife, then going back down and pounding the floor again, well, they became absolutely hysterical. I know laughter is contagious, but I had never seen the room hotter. It was literally hysterical.

He came off the stage thinking that he was the comedy God on this stuff. "On mushrooms I could do no wrong." He really barely had to do two or three bits and it covered his whole fifteen or twenty minutes and he absolutely destroyed.

So the next time he does mushrooms and goes up on stage he is thinking, "I am a comedy God." He is acting that way, too. He's acting like he is a God, strutting across the stage, throwing out his material without even trying to give it that much because these are gems of wisdom, and he's the God, and they are so lucky to hear them. But they weren't buying any of this shit. He looks at them like, "What's wrong? I am the comedy God." The audience was telling him, "Boo. You suck."

He started to get paranoid and ended up literally in the corner of the stage. People were throwing coasters at him, like baseball cards. "Why are we all fighting?" as they are throwing shit at him. "Where's the love?"

I was also there the first time he ever got drunk. It was me, and Dan Merryman and Bill. This was after he had already done 'shrooms. He asked, "What'll you think will do it? What will really get me drunk?" Merryman said Cuervo, and I agreed with him. "Yeah, Cuervo, that will do it." I don't remember exactly how many shots he did, maybe twelve, I think.

He was crawling on the stage after doing about an hour and a half – he was way over time – he was talking about, "You old people, you send your kids off to war, what the fuck do you care? You're fat and happy. Let the innocent die. You con them into doing your fighting for you. You fucking fat cats."

So this old lady, this nice 60- or 65-year old Texas lady, she gets up – and I'm sure she is already appalled at the crap she has had to sit through – and she goes, "Young man, I'll have you know we lost two sons in Vietnam. My husband fought in World War II and was wounded. And I don't appreciate being lectured to by a young, drug addict, alcoholic falling across the stage."

Then Bill crawled to the other side of the stage and goes, "Maybe I was a little out of line." He might have yelled back at other people, but that one woman really took the air out of his sails.

[*   *   *]

CHAPTER 5

Kevin Booth

David Johndrow had a friend named Mark. Older guy. Married. He was a swinger, or at least had all of these swinger stories, and other lurid tales of his sexual exploits. He also claimed to be going to prostitutes with some regularity and told David about a place off of Interstate 35, a few miles north of 183. Full of Asian women. For $50 you could get anything you wanted. Anything. David told Bill about it.

So after another episode in the seemingly endless series where I had had a fight with Jere, and Bill had had a fight with Laurie, we decided to pay a visit to this Asian amusement park. In the abstract, it sounded like a good idea. First, we were both pissed off and spiteful. Second, we were going to go have sex. Third, the women were Asian. Fourth, we were going to go have sex.

It's not an uncommon fantasy for a white man. And a women's reaction, specifically white, middle-class American women, is usually the same: "Oh, men are sexually attracted to Asians because they are subservient. That's sexist and gross." And what about American women? Bill used to joke that their fantasy was to have sex with a Frenchman while riding naked on horseback. On a beach.

The truth was that the attraction was also based on Asian

women's genitalia. By our understanding, we thought it was naturally less hairy and darker in color. Also, Asian women are notorious for being tight and muscular, vaginally speaking. And with Asian men being equally notorious for being poorly hung, we would seem well-endowed if only by comparison. We might have been trading off completely false conceptions, but that only made the mystery that much greater, the possibility that much more alluring. We just didn't know.

Bill was actually way more into Italian women – he liked dark skin, dark hair, dark features – but largely for the same reasons (i.e. dark, mysterious). However, there were no Italian "modeling studios" or "massage parlors." Asians were a more than acceptable substitute.

The whole cover that these were "models" was ridiculous. It was even something they used in pornography. Years later Bill would joke about picking up a copy of *Barely Legal* and noting how it would say on the cover that all of the models were over the age of 18. "These are models? Models? Tell me, Dusty, how is the cock being worn this year? Is it being worn in the ass or between the tits?"

It seemed like a great idea while we were telling ourselves to do it, and as we were driving up north of town; but once in the parking lot, I remember getting out of the car and thinking, "Oh man, are we going to go through with this?" I was even too broke to afford it. Am I gonna spend my last $50 to have sex, when, in reality I can go home and have sex with my girlfriend if I want? When I expressed my reservations, Bill agreed to pay for it.

We walked in, and it looked like a Denny's or a dentist's office. Very brightly lit, two rows of chairs facing each other. There were older, definitely married guys already sitting down. All looking guilty. All trying not to be seen. It was all Bill could do not to burst out laughing. It was funny.

These men all wore their shame on their sleeves, certainly; but at least these guys were willing just to do what they felt they needed to do. Hanging out in topless bars, which in the States was seen as an acceptable way to indulge but not cheat, Bill saw as wussing out. This was cheating, yes, but it was practical. Your sex life at home is awful and you need sex, then just go get it.

Bill had real disdain for topless bars for other reasons. He remarked how they had enormous homoerotic overtones. You sit in a room filled with super-horny guys, who are all going home alone at the end of the night. Kinda gay.

Bill always used to say, "Show me the pussy." It was his same complaint with *Playboy*. "I need to see the pussy." He couldn't understand why titty bars were so popular when all you could see were bare beasts. "I can see breasts in *National Geographic*." He would pull open his shirt, "I have breasts. Look, I have a nipple. Why would I pay to see a nipple? I need to see a pussy. I will pay."

"Tastefully done" was a cop-out for Bill. "Show me the pussy." That was one of his mantras. For that need, Bill was about to pay.

Clad in an unsexy negligée, the madam, an older woman, walks in and hands us menus. We're in this room that is like something out of a M*A*S*H episode. We are Hawkeye and Trapper in Tokyo. And the key feature here is that all the walls are made of paper.

A woman clocking in at about 45, not that pretty, with really bad teeth comes in, takes Bill by the hand, and walks him into the next room.

I'm sitting there by myself – well, by myself with a group of men waiting to renêge on their wedding vows – and Bill is right on the other side of the paper wall. I can hear him. He is talking really quietly, but I can hear every word he's saying.

Someone who had never been in a whorehouse could have written the script. "Why you no have honey? You cute. Why you no have?"

Bill. Poor puppy dog. "Oh, she cheated on me." Then silence. Thirty seconds. A minute. Then, "Ugh . . . ughhhhh."

The woman comes walking out from behind the paper wall, across the hallway to another room with an open door. There's a sink in that room. Without bothering to close the door behind her, she turns and spits into the sink. Right in full view of me. Right in full view of everyone else. Then she turns on the tap and starts gargling.

She walks back into the main room and asks me, "You want be next?"

"Uh . . . No. No, I don't."

Bill comes walking out with a big smile on his face and looking kind of sheepish. "You gonna do it, Kevin?"

"No. I'm gonna skip this one."

"I'll pay for it."

"No, let's go."

"No, you're going to do it. You're going to do it."

"I really want to get out of here."

We get back in the car and start heading home. "What happened in there? Did you get to see her pussy? What was it like?"

"No, she just kind of jerked me off, then put her mouth on me at the very last second, right when I came," Bill answered. "It was over before I knew what happened."

We later became obsessed with the Midnight Cowboy. There was this old guy, who owned the building that housed both the Comedy Workshop and the Capitol City Oyster Bar in Austin, and he helped nurture the fascination. This was another "modeling studio" in Austin, or, if you are bad with euphemisms, a whorehouse. It's been a fixture down on 6th Street in Austin for decades.

Bill and I developed a near-nightly habit of walking down to 6th Street where we would camp at the front door of the Midnight Cowboy. We would actually stand there talking to people we knew who were walking by. In reality we were just waiting. Is the coast clear? We didn't want anyone to see us going in. Kind of stupid in retrospect because the place had a back door.

To be completely accurate, it wasn't just the Midnight Cowboy. We were frequenting a few places. There was also a whorehouse on South Lamar called The Lady of the Eighties. We hit that place as well. Actually, one of the prostitutes working there would hang out

with Kinison when he was in town. Kinison's star was already starting to shine at this time. Bill's wasn't. Bill had to pay for his whores.

Basically, we were searching for girls who wanted to hang out and
party in exchange for drugs and money. We would also try to be nice
and act like we cared about their lives. We were interested customers,
even if a little creepy. More often than not, though, it seemed we
ended up at the Midnight Cowboy, usually after midnight and
usually on a weekend. Given the fantasy we were trying to fulfil, it
was monumentally stupid because that was rush hour. It was just a
factory of sex in there at that point.

Duh. What were we expecting? One guy right after another. To
add insult to injury, it was a line of fraternity guys. It was like forcing
Bill to watch reruns of his worst nightmare. (If he was ever openly
hostile to Austin it was because of the large numbers of drunken frat
boys littering the place.) People were being churned through the
place like they were on a conveyor belt, and there was Bill, trying to
have meaningful conversations with the employees: "How long have
you been in the States?" "What got you into this line of work?"

The girls had to be thinking, "God, what a fucking idiot." We
wanted to save these girls, but we also wanted to have sex. We were no
different than anyone else trying to get their rocks off; we were just
convincing ourselves we were different – which, in a nice parallel of
delusion, correlates well with what we convinced ourselves of when
we were doing drugs – that we were different.

One time we were there a stunningly beautiful Asian girl came out
and started talking to me. Perfect. After a few minutes she asked me
if I wanted to pick my girl. "Well, I pick you," I said. Instantly. Bill
shot me a look that said, "You fucker." I returned a look that said,
"Sorry, dude," but I wasn't sorry at all. This was working out better
than I could have hoped.

Yoko was her name. The point wasn't lost on us. The woman that
came out for Bill was this older, ugly, short-haired girl. She resem-
bled one of the Blue Meanies from *Yellow Submarine*. After he
finished, we walked outside and Bill said, "I need to go back to the

hotel, pour gasoline on my dick and light it on fire." The girl Bill had done it with was just nasty. Scary. Bill pantomimed his vision of the immediate future – pouring lighter fluid on his cock, taking a match, then "pwoof," flames burning off all the VD and crabs he had just picked up.

As bad as it was for Bill, my experience ended up being more depressing. When I finished, another one of the girls told Yoko there was a man at the back door for her. I came out of the room and she told me, "Ah, I need to go talk to husband." It was horrible. All of our fears about the women we loved being whores suddenly seemed a little less abstract. Just like Bill was so tortured by the things that Laurie had done, there was a dark part of him that was turned on by it at the same time. It was something Bill and I talked about for days.

We ran back to Bill's hotel and went straight to the pool. The heavily chlorinated water couldn't but help as we were trying to clean ourselves off a bit. We took a short dip, then, right as we had finished having sex, oh, about 20 minutes previous, two girls down by the pool started flirting with us. It was too perfect. Sex was the last thing on our minds, and we were being hit on. Women were indeed attracted to guys who didn't look or act like they needed it.

But Bill never forgave me for taking the good-looking girl. Especially when he paid for it.

We didn't go back to the Midnight Cowboy for months. When we did, we were all coked out to the gills. Kinison was in town. Bill, Kinison and I decide to go to the Midnight Cowboy.

Coke is such a weird drug from a sex standpoint. It makes you horny, but you can't get hard to save your life. Guys on coke are a prostitute's worst nightmare. An hour later you could hear the woman in Kinison's room: "Why you no get hard?" She probably lost ten pounds in water weight trying to suck his dick.

Then from Bill's room you'd hear a woman protesting: "No hiney. No hiney." Always from Bill's room. Bill was so into anal. He went well past fetish and fascination to the point of obsession. I remember when Bill got sick and I was searching for any explanation –

Why? Why Bill? – one of the more ridiculous notions that came across my head was the thought he got sick from tossing a few too many salads.

He talked about it all the time. It was one of his hobbies. There was an Indian girl Bill had an affair with. He would talk about sex with her and he would do skits about it. He would play the part of her asshole beckoning him to enter. Seriously, Bill would personify her ass, complete with female Hindustani accent: "Uoh, Beell. Beell, coom and take me, Beell."

Nasty. For Bill, things just couldn't get nasty enough. When it came to food or sex or whatever. Nasty. Nasty. Nasty. More. More. More. Action movies were never violent enough. Porn was never graphic enough. Drugs were never strong enough. Sex was never naughty enough. It was just who he was.

On the couple of occasions Kinison came into town – they had parties that started in one city, and ended in another a couple of days later – he just aided and abetted. All of Bill's disproportionate appetites, Kinison was only too willing to help feed.

Sam had long since moved to LA but was still coming back to Austin and Houston every now and then to perform and to party.

One night he was wearing a long black trenchcoat. It hung almost all the way down to his feet, down to the floor. Kinison sat there telling me that the jacket was his security blanket, the armor that he had worn since he had gotten clean and sober. It was his shield and sword that protected him from the demons, the temptation drawing him back into doing more drugs. It was a fucking beautiful speech, marred only by the fact that, while Sam was giving me this whole sermon, he was snorting gigantic lines of cocaine off the table.

He's talking about this jacket like it's his brother and his savior, it's the reason he survives the day without having to do more coke, while he's doing fucking ridiculous amounts of coke.

Cocaine. The big lie. No line of bullshit was big enough to keep you from doing a bigger line of coke.

171

Night after night. Party after party. It involved blow often enough that we kept David Cotton's number on speed dial because we were either doing blow or chasing blow. The Biggs House, the Villa Capri, Steamboat, the Workshop, the Annex, Houston House. It all coalesces into this one giant amalgam of a party you could call "1982 to 1988." There was very little to distinguish one night from the next.

Bill had spent plenty of time in Austin, both performing and partying, so much so that there are plenty of locals who think Bill was either from Austin or lived there. He wasn't and he never did, although he was always threatening to move there. One time he finally decided to make good on the threat. So what's the first thing he does? He goes out not to look at apartments, but to shop for pets. Honestly. He and I went out and shopped for pets. This was the guy who used to joke that he couldn't take care of a plastic plant.

Bill's decision not to move to Austin was largely financial. Right as he was contemplating relocating, Jack Mark Wilks scored a free place to live. If it came down to a decision between "live free" and "live in Austin," well, Austin was a pretty cool place to live at that time, but not that cool.

Wilks was the kind of guy who proposed toasts at weddings and made the big "It doesn't get any better than this" speech. So it's hard to hate him, because he really did cultivate the whole notion of brotherhood amongst his peers, but at the same time he was more than a little schlocky. Before Bill died, when he had asked people not to come see him, Wilks went anyway. Supposedly Wilks was trying to create this big sentimental moment but Bill didn't have the energy for a long goodbye. Bill was too far beyond sentiment at that point.

They had an amazing corner apartment at Houston House, which was a swanky address with a great view of the Houston skyline. Then Pineapple and Huggins moved in upstairs. Suddenly they were behaving like the Rat Pack. It sounds trite now because in the intervening years since Bill's death, so many people have tried to do it. It was a full-fledged fad in the Nineties: swing dancing, cigars, Capitol

Records-era Sinatra. Put on a fedora and suddenly be cool. But to be doing it a decade before that was actually somewhat original.

It's how they fancied themselves. They thought they were too cool for school. Literally. Bill was done with the idea of college, and at this point there was no chance of him going back. But so much about Bill was Sinatra-sized. His goals, his alcohol intake, his thirst for life. It was a goofy affectation, but something about it fitted Bill.

That apartment became party central (which, I guess, would make it like the Sands). Jimmy Pineapple's schtick was very much patterned on the mannerisms and lingo: calling women "dames" and "broads," etc. And most of them bought into the persona of the broken-hearted but good-time drunk. And when they got drunk, they'd spell out the associations: "Jimmy is Dean Martin. Bill is Frank Sinatra. Mark is Peter Lawford."

To some extent, Bill was also trying to become a "man," as in a proper adult. He was living in the kind of place that a proper adult with adult responsibilities would live, so he started behaving accordingly. Or trying to. He would get his shoes shined and go downstairs and get the paper from the doorman. They decked the apartment walls with some really great black-and-white photographs, most of which were taken by David Johndrow (Bill was always very proud of his friends and the people he knew).

At the same time, the apartment smelled like someone had puked and urinated all over the place. One night, I pulled the cushions off the couch, put them on the floor, and crashed. During the night, I rolled over to where my nose touched the shag carpet and it smelled like vomit. Actually, it *was* the smell of vomit. My nose hit the carpet precisely where someone had previously thrown up. It instantly woke me and left me with the feeling I too was going to puke. That smell permeated the whole apartment. Plus, the living room didn't have proper window shades, so the sun would shoot in during the early morning. Bright and smelly. It was impossible to sleep.

Bill was sporting the exposed-mattress look in his room. He accessorized with shit all over the floor – books, tapes, piles of clothes.

His bed was never on a frame. I once told him: "Dude, your box spring is supposed to be on a frame." For a pretty brilliant comedian and just a generally clever guy, his response was only memorable for how ordinary it was: "What are you? My mom?" He kept tinfoil over the windows and kept the air conditioning turned low. It was part-dungeon, part-meat locker. It had a really dark aura to it.

Behaving like someone with adult responsibilities and actually having them were two different things. Bill was having problems getting booked outside of Houston or Austin, so he was mostly working locally, which meant at some point he was probably scheduled to be at the Annex. He had a half-hour obligation somewhere in the neighborhood of 10 p.m. That was part of the act. "I love my job. I love the hour."

He could play grown-up all he wanted, but really Bill had no responsibilities. Plus, the apartment, it was a one-bedroom that he was sharing with another guy. Not like that. Wilks slept on a cot-type thing in the living room.

Bill would go through periods when he was playing roles from movies, especially when he was drinking heavily. He would see a movie with someone he identified with, or thought he identified with and co-opt that character. Sinatra-isms aside, he was going through a Peter O'Toole as the Errol Flynn-inspired Alan Swann in *My Favorite Year* period. He pictured himself as a glorious drunk. The classy guy with the style and the witty "I must get out of these wet clothes and into a dry martini" entrances. Always gets the girl. Always has the perfect comeback for an insult.

When Bill lived in Houston House, that marked the height of his drinking and drug addiction. At the time it didn't seem out of control, but looking back it was. Even though they were performing and had to be somewhat coherent and functional, everyone was getting drunk nearly nightly. There were toxic, scary nights, to the point where Bill would be obnoxious, talking above the room and yelling at some patrons as the others stared at him while trying not

174

to stare at him. Then from there we would go to the comedy club. There were nights – plural – like that.

Bill would warm up with a beer or two. During peak drinking days he might down a whole six-pack at the apartment before heading out. Once at a bar or the Workshop, his main drink of choice would be Jack Daniels; but people would also buy him shots. He would down whatever. If you handed him a glass of Everclear, he would drink it. If you handed him a glass of Mad Dog 20/20, he'd drink it. A glass of Schlitz. It just didn't matter.

Mix and match. Beer, wine, hard liquor. He'd wake up with a horrible fucking hangover, and wonder why it was so bad. I'd tell him, "Well, you drank a trifecta, Bill. Those things will clash." Bill just didn't think that mattered. Then there was the sheer volume of how much he put down the night before. He could easily drink a fifth of straight liquor every night. That wasn't untypical.

It almost sounds delusional to say it was social. It was. That was the intent anyway. Things just progressed to the point where they were out of control. People were out. Joking. Laughing. Drinks were flowing. They were the Rat Pack in their own minds, but a lot of people would see them as pathetic.

They were all fucking broke. They didn't drive nice cars. They weren't marrying movie stars. They didn't take a private plane out to Palm Springs for the weekend. Spiritually, sure, they probably felt the same kinship of wit and alcohol-aided camaraderie as the Rat Pack. But the "there's plenty of other fish in the sea and plenty of other dames in the place . . ." schtick became like a broken record. A self-parody.

But for that period, they really were brothers; and they were there for each other. Even if it was stupid shit. If one of them was saying, "Hey, I need a $100 for this hooker," another one would reach into his pocket and tell him, "Well, I've got this $100 to last me all week, but, shit, take it. I'll get by somehow." There was something laudable in that, skewed though it was, but when Bill went sober, and watched all those guys through clean eyes he had a massive awakening. He was able to look in the mirror and he didn't like what he saw.

There were parties at Houston House, but I wasn't around that many times when there were tons of people in Bill's apartment. He wasn't too into crowds in his place. A lot of people would come and go from there, it did become like a flop house. It was so much against Bill's grain; so the opposite of what he was like before. He was a private person.

It wasn't all debauchery. Sometimes when I went to Houston a lot of the comics who might otherwise loiter would disappear. Bill would put on a different face, and we would get to work on *Ninja Bachelor Party*. Much of it was shot at Houston House.

The roof shots we did by ourselves. We put the camera on a tripod and did some horribly bad kung fu fighting on the roof of Bill's building. David Johndrow, who was actually living in Houston for a time, helped us film some of the fight scenes in the streets. There was also a struggling comedienne friend of Bill's, who came out and shot camera for us as well. Those scenes were in front of Houston House. The fight scene in a gymnasium: that was in the weight room at Houston House. The scene with the large industrial laundry machines: that's Houston House. The scene where we go running into a lobby, that was the front desk of Houston House.

The experience was uniform. Friends and family or even bystanders would find out what we were doing and make a comment like, "Oh wow, you guys are making a movie . . ." They'd hang around long enough to see us running around in goofy costumes. That would put an end to the "Oh wow." The great first impression would give way to the reality that they were watching these two dumb guys behaving like idiots in front of a dippy little video camera.

We were acting like we were making this really serious movie, but that only confused the people we knew. They would look at us like: "Are Bill and Kevin being sarcastic? Do they not realize this is some horrible home movie they are making?" They didn't know whether to laugh with us or at us. Or course it got to the point where *we* didn't know, either. We were in so deep we couldn't turn back. We were going to teach everybody a lesson by finishing that thing no matter how stupid it got. The more stupid the better.

When he was living at Houston House, Bill also started dating hairdresser Pamela Johnson. She was a small-scale model of Laurie Mango, and bore a resemblance to Illeana Douglas. She was older and had two sons. Pam was a bit of a mystery woman, the girlfriend Bill kept a secret; not a good secret. I felt like I was segregated a bit from her and never got to know much about her.

Bill was jealous and protective over her, so he purposely kept her on the outer edge of the loop of his friends. Bill knew he could leave Laurie with his friends; he knew she wouldn't do anything with us; he knew we wouldn't do anything with her. Not so with Pamela. He was much more paranoid with her. She had already slept with Wilks. That's how they met. She was cutting Pineapple's hair, then started seeing Wilks. She became a sexual obsession for Bill, a little closet prize he was very protective of.

Later, when Bill started making money, he actually bought one of her sons a car. Then at some point when they were fighting I remember Bill saying: "My dad wouldn't even buy me a car and here I am buying a car for her son. How crazy is this?"

We all knew about her. But almost none of us knew her. Except maybe Mark Wilks. He was sleeping in the next room, oh, and had already slept with her. So he certainly knew her Biblically.

Bill never wanted to get tied down with any situation, and was careful about getting himself involved in something he couldn't get out of. He didn't accumulate stuff. If he wanted to up and move, it was a process that, by design, required about as long as it took to fill the car with gas.

That's what was particularly weird about his relationship with Pamela. She seemed to have a hold over him. I know it was sexual. She was an older woman but was this skinny, wiry brunette, like an older porn star. I actually shot some footage of Bill and Pamela French-kissing and put that in an edit of *Sane Man* in 1999. Mary

177

Hicks saw it and said, "Remove that right away. I don't want to see Bill kissing that girl." It was like she wouldn't even say her name. "That girl."

It's like a broken record, but so much of Bill's excess can easily be attributed to two things that were just part of his personality. First, he didn't do things timidly or with any restraint. When he went into something, he went fully. It's easy to see with chemicals; he was the guy who would say: "Hey, I got ten hits of acid here. If I take all ten, will that make me high enough? Okay, I'll take all ten."

I had been going to Mexico to buy drugs. One trip I picked up a bunch of boxes of Darvon to give to friends as stocking stuffers for Christmas. So one night Bill was actually going to take my parents out to dinner to atone for some other transgression. Before going out he took a couple of Darvon. Nothing. Took two more. Still nothing. Took eight. Now he's a little tingly. So, hey, eight more will be more tingly.

Bill ended up taking the whole box, and he ended up in the ER of St. Joseph Hospital with a Chinese doctor standing over him yelling, "You partyin' now, white boy? You partyin' now, white boy?" while trying to slap him back into consciousness. He obviously missed dinner. He told my parents he had the flu.

But he had that all-or-nothing attitude and approach towards everything. For example, one of the last movies that he was into before he died was *Reservoir Dogs*, and he wasn't just into it. He was insanely into it. "Look, Kevin, I can't even talk to you until you go see this movie. I got nothing to say to you until you see it." There just wasn't a lot of middle ground to occupy in Bill's world. Nothing in moderation.

The other trait that makes it easy to see how things got out of control for Bill was that he was the kind of guy that did not want to miss out on an experience. He was always the one who wasn't afraid to take chances.

That's what's still so puzzling about his passing up on a threeway. Laurie once offered Bill the chance to have sex with her and another woman at the same time. It was his dream, well, it's every guy's dream, but Bill talked about it enough to where his desire seemed a little more acute. But he turned it down. He said he didn't want to ever have to explain to his kids how he and mommy, the love of his life, once had sex with another one of mommy's friends. How could he ever even face his kids knowing *that* happened.

Maybe it's the exception that proves the rule. I can't imagine the temporary hit to Laurie's self-esteem.

[* * *]

Jack Mark Wilks

We became the tightest clique you can imagine. Six or eight very close people. So close that one would work, then would come back and feed the others. I mean that literally. We were often broke, so whoever had worked most recently and had money would usually pay for lunch. And we never left the loop; the inside of the city of Houston became our playground. We owned the city at night. Bill even wrote a bit about it: that one car leaving the city when you guys are all stuck in traffic trying to get in. That's us. And that one car that's coming in that open lane when you are trying to get out. That's us, too.

It was amazing, it was fertile for us to fantasize about what we could do with the place. We felt like we owned it and we felt like it needed an identity. Driving around at night in the Blue Cab, a 1966 blue Dodge Coronet that I acquired from my grandmother, we dreamed about making Houston the Third Coast and had endless conversations about the things we would do. "We should make movies here." We had millions of ideas. It didn't matter if it wasn't going to happen or not, we were entertaining ourselves. We were creating our own reality. Epstein even licensed the name Blue Cab Productions.

What made that time really special was that everybody knew it was special while it was happening. There were no doubts and no one had to say it. Every day was exciting to wake up to.

The things we dreamed about in the Blue Cab started to become true. We thought we should be the pets of the city. We loved it more than anybody else, so why shouldn't we be recognized? We started to get the run of the place.

We would go to Birraporetti's and get obscenely drunk. The comics would have fake fights in that place. Any self-respecting manager would have thrown us out. Instead there was an open tab there for the Outlaws.

Bill and I talked about metaphysics, and we made a spiritual connection in terms of what we believed. In Houston, I don't think he had anyone that believed in that stuff. So we started to talk and talk some more. Tripping brought out a lot of this, but I told him about the time I channeled a Hindu and I had an out-of-body experience. I had learned there was another dimension, and Bill's closet was filled with religious books.

At one point I asked him: "Would you like to be roommates?" And he said to me: "Out of all the guys, I think I could live with you the easiest." I said, "Great. Let's go find the best place in town to live."

At least the timing was right because in Houston in the mid-Eighties there was a glut of real estate space. As the same time, the resurrection of the Outlaw Comics started to take off. Shock had put together a deal with the local NBC affiliate to broadcast a packaged show of the Houston comics called *Texas Outlaw Comics*. And locally, Bill had been getting a fair amount of press off of his Letterman appearance. So we had a little bit going for us.

Still we spent day one out of our league, looking at $1500-a-month apartments, jerking off these real estate people. That night we were at the club, and I had one of my rare good sets, when there just happened to be two beautiful girls accompanied by an older gentleman at a table front and center. It was an unwritten rule that if there was a chance a guy could get laid in the club, no one was going to complain if he ignored everyone else and focused on the girls, which I did. So after my set, I went and sat down with the girls. Bill followed me. He had a great set, then joined us.

We got around to "Where are you from?" and "What do you do?"

THE GIRLS
We're in real estate.

BILL AND MARK
Oh, really.

THE GIRLS
Yeah. We work at Houston House.

181

Jackpot.

THE GIRLS

And this gentleman here, he's part-owner of Houston House,
but he lives in California.

Bill and Mark both grin wide. This was meant to happen.

BILL AND MARK

Well, what a coincidence. We were just looking at your
property today, but it's a little pricey for us.

OLDER GENTLEMAN

Boys, I tell you what. We got such a low occupancy over
there. If you guys want to live there, use my name and tell the
president of the property, tell him I said to give you one of
those apartments for half.

And now we've got something to work with. We schedule a meeting
with the building president. Bill lets me do the talking. He shows up
wearing his black T-shirt and black tennis shoes and just sits back,
breathing heavily through his nose and twiddling his thumbs. I was
selling Bill. I was selling Bill's friends. I was selling Shock giving a
sales seminar to their leasing agents. I was selling anything I could
imagine. "Jay Leno is going to be dropping by. Sam Kinison is going
to be dropping by."

We put the building president and his wife on the front row of one
of the Outlaw Comics' TV shows, which ran about every three weeks
on local television. I told them we would get shots of them in the
audience and mention him and the property in the closing credits of
the show. That helped close the deal. He gave us 2219, an $800-a-
month one-bedroom apartment on the corner. We had two glass
walls and an unbelievable view.

When the girls brought us the keys, they said we had cable, gas,
and electricity; and told us it would run to about $50 a month for
the utilities. I immediately went: "Hey! That wasn't part of the deal."

They caved instantly: "Okay. Pay nothing." After they left Bill looks at me and says, "Wilkie, that was the greatest move ever."

We went from no money, no job, I'm not funny, Bill can't work anywhere, straight to the 22nd floor of the Houston House apartments. I gave Bill the bedroom and I slept on a little pallet out in the corner. Almost immediately, Bill put tinfoil over his windows, so the sun couldn't wake him up. Elvis had done the same thing.

Management even let us have our housewarming party in one of the expensive three-bedroom places; and the party at that place was hopping. We had chicks, we had the whole audience from the Workshop, our coke dealer was there. The joke I heard was that on their way to the party – I think it was Reilly and Patterson – one of them asked, "How long do you think these guys will have this place?" And the other one said, "Better step on it."

We pulled off the TV show and two seminars that Shock gave the salespeople – some positive thinking bullshit, or whatever. We pulled off a couple of comedy shows in one of their party rooms. We got a microphone and a little amplifier. Bill, Jimmy and I all did sets. But we weren't paying a dime of rent, and the place became party central. We had a deli downstairs and they loved us and gave us credit. The concierge quickly figured out who we were, we'd call down and make a big show about whether so and so could be let in.

There was a lot of drinking. David Cotton and those guys were feeding us what, at best, could be considered cocaine; it was weak and wasn't the kind of stuff that carried you away. There was a lot of tripping – ecstasy, and guys would take mushrooms and sit on the balcony looking out at the city. Most of the guys at the Workshop liked to smoke pot. Bill was never into it. He found it boring.

In Houston we had a pretty normal routine. The only two multi-day benders I can recall were when Kinison came into town. They both started in Houston and wound up in Austin on 6th Street. As far as Bill goes, Kinison really fueled the party. Coke fueled Kinison and Bill went along for the ride. Austin was usually where it went sideways. They were long, long benders.

At some point during that time Bill and I started going out on the road together. I could sell myself pretty well if I was taking Bill with me, and Bill had me as his middle. Basically, we were feeding each other. I had a car that would make it. His car, the Chevette dubbed "Toad," was usually dilapidated, sitting with a flat tire in the Houston House parking garage. He had the draw to the club.

It was an education. The most monumental story about Bill and I working together was the week we did in Bossier City. For some reason we had a one-nighter in New Orleans on our way back to Bossier City, Louisiana. Bill met this girl – a beautiful, seductive, stunning Creole girl, more white than black, Italian-looking – who we picked up in New Orleans to take on the road with us.

Bossier City is an old horse-racing town across the river from Shreveport. It's old money. I had got us booked at a comedy club in a hotel there. So we get in there, and we are under the misconception that we have total creative control over our show. We assume that whatever else goes on in the outside world, we have control over how we present ourselves. It sounds reasonable enough.

Bill and I had added music to our shows. I had picked some play-on music, and Bill was coming on stage to the The Replacements' "Bastards of Young." We also had the idea to close the show singing "Young at Heart" along with Frank Sinatra. We were in love with that song.

The tape player for the club was behind the bar, and this becomes important later, but I would go back behind the bar and put in the tape for Bill's play-on music: The Replacements, and Sinatra. The emcee, who was a ventriloquist and now does ships and works with a duck, was giving me time after my set to get back to the bar and do this.

It's Tuesday, the first night, and the place is full of old people, the old religious people and the old power-people of the town. They have come to see the show; and it's going well enough. The little puppet guy gets up and does his thing. Then I get up and do my thing. I'm moderately funny – I do my preacher bit, and my anti-religious bullshit – then there is Bill.

Bill is doing stuff about Jimmy Swaggart and Pat Robertson and the televangelists. This was not long before Swaggart got nailed, so he hadn't yet been totally exposed as a fraud and a hypocrite. Moreover, Swaggart is from Ferriday, Louisiana, which is about halfway to Baton Rouge from Bossier City. You don't need to know too much about Louisiana geography to know that we were in Swaggart country. Bill goes up and they had never heard anything like it. They were shocked, and they were very vocal about it.

The old folks clearly went home and talked to their friends about what they had seen. Word got around; but word also got around to the kids because, Wednesday night, the place seems to be about half-filled with younger folks.

It's night two, and the alcohol is coming into play. We are going up on stage drunk. It's nothing new, but it's not going to help. It was a corner stage, and on the adjacent wall there were pictures of comedians who had performed there. During his set, Bill goes over to the wall. He takes the microphone and he goes through the pictures one by one and taps them. "This guy? He's not funny. This guy is not funny. This guy? He's kind of funny. This guy? Not funny."

They were super-cheap frames with super-thin glass. Bill tapped one of the pictures a little too hard and cracked the glass. He wasn't deliberately trying to break the picture. Of course, now the waitress is unhappy: "Oh, we love that guy."

They all hated us. They hated our music. They hated Frank Sinatra. They hated The Replacements. They didn't like anything we were doing or saying. We are sitting at a table and the manager comes over and yells at Bill, "Hey, you're going to have to pay for this picture."

I reach in my pocket, pull out a ten dollar bill and say, "Hey man, I'll pay for it." The manager replies, "No, he's going to pay for it," pointing angrily at Bill. Bill says, "It's okay Wilkie. It's okay," and tosses him some money. But that doesn't solve the problem or dissipate any of the tension.

The next night, it's Thursday and now it's mostly kids. We are also starting to feel like something is going to happen here, something not good. Bill and I notice there are a couple of plain-clothes guys from the hotel standing in the back of the room, watching what's going on. We figured they're cops or some security associated with the hotel, in either case they are not there for *our* protection.

So we take the offensive and at the end of the night go on stage to tell the crowd, "Hey guys, we gotta get a standing ovation or these guys in the back are going to beat us up." We get the audience to sing with us and Frank – "Don't you know that it's worth . . ." – and we get a standing ovation. We're also just really full of ourselves. The crowd is on our side, so we think we are safe for the time being.

Friday night the thing grows a little bit more; and Bill is getting further into a bender. The Creole girl is starting not to want any part of this. Friday turns to Saturday and the place is packed. The waitress hates us. The manager hates us, which doesn't make much sense because, antagonistic alcoholics aside, we have been packing the club. And the kids love us because we are dismissing authority.

Again, the same plain-clothes guys from the hotel are there along with uniformed cops. It's like a Lenny Bruce show; and we can't believe it, we are just feeding on it. The booze is flowing and we are feeling all of this power. It comes time to put on Bill's music. I come off the stage and hop behind the bar and I go to put on "Bastards of Young." The emcee goes up and a cop comes over and accosts me.

COP
You know I can put you in jail right now. Do you have a bar
license?

MARK WILKS
No.

186

COP

I can put you in jail right now. It's against the law for
you to be behind this bar.

MARK WILKS

Well, man, how about you come put on the
music then?

COP

I don't know how.

MARK WILKS

Well, that doesn't surprise me.

COP

I want to talk to you outside.

Bill sees this and bolts right over.

BILL HICKS

Hey, man. I'm the headliner and I need this
guy to help me do my show.

COP

(Points a finger at Wilks)
If you weren't on the show, you and I would
be outside right now.

Mixing alcohol and law enforcement was bad enough, mixing
sarcasm and law enforcement was way worse. And the police officer
is blatantly telling me he is going to take me outside and kick my ass.
We weren't even doing anything that radical. It's just that they hadn't
seen anything as powerful as Bill before. Even though he was drunk,
it was still very powerful.

So it's the first show on Saturday. Bill is on fire. He was brilliant,
and he was taunting the police: "Yeah. That's what we need more of
in comedy clubs. More guys with guns." The audience follows the
lead and starts catcalling the cops.

The cops, though, are fucking with him by turning off his microphone, but they are also getting nervous because we are on the verge of inciting a damn riot. On top of this Bill is getting very, very drunk, so much so I was afraid he wasn't going to be able to work the second set. The girl is drinking heavily as well. She's enraged at Bill as much as she is shaken by what he has got her into.

Bill gets to the stage for the second set, and the police are cutting off the microphone again. So Bill just comes out and tells the audience what's going on. "These people want to kill us, folks. They threatened my opener and they want to beat the shit out of both of us." The cops keep turning the microphone down and off, and Hicks keeps screaming, "Turn it back on. TURN IT BACK ON!" Then the audience would scream at the cops and the management to turn it back on.

The club has now stopped serving drinks to the people who are laughing. They couldn't stand that we were going down well, so the club completely turned against us. All we had was the crowd and the microphone. And at some point, an attorney gets up from his seat, walks across the floor to the stage, hands Bill his card, and tells him, "Hold on to that because you are going to need me later."

I go up and we sing "Young at Heart." And "sing" is generous. I think Bill might have been on key. And we get another standing ovation. But the room is hot, and I'm still shaken about the cop telling me he's going to take me outside. The cops are everywhere, and I overhear on one of their radios someone saying, "If they come out your way, you guys hold them until we get there."

We have just wagged our butts in the face of their authority and dismissed them as insignificant because we thought we had control over our comedy. That's all we wanted: creative control over our show. They were furious, and they were going to take it out on us.

After we finished "Young at Heart" people from the audience came up to surround us. The guys in Houston, our own best friends, wouldn't believe us when we told them, but it happened. They surrounded us and formed a barrier between us and the cops. Of course

Bill breaks out of that circle to go chase after the girl, who walked off down the hallway. So I have to chase after Bill and tell him we have got to get the hell out of there.

Bill is arguing with the girl, about what I have no idea, and the cops are closing in on us. I literally drag Bill back into the crowd that wants to shield us and get us out of there. It was practically a riot. The girl comes with us. We can't go back to our rooms, so the lawyer puts us in the car with him and his wife and takes us to a nightclub he owns. We stay at his club and we have more drinks. The excitement is buzzing. We are the celebrities and the guests of honor in the club. For this we get free drinks, which is probably the last thing we need.

After the club closes, the lawyer takes us to his house, his very nice house; and the wife is starting to get a little tired of this whole adventure. Worse, the evil Bill has come out. The attorney couldn't be nicer. He opens up his home to us and Bill thanks him by punching a hole in his wall. Bill just rammed a hole in the guy's wall in the hallway. The guy looks at Bill and says, "I'm going to bed. You guys stay here and sober up. Do not got back to Bossier City."

Bill had managed to piss everyone off. He said or did something to the girl, and she was so pissed off that she bolted; and supposedly for years after there were guys waiting for Hicks to come back to New Orleans because they were going to kill him for whatever happened between him and the girl. This is also the first and maybe the only time I've ever been fed up with Bill. I tackled him and sat on him in the hallway to try to get him to calm down. I'm trying to do this quietly so our hosts can sleep, but they are basically hiding in their bedroom.

The sun eventually comes up, and it's about six in the morning. I call a cab, and it takes us back to the Ramada. Our money is at the front desk. Our tapes are at the front desk. Someone has pulled out the entire length of the tape itself and wrapped it around the cassette case. We go to the room. It has already been cleaned. We spend about fifteen minutes going behind the Kleenex dispenser and whatever, thinking they might have planted drugs on us. We find nothing, and after a quick search we think, "We should just get out of here."

We hop in my car and Bill, ever the safe careful driver – I never once saw him go over the speed limit – drove straight back to Houston, without a stop, to tell our friends what we had done. None of them believed us.

The guy I booked the gig through called us at the apartment and said: "Mark, I will tell you this: I know that what I was told you did could not possibly have happened. But don't ever call me again. For a gig. For anything. And whatever you did, don't ever go back to that town." Then he hung up and that was the end of the story.

As much as Houston House was party central, things at the club seemed more out of control. The drinking was heavier. And when he was drunk Bill would say anything to a woman, even if her husband was right there. When he was too drunk, the anti-Bill would come out, but he would almost always go home and crash. He couldn't be who he was and be completely off the deep end.

Comedienne Diane Ford once summed it up, "the Houston comics are guys who developed a drug and alcohol problem over a woman they once had a cup of coffee with fifteen years ago." That's who we were. We were all broken-hearted. Bill was always busted up over Laurie, and always expecting to get back together with her. He knew she was the love of his life.

Of course, he was also a magnet for psycho chicks; he just didn't want any of them. I don't recall him having that many one-night stands, and if it has become a legend, well, we didn't get laid that much. I would know, it was a one-bedroom apartment we were sharing. There were a few. He had Joan. She was the one from the airplane. On a flight back to Houston from one of Bill's Letterman appearances she was another passenger I told how great Bill was. She had money and lived out in River Oaks, which was a swanky part of town. She wound up becoming a girlfriend of his.

Then Pineapple found the perfect girl for me, his hairstylist. Pamela.

I slept with Pamela. Then Pamela went for Bill, and they both came to me and said, "Look we want to be together." And I said, "Okay." I once told him to shave Pamela's pussy. When she came out of the bathroom, Bill couldn't stop laughing. It was the funniest thing he'd ever seen in his life. She got embarrassed, but he couldn't quit laughing.

The sad part is that after Bill died I saw Pamela in Houston. And I'm not proud of it, but I slept with her again. It probably doesn't make me look any better, but she wanted to rekindle with a comic. She liked the life of a comic and I was working again. She had even moved into Houston House after Bill died.

Bill kept a journal every single day of his life. I cannot remember him ever missing writing in his journal. And I'm sure every night in his notebook in his room he was jotting down comedy ideas. I'm sure of that. He had to have been. But there were times when I'd say, "Billy, that is funny. You gotta write that down." And he looked at me really, really serious – he really wanted me to understand this – he said: "Wilkie, I never forget anything funny." So I think he had kind of a photographic comedy memory.

He got to a place where there was no act any more.

He told me: "I close my eyes and walk out there and start. I don't even have an opening line any more."

[*   *   *]

Not long after Bill and Jack Mark Wilks moved into their new Houston House digs, the feds made ecstasy illegal. This was bad news. To say the Houston comics loved ecstasy would be an understatement. Everyone loved ecstasy. It was omnipresent in party circles. It was legal and cheap. The going price for a hit of X was about five dollars, less than the price of a couplathree drinks. A couplathree drinks, however, only laid the foundation for the Houston comics to build a buzz; a hit of X meant maybe five hours of euphoria. It destroyed your ego and heightened your libido. It seemed like the perfect drug.

Steve Epstein indulged often. In fact, Epstein was taking it so frequently it started scaring people. He was tripping on ecstasy almost daily. Most everybody else in the circle took it, but not with the same regularity or zeal.

"Dude, I think Steve is taking too much ecstasy. I think it's fucking him up. And I'm starting to worry about him," Bill cautioned friends. Hearing Bill getting worried about someone doing too many drugs, that was a red flag because he never talked about those kinds of things. If you thought you could handle it, then Bill thought you could handle it and it wasn't his or anyone else's business. But Steve developed strange and embarrassing facial tics. His eyes tweaked every few seconds; his mouth corner pulled out; he looked like Herbert Lom doing Chief Inspector Dreyfus. With Steve, Bill finally saw the negative effects of drugs manifest themselves and he even said, "Dude, we might want to take a little break away from doing ecstasy."

In June 1985, the United States Drug Enforcement Agency placed an emergency ban on MDMA – the chemical moniker for ecstasy – giving it a Schedule I classification. Schedule I drugs are narcotics that have a high potential for abuse and no medical usefulness. At the end of the month, ecstasy would be illegal.

So there was a July 1 deadline. And everybody was scrambling around to find out how to get their hands on as much of it as possible. Most of the Houston comics only knew end-user dealers, guys who just had a few odd hits on them at any given time. They needed someone who was trafficking.

Steve Epstein knew just the people. Earlier that year, Ron Shock had helped put together a show called *Texas Outlaw Comics* for the local NBC affiliate KPRC. During production, Eppy met a girl Kay and her boyfriend, Mark, who also had a connection to one of the major X dealers in Houston, and again, it was still legal at the time. The night ecstasy became illegal, there was a get-together at Houston House and Epstein decided to take acid and X together.

While tripping, he took a sauna with Tracy Wright; and in the sauna starts having impure thoughts about Kay. He recalls, "So, I decide, 'Well, the only way to take care of my impurities and make them pure is that I have to marry her.'"

Now he has wedding preparations to make. So Wright drives Eppy to Fitzgerald's where Kay is waitressing. If she's getting married, she probably ought to know. Only she's not at work. And nobody there knows why she's not there or where she is. "Now I'm really starting to get paranoid," Epstein says. "I called her house again, and I leave a message because I have this psychic flash that Kay is dead and in the dumpster at Fitzgerald's." Of course Epstein, in his drug-addled paranoia, realized that if she really was dead and in the dumpster, no one would believe that he had a psychic flash, but instead would think that he killed her and put her there. So he's thinking the cops will soon be out for him.

"When we get back to Houston House, right away I flush all of the ecstasy I had with me, that, at a wholesale price of about $5 a tablet, was about $700 worth. I was trying to tell the guys – and I think they were almost all asleep at the time, they had pretty much crashed out –'Don't worry guys, I flushed all the ecstasy down the toilet so there is nothing to worry about. The cops are probably coming, but the ecstasy is flushed.'"

At that point pretty much everyone wanted Eppy dead. And they wanted the pleasure of killing him. Comic Steve Moore did a bit about it, admitting the comics' collective bloodlust: "We all wanted to kill Eppy," he'd joke, "but that evening in Houston, the roaches were giving each other back rubs. They were picking up crumbs from cakes and putting them back on, 'I think you dropped this.'"

The next day when Epstein woke up, he started calling around trying to see where he could score more ecstasy. They were living in a fantasy world. They wanted to believe that nothing bad ever really happens to people who take drugs.

In late August, John Farnetti called Bill and asked him if he wanted to go to lunch. Bill said no, but asked Farnetti if he wanted to go to New York instead. Letterman's producers had beaten Farnetti to the phone and asked Bill up to do the show for a second time. Farnetti lent Wilks the money to come as well, and the three of them made the trip.

Before the show, while Bill did his pre-show preparations, Farnetti and Wilks hung out backstage. They talked to Robert Morton and Paul Schaeffer. Letterman walked by them, keeping his head down. He had no interest in a stop-and-chat. There was also a good-looking girl from Houston in the audience with her parents. When Bill found out he went up to her, put his arm around her and said, "Well come on, darlin'. Let's go out on the town." Bill loved women.

Backstage they brought the censor in, and Bill ran his material by them once again. They told him he couldn't do the wheelchair joke. "That would be to me somewhat unnerving," speculates Farnetti. "You take this big, popular chunk out of your six-minute set just before the show. It wasn't exactly hurried but you had to run it by the censor and change it right there."

Hard to imagine that it was unnerving at all for Bill, as this was the third time he had tried to sneak the same joke past them and the third time they had told him that he couldn't do it.

Taking the stage to the sounds of "Money (That's What I Want)" Bill was obviously more relaxed than the first time. The set was solid. Some jokes seemed lost on the audience, others got good laughs; maybe the biggest was for the suicidal girlfriend: "[She] tells me she's thinking about jumping in front of a bus and I'm not being very helpful . . . So I sent her a bus schedule."

Half full or half empty? It was his second appearance and it was Letterman, but he was a late call to appear on the show. The other guests were fashion designer Dianne Brill and Seth Miranda. Who? Exactly. Miranda grew the biggest pumpkin at the Ohio State Fair that year. This was scraping. When introducing Bill, even Letterman made a sarcastic swipe at the juggernaut Bill's career hadn't become. Said Letterman: "A few months ago my next guest made his television debut on this program and things have been going great for him since. So great, in fact, that he'll be working this weekend at Chip Flato's San Antonio comedy club."

Bill took the same shot at himself, joking during his routine: "Just got back from Oklahoma on my way to San Antonio. My career continues to wobble unevenly."

After the taping, Bill, Farnetti and Wilks went out and got looped. They hopped in a hansom cab and soon found themselves traveling adjacent to a rough neighborhood. A drunk Wilks shouted out to a group of could-be gangbangers, "Hey, I bet you wish you had all of our money." Odd, considering that Farnetti was the only one of the three with a steady income. The horse turned to stare at Wilks, before breaking into a brisk trot. Even it knew that Wilks had said the most shit-stupid thing possible and to get the hell out of there.

Not having to worry about a rent payment had allowed Bill's life to stabilize. He had done Letterman a second time, but still had a reputation out on the road. However, the appearance of living well in Houston was helping him get laid.

Vicariously emboldened by Bill's performance on Letterman, Wilks began to chat up one of the women seated next to them on the flight back from New York, "We're just coming back from the Letterman show . . . "

A few days after the second Letterman appearance, Bill had a series of sold-out shows at the Comedy Workshop in Austin that ran through the weekend. Saturday afternoon, David Cotton's little brother was playing in a golf tournament in Kilgore. Kilgore College is located near Longview, Texas, about 120 miles east of Dallas. It's a five-hour-plus drive from Austin.

David had planned to leave Austin at about two in the morning so he could get to Kilgore, spend the day with his family, and see his brother compete. Best-laid plans. David's first mistake was either going to Bill's Friday night show or going back to his apartment with Bill after the show.

David was originally just going to hang out for a little bit, run Bill off, then head out of town. So the two spent some quality time sitting in David's living room. They are hanging out and talking and having a good time. They are also doing blow. Cotton is mindful of his previous commitments. He's got his bags packed and sitting by the door. The whole time he's thinking: "I'm ready to go. I'm ready to go."

He doesn't lose track of the time, it's just that the middle of the night quickly becomes sunrise when drugs are involved, and David is still in his living room. With Bill. Doing lines. Recalls Cotton: "Now, it's six in the morning. I want to go see my brother play in the tournament in Kilgore because he's winning."

Without David saying anything, Bill recognized he has kind of fucked it for him. So, Bill grabs a phone book and starts flipping through it, and before David knows what's going on Bill is calling people. "We'll just charter an airplane," he says. Bill is dialing up service after service, shopping for deals. Finally he found one that for $600 would fly them to Longview, wait for them, then fly them back. And between the two of them they just happened to have six hundred dollars laying around.

So they loaded up. Says David: "We did not go anywhere without our medicine." They got little bottles of cocaine and put those in their pockets, then they filled flasks full of Rumple Minze schnapps and put those in the inside of their leather jackets. Repeat: leather jackets.

It was summer in Texas. Bill's dedication to his tough-guy-cool-man-in-black look took a willingness to endure a tremendous level of discomfort. At 6 a.m., the sun was barely over the horizon, but it was already heating things up. It was probably eighty degrees, and it would climb another twenty through the day. On the way to the airport Bill and David bought matching sunglasses.

They got to the plane and Bill hopped right in the passenger seat up front, only to discover that the pilot had also loaded up for the flight. Between the seats in the front sat a cooler full of beer. A bit after take-off Bill asks the pilot: "Can I fly it?" Pilot: "Yeah. Yeah, yeah."

So Bill takes the controls, keeps it level and straight before asking: "Can I take it to the right a little bit?" Again: "Yeah. Yeah, yeah." Bill darts over and down to the right. "Cool," he says as he breaks out in a huge shit-eating grin. Now he wants to go back the other way. "Can I take it back over to the left?"

"Yeah. Yeah, yeah." And the same thing back to the left. Then Bill asks, "Can I take a loop-d-loop?" And the guy grabs the stick back from Bill before the "d" is out of his mouth. "No."

They touch down in Longview and the pilot calls David and Bill a taxi. The taxi picks them up and drives them the half hour to Kilgore. David's whole family is there, including his grandmother. David's brother Jimbo gives David the bad news. The officials aren't going to give them a golf cart to drive. "I don't know if it was the leather or the fact that we don't look good," says David, "but they did not want us driving anything, not even golf balls." The good news is they found a kid, a teenager who they would give a cart to, and he was going to drive for Bill and David.

They spend the next few hours being chauffeured around the course, drinking schnapps and doing cocaine. The kid is right there the whole time. "I'm sure we gave him some," says David. When the round was over, they all went and had dinner with David's grandmother before Bill and David headed back to the plane. They flew back to Austin. Bill took a shower. Went and did the sold-out show, then partied the rest of the night.

The club owner was none too pleased when he found out his headliner had spent much of the intervening twenty-three hours since his last set hopping around the state of Texas in a single-engine plane.

Bill trod a fine line. Did he do anything damaging? Only to his body. Was he reckless? Well, maybe taking the controls of the plane was a bit chancy, but, with the pilot next to him, Bill didn't put anyone in imminent danger. Did he miss work? Nope. Now, some employers might have wished he'd never shown up, but with only a handful of exceptions, Bill didn't miss work. His job facilitated his lifestyle.

The next time Bill came to Austin to play the Workshop, Kinison turned up as well. Kinison had already made a couple of appearances on *Saturday Night Live*, so he was progressing toward legitimate fame. That Friday, Sam warmed up Bill with a guest set. He got on stage and started yelling and screaming about women, his wife and his divorce.

There was a sizeable group of fraternity guys in the audience; and frat boys were the lowest men on the evolutionary ladder by both Bill and Sam's reckoning. The college geeks represented everything the comics stood against. Sam's yelling about women soon turned into his yelling at the fraternity boys. That degenerated into "Fuck you" from the crowd and "Go fuck yourself" back from the stage.

At the end of the show the Workshop manager came up to Cotton and said, "We're going to have to get Bill and Kinison out of here." They raced them out the front door and hurried them into a cab along with Booth, Cotton and Steven Doster. And there was still a bunch of those frat kids standing out front – they had been escorted out of the club – behind the cabs and running down the street chasing them. Sam was yelling back. They wanted to fight.

They had just incited a near-riot with their friends helping them get away, and what happens to Kinison? In the dozen blocks between the comedy club and 6th Street, Kinison fell asleep in the cab.

The entourage went downtown to Steamboat. Sam then fell over a table, knocking it and the drinks on it over. It was clearly going to get ugly and the night wasn't half over. At four in the morning they got thrown out of Steamboat. Bill, Sam and David wound up at

David's house, where, by his recollection, "We did a quarter ounce of cocaine sitting there. Right about seven grams. At least."

By about 8 a.m., David was trying to clear the Wonder Twins out of his place. They've done all the blow and are trying to get David to hook them up with some more. He told them he was out, and there was no more in the house. They were having none of it. They were right, and David was lying. But he wouldn't relent. "Do too." "Do not." "Do too." "Do not." This went on for half an hour. Then, according to Cotton: "Sam was sitting on the couch next to me and he reaches down into his sock and pulls out this plastic bag. And it's just the most beautiful blue and pink flake. It was sparkling. I had never seen cocaine like that. It was more than an eighth but not a quarter. It was hard to tell because it was just big beautiful rocks. Pink sparkling rocks. I remember that like it was yesterday.

"The sorry bastard didn't share with us. He had it. A good guy would have said, 'Hey look what I got.' A drug addict mind: he's got to hold out, he's on the road." Bill and Sam were too paranoid even to get into a cab. Cotton called a lawyer friend of his, who came to pick them up and take them back to the Villa Capri where they did the rest of the coke, then showed up for their Saturday night gig in the same clothes.

13 February 1986. New York City. 30 Rockefeller Plaza. *Late Night with David Letterman.* Bill did the material about the pencil in the eye and the kid in the wheelchair – fourth time's the charm – and he did a bit about an increasingly favorite target of his: televangelists.

To anyone at the taping, nothing about the set itself would have seemed inherently unusual, but clearly something had gone wrong. The show is taped in real time, meaning that the hour show is taped in an hour's time. During the breaks where the commercials are dropped in, the band plays straight through for the studio audience. That's why there is music coming in and out of each break.

The break is up. The "Applause" lights flash. And Letterman says, "Hey, we're back. I want to thank my guest . . ." It's all plausibly live.

At the break after Bill's set, producer Robert Morton, or rather "irate producer Robert Morton" rushed over to Bill to berate him. The studio audience witnessed the verbal row. To audiences watching on TVs across America that night, the indication that something odd might have happened came in the form of a creatively edited program. It was blatant.

When Bill got to the line about breaking the kid's back, there was an abrupt cut. The word "wheelchair" never made it to air. Then during Bill's televangelist bit, there was another abrupt cut. Bill talks about a TV preacher taking donations meant for a hunger fund, and instead buying a new Corvette. "He said it would have helped him spread the word quicker, but – ." Instead of a punchline, there was a sudden swing of the camera to an audience shot.

What the viewing audience at home should have heard was a variant of: "Never trust a man who starts a sentence, 'What God meant to say was . . .'" Instead, the next shot after the jarring visual of the crowd-cut was that of Bill walking to the chair next to Letterman's desk. When the credits rolled, Morton again came out to confront Hicks. "Man, I'm sorry about that," Hicks told him. You could literally read Bill's lips.

Morton had his back to the audience. But the manner of his gestures clearly suggests he was none too pleased.

In Houston, John Farnetti was watching: "When they swung the cameras around, I thought: What the fuck?" One hundred and eighty miles away in Austin, Steven Doster had a similar reaction: "Right in the middle it just goes haywire. It's obviously a cut. So I called Bill up in New York, and asked him what happened."

What had happened was either Bill had done material that wasn't approved or there had been a misunderstanding about what had been approved. To Morton it was clearly a case of the former. Bill told Doster and all of his friends that he thought they had said the material was okay. Bill defended himself to the show telling them he hadn't had time to change the material and that he wasn't dumb enough to sabotage his own career.

However, from his two previous experiences Bill knew certain subject areas were pretty much off limits. He had ventured into two of them. And for a guy who wasn't trying to ruin his own career he did a solid job of it. Bill would have to wait 1338 days until he would get his next turn on *Late Night*.

The original "Outlaw" name was attached to that 1980 "On the Lam" show to raise money for the comics to relocate to LA. Shock's *Texas Outlaw Comics* show was well received and was put into a short-term rotation where it ran every three to four weeks late-night in Houston for the next four months. Then Epstein, realizing he had financed the original fiasco and so probably had as much claim as anyone to the tag, trademarked the Outlaw name. With some prodding from Wilks, Epstein also began to organize Outlaw-themed shows for the current stable of Houston comics.

After having done themed shows on politics and drugs, Epstein booked the first of the next series of Outlaw shows in Baton Rouge, Louisiana, in February 1987: *The Outlaw Comics Get Religion*. Baton Rouge (technically Ferriday, Louisiana) just happened to be the hometown of Jimmy Swaggart, one of Bill's anti-heroes. But days before the show was to go off, the club owner got nervous and cancelled it.

Speculation on behalf of the Outlaws was that Swaggart himself pressured the club. Bill commented: "What the guy in Baton Rouge didn't understand is that we went to Swaggart's hometown to promote the idea of freedom of speech. When he shut us down, he was acting against precisely what we were fighting for."

The Outlaws brought the show back home to Houston the first week of March, then took it to Austin six weeks later. In Austin, Bill told a local reporter, "I believe in Christianity; I just don't believe it's ever been practised. If you get the idea that [we] aren't religious, just consider how spiritual we must be to do a show like this."

David Johndrow had designed promo posters with the faces of the comics on the show – Huggins, Barber, Epstein, Shock, Farnetti and

Bill – and cut-and-pasted them onto the bodies of six cowboys riding horses. Plastering posters around Austin for the 17 April show, there was a certain joy in Bill. It was everything he wanted out of comedy. He was performing in a show with only his friends. It was being produced by a friend (Barber), directed by another (Booth), and the art direction was being handled by another (Johndrow). Johndrow had put together a photo montage of some of the religious figures to be pilloried. The shots ran pre-show to the Talking Heads' "Burning Down the House." Bill and his circle made the decisions, they had creative control, they got to keep what they made. And playing to a near-packed house at the State Theater on Congress Avenue in downtown Austin, they made out pretty well.

Then they took the show to Chicago, where they took a bath.

[* * *]

CHAPTER 6

In September of 1987, the magazine of the *Houston Post* declared Bill "Houston's King of Comedy." In the article Bill described himself as "Beaver Cleaver with the soul of Eddie Haskell." In the profile, Riley Barber said of him: "What Bill is doing on stage is a direct reflection of what Bill is. It isn't derived from anywhere else. There is no facade. Bill takes the truth and makes it funny."

Being declared King was perfect for Bill because the real King (read: Elvis Presley) was one of Bill's heroes. Bill loved Elvis. He loved Elvis almost as much as he loved porn (although in a completely different way). Whereas some idols faded (e.g. the primacy of Woody Allen gave way to that of Richard Pryor as Bill got older), Bill loved Elvis from beginning to end. From about the time he was seven until he was maybe 11-years old, every Christmas, every birthday, Bill asked his family for gifts of Elvis records.

When Elvis played the annual Houston Livestock Show and Rodeo in 1973, a 12-year-old Bill had to go. Even Bill's Elvis impersonations date back to that era. He had an assignment of some sort for his 1st grade class that he completed by getting up in front of the class and playing E.

For Bill, Elvis was the perfect metaphor for America. You start out young and cool. You're rebellious and insolent, and that's part of what makes you great, what draws people to you. But you get drunk on your own success. You get old and fat and become a self-parody of everything you ever stood for. And it was that fat Elvis that Bill really thought was a hoot. There was excess in all its glory. Bill: "He had everything he could possibly want and was still completely miserable . . . You judge a culture by how happy the people are, not by how much money they have."

Bill had taken to doing Elvis on stage. And he did it with varying degrees of verisimilitude, from toilet paper scarves and a cape of an enormous Elvis tapestry, to a bona fide "I hope this suit don't rip up, baby" Elvisian jumpsuit. The degree of gravity also varied. Often Bill played to the excess, giving away brand-new Cadillacs (in theory). Other times he paid homage to his right-hand man Charlie Hodge.

But Bill might have been the one-eyed man in the land of the blind, because outside of Houston he was no king, but was still known primarily as the guy that was a risk to book. He was ten years into his comedy career and was still in Houston. The silver lining? He was still only twenty-five years old.

His then manager, Sandy DiPerna, contacted Rick Messina. Messina had been running a talent consulting agency specializing in stand-up and was the talent buyer for thirty clubs nationwide. That year, 1987, he teamed up with Richard Baker and started Messina Baker management. Their star clients would later include Drew Carey and Tim Allen. Saying Messina had contacts in comedy was putting it mildly.

One of the clubs Messina booked was Rodney Dangerfield's place in New York. So when Messina mentioned that Rodney was preparing for an HBO special to showcase young talent, DiPerna started angling for Bill's inclusion. Messina had been a fan of Bill's, but Bill had also been fired from a Messina-booked show.

Rodney's HBO specials were coveted gigs in the comedy community if only for the names that had been launched from the show: Roseanne Barr, Jerry Seinfeld, Jim Carrey, and Bill's old "pal" Sam Kinison. It was no guarantee, but six minutes with Dangerfield could jumpstart Hicks' stalled career. After some lobbying, Messina agreed to give Bill a shot at a slot on the show. But Bill would first have to go to New York to audition for Dangerfield, then go to LA to do the same for HBO. If he made the cut, he would have to go back to New York for the taping. No problem. Bill would also have to stay sober. Problem.

Bill first flew to New York to audition for Rodney himself. And he bombed. Bill called DiPerna moments after his set to let her know it went terribly, then went straight to the airport to head home to Houston. Even Messina admitted to DiPerna that Bill's set was bad. But none of that mattered, because Dangerfield, the one guy, whose opinion meant anything, "loved him," in Messina's words.

Bill then went to LA and got the go-ahead from HBO. So Bill had two weeks before he had to be back in New York. Again, he had to stay sober for the whole week. He became the "performing monkey boy" he dreaded. The same set. To the letter. Bill had fewer restrictions on the content of his set, but he still wasn't going to be able to deviate from the script.

The comedians were supposed to bring their own one-liner for Rodney to use as an intro. John Farnetti had come up with one for Bill to use: "This next guy is so ahead of his time, that his parents have not even met yet." When Bill fed it to Dangerfield, the elder statesman told him it wasn't funny enough.

"No, that's funny. Try it." Bill insisted. Dangerfield used the line. It got a room laugh. The next day when Bill walked by Dangerfield's dressing room he told Hicks he was right, the line was funny. "What the fuck do I know?" Dangerfield said.

Bill had stayed sober for the audition, but afterwards he let loose to make up for the lost time. According to another comedian who had first known Bill from his earliest days in LA: "I know there were stories about how Rodney Dangerfield was a monster partier, did huge amounts of coke. And he made a comment about Bill. Bill did one of the young comedians specials and even Rodney told him, 'Whoa, kid. You gotta slow down.'"

The Outlaws had always talked about getting the message out, about doing comedy that said something, that was genuine, that honored your viewpoint, and that made people think. Bill had done it. This wasn't Letterman and NBC, this was Dangerfield and HBO. You could say, "fuck" on HBO. It wasn't just being crude for crude's sake: Bill detested that characterization of his act. But on HBO he could deliver a set that was representative of who he really was without having to look over his shoulder for the producer coming after him. If nothing else, he was just more relaxed.

> There is good news for smokers, I'm sure y'all have noticed. Surgeon General's warnings are different on the sides of each pack. That's pretty cool. Mine say, "Surgeon General's Warning: Cigarette smoking may cause fetal injury or premature birth." Hey, fuck it . . .
> Just don't get the ones that say lung cancer. It is your body, you should shop around I think. I can live with low birth weight, you know? I think that's nice of cigarette companies. Come out with different types of diseases, you find the one that you can live with, continue to smoke. "What are you smoking, Tom?"
> "Uh . . . Throat Polyps."
> "Uh, I'm going to stick with my Yellow Fingernails, buddy, thank you. I can live with yellow fingernails."

When Bill got back to Houston he and Pineapple had a private celebration at Houston House. Pineapple recalls, "It was just him and me in his apartment; we cranked the music up and just went crazy. We got so drunk. This was it. One of us got across and the message was out. And that was one of the greatest nights. I'm not a pessimist, I'm a realist; but that was one of the few moments I really felt optimism Bill was so up, and Bill never really got up where he thought, 'Okay, this is it.' He kept things on an even plane, but that time he was so up."

As monumentally hopeful as that was, reality hit Bill again when *Nothin' Goes Right* (as it was called) was first broadcast in early 1988.

Bill gathered with some friends in Austin to watch the show. He had been trying to get sober, and, while that was a constant threat of his, he was actually making more concerted efforts to make good on that threat of late.

Not tonight, dear.

For the viewing party Bill went out and bought a bunch of beer. Sobriety would have to wait a bit longer. A group of friends gathered at Booth's house. Everybody sat and watched Bill's set. The entertainment wasn't the Bill on TV but the Bill right there before them. He sat there and did a running commentary on himself in real time: "Nice job, Hicks." "Why don't you blow another joke, Hicks?" Bill's friends were laughing more at him criticizing his own performance than at Bill's performance.

The special also featured Dom Irrera, Barry Sobel, Carol Leifer, and a couple of others. One notable: Andrew "Dice" Clay. Clay came out and stole the show. Everybody in that room hit the floor laughing. Dice opened his set with the line, "So, I got my tongue up this chick's ass . . ." His schtick, though, was to take nursery rhymes and turn them blue. "Little Miss Muffet sat on her tuffet eating her curds and whey. Along came a spider and sat down beside her, and said, 'What's in the bowl, bitch?'" That was Clay. And as he got more laughs in Booth's living room, the look of sheer hell froze itself on Bill's face.

It might have been okay if it had just been six minutes long; if, once Dice's set was over, order was restored to the room and Bill could look his friends in the face again. But, no, Bill was now wed to Clay in some sense for the rest of his life. From that day on, he would have to deal with people recognizing him in public and saying, "Oh you're the guy from that thing with Andrew Dice Clay." Always the bridesmaid.

Pineapple put it succinctly: "Clay was the anti-Bill." Pineapple once lived at the Comedy Store house at the same time as Clay and thought the guy was "a joke."

"I actually almost felt sorry for him," continues Pineapple, "because I thought he was such a loser. I'd pass by his room and he would be doing Al Pacino in the mirror. He was a moron. He was fucking Mitzi's daughter, and was just an opportunist." There used to be an old joke: a comedian asks someone where they are from and they say, "Buffalo," and the comedian tells them, "Well, too bad you're not from normal parents." It's a bad joke. But Clay once asked someone in the Store audience where they were from. When they replied, "Oakland," he still went ahead and told them, "Well, too bad · you're not from normal parents."

Once dubbed "Fonzie with Tourette's" by another comic, Clay became the guy Bill loved to hate. Bill hated lots of other hacks, but he didn't waste time and money to go see them. He went to see Clay at least three times. Once when Hicks had a Saturday night gig in Austin, Clay was doing a Friday. When a reporter noted to Hicks that they were playing on back-to-back nights, he responded, "Consider me the antidote." Still, that weekend, Bill was booked into a club seating a couple of hundred people. Clay was at the Palmer Auditorium, which seated three thousand. He also sold it out. Bill went to watch. He paid $30 and stayed fifteen minutes. Two bucks a minute was the price he paid for having the pleasure of walking out. It was a zoo, though, mostly men. At rock concerts they bounce beach balls around the crowd. At Clay's show they were bouncing blow-up dolls.

In the summer of 1990, Hicks got an invite to the LA premiere of *The Adventures of Ford Fairlane*. In the two years since they had been on Dangerfield's special, Clay had landed a starring role in a feature film. Bill had landed in AA. Bill went to the premiere. It was free. The movie was panned almost universally by critics.

Bill spent New Year's Eve 1987 with Pamela and friends of hers, another couple. Bill got drunk, and when he and Pamela got back to his apartment later that night, he got violent. He held Pamela against the railing of his apartment balcony and threatened to push her over. When Bill woke up the next morning, he had a bump on his head, no girlfriend next to him in bed, and minimal recall as to what had happened.

He immediately called her. And was relieved when she answered the phone. Bill swore he'd never drink again. She swore they were done. They were both liars.

[*   *   *]

Kevin Booth

It was the most important event in Bill's life. It was the moment all the possibilities he believed in and had searched for became a reality. It seems like it was something we had been preparing for our whole lives. In a practical sense it was something for which we spent weeks preparing. Yoga, meditation, sensory deprivation: we did it all. We even did water yoga, where we floated in a pool wearing masks and snorkels, doing poses, floating and sinking.

Bill and I, and David Johndrow, we were clearing our minds. That was the "preparation." We didn't want our brains to be busy for what was about to happen. We didn't know what was going to happen, we just wanted to be calm and open so we could participate fully in the possibilities. We were mentally and spiritually aligning ourselves and we were meticulous, even watching our diet. No fast food, no junk food. Carrots, not chilli dogs.

As the day got closer, we went to a seminar where people were handing out literature on the significance of the Harmonic Convergence. They were explaining how the planets were going to align. They had astrologers. We got readings. Then, the morning of the Harmonic Convergence, we drove out to the ranch in Fredericksburg, Bill, David, Riley Barber, Epstein and I.

Originally we were going to go to Enchanted Rock. Just north of the ranch, Enchanted Rock is a massive granite batholith whose main dome rises some 300 feet over the surrounding Texas terrain. The people indigenous to the area thought it to be inhabited by spirits. It was supposed to be one of the main sites, along with Mt. Shasta, California, and Uluru in the Australian Outback, amongst others, for people wanting to congregate and share an experience.

But we had watched the local news and saw how many people were going out to Enchanted Rock. All of a sudden it looked like Eeyore's Birthday Party with a bunch of middle-class hippies going to hang out, take drugs and bang drums. We reconsidered. Fuck that.

That's the last place we want to go. We thought: if this is for real, we don't need to be around all of these people. Let's go with what we know. Let's just go to the ranch. We always have great trips there. If we really are going to tap into other minds or something spiritual, then it can happen there.

Part of the experience was that everyone else around the world was supposed to be logging on to the same metaphysical chat room at the same time. It was part of the mental telepathy. Everything uniform, everybody in sync. Except, of course, Epstein breaks stride. He had his own program. "I've got to read this passage from the Bible and this passage from the Koran and do this yoga." Epstein was playing with crystals and was getting bogged down with his New Age trinkets. Riley waited for Epstein, we couldn't. We had done our prep work. Bill, David, and I took our mushrooms and walked across the ranch down to the pond where we sat in a lotus position.

We took five grams. Five grams of dried mushrooms is a lot. If you wanted to punch a hole through the fabric of space-time, five grams is good. But don't try it yourself at home or at my family's ranch or any place unless you are ready and willing to cross the threshold.

We sat at the pond, the three of us, and focused on each other's energy. It wasn't uncommon for one of us to get up and wander away at some point. Bill and I had both done this. David stayed seated by the pond.

Bill wandered over to me and said, "I want you to explain Einstein's theory of relativity to me. I want to be able to grasp it." It was something I had been reading about before the Harmonic Convergence. And even though textbook explanations didn't always register with Bill, he wanted me to try to give him a technical "classroom" explanation. So we walked circles around the pond. I spent some time trying to explain to him what I understood, then went back and sat down in a space where there was a group of trees facing the pond.

We sat back down and the next thing we knew, we opened our eyes and we shared this UFO experience. From a descriptive standpoint, it's almost ridiculous to talk about as visually it did seem like something from a bad science-fiction movie. Cheesy. On some level when something like this happens – whether it's just in your own mind or whether it's actually happening – it might just trigger things already in your brain that allow you to identify or relate to certain energies or entities.

The inside of the ship was like a conch shell. I walked down a circular ramp through a hallway of light and headed towards a circle of light. The beings, they were glowing. Again, describing how things looked starts to sound absurd, but they looked like Mr. Burns from *The Simpsons*, specifically in the episode where he emerges from the forest looking like an alien. His eyes dilated and his body glowing green – the aliens were lustrous like that.

Bill and I were both in the ship. He was asking questions like: "Why are you here? Why is this happening?" I remember coming out with explanations of time travel and a firm belief that the barriers to time travel and communication were all inside your mind. Basically, anything was possible.

At the time I was thinking that my head conjured up this image just for me to see, then Bill indicated to me he had seen and experienced the exact same thing. Immediately after leaving the ship, we opened each other's eyes. We said a few words:

KEVIN
Oh my God. Did you . . . ?

BILL
Yes.

After that we realized we were able to communicate telepathically. It was way beyond just being able to make people laugh when tripping, like the experiences Bill first had when he took mushrooms and went on stage to do comedy, the time when he thought he was reading the audience's collective mind.

This was very specific. For the first time ever, Bill and I were able to say things and hear each other back, able to ask questions and get answers. We had a perfectly normal conversation without either one of us opening our mouth. We were perfectly in sync. It was like a miracle. We communicated like this for a while, neither of us saying anything.

We were snapped out of our place, for lack of a better term, when we heard footsteps crunching on the granite pathway. We looked up to see Epstein walking towards us. "Are you guys feeling anything? I'm not really getting off." It was so funny. "Dude, you missed it," Bill said.

"I just think mushrooms were a lot stronger back in the Sixties. I remember back in Berkeley . . ." Epstein was one of those people. Epstein. I was late getting here; I had to read a passage out of the Bible; I had to read a passage out of that Koran; I've got my crystals.

We were: "Oh my God. None of that matters. Let it go. Let it all go."

I kept picking up Epstein's crystals and clanking them together like I was trying to start a fire, like they were pieces of flint. It was too easy and too fun to tease him. He opened himself up to it. There were sparks flying off the crystals when I chipped them. "Stop disrespecting the crystals." And we would die laughing. "Dude, it's just a rock. There is nothing sacred about a rock."

He was so cluttered up with all of this crap that he wasn't seeing what we were seeing. It was funny and tragic at the same time. Jesus could have punched him in the face and he would have missed it. Sometimes he was so preoccupied with living in the moment that he was missing the moment. We were laughing at him, but we were also thinking, "We have to get away from him." We didn't even mention the UFO. We didn't want to ruin the place where we were. We told him not to worry. It was all going to happen. It was amazing. Enjoy it.

Then Bill and I walked back to the ranch house, just to get away from Epstein. It was still light outside and we were still tripping balls when we sat down at a picnic bench in the yard. We both crossed our arms on the table and put our heads down on our arms. We sat there for what had to be twenty minutes or more telling each other jokes . . .

without saying a word. Again, it was back and forth. And it was telepathic. We were making each other laugh like you can't imagine.

And there was something unusual about the jokes. They had depth. They had several levels of humor to them that we were able to share at once. It was like telling a seven-layered joke with one line. I remember we even joked about Epstein. We weren't making fun of him because he couldn't do it, but we were making fun of him because we wished he could be experiencing the same thing. We did it all without words.

That was only the start. It was still hot outside, so Bill and I went into the house to get some water, then laid down on the floor in the living room. Suddenly we were tapping into other people's voices.

BILL

Dude, do you get the feeling that we are meeting hundreds
of people right now?

KEVIN

Oh my God, yes.

It went from being the two of us being able to communicate with each other, to us being dialed into a network where now we were openly communicating with hundreds, thousands, maybe millions of minds at the same time. There was something identifiable in it, like we could trace where their voices were coming from and who they were. Everybody was sharing this moment because they wanted to. It was freeing. And it was unbelievable. We just laid on the floor and stayed tapped into whatever we had tapped into.

On the come-down we kept laughing our asses off.

Epstein stayed Epstein the whole time.

EPSTEIN

I didn't see anything. You guys saw spaceships?

BILL

Dude, they are all around us right now. There is one right behind you.
They are everywhere.

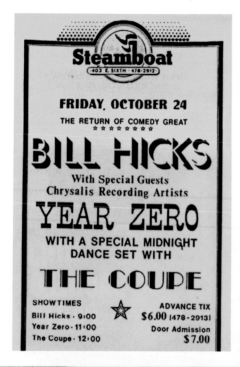

Left Poster from Year Zero record release, 1987.

Below Bill wearing *Sane Man* shirt, Jere Raridon, Gary Stamler.

Bottom Year Zero's dressing room in the basement of Club Steamboat, 1987. *Back Row*: Bill Hicks, David Cotton, Brent Ballard. *Front Row*: Kevin Booth, Jere Raridon, Lorain Larusso.

"Karate action so fast the camera failed to pick it up."

"...TWO THUMBS UP my butt and still I was bored..."
— Roger Ebert

SHOUT!!! It's finally out! After ten years in the making and cost overruns of up to one thousand dollars--- the epic karate opera NINJA BACHELOR PARTY is here. It's the story of a boy addicted to cough syrup who dreams of one day becoming a ninja warrior.

Follow Clarence Mumford as he is dejected by his parents, betrayed by his true love, and double-crossed by his first teacher, the murderous Dr. Death.

Only when he follows his dream and goes to Korea does he meet the one who holds the key...and only after he realizes the "Three Jewels of Wisdom": believe in yourself , dreams are real, and never trust anyone, not even your own guru – will he be ready to return home and meet death...head on!!!

"HOORAY, HOORAY..., PERFECTLY perfect,...a triumph...jump for joy...it felt good..."
— Rex Reed

WRITTEN, DIRECTED, STARRING, EDITED, MIXED, REMIXED AND DUBBED BY BILL HICKS, KEVIN BOOTH, AND DAVID JOHNDROW

© 1991 Bula Bula/Sacred Cow

BULA BULA ENTERTAINMENT & SACRED COW PRESENT

NINJA BACHELOR PARTY

STARRING
BILL HICKS
KEVIN BOOTH

Top Cover for *Ninja Batchelor Party*, 1984–1991.

Above left Bill and Kevin training on hay bails.

Above right Fighting on the roof of Houston House.

Above Dr Death dries off.

Dr Death poster that was used in *Ninja Bachelor Party*.

Pond at the ranch, 1987.

Above 'Satan has many faces!' Bill during a performance of *Sane Man*.

Left Headline from *Sane Man*, refering to an angry letter a woman sent in about Bill's performance.

Above Bill in Las Vegas before his performance on *Dangerfield*.

Right Bill watching his performance on *Dangerfield*.

Below Bill on the phone to his manager after watching *Dangerfield*. *Left to right*: Steven Doster, Bill, Bob Reily, Brent Ballard.

EPSTEIN

I don't think mushrooms are as strong as they used to be.

It was such a transforming experience. Bill started talking about it from the stage. "Yeah, we're crackers. Join us later. As soon as you get away from the smell of diesel from your buses, why don't you come out to the pond and I'll show you a fucking cow paddy that turns into a mothership at will."

And: "I leave this show tonight and I get on the mothership and I go to the planet Arcturus, where golden maidens with three heads line up on their knees."

I think the audiences were confused by it. Was it a metaphor? Was it a joke? Where was the punchline? But the first time he talked about it during a show, I was proud and amazed but also a little bit embarrassed. Maybe it was something we should keep quiet. David, even though he didn't have the same experience, he was fully embarrassed. He was against talking about it in public. But David didn't have the same experience as we did that night. He was watching the stars when we boarded. Bill, of course, couldn't shout it loud enough.

People really didn't know whether or not to believe him. Most people probably don't. Even so, it's enough to believe that Bill believed it. Bill believed everything. He wasn't the kind of person who would say, "Well, now I'm a Christian so I no longer believe in reincarnation." Multiple religious beliefs could coexist simultaneously. He was a Christian and a Buddhist. Bill didn't go through life adopting some beliefs at the expense of others, but instead was open to things that came to him or came into his consciousness.

But the spaceship, that was the most important thing that ever happened to Bill. He saw the "source of light that exists in all of us." Later he said, "God, I hope that was just the first of many things just like that."

The next time we tripped, nothing close to the UFO or the telepathy experiences happened. We were disappointed. It was

215

probably the wrong frame of mind to be in, trying to make it happen, wanting it to happen. It was a case of being the right place, right time for that moment. I think Bill always thought he could get somewhere else. This was the moment it was proved to him. It's easy to point out the obvious: you took 5 grams of mushrooms, of course you are going to see spaceships and all kinds of other shit that doesn't exist. That's why they call them hallucinogens. They cause hallucinations.

That's a valid argument. But we were taking hallucinogens to help boost consciousness. It was more like a key opening a door. The door was there without the drugs. What the mushrooms would do is they would allow two or more people to get in sync and open the door together and walk through it together and experience what's in the next room together.

Bill often referenced Terrance McKenna from the stage when he talked about the UFO experience. McKenna was once described as the Magellan of psychedelic head space. A true child of the Sixties, after graduating from the University of California at Berkeley he spent time studying native Amazon plant life and hallucinogens, particularly as they related to local shamanistic traditions.

McKenna thought that tryptamine-based hallucinogens, such as those found in magic mushrooms, were a vehicle for communication with other forms of life across the universe. He was particularly fascinated by a pronounced consistency of experience amongst people ingesting large dosages – he referred to these, greater than 3.5 grams, as "heroic" (Bill often alluded to this term on stage, and often exceeded that amount when taking mushrooms). People taking such large doses were, with noticeable frequency, reporting that they were all going to a place, a realm he described as inhabited by entities he termed "self-transforming machine elves."

The way these entities were perceived was based on the hallucinogen and the context in which it was taken. For example,

McKenna found that DMT, once extracted from plants, purified and smoked, invariably resulted in the user having a UFO abduction experience.

So when Bill talked about mushrooms and evolving and UFOs he wasn't joking. Okay, he found a way to get a laugh out of it – "That's why people in rural areas always see UFOs, they are always tripping on mushrooms that the cows just shit out of their butt"– but Bill wasn't kidding when he talked about it from the stage.

But the danger of using drugs as a crutch, something that he had seen first-hand with Epstein and Kinison, resonated with Bill, and it wasn't too long after the Harmonic Convergence that he got it into his mind, "God, I want to go sober, I have to go sober."

He wasn't done yet, though. Bill had to bottom out. It's analogous to someone trying to force a smoker to quit by giving him cartons of cigarettes to smoke. They have to smoke them all at once and put enough nicotine in their body to poison it until they are puking up blood. It has to become such a miserable experience that you un-ring the bell. It couldn't have been a conscious effort, but while Bill was suffering, he hadn't quite made it to hell yet; hadn't purposely hit the bottom. He would.

Bill knew he needed to get sober. And not the kind of half-hearted self-loathing sobriety that lasted a couple of days only to fail spectacularly. It was common knowledge in the clubs that if you hired Bill Hicks you were hiring a drunk, and there were better than even odds that he would go off. You no longer had a comedian on stage but an irate drunk who was pissing off the clientele that bought the drinks that kept you in business. So from a career standpoint, it became apparent that he needed to turn things around. There were a few things in the wind – an HBO special and a management deal – in spite of himself he was somehow getting to a position where he had things to lose.

But the first major catalyst was the UFO experience on the Harmonic Convergence. Bill believed he had direct communication with another intelligent life form that was trying to show him what the future could be like. And the future was all about love, light and acceptance. The drugs we took were not to be used as a crutch, and when you used them like that, you lost the whole point of it.

And that's the exact reason why we originally got into it.

[* * *]

Cole and Allison Johnston

Pamela Johnson's son and best friend

[**Cole:**] First thing you have to know about my mom, Pam, she was one of the most eccentric people you would ever meet. And if you asked her a story, you might not get the whole thing. She called her life a movie and she would make the movie play however she wanted. My mom didn't raise me either. I was raised by my grandmother.

[**Allison:**] Pam had seen him, Bill, before with the other comics. She never thought that much of him; said she thought he was dull. He didn't talk a lot. Then one day she went up to their place, Bill and Mark's, to see Mark. She knocked on the door, walked in, saw Bill sitting there and asked if he was alone. "I'm always alone," he said. And that's what started it. They started dating and spending a lot of their time together at the Houston House apartment.

[**Cole:**] The first time I met Bill, I had just woken up and he was sitting in our house reading the newspaper, sitting on my grandmother's couch in shorts and a T-shirt. I thought Bill was Chinese. His face was puffy. I said, "Mom is dating a Chinaman." I couldn't believe he was even there in the house. My grandmother was like Mary Poppins.

I was just a kid when I went to a comedy club with my grandmother and my brother to see Bill. We didn't really pay attention to the show, but afterwards, watching him rip the filter off a Marlboro Light, I'll always remember that, thinking, "Man, that is strange. Why not just smoke a Red?" It looked tough, though, I guess.

I didn't listen to the show. I was too young and spent the night trying to get drinks. I wish I had watched him. The first time I remember listening to his stuff was a little while after my mom and

Bill started dating. I was like, "Come on," the guy was just it. I loved it. "Lock arms and block cemeteries." It was brilliant.

My mom wanted Bill to be famous. She believed in him big time. She didn't want to be famous, she didn't even want to be in front of the camera.

[**Allison:**] She would always talk about how she wanted to be his concubine. She didn't really want people to know about her.

[**Cole:**] And he wanted her to lose her last name because he didn't like that she had been married before and had kids. He didn't like that.

[**Allison:**] That's why he called her Pamela K.

[**Cole:**] She was his "silent witness." That was her name. Whenever they went anywhere, she didn't talk. She never talked, she just sat back and watched people. And when it was over she told Bill what she thought about this person or that person. This is true of every-body; if you are going to be around an artist like Bill, you want to be a part, and that was her way of being a part of him. It made her feel like she was helping out. She and I had fights over that. I told her, "You were there as the girlfriend. He was the artist." I never should have said that stuff to her, though.

[**Allison:**] Being the concubine, that was the part she loved.

[**Cole:**] But she would tell Bill what she thought about people. I know nobody liked Peter Casperson but my mom. Of course, she always kind of had bad taste. She didn't like Bill's mom, Mary. Didn't like her at all. And my mom told me none of the things she left behind – the pictures, the journals, her souvenirs of her life with Bill – was to go to Mary.

But she really liked Bill's dad. She met them when they had dinner one time, just the four of them. I wouldn't be surprised if she flirted with Bill's dad. She was like that. She thought she was a southern belle. She'd put on the act.

[**Allison:**] There's a story that Bill went sober because of Pam. I think it was at Houston House. He was really drunk, and she got really pissed. She was so mad that she thought she could hurt him with her mind. So she left. She went home. And the next morning he woke up and had fallen. He didn't drink again.

[**Cole:**] Yeah, she went up to his apartment, he was really drunk. Maybe he got a little rough with her, but when she was on her way home she said, "I could have sworn I threw him across the room with my mind." And you could tell it was both of them feeding into things like that – with that kind of power – but Bill woke up the next morning with a bump on his head and he didn't know where it came from.

I don't know exactly what happened, if he did something, but there was nothing that she couldn't take care of herself. He did write a song about abuse but it might have been something he got from my mom, from hearing about her previous relationships, some of which were abusive. My mom was the kind of lady who, if you started shit with her, she would get right in your face and tell you what a prick you were. And if you hit her, you were going to keep on hearing what a fucking prick you were, then she would cut your throat when you slept. It was not a joke.

II

[**Allison:**] Pam and Bill moved into Hell's Kitchen, to a horrible apartment across the street from Lee Strasberg's Actors Studio.

[**Cole:**] When they got their place, my grandmother bought them a TV and a mattress to help them get set up – when my mom needed someone to bail her ass out, she always called my grandmother. And Bill wrote her this thank-you letter that she still talks about today. When she tells me about it, she beams because it was really heartfelt. This guy had such a heart, and you wouldn't know it if you just saw him on one of his tapes. When you see Bill on stage you can see his passion for his art, but you can't see his heart.

My grandmother was also really impressed by Bill because she couldn't believe someone could move to New York, and have to get a job every night. She would tell me that, "Bill has to go get a job every night." She was real impressed with that, real impressed with work.

[**Allison:**] In New York they both got really into reiki, which is the laying on of hands. It's a type of energy healing. What happens when you do it is your hands will get really, really hot. Say your foot is hurting and I have the power, then I can make your foot better by putting my hands on it. Pam went to school for it, took classes in it.

[**Cole:**] My mom would describe it, saying, imagine the universe, all the stars connecting, then the power flowing through your hands, like a white light. She healed me once when I came back to Houston. I woke up and couldn't even swallow. I was spitting. Totally ill. And the next morning I was completely healed, then I was a believer. Definitely.

[**Allison:**] They were both so into the supernatural. He was into it as much as she was. Pam was also real psychic. We were driving to LA and she told me I was going to meet Benicio Del Toro, the actor. I didn't even know who he was at the time. She kept talking about it, and finally I said, "Pam, the more you talk about it, the more it's not going to happen." So I was in a restaurant one day and my friend said, "Okay, turn around but don't freak out." He was at the next table.

[**Cole:**] They were also big into UFOs, or I know my mom was. She told me little stories, like she thought Bill might have been abducted in New York because one time he went out for a walk and when he came back he was different. He left one night and when he came back he wasn't as nice as he was before. There was also the Sedona trip.

[**Allison:**] There's one story where they were in Sedona and went hiking during the day. Bill picked up a rock that looked so much like an alien head that Pam freaked out, like it wasn't a coincidence but it was from outer space. "Put it back. Put it back," she said. He wanted to take it, but she told him, "No, put it back."

So they go back to their hotel, and that night they are asleep. She starts having a dream where she sees him, Bill, get on a spaceship. She wakes up and sits up. At the exact same time he sits up. They were having the same dream. They turn to each other. "I saw it," she said.

"I know. I'm going. Are you coming?" he asked her.

"No, I have children."

He went out in the middle of the night, out to the place where they had found the rock earlier in the day, and when he came back, she said he was never the same. Her theory was that they took him up, and left the shell, the body to live out.

III

[**Cole:**] I've heard some of the other Houston comedians thought their relationship was purely sexual. I can believe they were very sexual, but I don't think anyone could think it was just sexual. I mean, this guy paid for half my brother's car.

[**Allison:**] At some point, they talked about moving Cole and his brother Roy up to New York. Cole even went to visit.

[**Cole:**] I was there for a couple of weeks. When I left, I begged to stay. I loved it. Bill was out on the road some, but he was there for a while when I was. We played a little Nintendo. I also remember going with him to the laundrymat. He had wrapped all of his dirty clothes in a sheet, and he just walked down the street carrying this enormous ball of clothes. I thought that was pretty cool. He paid for us to go see *A Few Good Men*, and he also paid for us to go to Jezebelle's, a restaurant right by the theater district, and I know that place just had to be outrageously expensive.

Mom and Bill started talking about getting married. And maybe he started giving in a little by talking about me and my brother moving up there. But I think I understand why he didn't want to get married. A married artist? She didn't want to be left old and alone. She wanted to have something for sure. I don't know if she really understood the roles that people play. He sacrificed a lot for his art.

But she was living there alone while he was on the road, and she hated that. And he didn't want her to work. She did get a job at an auction house, but he had a whole song about that, about how he didn't want her to work, didn't want her to have a job. The lyric is: "Hate to watch you work." But she hated going on the road, I know she did.

[**Allison:**] She would always tell me she had to leave New York. She had to. She was so cold – she developed hypothermia – and tired of being alone all the time. She remembered walking to work with the wind blowing through her. She had to fight it just to walk. Her boss was really cool, but that was her only friend. She had to leave. She couldn't take it any more. That and she said she thought something bad was going to happen. She had a really bad feeling. That was another of the reasons she had to leave.

She came back and lived at the place on 2016 Main, before she moved back into the Houston House. I know Cole was going to the High School for the Performing and Visual Arts at that time. Bill and

Pamela were still off and on again with each other before she moved to Houston House.

[Cole:] We were living there when the Gulf War started, and she made us shut all the drapes because she thought we were going to get snipered. She loved to make things bigger than they were, just to make life more exciting.

Bill came to see us once more. They were talking, and at some point stopped. Then when we got the house in the Heights, he came over another time and it seemed like they were going to get back together.

IV

[Cole:] I wanted to be like him because I never had a father figure, and he was a real cool one because of what he did. He was nice to me because he saw that I was open and thoughtful – like, I'd hold the door open for someone. Little things. Bill noticed that. "Okay, he's not a total prick who thinks he's entitled to everything because he's in America."

When I was a kid, I heard he didn't even like kids, but I didn't not like him because of that. I just think he was willing to sacrifice everything for his art. I remember we were in the car one time, and we were driving some place. My brother gets in the car and puts on some disco techno bullshit. Bill goes, "Oh, it's teenie-bopper hour." And I'd always listened to older music, but I started listening to that stuff with my brother because it was the cool thing to do, but when Bill said that it dawned on me: "I am a traitor." I didn't really care about the "teenie" thing, but the idea that you had to sacrifice and be a martyr and say these things, to put your ideas out there to get cut off – I couldn't respect anything more than being tough like that.

There was the time we played Nintendo for three days straight. That was in California. Sam Kinison was around. He came down and

225

saw him. I know because Sam called and I answered the phone. I think that was the last time Bill saw Kinison, but I don't remember what the feud was over. Anyway, we got Super Mario Bros. and Nintendo didn't have a "save" function back then. It didn't matter, we just kept playing. We slept for maybe an hour here or there. You could pause the game, but as long as the machine stayed on you were okay. We were like, "Let's go to the end." So we did.

I was back in Texas when he came up to the Heights house. He visited us there, and I think he was living in LA by then. I don't know if he was doing a show or not in town, but he stayed there with us. We listened to Marble Head Johnson – it had just come out – then sat around and watched a movie.

V

[Cole:] We were living at the house in the Heights – my mom told me this – she said Bill had called and asked her to go to London with him. She was thinking about going because maybe things had changed. Not long after that, maybe a couple of months, he passed away. He didn't tell her he had cancer.

[Allison:] When Bill died, Pam's dad came to her – like an apparition. That's why she went down to the comedy club that night. She knew the only reason her dad would come to her was to tell her something important. So, she went to the club and Jimmy Pineapple told her Bill had just passed away.

[Cole:] After Pineapple told her that, she came home and she freaked out. She wanted to go to the funeral. She asked me to take her, but then she didn't think it would be cool because of his mom. Like I said, she never liked his mom. But when Bill was gone, that was the end for her. Their connection was so spiritual with my mom that she gave up. She was gone.

I remember the day he died. We knew it. I remember the sunset. I was on 288 and I was going to take a picture of it, but I didn't get out.

When my mom passed, it really was her emotions that killed her. I don't want to say too much about my mom that is really personal, but she was hard to talk to. After Bill died, she was gone. That was it. She left behind some things from when she was out of it and trying to remember. There's one book, kind of like a journal, but it's all nonsense. What she was trying to do was remember her life with Bill, and she was trying to write it down for me, because she thought it would help me in some way because I was an artist. There were some other letters that were explicit and sexual. My dad found them. He said those letters were disgusting and he tore them up.

[**Allison:**] She thought she had cancer for a long time, but she never even went to the doctor, she just went straight to the hospice.

[**Cole:**] She wanted to die. She refused treatment. They never even knew what kind of cancer she had or where she had it. She gave up. She wanted to go to heaven or wherever it is people go, to see Bill and her dad. When her dad died, she died a little. When Bill died, that was the end of her.

I have this tape, it has a love song to my mom. It has a bunch of songs, but there's one in particular, "Bird." It's a pretty cool song. Bill heard that I was listening to it, and that I totally dug it. And he got on the phone – my mom told me that he wanted to talk to me – and he told me, "Don't let anybody hear this." He didn't want anyone to hear it. Most people have this illusion about Bill and when they hear his music they don't understand. There is emotion in his music. I really wish people got it. I really do, but I think he knew people wouldn't understand. They are love songs.

But, oh man, my mom had the worst relationships. Bill was the only guy that was ever nice to her. He may have done some stuff wrong, but I really respect the guy because of the way he treated my mom. For sure. He made her happy. I could show you other pictures of my mom, you look at her and she doesn't look happy. You don't see happiness in her face. You look at pictures of her with Bill and her face really did glow. You can see it.

[*   *   *]

Kevin Booth

Bill was out on the road somewhere. It was the typical scenario where he is out playing a strip center in a town where nobody knows him. Fife, Alabama, maybe. Or Goldsboro, North Carolina. It was definitely the South and some place no reasonable person has ever heard of or will ever visit.

I was at the ranch. Bill called me. He called me a couple of times over a couple of days. The first was another one of the drunken rambling rants. It was one of the times when I literally put the phone down, walked away went and fixed something to eat – I made a sandwich – then maybe five minutes later picked back up. Bill hadn't even broken stride.

"The fucking idiots in the crowd." "Nobody gets it. Nobody gets me." "I'm fucking sick of the road." "This is the last time I go out on the road, when I get back to Houston, I'm done with stand-up."

It was either that or just out and tell him, "God, nobody cares any more, Bill. Just fucking stop it. If you want to quit, then fucking quit. But right now just go to fucking bed." Humoring Bill was part of the price of being his friend, but people were tired of paying it.

The next phone call, maybe a night or two later was different. Bill was lucid. He told me he had been having sex with a "big, 350-pound black woman." He described it to me in great detail. He did a skit where he was like a baby in her arms, sucking on her giant tit. "Oh man, I fucked Aunt Jemaimah last night. It was so great." He was the infant in the fetal position nursing on the black breast of humanity. He said it was like fucking mother earth. Sex with a giant white girl, that was disgusting; but there was something alluring about the idea of sex with a big black woman. It had soul.

Bill had done some rebirthing. He went to a hypnotist to do it. But this was the closest thing he could do in the real world that was physically akin to what he wanted to experience.

More important than telling me about his sexual exploits, though,

Bill had also been calling me to tell me how he had been getting really fucked up lately. No shit. But there was something desperate in the way and the frequency – "Kevin, I've been getting really fucked up lately. Seriously, Dude, it's getting out of control I've been getting wrecked every night." Then he broke down.

He broke down and told me how he'd injected cocaine.

That was the one thing. That was the one barrier. The big line we always drew with drugs was the use of a needle. It was okay to snort a few grams of cocaine. It was okay to maybe try smoking heroin. You could drink until you were blind. But shooting up, that was the one "never."

It was something we had talked about together. We thought people who shot up were low lifes. Shooting cocaine. This was the final low. Fuck. He was a comedian. Didn't the name John Belushi mean anything to Bill? Bill had done the worst I could ever think of him doing. He defended his actions; it wasn't as bad as it looked: "Kevin, we were shooting up pharmaceutical grade cocaine, it was real safe, we knew what it was. It was real clean. The needles came out of a wrapper."

God, was there even such a thing as pharmaceutical grade cocaine? It was almost surreal. I still wasn't sure how to react. "Jesus, Bill," I said.

"It was very controlled, of course these people I was with knew what they were doing," Bill was clearly convincing himself this was okay. It certainly wasn't for my benefit. "They wouldn't jeopardize my life. Kevin, these people are practically doctors!"

There was some truth to what he was saying. But it was a partial truth. His confessions got incrementally worse. It had to do with the people he was hanging out with. Chasing drugs and chasing a high you quickly ended up hanging with some pretty low-life people. Bill had found them. And when you're fucked up, their irrational behavior doesn't seem so unusual. Bill started peeling back the layers. They shot up cocaine. The next night they started running out of cocaine. Someone had some heroin. So they mixed it up with a little bit of heroin.

The night after that they started running out of heroin. Someone had some crystal meth. So they started mixing it with a little bit of crystal meth.

The night after that they had run out of everything. "Kevin, I actually put a needle of Jack Daniels in my arm." And that was the real truth. Bill had put some whiskey in a syringe and mainlined it.

Jesus fuck, Bill.

That was the final low. The final blow. And that was after many, many times of Bill waking up and saying he was sick and tired of being sick and tired, and asking himself what he was doing.

I couldn't believe it. My only was reaction was: "Jesus Christ, Bill . . ." Over and over. I knew I couldn't lecture him, and I knew that he knew it had to stop soon. If it went lower that was the end. As if he could. I had to be sympathetic more than anything else: "Well, what was it like?"

"It was horrible. It was fucking horrible. What the fuck am I doing, Kevin? This isn't me." That was the signature line. "This isn't me." Then who was it? This was the bottom.

Somewhere in the canon of Hicks lore is the story that Bill was backstage for a gig in North Carolina. Everyone backstage to meet him was either a dealer or a friend looking to score. It was then Bill decided he needed to get clean.

That might have happened. But Bill knew he had already hit the bottom. That he'd be dead if something didn't change. And soon. He was no longer himself. He had become someone different from the 14-year-old kid who stayed up until 2 a.m. to watch TV in his bedroom just so he could see Woody Allen.

The whole group of people in Houston, they had started out wanting to be breakthrough comedians. They dedicated their lives to pushing boundaries – both with comedy and with chemicals – sometimes just to see what was on the other side. Finally, it all caught up with them. And it became painfully obvious they were just a huge group of people trying to get fucked up every night.

They always were that, but initially it had this spark of naiveté about it. They were getting fucked up, but they were doing it to change the world, or to achieve some epiphany, or whatever bullshit reason they could convince themselves or others they were doing it for.

Finally the whole crowd just hit the skids. Even though Bill's career wasn't skyrocketing, he was definitely the most successful of the comics still hanging out in Houston. Kinison was long gone. He was in LA never to return. Movies and concert halls. Bill had the greatest potential left to fulfil, and the most to lose. And he was acting like a fucking loser; and he knew it. The next time I saw Bill he told me he had gone clean.

I don't think I believed him.

[*   *   *]

CHAPTER 7

Bill had an affinity for Raleigh, North Carolina. Once asked when he was happiest, Bill replied: "6 March 1986, 3:30 p.m., Raleigh, NC." That was during a week of shows he did at Charlie Goodnight's in Raleigh with Andy Huggins and Jimmy Pineapple.

In January of 1988, Bill was back in Raleigh. Back at Charlie Goodnight's. He was appearing with James Vernon. Vernon's first bona fide gig in comedy was opening for Bill at the Comedy Workshop in Austin. Vernon had been sober for about five years at this point and attended AA meetings daily.

After the second night's show Bill went on a bender, then had to go pimp himself at 7 a.m. the next morning on a local radio show. "I was up all night with the most satanic thoughts, thinking 'I have chosen evil,'" Bill said. He spent the duration of the radio interview thinking he was going to die.

When he got back to the hotel he found Vernon and asked if he was going to an AA meeting. Vernon told Bill he had been waiting three years to hear him ask that. The next day Bill went with Vernon to an AA meeting. That night on stage Bill was drinking Jack Daniels straight. "We'll start over again tomorrow," he told Vernon.

A few weeks later, Bill was appearing in Southern California when a friend introduced him to Jack Mondrus. Mondrus was a manager whose star client was a dummy. Seriously. Willie Lester is a ventriloquist and Tyler is his wooden sidekick. That was the marquee name on Jack's client roster when he was introduced to Bill. Lester had appeared in numerous variety specials as well as a handful of sitcoms.

Mondrus saw Bill perform at the Laff Stop in Newport Beach, about an hour south of Los Angeles. Mondrus said of Bill's performance, "I believed that he'd thought of every word he was saying right there on the spot. It was like that every time I saw him. I never thought he was doing material." When the two had a meeting the next day, Bill told Mondrus he wanted to get back on Letterman. The only television Bill had managed to land since the curiously edited Letterman show was Dangerfield's HBO special. Mondrus wanted Bill to do more television in general. He wanted Bill to make money while and where he could. And he was ambitious about the kind of money Bill should be making on the road. Mondrus soon found himself acting not only as Bill's manager, but as his booking agent.

Bill was immediately Mondrus' star client. Jack was also soon hit with the sober legacy of Bill's hard-drinking days. The residual reputation was still making him a wildcard as a booking. Bill still had a few allies on the club circuit, though, and by tapping into those he was able to showcase himself as something besides a combustible comedian with a short fuse. Within a year Bill was on the road nearly non-stop.

While AA didn't take after the first meeting, by February Bill was going to meetings in Houston unfailingly. His desire to reconcile with Pamela might have been part of his commitment to the program, or maybe his commitment to the program made it tenable for them to reconcile; but they got back together. And within two months, Bill was ready to get out of town and she was ready to go with him.

In April of 1998, he sold Toad. Fifty bucks. Cash deal, no questions. He moved out of Houston House and went to New York. Bill first stayed with a cousin, Joan Moossy, when he got to the city. Pamela was trailing him by a few weeks. She joined him at Moossy's, then the two went apartment hunting. Pamela's mother helped them financially to get set up in a Hell's Kitchen studio apartment, one that had a honeymooners' view of the neighboring building's brick wall.

Addicts often trade one addiction for another. Bill began filling the void with food. Ron Shock stayed with Bill and Pamela on a few occasions when passing through New York. How did they kill the time they used to spend partying? "We'd eat," said Shock. "There's a street in New York that runs a block and it's all Indian restaurants. Bill and I ate that street one week. We went to every goddamn restaurant there. We ate two meals a day on that street. Seven days. Fourteen different restaurants."

If food filled one of the voids in Bill's life, having Pamela around filled another. As the houseguest Shock observed: "She was fucking Bill's brains out. And he really needed that at that time of his life."

Pamela had willingly taken to the role of being Bill's concubine, but she was still somewhat of a mystery to Bill's comic friends. She was never very vocal in their presence and never seemed to share many of Bill's interests. She just didn't open herself up to them.

"Would I sit down and have long, deep conversations with Pam? No," Shock admitted. "Was I glad she came into Bill's life? Yes. Did we have fun, the three of us together when we were in New York City? We had a blast. But I don't think I ever had a very real conversation with Pam. Conversations with Pam were very superficial. Chit chat. Dogs and cats. And baby ain't it cold outside. Obviously there was something there because Bill stayed with her, but when I was with them in New York City, the apartment was so small they couldn't have a deep conversation without me being aware of it. I could hear them fucking, but I never heard them talking."

Bill was trying to put back together his reputation, or rather establish a different one from the only other one he ever had (translation: "don't hire") while trying to get some momentum going in his career. Not long after getting set up in New York Bill got a call from Rick Messina, offering him a slot in *Comedy's Dirtiest Dozen*.

It was a film being produced that would feature twelve of the most foul-mouthed comedians around. It was a peculiar thing for Bill to agree to, because he generally hated being pigeonholed as a "dirty" comic. "If you are shocked by a couple of slang words, that is your problem not mine. Quite honestly, being referred to as 'blue' not only bothers me, but it really shocks me."

Still, it was a movie that would allow Bill to appear in multiple rooms, simultaneously, over and over again, without someone telling him what he could and could not say. But the movie came and went uneventfully. Outside of Hicks' set, there were maybe two curiosities. First was the appearance of Tim Allen. Allen would go on to become the centerpiece of the long-running ABC family (repeat: family) sitcom *Home Improvement*. Second was the appearance of the then almost-unknown Chris Rock, who would end up on *Saturday Night Live* and use that as a launching pad to enormous popularity.

There were other shows like it, but there is tape to immortalize one particular night in Chicago and because of that, it might be Bill's most famous show. It's also ironic because while it's famous for how blatantly and ruthlessly he tore into a couple of audience members, it happened when he was no longer drinking. Most of Bill's friends and peers remember the drunk who would go up on stage and rant; say anything to anybody. That part of his stage persona never left him when he left the chemicals behind.

The difference was that now, even if he went over the edge, he could always find a way back. Just a few minutes into his *Funny Firm* set, a female voice from the crowd told him: "You suck." And it was sing-songy, the way she said it. The crowd reacted with a collective and crescendoing, "Ooooh." At first Bill tried to blow it off with a joke. "Thank you. That's my mother."

The self-deprecation lasted about three seconds. He couldn't resist. "You suck. You fucking cunt. Get the fuck out of here right now. Get out! Fuck you! Fuck you, you idiot! You're everything about

America that should be flushed down the toilet, you fucking turd. Fuck you, get out. Get out, you fucking drunk bitch."

It was on.

"Take her out. Take her fucking out. Take her to see somewhere that's good. Go see fucking Madonna you fucking idiot piece of shit. 'You suck, buddy. You suck. I can yell at the comedian cause I'm a drunk cunt. That gives me carte blanche. I've got a cunt and I'm drunk. I can do anything I want. I don't have a cock. I can yell at performers because I'm a fucking idiot because I've got a cunt.' I want you to go find a fucking soul!"

It was hateful and angry. Angry, angry, angry.

Still, Bill quickly tried to restore some sort of normalcy – "Sorry y'all had to see that" – and return to something resembling a set. He joked about it. At least half the crowd was on his side, cheering all the while. "I dug a real hole on this one, didn't I?" And he cackled at himself. "Is there a punchline coming? Is there a point of view there, Bill?" He turned back to the original female heckler, first told her it was taking too long for her to leave, then told her he didn't care if she stayed but not to yell at him. "I don't like to have yelled 'You suck' at me. I have feelings too."

A lull. Then a gentleman in the crowd yelled it: "You suck."

This time, Bill laughed. "That's okay because that's a nice fellow back there. He's sober and he thought it out." Finally he goes back to a set, talking about excessive masturbation: "Is it a bad sign when you come and nothing but air comes out? I don't think that's healthy." For about three minutes it's a stand-up comedy show again.

Bill starts ruminating over the notion that maybe he does suck, or at least there is a gap he's not bridging. He knows his sense of humor is dark; he knows America doesn't get him. He thinks he's lost the will to live. "I do suck."

The same woman: "You're right." Bill, not missing a beat, tells the guy at the table with her: "Sir, stick your cock in her mouth and shut her up." Big crowd cheer.

Again, and amazingly, he got himself back into some semblance of normalcy. But people are still yelling at him for requests. He bitches then obliges one or two. Lung cancer. Horror movies. Tepid puddle of afterbirth. "Honey, do you ever, like, look at your pussy?" And "Why don't you ladies like sucking your guys' cocks, and making it, I don't know, the focal point of your existence?"

About twenty minutes in, someone throws up the first call of "Kevin Matthews" from the audience, followed closely by "Freebird." Matthews was then a deejay on a local radio station, the Loop (WLUP-FM), in Chicago. He had helped speed the proliferation of people shouting "Freebird." It was a Howard Stern thing before Stern. Matthews used to goad his listeners to shout "Freebird" if they went to a concert or any type of mass gathering. That was his signature, and the inside "joke" was that if someone shouted "Freebird" it meant Kevin's fans were there.

"Freebird."

Bill threatens to leave. Then decides against it, out of spite. He has nowhere else to go. The calls continue sporadically for the next five minutes as Bill tells jokes. Suck your own cock. Empty stage. Arsenio. Jesus. Mr. Shirt-and-Tie. Bill improvs a song about how he has hours of dick and cunt jokes. The lady who first yelled at Bill is finally taken out of the club. He advises her and her partner not to procreate after they leave the club. There was much rejoicing. Dick Clark. The anti-Christ. John Davidson.

"There is no joke any more. Sorry, sir, there are none . . . Go back to Gallagher . . . Fuck you all, America. Go Saddam. Nuke everybody and fuck off." Michael Bolton. More people leave. Someone says they're not leaving because they paid: "I'll pay you the money. Just get the fuck out." Goat people. Jerry Lewis. Sheep people. Bill asks for his own money back. Goodnight folks.

Any attempt Bill makes at this point to re-establish a comedy show is completely ineffectual. He starts to sound like a Bill Hicks cover comic. He knows it, too. "Freebird" again.

Straw. Camel. Back.

And it's Round Two of Bill against a patron.
"Freebird"

BILL

Please, quit yelling that. It's not funny. It's not clever. It's
stupid. It's repetitive. Why the fuck would you continue to yell
that? I'm serious.

PATRON

Kevin Matthews.

BILL

Kevin Matthews. Okay, what does that mean? I understand
where it comes from, so do you, but what does it all mean?
What is the culmination of yelling that?

PATRON

Jimmy Shorts.

BILL

Jimmy Shorts. He's not here. He's not going to be here. Now
what? Now where are we? We are here at you interrupting me
again, you fucking idiot. You see where we're at? We're here at
the same point again where you, the fucking peon masses, can
once again ruin anyone who tries to do anything because you
don't know how to do it on your own. That's where we're
fucking at. Once again the useless waste of fucking flesh that has
ruined everything good in this goddamn world, that's where
we're at. Hitler had the right idea, he was just an underachiever!
Kill 'em all, Adolph, all of them. Jew, Mexican, American, white.
Kill 'em all. Start over. The experiment didn't work. Rain forty
days, please fucking rain and wash these turds out of my fucking
life . . . I pray to you, God, to kill these fucking people.

From the crowd: "Freebird." Bill chuckles and falls to the floor in
faux exhaustion, then he gets back up to facetiously lead a brief
chant: "Freebird. Freebird . . ." He stops and quips, "Well, I don't
think this is going to be a 'get laid' set for me." Abortion. The Lotto.

"Freebird." Shooting a syringe full of heroin into the vein under his cock. Jacqueline Bisset. How much longer until my contractual time is over? Kindergarten.

After fifty minutes Bill says, "Uncle." He literally says it on stage. About two minutes later he was off the stage. Half an hour after first floating the idea.

Bill was back in New York City appearing on a showcase with about ten other comics at the Bottom Line. Peter Casperson and Steve Saporta were there to see one of their clients and Allan Parker, the owner of the club, tipped off the pair that they'd be wise to hang around and catch this guy Hicks.

"It was one of those situations where everybody had twenty minutes and, of course, Bill did forty," says Casperson. Like many first timers, he and Saporta were blown away by Bill. Serendipitous that they were so impressed as the duo was also in the formative stages of putting together the plans for their record label, Invasion Records.

Invasion had released the first rave album in the US with techno they had licensed from Europe. They had also done some underground 12-inches and basically traded in things that weren't on mainstream radio. When they came across Bill, they had financing in place but still hadn't signed that many acts.

Says Casperson: "Even though it made no logical or practical sense to do a comedy record, we didn't look at it as a comedy record. We just really wanted to be involved."

They inked a deal with Bill to do a record, with an option to do a record, with an option to do a record. Bill got a modest advance of $2000. In front of an audience of about thirty people at the Village Gate Bill did the four shows which became his first live comedy record, *Dangerous*. The space was Art D'Lugoff's quasi-legendary showplace for jazz. Popular myth has it that Bob Dylan wrote "A Hard Rain's Gonna Fall" in the building's basement apartment.

Casperson and Saporta invited Bill McGathy to the Village Gate shows and he became a convert from the get-go. McGathy would have one of the big names in the rock radio format in Bill's corner when it came time to do promotion for *Dangerous*. On paper it looked like Bill's move to New York was paying off.

Frank Gannon worked as a press aide in the Nixon White House, and from a historical standpoint is responsible for some of the most in-depth and revealing interviews with the former President. He also has a PhD from Oxford. The perfect resumé for getting into television. But Gannon had been a segment producer on *Late Night with David Letterman* for a couple of years when he came across Bill performing at the Improv in New York City. He was more than impressed with what he saw. Yet Gannon had never heard of Bill, and couldn't understand why. He asked Robert Morton, now executive producer on the show, why Hicks' name hadn't come up in meetings when they discussed guest bookings.

Morton explained about the problems the show had with Hicks on his last appearance. Misunderstanding on Bill's side or not, he had, from the show's standpoint, done material not approved by the show. But after talking with Gannon, Morton agreed to give Hicks another shot provided that Gannon could guarantee that Bill wouldn't cause a similar problem again in the future.

On 12 September 1989 Bill was back on the *Late Night* stage. Sporting his black leather jacket and comb-over haircut, Bill looked like a Boy Scout trying to look tough. "I've been on the road for the past three years so bear with me while I plaster on a fake smile and plow through this stuff one more time."

Bill had accomplished two things. First, he got back on the show; second, and more importantly, he got back into the rotation as about three months later, on 26 December 1989, he made his fifth appearance on Letterman. To the sounds of the band playing The Doors' "Break On Through" Bill came out all in black again, but gone was the leather jacket, replaced with a sport coat. Bill cleaned up okay. Pamela's doing.

The set was fairly pedestrian. He did a bit about how he'd been channeling Elvis, coming to and having strangers around him expecting a brand-new Cadillac. The silence was uncomfortable. Going by audience reaction, though, the tepid set gained momentum. The laughs soon started spilling out a little more freely. Nonsmokers die every day. Love my job. Love the hour. Bill did the bit about bums, including what became one of his signature lines: "I could have been a bum. All it takes is the right girl, the bar and the right friends."

He also did the routine about having a boss and having nothing to do at work. "Well, pretend like you're working. Why don't you pretend I'm working? Man, you get paid more than me, you fantasize." He had done the same bit back on his second appearance. Bill was either retreading material or didn't even realize he was doing jokes he did on the show before.

It wasn't an isolated occurrence. Bill was back on *Late Night* the following October, and he did the bit about how he had been seeing the same girl for three years and was ready to pop the big question. "Why . . . are we still seeing each other?" He had also done that on his second appearance five years earlier. For a guy who could do ninety minutes easy in a club, he was having problems doing six on TV. Either that or he wasn't paying attention, or maybe didn't care.

He was also making concessions to the medium. Talking about smoking, he did his stuff about non-smokers coming up to him and coughing: "Shoot, you're lucky you don't smoke." He usually tagged it with a line like: "Shit, you go up to crippled people and dance?" Network TV. Handicap joke bad.

But he was getting edgier. For a few moments, it was actually a glimpse of what Bill Hicks looked like being "Bill Hicks" on Letterman. "You ever watch that show *The Love Connection*? Is that spooky or what? Adult human beings on national television groveling for dates. Have some self-respect. Stay home and masturbate . . . That show makes masturbation look like a spiritual quest."

People weren't making masturbation jokes on TV in America in 1990.

Bill's schedule of incessant travel was starting to wear on Pamela. She hadn't been working when she first got to New York with Bill, opting to go to gigs with him more often than not. But she got tired of the travel. So, she stopped. She got a job in New York City working with an auction house, but she was lonely. He wasn't taking breaks. She asked him to leave Jack Mondrus, to find new management. He didn't.

Bill was back in New York appearing at Caroline's. Pamela had told Bill earlier in the day that she couldn't take it any more. They were done. While it certainly wasn't the first time Bill had heard that, it must have had a greater sense of sincerity and finality to it, and his first set that night was pure wallowing. He spent the hour talking about his love life and his girlfriend.

Caspeson, who for years kept a tape of that show, recalls, "He just did a rant for the whole show about what it was like to be the guy who now had to envision his girlfriend allowing another guy to enjoy the crotchless panties he had given her on Valentine's Day. It was every guy's worst fears and worst insecurities about relationships, and he did it all spontaneously. I had seen many shows and there were always reference points, but he just did it. And it was spectacular."

Between that set and the late set, Pamela came running into the restaurant downstairs from the club, asking an acquaintance, "Where's Bill?" She found him backstage in his dressing room. After the door was closed for the better part of fifteen minutes, friends found Bill sitting backstage with Pamela on his lap. After Bill and Pamela had, uh, patched things up, the late crowd got a more normal Hicks set.

Pamela wanted to get married, wanted to have a child. Bill reminded her she had two children already, that she had left back in Houston. She told Bill that she wanted a child with him. "I am my own child," he responded. In March of 1990, Pamela packed up and left New York, returning to Houston.

Bill had written a number of songs about Pamela, but maybe more telling was one he wrote about the road being his home. It contained a lyric:

> Told me she's leaving
> Said she's not leaving me
> 'Cause I'm on the road
> I'm not there to leave

When *Dangerous* hit the shelves in 1990, the guys at Invasion wanted to treat Bill like a rock act from a marketing perspective; they even told some of the larger retail outlets that Bill was a rock artist. And with Bill McGathy in his corner, Bill Hicks had an enormous ally. McGathy had helped put together radio edits for the record so they could get *Dangerous* to FM stations. Yet, for all of the upside, the players still couldn't "break" Bill in America. Says Casperson: "The problem that developed was that the jocks loved what he did, but they always ended up taking a lot of credit for it, and they rarely back-announced it. They'd play him, but afterwards, you wouldn't know it was him."

Bill had also placed a sticker on the record that read: "Are we to have a censor whose imprimatur shall say what books shall be sold and what we may buy?" The quote was Thomas Jefferson. The question was rhetorical. It still had an answer: "Maybe so."

Bill was taking a jab at the Parents Music Resource Center. The PMRC was a group of concerned wives of congressmen and was headed by Tipper Gore, wife of then-Senator, later Vice President, Al Gore. Basically the PMRC claimed rock music was encouraging and glorifying drug use and violence, and wanted to protect parents and families from "dangerous" material by labeling, if not outright censoring records.

Under pressure from the PMRC, the Senate held hearings in September 1985. Before the hearings were over, the Recording

Industry Association of America bent and by 1990 had a uniform labeling system (although one, oddly enough, without definite standards) in place to slap the "Tipper sticker," as it was dubbed, on records with lyrical references to drugs, sex, violence and other potentially objectionable material. The sticker read "Parental Advisory – Explicit Lyrics."

One of the more prominent musicians to testify, Frank Zappa, called the PMRC's demands the "equivalent of treating dandruff by decapitation," while also pointing out that neither country music nor comedy records were being subjected to labels. Bill took it upon himself to label his own record.

According to Casperson, Invasion became the Bill Hicks company for a period, if for no other reason than everybody there fell in love with him. But even though the fledgling company had financing, they way overdid it in terms of what they should have been spending based on what was happening in the marketplace. "I believe we spent $150,000 marketing it," claims Casperson. "So, it was disappointing when you add up what came in versus what went out."

Dangerous sold around 5000 units.

Part of it might have had something to do with the environment the album was released in. Or that might have had nothing to do with it. Ultimately, it was a comedy record, and you couldn't really work it like a rock record. There was no single to take to radio. Even if you got radio play, it was a twenty-second snippet of interstitial filler. Plus comedy albums didn't sell well.

[*   *   *]

Kevin Booth

I've always thought Bill knew he wasn't going to live very long, although he didn't go around glorifying it like so many retarded musicians do with their dead heroes. "I'm going to live fast and die at 27, aren't I cool?" No, you're not. Life is too fucking precious, too beautiful. Bill didn't go around saying anything of the like, but deep down he really did know he wasn't going to be around as long as the rest of us. So it was important for him to leave behind not so much a trace of himself, although that was important, but a contribution. A contribution to comedy, to society, to mankind; something people could take and use to make their lives better.

It was that or keep drinking and end up a waiter who was legendary for failing his own talent as a comic because he was a drunk. In fact, when Bill went sober, it still took him a while to turn things around. He really had burned a lot of bridges as an alcoholic. He had done a lot of stupid things, had a lot of dumb drunken moments in restaurants and bars. I witnessed many, many nights where he would get up on stage and just yell at people. I could see what was making him mad – people really did rush to the lowest common denominator – on the other hand, I was like, "Bill, come on, shut up. You're embarrassing yourself."

There was this guy, James Vernon. He was an Austin comedian, and a total hack at that, but he was an AA guy. He hung around Bill when he was in Austin, and was attracted to him for the same reason most comedians were. But more important than anything he ever did comedically, Vernon was the first AA guy to approach Bill in a non-condemning way.

He wasn't one of these AA people who was going to give you the party line about being sick and tired of losing your job, your wife, all those dumb clichés. It was precisely what Bill was – tired – but he didn't want to be that guy or hang around that guy. Vernon approached Bill for the right reasons, as someone that cared, as someone Bill felt he could trust. So when Bill finally contacted Vernon to ask about AA, Vernon wouldn't even tell Bill: "You should go try it with me" or anything like that. He just told Bill about his own experiences.

He also saw in Vernon a model to assuage his own fears about sobriety. Bill had this huge fear of not being a part of the party any more. He had become everything he hated. In those adolescent years with Dwight, all he did was make fun of people who needed the party – they were losers and fools and wasting their time and their lives. Then Bill got into it, and he was Mr. Where's The Fucking Party. Let's get the group together, let's get as many drugs as we can afford, and pour as much alcohol into our systems as they can tolerate. Let's trip. Let's do this. Let's do that. As much as we can do, as often as we can do it. Push, push, push. Bill was not only the party person, but now Bill couldn't let the party go.

And for a misanthrope, he was social as fuck. Ironic, but there was an energy in those situations, and it fed him. There were fans and friends and girls. It all goes hand in hand: the women, the alcohol, the attention. It was another aspect of his transformation that had become complete. Back in 10th grade, it was, "Hey, you wanna hook up? You've got to get 'em a few drinks." The overly desperate romantic in him thought it was cheap to get girls drunk just to have sex. Now Bill and alcohol were both charming the pants off women.

Would he still have those things if he weren't drinking any more? It was a huge fear. He also had to deal with the fear of that environment itself, of "How in the world am I going to perform in nightclubs with people smoking, drinking, doing drugs, laughing, and having a good time if I'm sober? It's impossible." He loved it. He loved all of it. Too much.

That's why Vernon was like a prototype designed and delivered to save Bill. Vernon had the ability to hang out in the club and just have a soft drink while the others were getting fucked up. He could be at the party and enjoy it for what it was, but didn't have to be the party. Bill looked at Vernon. "Okay, if he can do this. I can do this."

Hendrix. Pryor. Allen. Chaplin. More than any other question I've heard: "Who were Bill's influences? Who were Bill's heroes? Who did Bill admire?" I used to think the answers to those questions were so obvious I couldn't even believe people who already had an appreciation for Bill would even bother to ask them. But maybe some of Bill's biggest heroes were the most ordinary of people; and maybe some of the people who looked like bit-players in Bill's life were more crucial to his story than they will ever know.

Going sober clearly wasn't just quitting drinking. Bill had to change a lot of things about himself. He went from a guy who spent his whole night in a club before and after his set to a guy who arrived in a cab five minutes before his scheduled time and stopped lingering too long after he was done.

One of the biggest "things" he needed to change was his friends. He couldn't hang around with that same crowd night after night. He loved them, but they were the people he got fucked up with; and, if he wasn't going to be getting fucked up any more, something had to give.

They were still his friends, but he just wasn't going to be a lifelong alcoholic. Some higher power told Bill it was last call. He knew he had to divorce himself from his friends if he wanted to survive and have a career that left some sort of mark.

It sounds so bizarre to people: to find some calm in his life, Bill went to the City That Never Sleeps. On the face of it, it looks ridiculous, but he had to get away from Houston. Plus, his career was no longer going to be a "career," which meant his choices were two: New York or LA. Bill's feelings about LA were no secret.

How could I not be proud of him? He made a positive change in his life, but when Bill joined AA, I was also sitting there thinking, "No way. There is no fucking way. If Bill starts preaching to me about the evils of alcohol and the joy of sobriety, I am going to fucking kill him." After all these years of him harassing me: "Drink more. C'mon, let's fucking party. Don't be a pussy. Let's get more drinks." Years of that shit – trying to pry myself away to get some sleep, or sucking it up to humor him and running around town until 4 a.m. became noon, trying to find another party, trying to find David Cotton. If Bill was going to turn around and start haranguing me, he was going to get a beating if not multiple beatings.

But he didn't. He was astonishingly non-judgmental. He might actually have been very judgmental, but he didn't say anything. He was even able to joke about it, more remarkable considering how seriously he took AA. And Bill was very serious about AA.

I never went to any meetings with Bill – although he did give me his twenty-four hour chip – but I got the impression it was like nobody in the AA world had a sense of humor. There were probably people who did, but the process itself was so serious. Humor was Bill's coping mechanism. He had to find something amusing in it. It's who he was. Comedy was how he dealt with everything in the world that was difficult.

If Bill ever got in a stupid argument with someone he would often turn around and write a little song about it – maybe just three or four clever lines about whatever the argument was over – then call them up and leave the song on his or her answering machine. That was his way of deflecting things and leaving everyone with a smile on their face. Bill had very few endings or bitter falling-outs. He was a guy that was able to maintain positive and constructive ties with most people. Pretty amazing.

But even better than the humor was that he went through it – the hard drinking, the excessive drugs, the non-stop partying – got clean and didn't become a hypocrite. Bill had spent so much time on the stage preaching about the good things that have come out of drug use – "the Beatles were so high, they let Ringo sing"– and the fact that it's nobody's fucking business what you do to yourself as long as you are not harming others, that he had set himself up to look like a complete ass. But he never did.

Of course, Bill also saw the hypocrisy in AA, how half the people there are ridiculous chain-smokers. Nicotine is a drug; cigarettes kill more people than alcohol.

One of the very last times I was ever backstage with Bill was in Austin when we were finishing the recordings for *Rant in E Minor*. David Cotton came back with several contact sheets with pictures of Bill and was showing them to him. Or trying to. Usually before Bill went on stage he would be meditating or pacing around. He was in that mode, trying to prepare himself. There were people on stage about to announce him and he was trying to get in the moment. Suddenly here is David Cotton saying: "Bill, look. I got these pictures." Bill told him, "I can't talk, David. I can't talk right now. I'm about to go on stage." But David just kept going at him, "Look. Look. Here's one of me and you. Would you like this one blown up?" Bill was talking back to him, but David wasn't hearing.

David Cotton was still partying. Bill wasn't. And got upset with him: "Man, I don't want copies of these pictures. That's me as a drug addict. Why in the world would I want pictures of me as a drug addict? See that? That's me as a drug addict. That's not me any more. I'm over that. I'm through that. That part is gone."

The hard living? He got through it, and it is okay to talk about it. The drugs were something that Bill put behind him, that didn't exist any more. And he didn't talk much about it. Nor did he seem to struggle with it outwardly. No, "God, I just need a drink." But when Bill was dying, he probably started worrying about how he was going to be remembered. When David Cotton came up to him with all of these pictures, it was horrifying and embarrassing: "That's not me any more."

It wasn't. Past tense.

I started telling Bill, "I just want to make a video of you." He was like, "Great." Kind of a hard offer to turn down. He was never opposed to the idea, it was more of a time-money thing. We usually had one or the other. Bill had finally come back to Austin after getting sober. I went to his shows and hung out but I still wasn't convinced he was going to make it. It hadn't been that long since the last phone call when I had been up at the family ranch doing construction and he was on the line drunk and blithering.

When he came to Austin, I just sat there and waited for the other shoe to drop, waited for him to break down and say, "Hey man, let's go get some blow," or "Let's go to a bar." He never did.

Fucking cool. Bill was really sober. I mean, Bill had always talked about this moment. It had even taken on a kind of romantic quality by its never happening, but it had finally come. I started thinking, "Shit, we better make this thing now. Before he starts drinking and drugging again." It sounds like I had no faith in him. Not true. But nothing with Bill was permanent. I had seen him try to quit many times before. Bill didn't fall off the wagon, he usually jumped off, double fisting.

We had to assemble something different or, rather, better than what we came up with for the production of the Outlaw Comics show. I went out and purchased a multi-track recorder. I also tapped the resources at Austin Access. To get their multi-cam video set up we pulled a bit of a scam. I wasn't certified to use it, so we had someone else sign it out for us.

In the meantime, Bill and I were doing some pre-production. I became the overbearing producer. "What are you going to wear?" "Are you sure you want to open with that bit?" Etc. He kept telling me off. "Kevin, I know what the fuck I am doing. What do you think I am doing for 300 nights a year?" Despite the unnecessary tension, Bill and I managed to keep focused on the aesthetic that we wanted. And that was basically to rip off the look of 1979's *Richard Pryor: Live! In Concert*.

We shot two sets, and most of what ended up in the final edit of *Sane Man* came from the second set. The biggest difference wasn't the material. The biggest difference was that Bill's parents were in attendance for the first set. Once they were gone, he was able to exhale, to relax, to tell suck-your-own-dick jokes without having to glance at mom from the corner of his eye. So the second show was live.

Jimmy Pineapple opened the show. It was bittersweet because he had followed suit in getting sober with Bill. There's the shot at the beginning of *Sane Man* where Bill was backstage, pacing around, smoking. He looks like he needs a drink, but that's not what's going on. Again, once Bill quit alcohol, I just didn't get the feeling he struggled with it that hard on a daily basis. I don't think he walked around craving a drink. With cigarettes he had more of a problem.

Jimmy was different and that night he finally hit that point of, "Fuck it," and couldn't take it any more. We actually filmed him falling off the wagon. The bartender poured him a giant glass of whiskey. We rolled camera as he took the drink. Part of me, the shitty part was thinking, "Woo hoo! It's a party night." The other part was praying Bill didn't do the same because I knew he walked with the same crutch.

But no. Water. Bill drank nothing but water. And he was great.

We went back and picked up shots for the intro. We had a timer built to do the time-lapse shots for the intro. In part of the sequence, you can see Bill come up to his mom and give her a kiss before they head into the club. We also did some shots on Super 8 of Bill at his hotel – bumming around the room, getting in and out of an elevator, walking to the parking lot and getting into his rental car.

Hands down the coolest shots were for the sequence where it looks like Bill is riding a bicycle through Austin. We had him sit on the tailgate of the Blazer, mounted a Super-8 camera in the back, and pointed it at him so that all you could see was his face. We put the camera in time-lapse mode and just drove all around Austin.

He did other physical comedy bits – impressions, Chaplin's microphone dance, flipping a cigarette over his back and kicking it in the air. Bill had a real silent-film-star quality about him in that footage, and his gift for physical comedy is always overlooked.

Then David Johndrow and I went to the edit bays at Austin Access and spent the next five months putting it together.

We started sending out rough cuts to Bill. He sent one of them to HBO. Bill called one day, "Great news, Kevin. HBO wants to do a *One Night Stand* special with me." You're ecstatic for your friend, but you look at all your work and all you can think is: "Great, well this is now a waste of time." Bill wasn't the guy who was going to pretend like he didn't know I was disappointed. "So does that mean we're not going to finish this video?" I ask. "It's all I've been doing for the last five months."

"No, no, man. Finish it. We're gonna put it out. It's gonna be great. You've done so much hard work. We're gonna put it out."

He had been telling me he was going to get HBO to have me co-direct the special. Of course, I knew it was complete bullshit. He was only trying to be encouraging. Sometimes it had the opposite effect. I truly believe it's what Bill wanted. If someone at HBO had thrown Bill the keys and said, "Do whatever you want," his first call would have been to me. I don't say that out of ego. Bill was loyal. And given the choice between working with friends and working with strangers who might not even get who he was, it was an easy choice. But HBO doesn't work that way. He knew it.

Bill called me one day: "Kevin, the producers at HBO are really stuck on what to do for the intro." I started thinking about the things I wanted to do for *Sane Man* but didn't have the resources; and I remember sitting in my house smoking a joint and telling Bill about doing a time-lapse stop-action sequence of him going through the airport. I rattled off a detailed account of what I thought it should look like while Bill sat on the other end of the line and wrote it all down. When Bill's HBO *One Night Stand* came out, it was exactly what I had told Bill during that phone conversation. Every last detail. It was on HBO.

Sane Man was finished right at the same time they aired that first *One Night Stand*. It was shot in Chicago. Bill looked like Jimmy Swaggart. I remember sitting in my house while Bill and I were finishing *Sane Man*. FedEx knocked on my door but I wasn't expecting anything. Bill hopped up, "Oh, I think that's for me." We open up the box. "Hey, this is the first cut of my HBO special."

Me: "Oh. Cool."

Not cool.

It was another one of those things that, if he had thought about it, he probably would have realized that having the package sent to my house really was adding insult to injury. I was hurt. But he knew he was going to be at my place. Where else was he going to have the tape sent?

We sat down to watch it. The opening was not only my idea for the visuals but also had a nearly identical monologue to the one we had worked on for so long. The set also had tremendous overlap with the material on *Sane Man*. It was just one of those things. After we watched it, Bill turned to me and said, "Look, Kevin, I know you and David have put in a ton of work. Whatever you can do with this thing, you're welcome to it. I want you to be able to make some money off of this thing. I do kind of feel bad."

David took some great pictures of Bill against the Houston skyline. We used those for the artwork. And when it was done in February of 1990, it was *Sane Man*. I'm sure I'm biased but I think it's the best, most representative show of Bill's ever put on tape. It really captures him at the top of his game and just enjoying the moment.

While David and I worked on finishing *Sane Man* I didn't see too much of Bill for a while. He was living in New York with Pamela. His time was mostly divided between her and the road. And as the months wore on, Bill seemed to be doing more of the road than of Pamela.

Bill was still a hardcore phone addict, but it was a far more pleasant experience, primarily because there was a rational person on the other end. The hours were also more compatible with something resembling an adult lifestyle (although few of Bill's friends were adopting real-world adult responsibilities), and Bill wanted to talk. It became bi-directional, and was an actual exchange between two people, not a blithering drunk airing his grievances with the world to people who had absolutely zero power to do anything about any of it. He was still upset about how the world was put together, he was just expressing his displeasure with greater elegance. It was fun to be Bill's friend again.

[* * *]

James Ladmirault (Jimmy Pineapple)

My first night, I saw Sam Kinison there, and he had also started just a couple of months before. So I remember meeting Sam and a couple of other guys; but Sam pulled me aside and said, "Listen, I don't know where you are from or what you do for a living, but you should quit that and move here to do this, because you are good. It's what I did."

I started October '79. I moved from Louisiana and I knew no one. A few weeks later, I distinctly remember meeting Bill. He started a few weeks or a couple of months before I did at the Annex. This was when he was maybe 17, before he had ever gone to LA. I'm not that outgoing when meeting people and it takes me a while to get to know them, but Bill was immediate, especially for someone who was a kid.

It was at the very end of when Dwight and Bill stopped doing their act together. I saw Dwight and Bill, but I came when Bill was just starting to take off on his own. So I knew very little of Dwight. Every time I've seen him in more recent history, he's always been great. We talk about Bill a little bit, about certain things, but I think the last time we talked it was about our mutual obsession with Tonya Harding's butt.

Anyway, I don't remember what was said – me and Bill – but it was definitely an immediate thing. We liked each other right off the bat.

It was hard for us to judge whether the amount of drinking we did really was that bad or not, because that was our lives. We weren't in general society. You put us around other people, yeah, I guess it would have stood out, but we hung out with each other, and it was what we did. So we never thought it was bad or excessive.

It started hitting us, though, when other clubs began opening up across the country and a circuit was starting. Other comics from other cities were now coming to play Houston, and they started going, "God damn, those Houston comics really drink and party."

We began to get a reputation around the country, but other comics used to love to play Houston because they wanted to come hang out with the Houston comics.

I guess that was kind of fun, but what I was most proud of was that the Houston comics also had a reputation for being the best comics in the country. We were doing stuff that other people weren't doing. You went to LA and New York, and they were preparing to do TV. Clean. Six minutes on Carson. Network shows. Stuff like that. So everything had to be sanitized.

We were stuck down here, just speaking our minds and having fun. I'm not saying we broke any new ground, because Carlin had done it, Pryor and Bruce had done it; but when we came along it seemed it had stopped. Instead there were all of these really smooth airline-joke comics. We despised that shit. We just couldn't stand it. So we were doing stuff that we felt – that came from inside – people responded and it would come out. We didn't get a lot of work at first in other places because people were scared to hire us for fear of what might come out of our mouths. You never knew what was going to happen. So, as I recall, it was all the clean, TV-type comics that were getting all of the paid touring gigs while we got more resentful and more bitter. And the cycle continues.

But we took our lifestyle and put it on stage. It wasn't phony at all. Especially Bill. That's why I liked him. He was so real. For instance, when he had just started and was still in high school, he used to cut his own hair, almost every day. And he didn't do it for an act. He talked about it on stage and made it funny. But he didn't go, "Oh, this is a funny bit. I'm going to fuck up my hair." Something drove him to cut his hair. I remember him in the green room, he was always pulling at it, and he just hated it, so he cut it. And it was always, well, not punkish but it was just a horrible bad haircut almost every day. Then, I swear to God, another comic started doing that.

What the comic saw was that Bill was getting laughs from it. So he started doing it, started cutting his own hair, then started talking about it on stage. I couldn't believe it. I thought it was kind of naive in a way. "Jeez, you're up here because you think you're funny, but if you can't write your own material why are you even doing this?"

This is the thing people don't remember, though: they always think of Bill as this legend, but they don't know how many times Bill cleared the fucking room. Even when he wasn't drunk, he'd be so angry some times, or he was off on some tangent. And someone in the audience would piss him off. He'd just go off. And you almost felt sorry for him.

It was fun for me, though, because I knew what was coming. I'd grab a drink and pull up a chair. That was when the show started.

Back then nobody looked at Bill as some kind of god. He was one of the guys. He had bad shows like everybody else. And he had as much respect for some of the other comics as they did for him. But I used to love to follow Bill because it pushed me. It was a good competition, a healthy competition. Bill liked to follow me for the same reason. Same thing with Kinison. I had no fear of following Sam, nor did Bill, nor did we resent Sam for doing what he did; and it was hard to follow him because he didn't do a standard stand-up set.

Kinison could be very funny. But the second he started making it, he turned into a sell-out. His whole thing was be a celebrity and not a comic. We saw him as wasting the opportunity. We used to talk about "getting the message out." The first one to break out there had to get the message out, had to change all of the shit going on in comedy. He was the first out, and he didn't do it.

We believed it was all about the stand-up. That's why I absolutely loved Bill. We were almost comedy soul mates, because we believed it was all about stand-up. We had such a passion for it. The image of Bill as a preacher, Bill as a social activist, Bill as a whatever, I don't think Bill would have liked that. Bill wanted to be known as a stand-up. That's what Bill was down to his core: a stand-up comic. He did these other things, but essentially he was a comedian. I read all of this other stuff about him, and I never get that.

Every time we went on stage, we were always trying to learn. No show was ever good enough. I don't care if we killed or destroyed, something could have been tweaked, we could have got more of a laugh out of this joke. A lot of our conversations were about that: remember what this show was like, remember how that show could have been better.

That was another difference between the Houston comics and comics that came here from other places, the comics on the road: they were always talking about getting this job and who was hiring; we talked about comedy. It just annoyed me when other comedians talked about work. And they were right in a way because they had more successful careers. They were obsessed with getting work. I was obsessed with being funny. And they went a lot further. They got work. But I believed it was more important to be a better comic. And that's absolutely the way Bill was.

That's probably where we messed up. A lot of comics used to say, "We could just follow Pineapple and Huggins or Hicks around and take their ideas." The stuff we talked about offstage, we just threw these things out. We came up with great ideas but never said: "Hey, this would make a great TV show." When that's what we should have been doing.

When Bill died, it took a lot out of me. It is very hard to find someone like that to work with. The comedy, that's what it was all about. God, we had a lot of fun. We talked about everything under the sun, but a lot of it had to do with comedy and other comics.

I liked going on the road with Bill, but we were both headliners, so more often than not we split ways, but I did not mind either co-headlining or dropping down to the middle to work with Bill just because it was so much fun. I had no ego about that headline crap.

There was one time where we did Raleigh, North Carolina. Andy, myself and Bill. It was one of the greatest weeks of comedy I ever did. Ever. You've got three people who just cared about stand-up, and we were having a great time. From the moment we got up in the morning, or sometimes afternoon, until the time we went on stage, we hung out together, we laughed, we were ribbing each other.

We were just being our normal selves, doing the stuff we do all the time, and it just flowed from that.

When Andy was on stage, Bill and I were backstage still joking around. We were doing it up until the second we were on stage, and we would just take that energy up there. Every night. Andy was basically a headliner, and he opened the show. Then I had to follow that. That means he took it to a level that I had to go beyond. Then I took it up to a place where most people think it's the end of the show, then, shit, Bill comes up.

And Bill and I and Andy used to talk about it, every night, when that show was over that there was no show anywhere in the country, any place in the world, as good. It was the best comedy show that night. Period. It was just taken to such a high level. Every night we decided we were going to top what we did the night before. We were just having so much fun.

They had a rule in that club that you couldn't drink on stage. Something about a city ordinance or something, but they were always very strict about it. You could drink in the club – and I thought this was absolutely ridiculous – but the comics actually had to step offstage to take a sip of their drink.

Of course all of the comics played that, and made a joke about it. I basically said, "Fuck that. This is ridiculous." And I just took my drink on stage. The place went wild. There were regulars in there, and the owner, who I thought would probably send me packing, but I looked in the back and the owner was laughing. He thought it was great. This is kind of the way the week was.

And I remember a lot of drinking. Beyond what was normal. I used to call Jack Daniels "brown." And they knew my terminology after the first night. So I said, "Give me the biggest fucking glass of brown you can." I just wanted a drink, and they poured me a tumbler of Jack Daniels.

When Bill realized he wasn't going to beat cancer he called me, and it had to be one of our last conversations, but he said, "Esquire, we've been best friends for sixteen years and we never ever had one fight."

"Well, Bill, there was that one time in Raleigh . . . " After this absolutely magnificent week we had, we just had this huge blow-up over getting paid. Here we had been as close as could be, like the Three Amigos all week, and we just blew up at each other. Screaming at each other. It only happened for like a minute, then we laughed it off. It was about the money. I usually don't question it, but it's never what they say it is going to be. That's what it was coming down to, and we started screaming, at first just me and Bill. We were screaming about whose fault it was; and it was alcohol-fueled and there was frustration from being broke. It lasted about two or three minutes, but in his mind, it wasn't a real fight. He was right; in that whole time, we never had any kind of blow-up or any kind of nastiness or resentment.

If I were to go on and do HBO, or whatever, years from now I would look back and still say that was the best time ever, the best comedy ever. And Bill talked about it like Andy and I did. It wasn't about fame. If you were a comedian, you were there to do the best work. I would love to do that again now, sober, with Bill and Andy because I feel my material is better, but at that time the material that I had, it didn't get any better.

I just remember every time I was with him, it was always fun. I always laughed. I can't say that about anybody else I've ever met. Like I said, comics from other cities used to love to come to Houston, and it certainly wasn't for the weather.

The one time I made Bill laugh probably more than any other – he had that "Ha! Ha-ha!" belly laugh – was when he was giving me his sad song about some girl and about how she dumped him or wasn't going in the same direction he was. So Bill asked, "Esquire, we're good guys, and we're the best at what we do. So why don't women like us?" And I said, "Because, Bill, women like guys with a sense of humor." That one just hit right at the nail. "Ha ha-ha."

But there's not a conversation I ever had with Bill where he didn't make me laugh. Even in something serious or painful, he still made me laugh without even trying. Any time he called me to commiserate about women, it was always funny. It was an ongoing story, it just depended on who he had at the time.

I actually knew Pam before Bill. I brought her there for Mark Wilks. Pam and I were friends and I said, "I have this guy I want you to meet, he would be perfect for you," and it wasn't Bill. I thought she and Wilks were made for each other. She was a nice girl, but I never saw her as Bill's type. I always saw her more as Wilks' type. I don't want to go into the reasons why, it would be somewhat derogatory to someone who has already passed. Not to Mark, I don't think you can offend Mark.

Bill and Pam had almost a love/hate thing. I don't know about love/hate because he didn't hate her, but it was not healthy. They kept getting back together, but I could tell he didn't want to. Then when he wasn't with her, he was bitching about being apart. But, like I said, every time we ever talked he made me laugh, even when he called me to tell me he had cancer. He asked me if I knew how to get a hold of Pamela, I said, "No." And he told me, "Well, I've got to get a hold of her because I have a tumor the size of a golf ball on my pancreas and it's got her name it." So that's not love, it's some sort of a tumor.

Then there was Joanie, another one of Wilks's concoctions. They were flying back from someplace and Wilks met her on the plane. Once again it was Wilks that was trying to pick her up. And once again, she just bypassed Wilks and went straight to Bill. Bill had this magnetic personality, no doubt about that, because I don't think he was really trying. But I can imagine on that plane, Wilks was so obnoxious she just clung to Bill.

Joanie was absolutely nuts. She was another one that just didn't figure to me, she was a lot like Pam in that she just didn't look like Bill's type. She was the rich one from River Oaks. I don't remember what she did. I remember there was some other girl from Arizona that he was crazy about for a while. Her name was Sedona. We used to joke about that. Her name was Sedona. She had to be from there.

It wasn't just women that were nuts, though. Fallon Woodland, who he worked with on the TV show for England, he was also kind of strange. I know one of the things that I guess Bill was attracted to, or why he allowed that guy to hang around, was that he was hugely into video games. Bill loved video games. Now I don't know if he got into video games to hang around Bill, or if that was one of his things he was already into, but Bill kind of had a soft spot for psychos.

And all he did when he finally started talking to me about Fallon was complain about him. When they started working on the London thing that was all he did. Complain. "He does nothing. As soon as this thing gets off the ground, I'm going to get rid of him."

But Bill was very loyal. He could have dumped Fallon. Even though there was nothing legally binding about it, in Bill's head he would never screw anybody around. He was at the inception so he goes along for the ride, but he was contributing nothing and Bill was complaining about him. "He didn't write anything," or, "He's not funny."

It was funny because during that time in Houston, Bill also had his big loves, and the rest of us hardly had anything. But I heard sexual stuff about Pam, and I heard about Laurie "love of my life." Of course, Laurie was earlier on, but my take on it is that she, Laurie, was just that.

I couldn't get Laurie. I know how she felt about Bill, the way Bill felt about her, but she always seemed to complicate things. I know Bill wasn't the easiest guy in the world. For a girl. For a guy, he was the easiest guy in the world to get along with, but for a woman, I can't imagine. But I'll always remember: "Esquire, she's the love of my life. I've got to get back with Laurie."

The strange thing is that Bill talked about all of his women, but Colleen was a big surprise. It wasn't until towards the end when he told me he was sick that he even started talking about Colleen, and that he was living at her place. Before that he never mentioned her. In the last year of Bill's life we had got away from being adolescent

263

high-school boys discussing our one-night stands. We had passed through that phase. He was taking women and relationships a tad more seriously. Don't get the wrong idea, he wasn't calling to brag about conquests. Bill always analyzed and asked for advice.

But Colleen was an anomaly. And Bill was an enigma in certain ways, even to his best friends. Colleen he didn't say anything about until the end. He compartmentalized a bit. And I think in a way, especially with me and Andy, he didn't want us to know things. I think he thought it might have changed the way we looked at him.

This is only my perception because it was kind of a running gag between Bill and me that I was always his relationship guy. He would always call me for advice and tell me everything, even about his one-night stands. Colleen came up – and I'm thinking she insinuated herself into his life. This was never said to me, but when he was sick, and I heard she did a lot for him, that sounds to me more like gratitude. Not only that, she looks nothing like a Bill woman.

Maybe Bill just put her up on a pedestal and thought she could do more than she actually could. But she wasn't doing enough for him when he was alive. Look at who he was. He could have been huge. So whatever she was doing, she was bungling. Colleen wasn't family. She was someone Bill knew. I did not even meet Colleen until I was at the services.

At the point where we were both headliners and rarely worked together any more, we both still knew where we were – LA – and Bill would get as many phone calls from me.

We both had this obsession with Jay Leno. So a lot of the conversations were while we were watching *The Tonight Show* from different parts of the country. Leno would say something and I could almost put my hand by the phone. "Can you believe that piece of shit?' Whatever it was he'd said at the time. Then we'd analyze and dissect that garbage, put the phone down, then I'd call him back. "Did you hear that?"

There were a lot of hacks we weren't obsessed with, but Leno was the biggest sell-out we ever knew. Early on, we respected Jay as a stand-up, but the worst thing you could do was betray Bill. He would get really vicious after that. And not ever forgive. That someone as good as Leno could do as he did, that was the big betrayal. And we never understood why, because he got the gig.

It influences things. The standard drops and it makes it harder for other comics. Here was a guy who was a stand-up, became a star because of *The Tonight Show* and as soon as he took over *The Tonight Show*, he cut the rope bridge and you didn't see stand-ups on Leno much any more, and they were usually pretty bad when you did. That's one of the things Bill and I used to talk about, this strange insecurity.

The Tonight Show was sacrosanct to all of us. It was every comic's dream. *The Tonight Show* with Johnny Carson. Everybody talked about Carson. You never hear that now, you never hear comics saying, "I want to get on Leno's show." Leno saw that he stole Carson's job, so if he puts a good comic on, maybe his job was in jeopardy.

Bill hit his bottom long before I did, but he was never that great a drinker. He would have a couple and his whole personality would change. It appeared like he drank a lot, but it didn't take too much to get him to look like that. So sometimes it was deceptive. He could look like he was falling-down drunk, like he had been drinking all night, but really he'd just had a few.

He had had enough. And Bill was very decisive. When he decided to do something that was it. He went to AA. I asked him one time about why he first went to AA – I can't remember where he was, some city – and he remembered he was so sick and tired. He found an AA meeting and when he went in there, he just looked at the faces of the people, and the looks on their faces were saying, "You're finally here," and "Welcome." He said there was nothing but love in that room.

So when I finally went in, Bill was my sponsor. And the strange thing was, he died a year and a couple of days after I stopped. My AA birthday is February 23rd; Bill died February 26th. But in that year, I was never in Bill's physical presence – he was in London for quite a bit, and in Australia for a while. He lived in LA, I was in Louisiana. And it was a very hard year for me. Alcohol, my whole act was centered around it, my whole lifestyle. I didn't think I could be funny without it. I thought I was going to have to give up my career. It got to the point where I knew it was affecting me. That was the reason I stopped. I always wanted to be the best stand-up I could and I knew the booze was interfering. I knew I couldn't think as quickly as I used to.

That was the reason I quit. I had to get my stand-up back. And it was tough. Bill walked me through it the whole way. But the thing was, it was all by phone. And probably in that year he and I grew closer than we had ever been before, even though we were never in the physical presence of each other. I remember, I said, "Bill, I can't do this. The reason I stopped this was for my stand-up, and I am bombing every night." And he told me, "Listen, when I stopped, I bombed every night for six months. You are just going to have to go through that. It's going to be hard."

And for six months I bombed every night.

But it was just like Bill said. And it was almost six months to the day. It opened up for me. I went on stage and everything was clear, and I was clear. I just started killing. I was falling apart until one day it was clean and clear.

If it wasn't for Bill telling me that about the six-month thing, I probably would have started drinking again. Of course, I learned later on that he was dealing with his own stuff and not even telling his closest friends about it at the time. He was still able to walk me through my drunken shit.

Bill always kind of took care of me because he knew I was a complete fuck up. I hated club owners. Club owners hated me and I hated club owners. Agents, they wouldn't come near me. So Bill knew I needed some help that way. He told me that when he put together his record label the first thing he wanted to put out was my comedy album, *Jimmy Pineapple Plays Songs of Love.*

That really touched me. And the fact that it never happened – that he died and the album never came out – it doesn't bother me because of the fact that that was what he wanted.

[*   *   *]

Len Austrevich

There was something about him. It wasn't that he was outrageous, it was his point of view, and certainly when I got to own the Funny Firm in Chicago and see every comic in the world and travel all over – that's all I did for the first year or two of my club was go to New York and Los Angeles and watch comics, because I wanted the personality of the room to be booked from the comic's standpoint – that's when I started to realize there was something special about this guy.

But when I was a punk just starting out in comedy I moved out to LA. I was really young. I used to hang out at the Comedy Store. That was the training ground if you wanted to be a comic. And it was just like the stories – on any given night it's Robin Williams, or Richard Pryor, and on and on and on. So I got to be friendly with Riley Barber, who was the doorman at the back door of the Store. The comics would always come in through the back, that's how you got in for free. Riley, and I'm sure he doesn't even remember this, he told me, "Hey, you've got to check out this guy Hicks," who was also young like me.

That's the first time I saw Bill, doing stand-up out there. I was enamored by watching this young guy just destroying. It wasn't the Bill Hicks we know from later on, but that was the first time I got to see him.

I was mainly doing open mics but I was getting spots at the Westwood Comedy Store and doing open mics at the Improv. There were a million places and you could work twice a night if you wanted to hustle around. I wasn't a regular at the Store but I was getting stage time – four minutes, three minutes.

He was on stage from the beginning, which is remarkable. He had the right combination of being really funny and young, because Mitzi was looking at everything from the point of view of the business, and this guy's hook was that he was funny and young. He wasn't "Bill Hicks" but he was a very solid comic. He certainly wasn't

268

political, but his humor – I remember the bit about the kid in the wheelchair – that's fairly edgy, making jokes about people being crippled. I can't name other people that were doing that kind of stuff, and as mild as that is by today's standards, it's the kind of thing that stood out then to another comedian. He's making jokes about someone getting a pencil in his eye, everyone else is doing McDonald's and relationship and airline shit. This guy is pushing the envelope, making you feel a little uncomfortable.

And the way he acted it out. He would do the whole pantomime. He was almost old-school using his physical comedy. Aside from his political statements and his edge, the way he worked on stage was almost ballet-like. My background was theater and I went to acting school and here I was looking at a guy who was pulling this into the stand-up world. It was certainly part of what I was attracted to when I saw him. His ability, not to sell a joke, but to really take it to that next level. There are very few people who can do that. So he wasn't edgy and political at that point, but he certainly was different. And just funny. Really, really funny.

Two things about Bill Hicks stand out for me. One time I remember picking him up at the airport and he says to me, "I gotta talk to you. I gotta talk to you." When I was doing stand-up, I was known for this porn bit where I'd do the "Waka-waka," the sound of the wah pedal in the background music of porn; and I used to have a band and the whole band would come in. It was a running gag throughout my whole act.

So, Bill came to me and said, "I gotta talk to you. I used your waka-waka sound on an album and I didn't ask your permission. I'm sorry." I was totally taken aback by that. In terms of loyalty to a friendship, there are other people do that, but here's a guy who has already reached a certain stature, but he still had the class and the loyalty to admit to that and apologize.

Then I remember one of the last times I saw him we were working in West Palm Beach. I think he was sick then, I'm not sure because he didn't tell anybody for the longest time. So we were writing this screenplay together and batting ideas back and forth. The plot line of the script is that of someone going around killing hack comedians. They are trying to figure out why all of these comics are getting killed, and it turns out that the killer only kills impure comics. So Bill was helping a lot with the dialogue, and we had worked back and forth on this.

I was working the Carefree Theater, and Colleen McGarr used to run the Comedy Corner which was the club adjacent to the theater. So I asked Bill, "Hey, can you come check out my set?" And this is pure Bill Hicks. I get off the stage and he goes, "Man you are just one of the funniest fucking people I've met. I can't believe how intelligent you are. We've got to do some writing together." Then he just flipped it around. "So why do you do that fucking shit on stage?" He was completely honest. "Why are you doing hack crap that is offensive to you?"

He built me up, then ripped me up because he was that honest and dedicated to the art. He was a purist and wasn't scared to say things like that. And after he said it, it hurt my feelings, but I knew he had so much respect for the art form that it superseded everything. As much as I was hurt, at least he gave a shit enough.

Bill could eat with me. I'm a huge eater, and that was our thing. We used to go down to Stevie B's for ribs. We also went to Twin Anchors, which used to be a Sinatra joint, but Bill definitely preferred Stevie B's. It was so weird because you would sit down and eat with him, and he was so focused on his food. I remember chuckling, going, "This guy eats like an Austrevich." He'd get the huge double slab of ribs and his face would just be covered with the stuff. I just looked at him and laughed. He was totally into eating. But he wasn't fat. He'd always go, "Gonna put a little paunch on," and rub his belly.

I used to take him to get steaks. He was a big meat eater. Stevie B's, the Steakhouse and the Polish sausages were his big things. Oh God, he loved these Maxwell Street Polish sausages to the point where he was addicted. If he was flying through Chicago, I'd go get them and bring them to him at the airport. We would go after shows. It got to the point where, well, the worst was the time he came into town for a show and right after I picked him up at the airport, we went and got a Polish sausage. He did the show, and after the show we went and got a Polish sausage. We were up late bullshitting after the show, then went back and got a Polish sausage. Three times in one day. You see on his albums he gives a special thanks to Jimmy's Maxwell Street Polishes.

You go down there and you are always accosted by street guys, trying to sell you shit. It was freezing out, it was like 5 degrees, and we were sitting there eating the sausages, and the guys come up trying to sell you tube socks or anything. One was selling pornos. He had all of this porn, and there was one that was like, "Cum Liking Black Whores." It had this enormous naked black woman with giant boobs, and the guy is going, "Porno for your lad

My big joke to him was, "I can tell you in four words why you should fire Jack Mondrus."

"What?"

"Willie Lester and Tyler."

The dummy act, the ventriloquist. That was the only other act Mondrus had that anyone might have heard of. I told Bill, "He's a fan, but does he really get what you are all about? Is he really going to take you to that level?" You talk to any comic and that's the bitch. That's the complaint of every comic: "I've got shit representation." But his was conflict in terms of, "Do they get it?"

He was feeling worn out and he was telling me, "Man, I go from gig to gig to gig." And I told him he didn't have to do that, but he was almost childlike in his approach in that when he got into his art, he just didn't get the business. He was blinded by the fact that in the early stages he was manipulated by managers and other people. I think he was loyal to Jack to a fault too, but Jack wasn't servicing Bill well.

You can achieve the same thing he did working the road, without working it that hard. Jesus, you can get your manager to negotiate knocking off the Mondays and Sundays. Bill was literally doing back-to-back-to-back gigs, working fifty weeks, taking no time off. So at that point it was: "Bill, he is killing you. There's no reason for you to be working like this."

I always felt that Bill never really had a home base. If you ever saw his apartment in west LA, it was just shit on the floor. It wasn't a home. I always felt bad for him that he didn't have a cool place where he could just chill. He was this consummate road monkey that went around and around. It was not disheartening but kind of sad. You felt for the guy. "Take some time off, Bill."

I almost think Jack holds me responsible for his getting booted by Bill. He was one of those guys I was friendly with, but I think in the heat of passion, well, I tried hardcore to get him away from the guy. I certainly had a hand into putting a nail into that coffin.

I can remember it like it was yesterday. We were standing in the back of the Funny Firm. Bill was on stage. Mondrus was there, looking at him, watching him do his bit and he was mouthing Bill's bits as he does them. That's how obsessed he was. And I told Bill that night, "You've got to get away from this guy." There's a fine line between a passion for someone and being obsessive. I said to Bill, "Tell the guy I told you." And I think Bill may have said, "Well, Len said . . ." He treated me differently after that, Jack did. It was weird, but I gave a shit about the guy, Bill. We had become friends.

The sad thing is that Mondrus really loved him. It's the Hollywood thing: the guy gets discovered and he moves on, and you have to move on to get to the next guy who is going to take you to the next level. The sad thing is, for Jack, there was no maliciousness except for the greed. I think the guy was riding Bill and making him work so hard because he was making money. And that was another thing: "Why is this guy collecting commission on you? You and I are just doing this ourselves. I came to you. He never did anything." I always just paid Bill, nobody ever negotiated anything with us. And I think I was paying him, shit, $5000 or $7000 for the week. Nobody was paying that. But he deserved it. I didn't give a fuck.

And that was another problem I had with my partners, that I would book guys like Bill and just pay them great money.

I never knew Bill at all when he was a drinker. He was always straight. He always seemed to be in control on the stage, but I do remember one time we had this party when he came in to play the Funny Firm on an overlap week with Danny Bonaduce.

They all came over to my house one night. I used to have parties, get-togethers, with the comedians and friends. So Danny was holding court at this party and there were about ten musicians also hanging out. And I remember Bill pulling me aside and saying, "You've got to get me out of here" – and this is how naive I am because I don't drink or do drugs. So I ask him, "What's going on?"

And he tells, "Man, those guys are fucking doing drugs." And he got angry because I had put him in this environment.

So the point as to why didn't he do that is that you get entrenched in your career and you are blinded by it – you're blinded by the drive and the adoration – and it takes an obsessive compulsive behavior to be a drug addict, or whatever your weakness is. So in that regard, maybe that's why he did it. But he was also always reaching out. He wasn't always that strong guy.

He did get pissed at me another time. I did something. He sent me his porno collection. You know that bit he does about his mom finding his porn collection: "I wonder what's in this box over here?" He sent me all that porn. That was another connection we had. We used to talk about porn all of the time. He used to tell me about how when he was in New York he would go to the porno places. But he bequeathed me all this porn. I wasn't at the club or I didn't accept the package when it arrived and my assistant opened it. So when I talked to Bill later, I made a flip comment and said, "Oh yeah, I wasn't there to take the delivery but Chuck got it."

"Chuck got it? Are you crazy? Do you understand what was in there?" There was also a letter in there. It said something like: "Herein lies the depravity of man . . ." But he was mad at me because I had broken confidence by letting someone else see the stuff.

It's weird the bits and pieces you do remember. Some things are still very clear, very vivid. I remember when I had just got a cell phone – this is back when cell phones were still enormous – I was driving up the Pacific Coast Highway, and I called Bill. It was a beautiful night, and I was out in the middle of nowhere on the California coast and I could still talk to my friend. And he told me, "That thing is going to give you cancer."

God, he could talk and talk on the phone, though. I used to sit on the phone with him for hours and hours and we'd watch COPS together and Leno. I never quite got the fascination with COPS, but he was obsessed with Leno. "Look at this clown. Can you fucking believe that joke?"

We'd talk for hours, and, beyond his obsessions, we just laughed a lot. He generated laughs, but Bill was very generous with his laughter too. If you were sitting around with a bunch of guys, he'd give you laughs when you were funny. And that's important to a comedian, not only to hear laughter but to be made to laugh by other people. He was a hard laugh. He didn't laugh at just anything, but he was one of those guys that if it was good, he had a belly laugh and he'd roll on the ground.

[*   *   *]

CHAPTER 8

I don't want butts in the seats, I want minds in the room. I'd
rather have one mind in the room than a couple hundred asses.

– Bill Hicks

Bill felt like he was getting overworked. Not taking time off. Jack
Mondrus made it clear to Bill that he didn't have to take the bookings if he didn't want to. On one hand it was taking a toll on Bill. On
the other hand, it was exposure. And exposure begat exposure. And
in the summer of 1990, the incessant touring began to pay off.

Montreal's *Just For Laughs* comedy festival began as a sixteen-
performer, two-day event in 1983. In a handful of years, it had transformed itself into perhaps the most important comedy festival in
North America, covering over two weeks, dozens of local clubs, and
featuring hundreds of comics. And, in the *Seinfeld*-sitcom era, *Just
For Laughs* also became a hunting ground for TV producers looking
to do development deals with the next hot property.

Bill got scheduled to play an event called "The Nasty Show" and
also got a slot at the festival's main gala event at the 3000-seat Theatre
St. Denis. Despite his standard reticence at being dropped down the
pigeonhole of profanity, Bill was the highlight of "The Nasty Show"
in Montreal. Local media had helped generate a buzz about him
before his appearance, and Bill took full advantage.

While expressing general disappointment with the final Saturday night gala, *The Independent* called Hicks a "particular revelation," singling out his material on drugs – "I just cannot believe in a war against drugs when they've got anti-drug commercials on TV all day long, followed by, 'This Bud's for you'" – and calling it "disturbing" and "subversive."

Increased interest from HBO after his appearance eventually netted Bill a *One Night Stand* taping. In the late Eighties and early Nineties, HBO featured fifty comedians over the course of the series, including Kevin Meaney, Ellen DeGeneres, Bill Maher, Norm Macdonald and Martin Lawrence.

More importantly, amongst the Montreal crowds catching Hicks for the first time was a British producer named Bill Hyman. Hyman was scouting for a show *Stand-Up America* that would feature three American comics a week for a six-week run in London's West End. Correctly expecting the word of mouth to build over the course of the weeks, Hyman scheduled Hicks to perform at the end of the run.

Bill and London made good first impressions on each other. He loved it. He loved the city. He loved the people. He even loved his Queen's Theatre digs where he was scheduled to perform. More importantly, the audiences were two things that American audiences usually weren't: large and receptive. They appreciated someone who talked so frankly about the ills and inconsistencies of America. They were more surprised that it was an American saying it. Best of all, he was brilliantly funny.

He was abruptly woken from his dream. Straight from London, Bill went back to Los Angeles to do some TV. *Comics Only* was a show hosted by fellow comedian Paul Provenza. It was extremely representational of Bill doing a lot of media. As a general tendency it was: insert joke A into slot B. When doing interviews, Bill usually wasn't very candid and wasn't working from the cuff. For a guy who could be quick, he was instead usually lazy, and just converted bits from his stand-up to answer quasi-leading questions. It's not uncommon for comics. Most do it at some point, if not regularly. But for a guy to whom authenticity and sincerity were so important it was peculiar that he did it so regularly.

Cigarettes. Fetal injury. "Bob Hope doesn't need to use the F-word." UFO tour. Waffle House. It was like watching Bill do his stand-up routine while sitting down for an audience of one: Provenza.

Maybe he was just tired.

Bill followed up the *Comics Only* performance with another appearance on Letterman in October. He opened by talking about going sober. "When you are using Mescal as a chaser, you've crossed the line." The door is ajar. We're Christians we didn't like what you said. "If it's a choice between eternal hell and good music and eternal heaven and New Kids on the Block, I'm going to be surfing on the lake of fire."

Pretty average? It was maybe his least inspired performance on the show ever. Even doing his favorite show on TV, Bill seemed to be dragging.

Starting in 1986, Channel 4 in the UK began sending a TV production crew to sample the *Just For Laughs* festival in Montreal. Since 1989, Tiger Aspects had been responsible for the task, making six half-hours sampling what was happening over the fortnight. But in 1991, Tiger Aspects was struggling to find anything worth covering.

According to Tiger Aspects director of production Charles Brand, "What was increasingly happening was the comedy festival tended, because of its American broadcasting connection, to want to book what I would call second-leaguers from American sitcoms, who were not that good in their own league as stand-ups, but helped the American broadcasters. So we were pulling our hair out as to how we were going to fill up six half-hours for the acerbic, dangerous-type comedy that Channel 4 had been able to find there."

Enter our hero.

Gillian Strachan, researcher for Tiger Aspects, saw Bill doing his one-man show at the 200-seat Centaur Theater, then went rushing back to the hotel to tell everyone else they had to see Hicks. He was the "it" boy, far better and far more interesting than anything else anybody had seen to this point.

Bill wasn't exactly a secret, though. Following his success at the previous year's festival, Mondrus had lobbied *Just For Laughs* programming director Bruce Hills to get Bill a one-man show in Montreal this year. The angling paid off and Bill was given a stage to himself.

He put together a theme, calling the show "The Evolution of Myth," and saying of it: "The world appears to us a certain way because we believe it to be that way. When we change our beliefs, the world will change as well." Bill went for a minimalist approach to the show. Almost no décor to speak of, unless a black curtain counts as art direction. Some star slides and Beatles music (courtesy of NASA in Houston and John Farnetti) to literally set the stage. Very stark and dark. Bill and a single spotlight against a lot of black. Comedy noir. There was nothing to distract or detract from Bill. He sold out all seven nights.

Bill was "thrilled" to have the extended spotlight and time to stretch out material. But it wasn't just time for the sake of time, equally important was that he wasn't splitting it with another comic. Bill had a monopoly on the message, saying of the format, "It's the only way to change the venue so that people don't come out and they see an opening, a middle act and they get all of these different points of view and all that material."

There was just Bill's point of view, and coming only a few months out of the first Gulf War and Operation Desert Storm, Bill had a lot of new material.

The rest of the entourage from Tiger Aspects, including Clive Anderson, who would host that year's series of shows for Channel 4, went to see Bill and were absolutely convinced he was the best thing in Montreal. Brand quickly reached an agreement with Mondrus – described by Brand as a "rather colorful character" – to shoot the whole of Bill's performance.

The problem was that Tiger Aspects had a small budget and

only brought over a crew of two. So they actually had to go out and hire an additional camera. The director manned the additional camera, and the cameraman shot the main camera. There was a remote put at the back of the theater to give a wide show to cut from. But that was it, as they weren't allowed to interfere with the show's minimal lighting.

The original idea was to use parts of Bill's show throughout the six half hours. But when they got back to the UK they were so excited with the footage they had that they went to the Channel 4 commissioning editor, Seamus Cassidy, and asked for a one-hour special. That became a one-off show unto itself.

Straight off the success in Montreal, Bill spent early August in Edinburgh, Scotland, playing the Festival. Bill was scheduled into the Dream Tent. The buzz around him built, and he ended up selling out the "venue" before taking home the Critics Award from the Festival.

Bill also did tapings for a number of TV shows in Scotland (including *The Funny Farm* hosted by Stu Who for STV) as well as in Manchester and London. The most peculiar was a pairing with host Denis Leary for a set on London Underground. Leary had become easily more popular in the States than Bill with an irascible act that was similar to Bill's. Strikingly so. In fact, Leary had been accused of doing Bill's material. But when friends of Bill in London pointed out the "similarities" and asked him if he noticed that Leary was doing a lot of his material; Bill would just smile in return.

Whenever the subject came up, Bill usually took the high road. Usually. In 1992 Bill took a jab at Leary when he made an appearance on *The Dennis Miller Show*, Miller's short-lived syndicated late-night talk show. When Bill told Miller that he was on his way over to London for a month, Miller mentioned, "Leary's big over there, isn't he?"

Bill replied, "Yeah, it's weird. Their comedy scene is where ours was five years ago." The pair laughed, Bill hard, and Miller looked to the camera and said, "Sorry Denis." Bill kept laughing. Harder. He came out of his seat he was laughing so hard.

To his old friends Bill was sometimes less diplomatic. He cursed Leary's name and on more than a handful of occasions openly bitched about Leary's material.

With its adoring audiences, England and Bill were getting along fine. Jack and Bill were getting along less fine. Tension was increasing between them, or at least Bill's unease with Jack was causing him to feel more tension. Jack Mondrus was the annoying American. He said "Edinburg." Mondrus thought it was all coming together, everything he had planned for. Bill didn't see it that way. The success was what Bill wanted, but it was what he wanted from long before he ever met Mondrus. He didn't see Jack as the reason it was happening, instead Jack was looking like a hindrance to bigger things.

When the dysfunctional duo returned to the States, Bill went back out on the road and not long after Mondrus went to Splitsville.

Dangerous had not done well, at least not up to perhaps overly optimistic expectations. So when it came time to work on a second record Bill wasn't given an advance. He was given a DAT machine. It was not only a far more fiscally conservative gesture, it was tantamount to telling him: "Not only are we not going to give you money, we want you to go do the work you hired us to do yourself. So, here, go tape your own shows."

But with Mondrus no longer servicing Bill, Steve Saporta and Peter Casperson still had designs on handling Bill's career. With Bill's burgeoning popularity in the UK, they had channeled resources into a London office to help promote *Dangerous* and were helping push other aspects of his career. And Bill let the guys at Invasion know they were amongst the few people that understood him, that got him. But they never got a commitment from him.

In November, Bill went back to Austin's Laff Stop to record the shows that would make up *Relentless* (the CD not the live performance video). He also gave Invasion a copy of Marble Head Johnson, which was an album of original music he had recorded over the course of 1991. They were not excited. Everybody in the business thought of Bill as a comedian and a comedian only. But there was a song on Marble Head Johnson called "Chicks Dig Jerks" that was also included on *Relentless* as a bonus track. It was cheeky (as in "tongue-in"), but it was a song.

> *Hitler had Eva Braun*
> *Manson had Squeaky Fromme*
> *Ted Bundy got lots of dates*
> *I wonder what I'm doing wrong*
> *I don't pretend to understand women's little quirks*
> *Just one thing I know for sure, chicks dig jerks*

When Casperson heard it, he took it to Bill McGathy, asking, "Could this be what we are looking for to break rock radio?" McGathy told him it was headed in the right direction but was underdeveloped and needed more work. When that constructive bit of criticism made it back to Bill, he was having none of it, telling Casperson: "No way, I'm not changing anything. It's perfect as it is." Bill was convinced that *Relentless* would be a breakthrough as was. He picked up a scrap of paper, wrote a number on it, handed it to Casperson and said, "I guarantee you the next record is going to sell 100,000 units."

Relentless came out and Bill couldn't get it going with "Chicks Dig Jerks." It sold in the neighborhood of 5000 units. Casperson recalls: "When Bill came in to talk about the next record, and I felt the same way about the next record – that it needed more work and was about three-quarters done – he said, 'No, it's done. That's it.' And I said, 'Well, what happened with the last one? I thought we were going to sell 100,000 units.' And he said, "I didn't say how long it was going to take."

Bill was infinitely more talented as a comedian; but he was also more interested in being a musician. Invasion tried to massage Bill when it came to his desire to do music. They were trying to move him upward on the comedy front and put together a meeting with Johnny Podell from the William Morris Agency. William Morris is one of the three or five most powerful talent agencies in the entertainment world. From there you could move maybe laterally to a CAA or an ICM, but you couldn't really move up.

So this was not a dippy little lunch date. This was serious business. During lunch they talked about putting Bill into a venue to do a one-man show. Podell was going to get *Saturday Night Live* producer Lorne Michaels to come down to see if they could create something along the lines of a Bill Hicks "Moment" on SNL, his own weekly segment on the show.

Podell *et al.* put together the whole plan, and Bill's response was unequivocally enthusiastic: "This sounds fabulous. This is what I've always wanted to do. What I'm going to do is I'm going to buy a Jeep and drive across the country and think about it."

The showcase never happened. Says Casperson, "The next thing I know he's moved to LA, got a new manager and he's hanging out doing yoga and waiting to do sitcoms."

[*   *   *]

Kevin Booth

Just like Opie and Andy Taylor, Marble Head Johnson came from Mayberry; and it was the biggest fish known of in those parts.

By 1990, Year Zero had completely fallen apart. The Big Rock Career was over. Several months later I was jamming with drummer Pat Brown. It was just friends having fun. But we were playing around with some heavy bass grooves, some funk things. Before we even thought we were doing anything, Pat and I had put together several songs: "Chicks Dig Jerks," "Lay of the Land," a couple of others.

We started calling it Marble Head Johnson. Like I said, it came from Mayberry, North Carolina, the small-town setting of *The Andy Griffith Show*. But it was also something I picked up from my brother: I went fishing with Curt, and he said he was trying to catch Marble Head Johnson.

The previous summer, Iraq had invaded Kuwait, and the United States had been amassing troops in the Gulf region. Bill and I were long-distance CNN junkies. We'd watch it for about twelve hours a day and spend the remaining thirteen hours on the phone talking about it. Bill had outrageous phone bills. Most guys bragged about the size of their penis, Bill bragged about the size of his phone bill. He used to joke that, anatomically, he was "hung like a seahorse." His phone bills, however, they were enormous.

January 1991 was the eve of the first Gulf War, Operation Desert Storm. Bill decided to fly to Austin. We were having the premiere for *Ninja Bachelor Party* and Bill was doing a show in town. But that very night America started dropping bombs on Iraq, that was the first night Bill played with us as Marble Head Johnson. We were jamming over at my house and playing a lot of the songs Pat and I had started writing. It just fell together. It was effortless. Organic. Bombs kept dropping and we kept playing. We rolled tape all night and filled up dozens of reels.

It felt great. For all of us – me, Bill, Pat Brown, David Johndrow – it was an electric night. And not just because we were watching the US bomb another country back to the Bronze Age in real time. It was the first time that Bill and I had worked together since finishing *Ninja*. *Sane Man* was more of a collaboration between David and me than Bill and me. I put together the crew that went to the Laff Stop and did almost everything in pre-production, production and post-production. Bill was the star. It was Bill's show. But from his perspective, it wasn't much different than any other night of work on the road.

I was hoping to put back together the pieces of my professional music career; and when Bill came into it, it was the missing ingredient. Without even knowing it, this was what I wanted.

Be careful what you wish for. Bill stepped in and he took over. Pat started taking his orders from Bill because Bill was the famous comedian flying in from out of town. As Bill was having more and more fun, I was having less and less. But I put on a brave smile and played the part of happy sidekick bass player. Quick joke: "What do bass players use for birth control?" Their personality. Self-deprecation beats frustration any day.

Things gradually working out with David. With all we had done together, something suddenly seemed different. There was always this strange energy between David Johndrow and Bill. I'm an air sign, Bill is a fire sign and David is a water sign. Together the three of us had this great energy; but with Bill and David in isolation, there was now a weird vibe, and things just stopped working out. One day Bill announced to me that he didn't want to work with David any more. He said, "I love David, and he and I will always be brothers, but something about the energy of working with him. It just doesn't work for me any more."

Maybe David felt it too. When he had an opportunity to move to Tokyo he took it.

After David left for Japan it seemed like Bill just started coming to Austin much more frequently to work. The tension had hit this level where it had become stressful for Bill to come to Austin. Shit, maybe Marble Head Johnson should have been called Stress. It seemed like Bill wasn't interested in hanging out with anybody. He wanted to work and didn't want it to be unpleasant. So when David left for Tokyo, it was like, whew, the coast is clear.

Instead of going with the flow and just accepting Marble Head Johnson for what it was worth, I also started having some issues working with Bill. I started resenting him maybe for the first time because he had power and he was exercising it. We kept playing, though. We had tons of 4-track material when finally I started asking: "Where is this going? What are we gonna do with this? I'm putting a lot of time into this and not doing other bands because of this."

Maybe he meant it, maybe he wanted to call my bluff, maybe he just wanted me to shut up and play my (bass) guitar. But Bill said, "Well, I'm going to quit comedy so we can do Marble Head Johnson full-time." First, I thought he was full of shit. Second, I didn't want him to quit comedy to do Marble Head Johnson full-time. Third, I thought he was full of shit. Who was he kidding? Bill's future was in comedy, which is a twist because back in high school I was completely shocked when Bill said he was leaving Texas to go to LA to do comedy full-time, because I thought Stress was going to be the future.

I know he was tired of touring, and maybe the idea of being in a band was suddenly appealing. But what do bands do? They tour and tour and tour. Plus, in a band there was shit to lug around.

The blues – that became the source of the friction. It's all Bill was playing. Each and every one of the songs he came up with was a 1-4-5 chord progression. And they were either in the key of E or A. Very basic. It's like playing "Wild Thing." It became an issue and we started arguing. His position was, "Well, if you're going to do music, you should start off with the basics, you should start off playing 'Johnny B. Goode.'" My response was, "Well, if we were going to start off doing

287

comedy, does that mean we have to start off doing fat housewife jokes?" In hindsight, I was being an ass.

But for all the tension, things never imploded. Instead we upgraded. We went to Cedar Creek Studios, which is a big, expensive, 24-track studio in Austin. Bill was living out one of his dreams. He had never made a real record, never got to hang out in the studio, never sit at the board, etc. With Marble Head Johnson he was playing out his rock star fantasy.

On one hand it was great to see Bill so excited, on the other he was bossing me around. So that kind of put a damper on the fun. Plus, we could only afford a few hours here and there. Working piecemeal on a record is horribly inefficient because you feel like you spend a good chunk of time trying to find where you just left off.

It appeared to a lot of people that he was the one who was shelling out the cash because he paid a studio bill or bought a tape. I guess, what, the studio we used for the initial tracks in my home built itself, and the equipment put itself in there? Bill bought studio time, but I ended up mixing it by myself. Nobody paid me anything.

Marble Head Johnson recorded ten songs in the studio, which was all we could afford to do at the time. We had far more material than that, but it added up to about thirty-seven minutes. Bill came back in town for one day of overdubs. When we finally finished, we ordered 400 cassette copies. I had to sit in my living room by myself putting together every single cassette case and insert by hand. Meanwhile, Bill calls me from out on the road, talking about how he's getting laid, and having a fucking riot of a ball. And I'm thinking, "Why the hell am I doing this?"

So when Bill came back to me and said, "Let's do another Marble Head Johnson album," I told him, "No." I was unequivocal. It was the first time I had ever turned down doing a project with Bill. And he couldn't believe it. I told him I wasn't having fun and I didn't like the music. I just let him have it. When Year Zero was signed to Chrysalis

288

I was like the Colonel to Bill's Elvis; now he was turning me into his own private Charlie Hodge. Suddenly, I was the loser taking orders. And I wanted to rebel against Bill.

Then Bill retaliated against my rebellion. We really could be that childish. He hooked up with Fallon Woodland. Fallon was this hugely overweight guy, a comic from Kansas City. You know how you get in a cab and the cab driver looks like he lives in it, looks like he cooks food and watches TV in the cab? That was Fallon.

At the tail end of Marble Head Johnson, when I decided I didn't want to be stuck behind 12 bars, Bill trotted out his latest acquaintance to see if it was going to bug me. I was telling Bill I wanted space. So he came back and told me he was going to be doing things with this other guy, Fallon Woodland. "He's the weirdest guy." That was Bill's description.

There was a club in Kansas City called Buzzard Beach; that was Fallon's hang out. Bill would call Fallon, and he would do it in front of me to make a point. It wasn't a casual thing either. It wasn't us sitting around on our asses and him trying to kill time chatting up people. It was Bill suddenly becoming super-busy and his needing to talk to Fallon was an integral part of whatever was so pressing. So Bill would call him with me standing there, and he would just get his answering machine.

Ring . . . Ring . . . Ring . . . "Hey, it's Fallon, I'm not here. I'm at Buzzard Beach. Leave a message." Beep. He suffered the embarrassment at his own doing.

Even when he did get Fallon he would turn around and bitch to me because he'd be trying to talk to Fallon about the TV show they were going to do, and Fallon wasn't taking it very seriously. The show was *Counts of the Netherworld*. The idea was for Bill and Fallon to sit in a Victorian salon and just discuss ideas.

Where Bill was acting like, "Hey, I'm giving you the opportunity of a lifetime, and you better get serious about this," Fallon was, to Bill, very blasé. And that drove Bill crazy. If you wanted to make Bill insane, the easiest way was to not match his intensity or his enthusiasm when it came time to work. Fallon did it better than anyone.

The truth is that, even though his befriending Fallon was Bill's way of irritating his older circle of friends, I ended up really liking Fallon. He was funny, even though he was kind of creepy. Bill's whole joke was that he was a stalker. I thought he was a pawn. He wasn't just a pawn. Fallon was someone Bill genuinely liked, but there were definitely asymmetrical overtones to their relationship. Bill got involved with Fallon in part because he was someone who Bill knew would drive everyone else crazy. Bill liked to push buttons. Come on, he would antagonize audiences, don't you think he liked to try to do the same with his friends even if to a much less abrasive degree?

"Why? Why is Bill working with Fallon?" I heard it from David, from Dwight, from Jimmy. They were low-volume grumblings while Bill was alive. People would say it to me and to each other, but not to Bill. It's almost like no one ever wanted to challenge him. No one would confront him.

Once Bill died, they freely upped the volume on their complaints. "What the fuck did Bill see in that guy? I should have been the one in *Counts* with Bill. It's an idea we talked about our whole lives, about doing, like, a talk show." Nobody understood, but they never held it against him. Still, the fact that Bill pulled Fallon out of a hat and kind of threw him at us, was a slap in the face to all the Houston guys.

Counts was, at its most basic core, an attempt to put Bill in front of the camera, roll tape, and capture this alleged magic. Bill had the Manifesto, and we shot a pilot in Austin. We had a friend who had the decor to make the studio at Austin Access look like a Victorian parlor. Fallon sat behind a desk with a dictionary opened up in front of him. Bill sat in a chair next to the front of the desk and they started talking.

Bill joked about how funny it was that every one of his friends' initial impression of Fallon was roughly: stalker. Besides *Counts of the*

Netherworld, Bill wanted to do another TV show that involved Fallon sitting in his car, parked in front of women's houses talking to them on a cell phone. He would just sit there, sitting in his car but having these long rambling conversations with the women inside. They'd have no idea that he was sitting outside their house.

[*   *   *]

Fallon Woodland

In 2003 Fallon Woodland ended up in federal prison after a guilty plea to a charge of travel with intent to engage in a sexual act with a juvenile. According to the plea agreement, Woodland admitted he had traveled to California with the intent, and for the purpose, of having sexual contact with a juvenile female whom he had met in an Internet chatroom.

Woodland was contacted by mail at the US Medical Center for Federal Prisoners in Springfield, Missouri. He agreed to be interviewed, and sent the relevant paperwork for visitation permission. After the paperwork was filled out, no further notification was ever given by the USMCFP either permitting or rejecting the request to visit Woodland.

During this period additional letters were exchanged. As the deadline for the manuscript approached and there was no indication that permission to visit would be granted, two letters were sent making an appeal to Woodland to take the time to write out the important details of the story of his relationship with Bill. That information would be used in lieu of in-person interviews.

The second of these letters was very brief. What's printed below is part of Woodland's response to that letter.

In a subsequent letter to Kevin Booth, Woodland maintained his innocence.

> In regards to your curt letter:
>
> "Never heard anything back on the status of the request to visit." Neither have I! That is why you have not heard back. "Never heard back after the last letter asking that you simply write out the highlights of your experiences with Bill." No you haven't heard back and you won't! I tried to arrange a visit for you, to help. I have done all I can. Have I been at all busy? Well, since you did not ask, I have four college classes a week

of 2 ½ hours class time and several hours of homework per
class, three computer classes weekly of 2 ½ hours each, typing
– 2 hours, a marketing plan that has taken all of my time,
teaching myself Pre-calculus and Calculus with college
textbooks, and my grandmother died and I could not leave
this place to show my respects. Thanks for asking . . .

"Here is Bill's story. Bill was so protective of me when it
came to getting hurt in relationships that he would want to
know everything about any new "her." If she crossed me,
betrayed my confidence, or hurt me, Bill had one standard
reaction. He'd say, "She's cut from the team!" Well, after your
snippy letter – "You are cut from the team!"

I deserved better,
Fallon

CHAPTER 9

More exposure. What kind, I don't know. I'm moving out to LA
What I want is to make a lot of money and get out of the business forever. I'd like to be more like the J.D. Salinger of comedy.
I'd like to produce one book that every year 30 million people
buy again.

— Bill Hicks

Bill moved to LA. Of all places.

West Los Angeles to be more precise. West LA is a strip of strip-
malls wedged between the 405 and the increasingly chi-chi zip code
of Santa Monica. He also signed on as a client with Moress Nanas
Shea.

Bill still hated Los Angeles, referring to it as a "nightmare city" but
the road was no longer his vehicle of choice. TV and maybe movies,
that was the way. His new management firm had represented
Roseanne Barr, who was one of the first to get a self-starring sitcom
based on her stand-up persona. *Seinfeld* and *The Simpsons* (and not
Roseanne) were amongst the few shows Bill ever singled out to admit
enjoying but he had respected Barr for making the transition to TV
without changing who she was.

But the bar for TV was also low. Even a middling comedian could
get a development deal with a network to do a sitcom pilot.
Depending how it was viewed, Bill was either reprioritizing to

reduce the touring load or quickly becoming everything he detested, actively pursuing work in a medium he had spent half a decade deriding. "Watching TV is like taking black spray paint to your third eye," he had said.

The whole business of TV didn't really fit with Bill's anti-marketing *Weltanschauung* – "By the way, if anyone here is in marketing and advertising, kill yourself." That was the line from Bill's stand-up. Also, the same month Bill moved to LA he told an interviewer, "Everyone should wear blue jeans and [own] three T- shirts, and eat beans and rice and break every fucking company. Break 'em. Don't buy McDonald's. We're going to break your ass Big Mac, okay? Quit making such shit." TV was an advertising-supported medium. McDonald's advertising dollars pay the bills for TV production.

It wasn't the medium so much as what people chose to do with it. Robert Altman's movie *The Player* was reflective of how Hollywood really does operate. You have to be able to walk into a room and say: "It's *Pretty Woman* meets *Out of Africa*." LA is a game. You have to play it. You can aspire to make something valuable that also delivers you piles of money, but you've at least got to find a way to package it.

Bill was not a game player. He was too binary. For him to walk into a pitch meeting and say: "I want to make a TV show that helps people evolve ideas" was insane or stupid, and Bill was anything but stupid, but doing that was as certain a way to turn a potentially good meeting into an early lunch, and Bill was smart enough to know that. Still, that summer, he and Fallon Woodland began codifying an idea for TV Bill had been kicking around called *Counts of the Netherworld*. They penned both a treatment and a manifesto to explain the idea. The counts, Bill and Fallon, would "encourage the spark in every mind to join them in illuminating the Netherworld of our Collective Unconscious."

The idea of the collective unconscious was something Bill had picked up from reading Carl Jung. Jung, like his mentor Freud, posited the existence of a conscious and an unconscious mind.

Thinking about the mind like an iceberg, the conscious mind is the part of the iceberg that sits above the surface of the water. This is the part of the mind where we think, and feel, and sense; and the part of the mind that we "live in," so to speak.

The rest of the iceberg, that hidden below the water's surface, is called the "personal unconscious," the home of thoughts, feelings, and urges. The contents of the personal unconscious are things that are developed environmentally – who your parents were, what books you've read, where you live. The collective unconscious, however, is a little different: one conciousness connecting everything. It is the part of the mind that is determined by heredity; something pre-figured by evolution.

So awakening the unconscious mind involved Bill and Fallon sitting in a lushly decorated Victorian-era salon to explore ideas and "celebrate" the ones that free the human sprit while "skewering unmercifully" those that don't. That was the idea, but in translation to tape it meant Bill and Fallon sitting in a room talking:

From the treatment:

BILL
Did you get all that?

FALLON
(Looking up from writings)
Hmmm? Get all what?

BILL
(Incredulous)
The Poem!

FALLON
Sorry, no. I was just writing this girl I met who works at the
fishmongers.

Bill glares at Fallon, then leaps away from the French window and storms over to the red velvet couch where he plops down boredly.

FALLON (CONT.)
I think she works at the fishmongers . . . either that or she
likes me a whole lot more than I first imagined.

Bill is holding a book of Carl Jung's work, which he is leafing
through thoughtfully.

BILL
You see. Jung has this idea of a Collective Unconscious which
mankind shared. . .. and I agree. But! I think this Collective
Mind is supposed to be conscious not unconscious! And that
is our job as Agents of Evolution – to enlighten – to bring
light into the dark corners of that Netherworld and thus
awaken our Mind to Truth and complete the circle that was
broken with the dream of our fall from Grace.

As Bill is saying this he is leafing through a copy of the Madonna *Sex*
book, which sits on the coffee table before him.

This opening segued into a brief discussion of how banal and
unshocking the *Sex* book actually was, and that segued into the
introduction of the first guest. Discussion would follow. That was
the template for the show.

In addition to the *Counts* pilot, Bill was also developing script ideas.
Selling a feature-length script was a six-figure return on about
20000 words' worth of work. *The King's Last Tour* was a story Bill had
come up with where Elvis Presley returns but, amidst the throngs of
Elvis impersonators, can't prove he is indeed The King. Bill and Len
Austrevich were also kicking around an idea for a dark comedy
about a serial killer whose targets were bad comedians.

Bill worked out *The King's Last Tour* on his own, but even though
the industry had modernized significantly since he and Dwight were
teenagers holed up in their Valley apartment, Bill hadn't adapted. He

wrote *The King's Last Tour* longhand on legal pads, and had a secretary type it. Fortunately Austrevich was tech-savvy enough to relieve Bill of the simple task of typing on a computer.

The AVN Awards are known as the Oscars of porn. Oxymoronic as that sounds, the awards exist. From a small ceremony in 1984, the AVNs had grown to an event with 2500 attendees held at Bally's by the time Bill was a guest performer in 1992. Talk about a kid in the proverbial fucking candy store. One of Bill's heroes was Bruce Seven, of the Buttman movies fame. He got to meet him; he got to meet all of his faves in porn. He not only met them, but he got to get up in front of these people that he had watched a million times – he had probably come on a few of their faces, if only on a TV screen – and for once they sat there and watched him.

So the AVN Awards were cool: first, because it was porn, and Bill loved porn. Second, it was the first and only time Bill got to perform as Elvis with a live band behind him. No jumpsuit, he was wearing a tux for the show. But he got to be Elvis – "Brand new Cadillac" – with a threepiece backing him.

Bill came out doing "Mystery Train," then walked the crowd, gave away his scarf, commented on the unfortunate circumstance that all the people up front were men, then did a few bars of "Suspicious Minds" before doing about a fifteen-minute stand-up set. He was visibly nervous to start. And the laughter was tepid until he did contextually appropriate material: talking about Vegas and talking about sex.

"I love it when they ask you that, 'Hey, you been gambling?' No, gambling implies the possibility you might fucking win. I have been donating quite regularly to the splendor of Las Vegas . . . I did find a way to break even here, though: you can play the change machines. You don't lose anything. You're a part of the action. Fuck it. I've had people ask me my system. I recommend dollar bills face up."

Then he started to get nasty, and the nastier he got the more the crowd loved him. The more the crowd loved him, the looser Bill got.

After the show, Bill went into the bathroom, he found himself at a urinal with Ron Jeremy on one side of him and Peter North on the other. Don't look down, Bill. He didn't have to. Peripheral vision was good enough. He called his friend in Austin after the show, "Kevin, I am hung like a fucking seahorse. These guys pulled anacondas out of their pants. Damn. And, man, a lot of these guys are ugly, too. They are ugly, schlocky guys, but the girls are just loving them. Size doesn't matter my ass."

Out of the thousands of shows Bill did in his life, performing at the AVNs was a huge milestone for him. He was hugely proud of it. Bill was the porno connoisseur par excellence. His jokes about his love of porn were not jokes. On the rare occasions Bill had time off from comedy – maybe a break of three or four consecutive days – he would rent a pile of porn and hole up in his place. Picture Bill locked by himself in his LA apartment for hours straight. He joked that his neighbors could see what he called the "blue unholy light" emanating from under his door. That light was a combination of the warm glow from the TV tube and Bill's forearm moving back and forth to cause the flickering fallout.

From his stand-up: "Anyone could go to the video store near my house and see what I've rented the past year, it's fairly frightening. Unbelievable evidence of an emotional digression going on here: porno movies and video games. What am I, thirteen emotionally? You know what I mean? I'm sitting there looking at this receipt I got from them, it's like: 'Clam Lappers' and 'Sonic the Hedgehog.' That was one weekend. That was Easter weekend."

Again, it was part of his stand-up routine, but it was no joke. He really spent an Easter by himself celebrating the holiest of Christian holidays with porn and video games. Bill remarked that by the end of the weekend he was shooting nothing but air.

But he was more proud of the AVN Awards appearance than any of the *Letterman* spots. For him it was fun. He got to hang out and meet all of these people that he idolized in a weird way. He got to be

Elvis. And he got to be as nasty as he wanted to with his jokes. Unlike TV, there were no censors to get through. Bill could say whatever he wanted. The more off-color he got, the more they encouraged him. This clique was totally different than other comedians or rock stars and to be invited in was one of his more cherished memories. Bill barely ever talked about the *Letterman* appearances to his close friends. He never stopped mentioning the AVN Awards.

A couple of months later, on 26 March Bill was back on *Letterman* and back in a constrained environment. He came on stage to Nirvana's "Smells Like Teen Spirit" and exited to Zeppelin's "Misty Mountain Hop." In between, lesbianism was about as far to the edge as he went. He did his joke about the girl-girl sex scenes getting cut from the movie *Basic Instinct* after rating poorly with test audiences. "Boy, is my thumb not on the pulse of America." He added that if he had been in that test audience Michael Douglas would have been picketing the movie to get his part put back in.

Letterman flashed *Relentless* (full-on vinyl, no less) which was due to hit stores in just a couple of weeks. It might have been the best exposure the record got.

It was something he had probably dreamed about, but never expected to see in his life. When Bill was on an airplane headed to the UK for a seventeen-day tour starting the end of April 1992, LA burned. It wasn't funny. Of course, Bill did find jokes in it. Fucking good ones. But there were massive riots that started in South Central Los Angeles and spread to other parts of the city.

The catalyst was the verdict in the Rodney King case. Four LAPD officers were charged after video of them beating King surfaced and received national media attention. One of the officers was convicted of using excessive force. The other three were cleared of all charges. Within moments of the verdict's live broadcast, chunks of the city were on fire and people were rioting. For three days violence reigned.

While LA burned, Bill joked on British radio, "Did I leave a cigarette lit?" (Bill had actually recently stopped smoking as part of the healthier lifestyle he had initiated that coincided with hid relocation to Southern California.) For two and a half weeks Bill packed theaters across the UK for his first major tour – Glasgow, Edinburgh, Liverpool, Manchester, Leeds – on that side of the Atlantic before finishing up in London where he sold out the 1000-seat Queen's Theatre.

That spring trip had been so successful that he returned to take a victory lap. Twenty-three shows. England, Scotland, and Ireland. He drove himself between many of the gigs, listening to *Tommy* in his rented car. Did some TV here and there. He was even paired with Cindy Crawford to talk about the US presidential election. Bill said that if the elder Bush was re-elected, he would stay in London and start looking for a place to live.

He loved that the British loved him. He loved feeling appreciated. He should have been happy, but in Britain he was preaching to the converted. Bill was about the struggle. He was about the fight. He never let go of that preacher part of him. He was like a missionary, and that job demanded that you convert people. It was work, and usually thankless at that. So while Bill toyed seriously with the idea of moving to Britain (Bush's defeat to Clinton meant Bill never had to make good on his threat) he never called anywhere but the United States home.

But even with the president's overthrow, Bill was skewering the outgoing Commander in Thief. From the stage in Oxford:

> "He's a Hitler. He's a Hitler. Saddam Hussein is a Hitler." What does that make you? Goebbels? Quit arming him. "He's a Hitler." He was your friend last week. He's a Hitler now? Trying to motivate people, you know. It's unbelievable how they got them. People were just like: "He's a Hitler." Yeah, Bush. Get real, man.
> "You like dogs, don't you?"
> "Yeah, we love dogs."
> "Well, we have an intelligence report that says here Saddam Hussein likes to fuck dogs in the ass and then take their spine out and use it as a toothpick."

"You're shitting me. Let's go kill this guy. I had no idea he was that much of a maniac. This is for Rover." (Bill makes a gun noise.)

"That's what the intelligence reports say. He's a Hitler. He fucks dogs. Um-hmm."

"I don't know. You sure that's true?"

"You like kittens?"

"Yeah, I like kittens. They are cute."

"He boils them and eats them."

"Fucker. This is for Fluffy."

Bill, in his critique, understood all too well the charade that governments play, and as comedy it cut so close to the truth that it was as much about educating people as it was making them laugh.

As a finale for his November jaunt through the UK, Bill's management had put together a deal with HBO and Tiger Aspects to do a taping for another TV special, this one at the Dominion Theatre in London. Herb Nanas and Bob Shea arrived in London to join Bill for the occasion, but he was none too pleased with how things began unfolding then.

Nanas and Shea were 100 per cent LA. They flew first class. They stayed at the swanky Chelsea Harbour Hotel (while Bill stayed at a rather ordinary and unassuming hotel). They took a limo. It was everything Bill didn't like about the business and it was causing tension. Bill had assembled a small group of people he had confidence in and a good working relationship with. His managers showed up and they wanted to call the shots. Even the local staff were starting to notice. Bill's managers were telling producers Bill had chosen to help on the project to get them coffee. At one point, during a rehearsal Bill had jumped from the stage to avoid even having to talk to Nanas and Shea. He slipped and hurt his wrist. It was nothing serious, but the lengths to which he was willing to go simply not to have to see his managers was clear.

Come showtime, Bill had a cold and a bum wrist, and he was even worried about the set décor. He thought it was too big. If ever Bill was set up for a let-down this could have been it. Brand and Tiger Aspects again produced the show for Channel 4. Says Brand, "In my view it wasn't as exciting as the original show from Montreal, but still a great hit. What was complicated in terms of where he was going comedically was that he did a lot of material in that show around his fascination with sex."

For years Bill had referred to himself from the stage facetiously as Randy Pan the Goat Boy at times, crossing even his imaginary line of good taste when it came to sexually explicit material. But now there was no apologizing for it. Bill had broken out a full-fledged character, his alter ego of Goat Boy, who was every sexual urge brought to light. Recalls Brand, "At that time in England the people who were his big fans were very much sort of left-wing liberal folk, who in those days had a quiet, sort of puritanical attitude towards sex, and certainly a very feminist attitude. Bill did this whole Goat Boy routine, and you could feel half of the theater go, 'What's he saying? He can't be saying this.' That made life more intriguing and more dangerous, which is what Bill always was."

Still, the show – which was aired with the title *Revelations* – was an unqualified success. Bill not only played to the biggest paying audience of his career but also got paid better than he ever had. Tiger Aspects was keen to further the relationship with Bill, wanting to know what he wanted to do next. The probability of Bill doing a show of his making in the UK was much greater than at home, so he brought Tiger Aspects his idea for *Counts of the Netherworld*.

The day after the Dominion show Bill met with writer John Lahr at his house. It was Lahr's son, Chris, who had brought Hicks to the attention of John while watching *Relentless* on Channel 4 the previous January. Lahr had written of the special in a brief review for *The Independent*, saying Hicks had "set a high-water mark for mischievous laughter." Lahr, who had attended the show the night before, was working to do a profile of Hicks for the *New Yorker*. Chris came into the room while the two were speaking and said to Bill, "I don't know how you have the courage to say those things."

The fact of the matter is that Bill reveled in it. In a later interview he admitted, "I get a certain kick out of being an outsider constantly. It allows me to be creative. I don't like anything in the mainstream and they don't like me." True, it was a year later that he said this, but it wasn't like Bill had suddenly been marginalized. If Bill had ever been in the mainstream, it's only because he was the salmon.

When Bill came back to the States he was fuming. He complained to a friend in New York that, aside from the fact that his management acted in a way that was appalling, they didn't get it, and they didn't get him. He wanted his people to push his projects, instead they were sending him out to read for bartender roles on someone else's sitcom. So he fired them. He fired his managers and also fired his agent at William Morris.

Now a free agent, Bill headed to Austin to do some shows that would from the basis of his next record, *Arizona Bay*.

Bill had been shopping for new management, but still hadn't made any formal decisions about it. He was leaning more and more heavily on clubowner Colleen McGarr and her business partner Duncan Strauss. According to Casperson, Bill had previously brought her into the Invasion offices and said he wanted them to represent him while Colleen would do anything to help.

Bill was in New York appearing at Caroline's when Casperson approached him and told him he needed to stop waffling about who would handle his career. Invasion had kept UK offices open longer than they would have normally just to support Bill, but despite Bill's growing popularity, the revenues from record sales weren't commensurate.

Simply so other people could make decisions, Bill needed to make a decision. Well before the string of shows at Caroline's, Bill had given a copy of *Arizona Bay* to Invasion. They told Bill they didn't think it was finished and weren't going to put it out. He was done with them as a record company, and that probably didn't help Casperson and Saporta in their desires to manage Bill. After that night at Caroline's, Bill hopped on a plane for Australia. Invasion was out of the picture, and Bill hardly had contact with them again. He was a client of Strauss McGarr.

"If you read Colleen's take on it, she ran the whole thing for ever," says Casperson. "She seemed like a club owner who was madly in love with Bill. That was my impression. And he loved that. He had many women in my office that were madly in love with him, who would basically do anything for him. They would drop everything and run across town to bring him a sandwich. They were Bill freaks. He definitely was a Pied Piper and everyone who got him, got him.

"We had issues creatively, where we didn't always agree. There were people that were 100 per cent Bill and there were people that were less than that. I would say he didn't seem like the kind of guy that wanted yes-men except for that he had them. And I think Colleen was the same thing, and we weren't."

Bill was opening his shows at this time with a bit about how that night would be his last performance because he was getting out of stand-up. "The fact of the matter is, the reason I'm going to quit performing is that I finally got my own TV show coming out next fall on CBS," he started.

"It's a half-hour weekly show that I will host entitled, *Let's Hunt and Kill Billy Ray Cyrus*. So y'all be tuning in? Cool.

"It's a fairly self-explanatory plot. Each week we let the hounds of Hell loose and we chase that jarhead, no-talent, cracker asshole all over the globe, until I finally catch that fruity little ponytail of his in the back, pull him to his knees, put a shotgun in his mouth like a big black cock of death . . ."

[Bill makes the sound of a shotgun.]

"And we'll be back in '95 with *Let's Hunt and Kill Michael Bolton*."

Curiously, Cyrus and Hicks practically passed each other coming out of and going into the country respectively as, the day after Hicks arrived in Australia, Cyrus was finishing up a press tour down under.

The Melbourne Comedy Festival had Bill booked for three weeks in April. Bill was spending unusual amounts of time lying prostrate in his hotel room. He was feeling alone and "weird." Bill thought the pain in his abdomen might have been from the Chinese food he was eating or that he had maybe picked up a tropical parasite. Not likely; he had complained in LA about the same pain weeks before. It was something he felt acutely during yoga, and thought he might have pulled something. Friends told him to see a doctor, Bill was hoping that it would clear itself up.

When Bill was in Australia, his medical insurance lapsed.

[*   *   *]

Kevin Booth

The whole time we were working on *Arizona Bay*, Bill kept complaining about a pain. But we ate so much ridiculous food during that time that I never gave it much thought. Anybody who hung out with Bill knew he was on a relentless tour of restaurants. After eating major Mexican food for lunch, he'd want to go have super-spicy Korean food for dinner. "Kevvy. El Azteca? Number 5? El Azteca? Kevvy?"

It got to be absurd. "Ugh. C'mon, Bill. We ate there for lunch yesterday." When Bill was in town to work on *Arizona Bay*, we must have eaten at El Azteca, this Mexican food place on the East Side of Austin, at least five times a week. Six more likely.

The way we were eating, I never would have thought it was anything but the same kind of pain I'm sure I was having every now and then. Plus, he was just so into the work, so focused on doing this record, it had rubbed off on me; and I just didn't give much thought to things that weren't about getting shit done. I made occasional suggestions that he go see my doctor, but he waved them off. By the time he was finally diagnosed in the summer of 1993 doctors gave him about three months to live.

We had been talking about *Arizona Bay* for a good five or six months before we ever stepped into the studio. Bill's original idea was to do a rock opera about Jack Kevorkian, the notorious euthanasia doctor who had single-handedly caused a minor constitutional crisis in the United States by assisting a few terminally ill patients in moving on to the next world, or out of this one, anyway.

At the time Kevorkian had been in the news pretty regularly; and Bill wanted to expand on his bit from *Relentless* about using terminally ill patients for stunts in movies. "Do you want your grandmother dying like a little bird in some hospital room . . . Or do you want her to meet Chuck Norris?" Gereuthanasia and comedy were a perfect fit for Bill. Plus, he simply had an obsession with death.

The idea, though, was to make a different kind of comedy album. Jokes don't always wear well. After so many listens, they just stop being funny. You know the punchline, you know the timing. Music is a more fecund matter. Melodies can give birth to emotions over and over again; or in the case of just huge fucking guitar riffs, 10,000 listens later "Whole Lotta Love" still sounds feral and raw. Bill wanted to marry the comedy and the music, so you had the kind of comedy record that you could listen to over and over again. When we finally got to work, the plan was to make a music record first – just a normal album – then Bill was going to stand in the studio and perform comedy right over that music.

About the only thing I recall from the first recordings was one song where Bill was repeating this lyric along the lines of "Red-eyed predator," which was a not-so-subtle metaphor for Los Angeles. Bill's hatred of Los Angeles fueled the whole project. Whenever Bill performed in LA, the clubs weren't packed. It just wasn't his place. He had plenty of friends there; and he had a good time when he was out there, obviously. It was more about what LA stood for – this factory of banality, pumping out all of this crap, which he saw as basically responsible for the world falling into a type of chaos. Los Angeles was the anus of all the shit being pumped out into the world.

On numerous occasions Bill would retreat to Sedona by himself to meditate and do mushrooms (and wait for UFOs). It was spiritually cleansing for him. So while the imagery on *Arizona Bay* is that this festering sore gets cauterized off the planet and we are left with the idyllic spot, Arizona as a place in the real world had a special place in Bill's heart. Moreover, Bill wanted to connote the notion that Arizona Bay is a state of mind – a peaceful place that could be.

We started work on the album in Austin in the fall of 1992. We kind of barricaded ourselves into the studio at my house; Bill played guitar and I did everything else – producer, engineer, drummer, technician. At that point it was still more or less a rock opera. We laid down some tracks, then Bill started going over it – doing some of the

309

comedy routines that he wanted on the record, and just talking about LA spilling into the Pacific.

When we finally had something that was anything, it was painful.

We listened to it and played it for other people and quickly realized that, as fun as it was for us to make and as much as we loved the idea, it just wasn't going to fly. It wasn't going to be anything that anyone would want to listen to.

I felt we had failed. We were close, but we ultimately failed. Bill was far more optimistic. He thought everything was great. Musically, though, things still weren't quite right. As much as the original aim was to make a rock opera, Bill really wanted to play this kind of light jazz, such that the music we were writing ended up having more of a Pat Metheny feel to it than anything you'd call rock 'n' roll.

From a music appreciation standpoint, it's like the cancer was already accelerating Bill's life. In a short span of time he went from liking the kind of music that a 30-year-old would like, to liking the kind of music a 50-year-old would like. So jazz, or some reasonable facsimile thereof, it was.

Bill had become my own personal slavedriver. All during the making of *Arizona Bay*, friends would be calling – and these weren't wannabe friends, or even friends of friends, but these were true friends of Bill – and they would call saying, "Hey, I hear Bill is going to be in town." I had told some people, "Yeah, he'll be here on Monday. Come on by."

Monday comes. They show up. Bill gets furious about it. He didn't want visitors. He didn't want interruptions. He wanted to work on the album. It was the first time Bill told me to lie to people about him coming to town. And I did. For him.

After Bill went sober, he was a man on a mission. He had wasted so much time drinking and drugging, and a lot of that time was in Austin. You make these drinking buddies that don't go away. You may have gone sober, but they still want to hang out. You can't always do that.

As long as I knew Bill he had weird habits and obsession patterns. For example, he loved to change his guitar strings, and he did it with

310

Left Bill heads out to do a set, New York, 1999.

Below Bill's 24 hour chip from AA.

ONE DAY

AT A TIME

Above Bill drunk watching *Dangerfield,* just before he stopped drinking.

Above Bill at the beach on the Gulf Coast south of Houston, 1989.

Left Bill nurses a swollen knee, 1989.

Above Bob Reilly, Bill Hicks, Pamela K. Johnson.

Right Bill before the Adult Video Awards in Las Vegas.

Above left Stopped by state troopers while trying to enter the Waco compound.

Above right Bill and the plastic dinosaur taken on the tour of Waco.

Left Kevin and Bill recording before the massacre took place.

Below Using Bradley tanks, the Davidian compound, packed with women and children, is burnt to the ground by the FBI and BTAF, 1993.

Above Bill with UK fans, 1992.

Left Bill out and about in London, 1992.

Left Bill sits on ladder posing for picture.

Above Bill's pilot for *Counts of the Netherworld*. Fallon in the background.

Comedian is ill

Bill Hicks, the outspoken comedian, is very ill with pancreatic cancer. For several weeks, the 32-year-old Hicks has been resting at his parents' home in Little Rock, Ark.

A member of Houston's "outlaw comic" gang, Hicks drew a devout Austin following over the past decade. He is even more popular in Great Britain, where he made frequent appearances on *London Underground*, the cable comedy show.

In November, Hicks was the subject of a long, flattering piece in *The New Yorker* by theater critic John Lahr. Earlier, the censorship of his routine on *Late Show With David Letterman* made national news. In a recent, taped performance at Austin's Laff Stop, he skewered widespread American hypocrisy regarding music, drugs, religion and sexuality.

He's perhaps best known locally for his work with Austinite Kevin Booth in the hourlong video *Ninja Bachelor Party*, which continues

Bill Hicks made news when his routine was censored on *Late Show With David Letterman.*

to enjoy brisk rentals. Hicks recently received his third consecutive nomination for the American Comedy Awards, to be held March 6.

Top right and left Bill's final Austin performance, recorded for *Rant in E Minor*, October 1993.

Left Article announcing Bill's diagnosis.

Below Bill backstage at his final Austin performance, October 1993.

Picture taken by Chris Saunders whilst Bill was in the UK, 1992.

Left Bill Hick's grave marker.

tribute to
BILL HICKS

Cap City Comedy Club
Feb 26th

Commemorating 10 years since Bill left our planet
Hicks impersonation contest, rare video screening
& special guests

All proceeds to benefit the
Bill Hicks Foundation for Wildlife

for more information
sacredcow.com

Above One of the many tributes in Bill's name organised by Sacred Cow. On the 10th anniversary of Bill's death there were over 20 tributes simultaneously taking place across the US, Canada, Australia and the UK.

unusual frequency, even for a guitarist. On top of that, he had a real thing about people playing his guitars. It was a chemistry thing, and a lot of it had to do with feel. You put on a new set of stings, and the way they twang and snap under your fingers, God, it makes playing feel effortless. Then you let someone else play it. You pick it back up and now the strings have this dead, gross feeling to them.

Changing strings was his being anal about something more or less inconsequential. *Arizona Bay*, however, was the first time Bill ever became anal about something that had a little more artistic weight to it, specifically, the actual production itself. Before, Bill always had the, "Aw, fuck it. It's good enough" attitude. When we did Marble Head Johnson, when we did *Relentless*, when we worked on *Ninja Bachelor Party*, I'd always play things back and think, "That one note is a little off." And Bill wouldn't think it was worth sweating over, "Dude, it's rock 'n' roll." Mistakes were not just an inevitability, they were an essential part of the final outcome.

But not for *Arizona Bay*. We would do take after take after take; and we would spend days on just one little piece of music. Every note had to be right. Every tone had to be right. Every vocal inflection had to be right. Playing jazz music, I was a fish out of water. The whole time I'm telling Bill, "I'm not a good enough drummer to pull this off." But give Bill credit as the optimist, he would keep telling me, "No, stick in there. It's gonna be great. It's gonna be great."

We'd work straight from ten in the a.m. until about six at night, go have dinner for an hour or two, then come back and work until around 11 p.m. Like I said, dinner was usually something unnecessarily spicy; it was also something that usually involved just me and Bill. One of the rarest exceptions proving both of those rules was the night we went to eat at the City Grille, a seafood and steak place in downtown Austin, and Bill brought this girl Davine along with us.

Bill was something of a star at this point. He was a bona fine star in Britain, but even in the US he had had the HBO Specials and done Letterman a number of times. So people knew who he was. Some people, anyway. Bill started to take advantage of it. And he used it in a manner consistent with why many people crave stardom in the first place – to have sex with girls without exerting much effort.

Davine, to me, was the Waffle House waitress – the girl from Bill's "Whatcha readin' for?" bit. Very Brett Butler. Very Southern white trash. But still sort of attractive. I just remember that dinner being uncomfortable for me. The subtext of the entire meal was Bill saying, "Kevin, this girl is here because she and I are going to go have sex later."

Bill was using his power with women in ways that I wasn't at all comfortable with. Other times he did it in ways that not only didn't make me proud of my friend but also made my life straight up miserable. There was another girl, who was the girlfriend of Kevin Pearson, who was the new drummer in my band, what was loosely being referred to as the New Year Zero. And Pearson already had jealousy issues with her.

Moreover, Pearson and Bill didn't care much for each other. Of course I was the intermediary through which that lack of kinship flowed. Bill didn't like this guy for a couple of reasons. First, Pearson had come on board with this singer Mike Moyer – and Moyer replaced a guy Bill went to high school with and really liked. On top of that, Bill had it in for them because I was playing with them in a band, and Bill also had jealousy issues. Finally, Bill didn't like Pearson (and Moyer for that matter) because, well, they didn't like him.

I was partially responsible for that. I would play them the music Bill and I were doing together. Their reaction was uniformly and categorically, "Dude, that's horrible." The music was bad. The guitar playing was lame. Bill can't sing. The lyrics are insufferable. Any criticism you can think of, they leveled at it. I remember Mike Moyer made this comment that comedians just don't crossover and said, "Bill needs to decide whether he wants to be a comic or a musician."

I told Bill, "You know what Mike said about you?"

Bill would obsess about critiques like that. He came back and told me he had written this song called "Crossover Rule." In the song Bill just rifled the attitude that people had – especially the people in the entertainment industry – that you could only do one thing. You were either a comedian, or a painter, or an accountant, or a shepherd, or you worked in a box factory, or whatever. But God forbids you be a shepherd that also paints. So "Crossover Rule" was Bill's way of saying "fuck you" to people who want to put him or anyone into a bounded, well-defined category of skills.

Anyway, Bill went after this girl mainly to show me that the balance of power was tipped in his favor. He simply had more power than my other friends and the other people I chose to work with. He never wanted me to idolize him or put him on a pedestal, but it pissed him off whenever I put other people as a priority over him, particularly when it came to doing things like music. Whenever Bill came to town and wanted to work, I had to cancel any other plans I had to work with any other people. I would juggle everybody else around to be available for Bill, even if it caused problems. And it did.

There was one night Bill was hanging out with this girl – really parading her around, and she was happy to be the parade float. She wanted to be seen with him and wanted everyone to know she was fucking Bill, just so it would get back to her boyfriend. At the same time, I'm playing in a band with her boyfriend, and working with Bill, and there is no way it's not getting back to this guy. I don't think she was a girl Bill was really even attracted to, and certainly wouldn't have pursued. He did it to exercise his new-found power, and prove to me he had it. "I know you think your friends who are playing the Back Room are cool and all, but their girlfriends just watched me on HBO; and later tonight one of them is going to fuck me." It wasn't humanity at its best.

Fortunately, it failed to blow up the way it probably should have.

Some time in early to mid-December of 1992, after about ten solid days in the studio of playing parts over and over, we wrapped *Arizona Bay* take 2. A few days later, I was driving to Houston with Jere and playing some of it for her in the car. She just rolled her eyes.

She always had been a real unsympathetic critic of everything I had ever done, but she really didn't like this. I was still insisting, "No. It's good. It's good."

Then I played some for my brother, and he wasn't crazy about Bill's voice or his lyrics. He thought they were kind of stupid. Bill even played some of it for his record label, Invasion, and they were none too thrilled with it. They thought it was cool he was doing stuff with his friends, but they weren't interested in Bill Hicks the musician at all.

I was managing to stay defiant, taking the attitude, "Oh, you're just jealous because I am doing this thing." And the people I played it for had their own agendas. I thought anyway.

On New Year's Eve, Bill performed at the Laff Stop in Austin. Our original intent was just to record the crowd sounds for later use. But we were back to square one. If that. We still had the idea that we were going to fuse comedy and music, but we didn't even know what form that would take, so we weren't sure how to even attack the problem at this point.

They turned out to be really great shows. They were the catalyst that helped us realize the comedy was going to have to be the meter. In rock 'n' roll, or just about any kind of music for that matter, you have to pick the foundation that everything else will be built on. Almost universally that turns out to be the drums and the bass. So we finally figured out that the comedy had to be our "drum track." We just turned the basic structure on its head. We had been wanting to lay down the music then put the comedy over that. But it obviously wasn't working. There is sort of a "duh" quality to it now, but maybe we had to fail several times the other way before we could admit to ourselves what we probably knew in the first place.

After the turn of the New Year, we had a much better handle on what we were doing. Things were going well in the studio; we were making real progress. Things also started happening outside the studio. Bill had been having discussions with Robert DeNiro's production company,

Tribeca, about several ideas, one of which was a script idea called *Public Access* that Bill and I had been kicking around. Another project they were discussing was *Counts of the Netherworld*, which was already on a development track in England.

When DeNiro heard that Bill was making a music/comedy record, he wanted to hear it, and expressed interest in possibly distributing it. I went nuts. DeNiro was going to listen to *Arizona Bay*? So what do I do? I go out and buy a whole new mixing console. It was part-overreaction, part-rationalization. I had wanted to buy a new mixing console anyway, but, shit, Robert DeNiro.

Bill continued going back and forth between Austin and LA, which was just his base of operations. Once there, he would maybe go to San Francisco to do a gig, or maybe fly to Phoenix and do a gig, or stay in LA and do a couple of nights at a college. The joke was that he couldn't even take care of a plastic plant. It wasn't really a joke, though. He had one plastic plant in his apartment and even that melted.

The other thing that happened around this time, besides DeNiro, was that the Bureau of Alcohol, Tobacco and Fireamrs (the ATF) decided to pay a visit to a small group of folks outside Waco, Texas.

Bill and I had been news junkies since the first Gulf War. We were either watching it, or talking on the phone about what we had just watched on CNN. When Waco happened in February, it was everything we could ever want out of a news story: a cult figure, the frustrated guitar player, an armed confrontation between the law and normal citizens, black helicopters, a siege. And it was right in our own backyard (Waco sits about ninety miles north of Austin). We had to go.

Bill actually changed his travel plans to get back to Austin earlier than he had originally scheduled. We talked and talked about it and he wanted to know, "You really want to go through with this?" Yes, I did. And I knew he did, too. So we tried to figure out how close, physically, would we be able to get to the Branch Davidian compound. I started calling news stations around Waco to find out. Bill flew in. We rented a car and drove up. It was Day 7 of the fifty-one day siege.

Our friends were telling us. "You're crazy. You're gonna get shot," which was just ridiculous. I had to remind them it was a standoff. There were no bullets flying. Plus, there were thousands of news people everywhere. I guess my friends thought we were going into some kind of a war zone. At the time I was thinking, "I hope we get shot at. At least then it will be interesting."

We drove up to Waco and, of course, it was a comedy of errors. It took us for ever just to find the compound. Then when we finally found the main entrance road in, it was blocked. The law enforcement officer blocking the road asked us if we were with the media. We told him no. He informed us that we needed to turn around and go home. We had absolutely no intention of doing that. The FBI had staked out a mile-long stretch of road in front of the Branch Davidian compound and they blocked the road at either end of that stretch. But this is East Texas. We knew there had to be a number of rural roads crisscrossing the area, and one of them had to feed into that road some place between the two points the Feds had blocked off. It was only a matter of time. Finding that access point didn't worry me nearly as much as surviving the search. Driving with Bill was like being held hostage. And he drove the piece of shit rental we had like he was trying to beat the competition to Dakar.

Of course, when we did finally find a tiny farm road that hooked up with the road into the compound, that's also when I realized I had an Austin Access producer's card. It was an Archimedes moment: "Hey, that's Press." So we went back and used that, and they let us right in.

Once we got near the compound, we pulled up to the row where all of the other media members were set up. They had trucks with satellite dishes, small armies of cameramen, summer-league softball teams-worth of reporters. We had a camcorder and an inflatable dinosaur. Bill bought an inflatable dinosaur in homage to his "Dinosaurs in the Bible" bit on *Arizona Bay*. He inflated the thing and went running around acting like a nut. Everyone wanted to know, "What's the deal with the dinosaur?" We'd tell them that it was a long story. Still, we were supposed to be press and, in addition to Bill running around with a large piece of plastic, we had set up our camera. A rather dinky-by-comparison Hi8 camcorder. People would take one look at us, and the expression on their face was, "Who are you with? And why are you here?"

"Uh . . . we're the retard network." That probably answered both questions.

The rest of the adventure consisted of Bill wandering around, talking to news and anchor people. It was relatively uneventful. At the end of the day, we took down our "gear" and "loaded up." We headed out to leave through the main entrance – the one where we had first tried to get in through – and the officer who had first turned us away recognized us. Suddenly we're telling him, "No, really. We are with the press." And he's just looking at us with this expression: "Yeah, right."

On the way back to Austin, Bill played me a tape of Denis Leary. It wasn't a fun listen. Bill had handed Leary a tape of Marble Head Johnson during the previous year. So when Bill heard Leary's *No Cure for Cancer* he was more than a little peeved. The album opened with a song called "Asshole," which was about what an asshole Leary was. Leary meant it in a tough-guy, John-Wayne-cool, do-what-the-fuck-I-want kind of way. Bill thought Leary was just a plain old garden variety asshole.

Many people had noticed the, uh, similarities between some of Bill's bits and some of Leary's. The latter had almost pilfered from the former verbatim. But theft was nothing new in comedy. It was part of the gig. Even Bill's friends (okay, Wilks) had, well, borrowed from him. Now, Leary's doing a song that really pissed Bill off. Really. Leary had taken shameless rip-off to a new low. Bill didn't own the idea of doing music, or even the idea of doing music and making something comedic with it, but clearly there was no idea Bill hadn't had first which Leary wouldn't co-opt as his own. Shameless.

317

When we got back to Austin we had dinner at Landry's. On the way there we ate barbecue, and when we got home we had crawfish. That's why I never thought the pain in his side that Bill often complained about was anything but a result of diet. Who says, "Hey, let's have some barbecue ribs, then go eat a bucket of crawfish." It was just ridiculous.

As tame as the trip was, the whole Waco fiasco ended up being a pivotal event in Bill's life. At the time of the siege we had no idea what was really happening. But no matter what you thought of David Koresh, you had to think something was just wrong about how this was being handled. There had to be a million other ways to get him. That was a house full of women and children, not to mention adult males who hadn't been found to be guilty of anything. The ATF agents endangered everyone, just to get a man they could have picked up walking in the streets of Waco. It didn't make any sense.

I remember shooting Bill with the compound far off in the background and he said to the camera, "There is a new breed of Christianity here in America, one that suffers no quarter, one thing's for sure when Dave makes his final move for the Lord there is going to be hell to pay all around."

Not long after the standoff ended, some rather curious video footage popped up on Austin Access television. I think the video was originally put out by the John Birch Society. Someone local had picked it up and was showing it. I never saw it anywhere else. It was a tape of one of the tanks – a government vehicle – shooting into the Branch Davidian compound. I happened to catch it one night and I taped it.

I showed it to Bill; and I think that was a seminal moment for him. Come to think of it, that video took him from just making the Kennedy assassination jokes, and "boy, our government sure is bad," to where he was on *Rant in E Minor* with the disposition: "'You better do what we want, or we'll fucking burn your house to the ground. You are free to do as we tell you.'" A lot of the bitter attitude towards the government came from watching that video. He saw that the government, from the career bureaucrats all the way up to the Commander-in-Chief, was lying to everyone's face, and it wasn't "Read my lips. No new taxes," type of lies. This was: "We will kill you, lie about doing it, and get away with it. Have a nice day."

Bill would actually play that Waco footage at shows. If the club had a projector or even a TV cart and a VCR, he would play it and tell the audience, "Do you see that? You are being lied to. Right there. There are flames coming out of that tank." We had got to watch the whole thing unfold before our eyes.

After Waco we went back to work. Again, it was hour after hour holed up in the studio. Cutting tracks. Recutting tracks. Re-recutting tracks. At least we knew what we were doing. We knew what the end product would sound like. It was just a matter of how long until we got there. Bill went back and forth from LA to Austin a couple more times, but when he was in Austin we were either in the studio or in a restaurant. The siege in Waco was still going on, and much like the Davidians we were holed up in our compound as well. Only ours was by choice and we were free to go eat at El Azteca. Still, it was an obscene amount of time in close quarters with just him and me. It's almost amazing in retrospect how relatively friction-free the whole experience was.

I do remember one instance where we were almost finished with the recording and Bill was pointing a gun, unloaded and more importantly fake, in my face and he said sarcastically, "I don't think we got too much cabin fever at all." Then he turned the gun on himself, pointed it at his own head, pulled the trigger and made a blast sound. I actually captured that moment on video. Bill is just out of the frame.

We wrapped at the end of March. All throughout recording Bill had promised me that when we finished, he would take me anywhere in the world I wanted to go. Even though he was saying it facetiously, I knew that if I turned to him and said, "Bill, take me to Bali," he would have done it.

But we never went to Bali. I never would have taken advantage of my friend's material success. Instead, we went to Kenny Rogers Roasters. Seriously. The *Arizona Bay* wrap party consisted of Bill and me eating chicken. I think it was the only place we could eat that allowed us to indulge in both irony and sincerity at the same time. Sincerity because it was really good chicken. Most people I know have never eaten there, but it is absolutely fucking delicious. Of course the reason they've never eaten there is because it's got Kenny's name on the place. Musically, the guy represents all that is wrong with popular music, and, perhaps more importantly, he's just kind of a cheeseball. Bill made endless fun of Kenny Rogers. So there was something kitschy about the experience. It wasn't true irony, but Bill was putting money into the pocket of the very type of person he thought to be part of the problem.

For all the mediocrity Kenny Rogers put out into the world for people to consume, he still had something on Bill. I remember at the restaurant there was a replica of one of Rogers' gold records hanging on the wall. I don't think Bill knew I saw him looking at it, but there was envy in his eye. Someone as insipid as Kenny Rogers had something Bill wanted. And it wasn't a chicken recipe. When I asked Bill what he was doing, he made some joke to disparage Rogers, but the expression on his face belied his derision.

That Kenny Rogers Roasters is gone. Bill is gone, too, but Arizona Bay exists, both as a record and as a place that might be.

[*   *   *]

Steven Doster

I first saw Bill at the Comedy Workshop in Austin, the original one. He came out on stage and said, "Good evening ladies and gentleman, my name is William Melvin Hicks . . . Thanks dad." Right from the beginning this guy had it.

I was playing gigs almost every night, but the shows at the Workshop were earlier. They were usually around eight and I wouldn't go on until around 10:30 p.m. So I went back to see Bill the very next night, and I remember the first time I spoke to him he went, "Dude, weren't you here last night?" I said, "Yeah, I came back to see you." He said "Get a life. Why would you want to come back and see me twice?"

I got to know Bill better after I moved in with Johnny Torrez. He was an emcee at the club, and became known locally as the Commissioner of Comedy. We got a call late one night. I answer the phone and the guy on the other end goes: "Who is this?" and I say, "Hey, man, who is this? You're calling me in the middle of the night." "It's Bill Hicks. Is Johnny there." I said no and told him it was me.

I quickly found out what an incredible phone talker Bill was. He would get you on the line and it was difficult to get off because it was so interesting, but I should have known it was an omen. He talked and talked, mainly about girls that first conversation, for over an hour. Both of us were talking about our first loves. He talked about Laurie. That was how I got in with Bill.

He soon started calling me on purpose. This was in the days before talk-as-long-as-you-want cheap long-distance. So, I'd go, "Bill, tell me you called me, please." He'd say, "Yeah, I called you, Steven. So anyway . . . "

For the next few years, he would come into town and give me a ring to let me know he was here. I'd go to his show, then he'd come to mine. I usually had a gig, a lot of times at Steamboat. Some of the shows were with the Austin All Stars, some were with my band. The

All Stars was a regular Sunday night gig. We would play a lot of covers. The most fun times were with the All Stars because we would have people come up on stage and play with us, and Bill would come up on stage.

As much as anything. Bill and I would talk a lot about music. I was pretty surprised when I first met him, I couldn't believe a lot of the things he hadn't heard or listened to, although he was barely 20 years old. His interest in music was really fast guitar playing. I was surprised at the people he hadn't heard of. I turned him on to Bob Dylan. I remember very distinctly one time he came over to the house, I made him sit down and listen to what I thought was a really profound piece of music: "It's Alright Ma (I'm Only Bleeding)" (Dylan from *Bringing It All Back Home*).

It's a very long song, and there were other people sleeping at the time, so I made him wear headphones. I sat there just watching him. So, after listening, he shrugs his shoulders and says, "I really don't get it. It's a couple of chords." I said, "What do you mean, Bill? Didn't you listen to the words?" He said, "No, I don't listen to the words." And I thought, "Oh my Lord."

A year or two later he comes back and he's got everything Dylan had ever done, and he starts to play me the same song, as if I hadn't heard it. I asked him if he remembered the time I played it for him. He said, "Yeah, I do. Please, don't tell me what I said." It actually ended up in one of his bits: "Dylan . . . G to C. G to C. Do you people realize he has lyrics?"

Bill would confide in me a lot when it came to music. He would tell me Kevin wanted to do this and he wanted to do that. My feeling was always that music was the one area where Kevin had equal ground. If it was comedy, Bill Hicks had the final authority. But a number of Bill's other friends had artistic talents, and sometimes they had expertise that exceeded Bill's.

It would piss him off a lot. I remember when he played me the first version of *Arizona Bay*. The music was going on all the time. It just really killed things in my eyes. Bill wasn't one to welcome criticism from people, either. But I remember talking to him about that and telling him he should do them separately, the music and the comedy. The new-agey type music, which is what it was, really drained the comedy of its weight, its profundity.

I think on a musical level, it was a lot better than anything he had done before. He really just played terribly when I first met him, but there was still a better way to get to where he wanted.

As a comedian, Bill was really unbelievable then, when he was 20. He didn't drink, then of course within a year or so he started drinking. And for about four or five years he drank excessively. It was kind of fun at first, then after a while it was anything but, especially to people around him. To begin with, he was really funny all the time. It didn't matter how much he drank. But I don't think he could have written the stuff he did when he was young. He wasn't insightful about people, about human nature, but he got out in the world. He was ready to take it all in.

Eventually it just went over any kind of edge you'd want to stand on. He had got into a fight in Houston where a guy broke his leg. I remember calling him at the hospital. Like a macho big brother I ask, "Do you need me to take care of this guy? Let's fuck this guy if he broke your leg. We break his leg." "No Steven, I pretty much had it coming."

There's also a tape of one episode we lovingly called the "Fuck Your Lord" show. He's doing the bit about fundamentalist Christians trying to determine the age of the earth by counting back books of the Bible. A woman in the audience yells to him that he can't talk about her Lord like that. And Bill, immediately and with great conviction and force in his voice, snaps back at her: "Fuck your Lord and fuck all of your quaint superstitions." Then he launched into the material about how he had cut out the middle man. He spoke directly to God.

I always thought Bill was very Jesus-like. Jesus at his most angry.

If he had only lived another year. Jesus made it to 33, right? I don't want you to think I saw him in some light, other than what he was: he was just a regular human being. I always thought he was a good guy, but he was far from perfect.

On the other hand, Bill was always very generous to his friends. Not in monetary ways, but in giving you his time. It's remarkable because he was such a hard cat to pin down. I have a picture in my head of him being continually in an airport. He didn't ever really stop. At one point we even talked about him taking some time to do normal things. I asked him about that and he said, "Yeah, I want to try to do some other things. I've just been touring non-stop my entire life as an adult." In reality I don't think he ever did any of that.

Steve did tell me one time that he'd got a call from Bill: "You'll never believe where I am." "Where are you?" "I'm on the beach man, I'm sitting on the beach and reading a book . . ." Bill had never been a beach person, or even an outdoors person. He had a joke about how the beach was just where water met dirt. He had a bathtub and an imagination, so he didn't need to go to the beach. This was after he was diagnosed, so I think his spending time on the beach had something to do with his being with Colleen and his treatment. But I'm sure that was one of the things that hit him the most by the end – that he never got to take any time to lead a normal life. It never stopped him from keeping close to his friends, though.

About a year before Bill died, we had a really interesting talk. The last five years of his life, when he wasn't drinking or doing drugs, eating became big on the priority list. He was in town and called and came over. We went to have lunch at an Indian restaurant on South Lamar. It was a very moving luncheon. He had written a poem – one that no one has been able to find since – something that he was thinking about using for *Arizona Bay*. It was about LA, and it was humorous but also very impassioned and angry about what he had seen there. Bill, I don't think he could even fathom why anyone would sell out their integrity or not do everything they possibly could to live their life on the highest moral ground. He couldn't understand how anyone could make music for purely commercial reasons.

He read out this poem. It was very moving. I remember coming home and my wife asking how it went; and I said to her that the guy has so much integrity and fire, where does he go from here? But I also remember him having trouble with his side, grabbing his side. "Are you okay, man." "Yeah, I'm all right. I'm okay." But I feel like he took me there to talk to him. We talked about things that were important.

He said to me, "I understand why you stayed in Austin and had a family. That's a beautiful thing. I never got to do anything like that." "Yeah, it is a wonderful thing," I replied. "I might not travel as much or have the same ambition as when I was younger but it's really special."

"I do what I do so people won't feel alone," he said. He realized he was a voice for a lot of people. It hit me heavy when he said that. I'd like to think that people like Bill or Jimi Hendrix have this purpose, but they come in and they flame out so fast. We're all on this road to enlightenment, but Bill was speeding down that road. He was at the speed of light.

"What we are on is an Art War. You're either on the side of telling the truth and trying to make the world a better place. Or you are on the side of selling garbage to people." All of us, no matter how successful, or no matter how people view success, if you don't have your integrity, what do you have?

Saying he didn't want people to feel alone, he meant it. He didn't want people to feel they were the only one thinking the way they did because they were never going to hear things on television that reflected their mores. "I believe most people think the way we do, or the way I do," he said. "And I just don't believe you hear that point of view." He was more right than wrong. When he went on TV, they wouldn't let him say anything.

For example, I think he kept pushing to get the strongest stuff on *Letterman* that he could. He did know what was funny. And he knew

325

if he went out there with unfunny material he was going to be in trouble, so he fought like the devil to get as much stuff through as he could. But it wasn't just the jokes. There was a message he wanted to get through. He was ambitious. There's nothing wrong with that and I don't think he thought being successful was selling out.

But he had problems with *Letterman*. There was the episode where they cut parts of his jokes out of the show. Right in the middle it just went haywire.

Then there was the time, his last appearance, where his entire set got cut from the show. I bet in some way it was kind of liberating to get tossed off the *Letterman* show completely. Bill kept saying that they were just jokes. But they weren't just jokes.

Kevin did everything but tell me Bill wasn't going to be around much longer. I didn't know about the cancer. I hadn't seen him in a few months. The last time he was in town he was on Access and looked pretty haggard. I just didn't put two and two together. Still, he looked pretty damn good for a guy that was about to die.

I called the hotel, called Bill, and he's going through chemo and is under medication, so he had to be suffering, but he was very sweet. He just told me he was trying to get a nap before the show. I told him that I couldn't make it out. Babysitter, etc. And he said, "That's okay. Just make sure Kevin gets you a tape. It should be a good show tonight, but I understand."

He let me off the hook, but I obviously regret not being there.

[*   *   *]

Susannah Bianchi

Susannah Bianchi was a comedienne living in New York in the early 1990s when she met Bill Hicks. The two had a brief but intense relationship between October 1992 and April 1993 in the period just prior to Bill's being diagnosed with pancreatic cancer. This is the first time she has ever spoken about her relationship with Hicks.

It was very clear to me that Bill never wanted me to know he was sick because he left me very abruptly and I never knew why. I thought it was because he met somebody and didn't have enough nerve to tell me. I spent the eight months before I heard he was sick hating him to such a degree I can't even tell you.

I met him a year and a half before he died, give or take a month. It was October. I met him because, I was doing stand-up at the time – I don't do it any more – but all I heard about was the great Bill Hicks. And I wasn't ever one to go to clubs at night unless I was performing because it was too much to go to a club on your night off. But friends of mine who worked at NBC were going to see the great Bill Hicks at Caroline's. And they kept bugging me to go.

I couldn't get over him. I can't even tell you what it was like to see him for the first time. I hadn't ever heard him or seen him on TV, I just knew the name. But I had brought him something that I left with the bartender to give him. I had brought him a gift. I wanted to bring him something as one comic to another – just another weird thing I did – even though I had never met him.

There was a fellow there I hadn't seen in a long time, who was actually courting him as a manager, Steven Saporta. I hadn't seen Steven in – I can't tell you how long – but after the show Steven said to me – and I thought this was amazing – "Do you want to go back and meet Bill?"

I said, "Sure," and that was it. It was like thunder on both ends. I don't say it because I am making that up and want people to think it was this great thing, that is just how it was. It was sexual right away, like when you meet someone who changes things for you in an instant. Not just on my part, but for him too. That's why it was always so odd for me when he suddenly disappeared. I didn't understand what happened.

It was on a Thursday night. I remember it well because I saw him on Friday. He called me up and asked me if I wanted to have tea or something. The thing about him was that he was so well-mannered. You can throw in all of that other stuff about him – the toughness, the arrogance, the opinionated personality – but he was still probably the most well-mannered man I ever met. He was from Texas, and he just had that way about him, that southern gentleman. He would never let me meet him anywhere, he insisted on picking me up. Even if we were going to where he was, he would always come to get me. I never knew a man that did that. I think it was because – I'm told – Texans are that way. I never knew one before.

The romance started right away. It became this thing. Bigger than I ever could have imagined. You meet somebody and you like them and you are attracted to them and you go out and you think, "Well . . ." but you have no idea what it is going to be like. It became this big thing right away. I saw him at Caroline's again on Sunday. We hung out and I stayed with him.

Then he went to London for a month. We wrote letters, a lot of calls. It was very romantic. I remember him in a very romantic way because it never had a chance to be anything else. It was romantic, then it ended.

When he was getting back from London, I went to meet him in Florida. He sent me a copy of his favorite book, *Confederacy of Dunces*. He sent it to me when he sent me my plane tickets. He would always pay for me. He didn't talk to me for three days when I offered to pay my plane fare, because I didn't expect him to pay for me.

But he sent me my plane tickets and a copy of that book because he felt so bad that I had to switch planes to go to Florida. There was no direct flight. I still have the copy he sent me.

So I was with him in Florida before Christmas in the year I met him, which I guess was 1992. It was a week after his birthday. He was playing at the club down there. Colleen was running it. And there was a condo next door where they would put up comics. We stayed there and had a great time: fooling around, renting movies, going to lunch. I'd go to the club every night and watch him perform. It sounds dreary but it wasn't. It was great. We were having a romance.

Colleen was around. She was at the club at night. I knew how loyal she was to him. She did a lot of work for him, but I never felt there was anything between them other than the fact they were friends. Maybe I'm stupid. Maybe there was something I didn't see, but he was very much with me and she knew about it.

He did so many things for me. I always keep a rose by my bed, and when I walked into the condo there was a rose by the bed. He liked the cream I used, the vanilla cream I was running out of and was upset that I couldn't find. He had stolen one of my jars and found out the distributor and ordered, like, fifty jars and put them in the medicine cabinet in one of the bathrooms. I remember how on edge he was, impatient for me to find it. Ten years later, I still have jars of the cream.

The last time I was really with him was in Montreal. I knew something was wrong with him because his stomach was bothering him. He was already complaining about pain in his abdomen. He ate so badly – he ate like a goat – that I just thought he had an upset stomach. I had no idea it could ever be cancer. You don't think like that. You think, "Well, he's sick," or "He has the flu."

We had made plans to meet in New York two weeks later. After I left him, I went back to New York, he went back to California. I got a call from him and he said he had decided he was going to go back to Austin to work on *Arizona Bay*. I didn't understand and I felt real upset. He promised me he would come to New York after he was finished there.

When he came to New York, that was the last time I saw him. This was right before he left for Australia. He was in town and he played Caroline's. I went to see him and I didn't stay. It was a weird thing. Something told me to leave. I couldn't face him because I thought he was going to reject me. But he actually called me later and we saw each other that night.

We had a terrible evening together, and I realized he wanted me to go away. He wanted me to see him, but he didn't want me to see him sick. You have to remember we were very romantic and very sexual and I think he didn't want me to see him that way. I know it sounds like a stupid explanation, but it's the only explanation I can come up with. He got very abusive at the restaurant with me to the point where I almost got up and left. He walked me home and said terrible things to me at my door. I don't remember what they were but they made me cry.

You know, Bill was the sweetest and the meanest man I ever knew. I'm not going to paint him as a saint because he wasn't. When he got mad at you it was scary, because it wasn't just a little storm, it was biblical.

He would say terrible things to me and make me cry. And he would say that fighting with me was like fighting with Bambi. It was no challenge. That was a big line of his and I would cry more. Then, of course, he would feel bad, then he would get mad at me all over because he was feeling bad that he made me cry. He'd say, "You know what? I don't want to like you. I don't want to have to make time for you. I could be reading my book." He would do this whole thing and I would cry more. He didn't like the fact he had a connection to me, then he would apologize again. It was a terrible cycle.

That ability to be so mean, then be so sweet, was part of what was so confounding about Bill. Audrey Hepburn was my idol, okay? Audrey Hepburn died that year, I guess it was 1993. My friend at NBC called me up to tell me that the story came over the wire that she had died. My idol is dead. I'm a mess. I'm crying and crying. And in the midst of me mourning and crying, Bill called, "What's the matter?" And I tell him. He doesn't even know who she really is, and he starts to tell me what an idiot I am that I am crying over this woman that I don't even know, which of course makes me sob even more. I hang up on him because I am so upset.

I don't hear from him for the whole day, which makes me even more upset because there is no compassion from him. He calls me up – again no "hello" – he just started talking, and he says, "Well, I have just spent 12 hours watching Audrey Hepburn movies" – he had gone to the video store and rented all these Audrey Hepburn movies – "Now I understand why you were crying." Simultaneous to this, the doorbell rings. I get flowers from him apologizing and telling me he understands why I was upset and that I was just going to have to carry the torch.

He could have been very nasty and inconsiderate, then turn around and do something like that. Do research, admit he was wrong, and send flowers, "Would you forgive me?" He did that all the time.

He wanted it his way, and if he didn't get it he got angry. And if he still didn't get it, he got abusive. He would do that with everything. That's just how he was. You couldn't negotiate with him. It was his way or no way. He would lick his wounds and come back, but he wasn't a businessman. He didn't have any business acumen at all. He was a creative person from start to finish, and that's part of what got him into trouble.

People would always say that, "Oh, Denis Leary was just like him." Nobody was like him. You know why? Because he meant it. When he said, "I hate Billy Ray Cyrus. I hate Whoopi Goldberg" – who he would refer to as a myth – he meant it. When Leary said that, it was only an act. Bill hated so many people. It wasn't, "Oh, this is part of my act." He hated them. Denis Leary would always say he hated Danny Thomas and the St. Jude thing. I bet you Leary sent them money, because he said that in an act and he had a very sick son at one point. He didn't mean any of that. That was the difference.

People say Bill Hicks was angry. He wasn't just angry. Bill Hicks was also a sensitive man. He couldn't go on stage and cry. He'd go on stage and rant, but when he went to see the movie *Of Mice and Men* with John Malkovich and Gary Sinise, do you know how much he cried? He called me up crying when he came out of the movie. He said he was sitting in the movie saying, "Put the rabbit down," and of course if you read the book, you know it doesn't happen that way, but he called me crying over that. He was a sensitive guy in a masculine guy's body. He didn't run around telling people that, but he was.

Bill Hicks took everything to heart. And that's what got him sick, because his anger was real. Everything was authentic. A lot of times he didn't let things out the way you are supposed to. He phoned nothing in. It was a responsibility and it was a burden. I believe when you combine that with the fact that he abused his organs, this is why he got sick. My theory.

We spoke one other time, just a night or two after he had been so abusive. He used to love Roger and Gallet Sandalwood Soap; and I used to buy it for him. At the time, they weren't importing it any more, so if I found some in a store I would buy it for him. Consequently I had 12 boxes of Roger and Gallet soap that I had accumulated. I didn't want it. I was angry at him. So I brought it to him at his hotel. He was staying at a hotel on Central Park West and appearing at Caroline's. When I knew he was safely on stage so I couldn't run into him, I brought the soap to his hotel.

He called me when he got finished. He was leaving for Australia the next day, and he was excited because he had got new luggage. He said to me, "I'm sorry for everything," and that I shouldn't have brought him all the soap. I said that it was his soap and I didn't want it.

He said, "I promise I'll call you."

"Okay. Take care of yourself," I told him.

He said, "You too."

Then something made me say it again, "Bill, please take care of yourself." And that was the last time I ever spoke to him.

And I was so mad at him because, number one, he was awful to me; and women only know one thing and of course it was normal, but I figured he met somebody and he didn't know how to tell me. How was he going to say, "I met some other girl." I was a lot younger. Why would a guy who was mad for me turn on me like that? You don't think, "Oh, he's got cancer." You just think he's a son of a bitch like everybody that preceded him and fuck him and I wished he were dead. You know how many times I wished that? How badly I felt to find out that he was really going to die?

Then he disappeared. He didn't call me, he didn't write me – this was a guy I heard from four times a day, wherever he was. I got letters. I got presents. I got flowers. He was so kind to me, and so romantic with me, then it all stopped. He wouldn't take my calls. It was awful. I know now he must have in that time-frame realized or found out that something was wrong.

[*   *   *]

CHAPTER 10

In 1993, Bill got home to the States to find he had been named *Rolling Stone Magazine*'s "Hot Comic" of 1993 in their annual Hot issue.

Bill remarked on the honor in a radio interview: "That's incredible considering the fact I wasn't in the country at all last year. And if this is any hint at how I should conduct my business, I will completely disappear and see if I can't be a big star here." As much of an honor as it might have been, and as much as Bill desired the recognition in his home country, it was what it was: just a mention in *Rolling Stone*. That year's Hot Band was the American Music Club. Who? Exactly. The band was a favorite amongst indie rock fans, but the exposure in the same issue didn't springboard the AMC to stardom either.

Back in the UK he was also getting some unexpected attention, and a little more personal attention at that. *Revelations* aired in May, and managed to piss off at least two priests. Enough so that they wrote letters to Channel 4; and the letters were forwarded to Bill. "His continued use of the word 'fucking' to describe the fundamentals of the Christian faith was dangerous, thoroughly and deliberately disrespectful and obscene," wrote Reverend Clark of St. Leonard's Baptist Church.

The other found *Revelations* similarly objectionable and requested a video copy of the performance so it could be reviewed by the church leaders. It was just like the Woody Allen joke: "The food here is awful." "Yeah, and such small portions." But never one to miss out on a good exchange of ideas, Bill responded with his own missive. He didn't just fire off a knee-jerk angry letter, however: he actually put substantial thought into his response.

He was in Houston the first week of June when he was cornered by a couple of zine writers and talked at length about the whole incident, saying: "I find it interesting how they find their beliefs threatened when I guarantee they've never received one letter asking them why they have the right to say what they do. Yet, here I am receiving those kinds of letters. No one ever calls up going, 'I was watching this religious program. Listen, I'm a physicist and I'd like to explain a couple of things." In his letters Bill defended himself basically by saying that he didn't have to defend himself. Anyone actually listening to what he said who understood his beliefs – less money on war, more to help the needy and poor – would have realized Bill was espousing real Christian values. Plus, they were just jokes.

"Where I come from – America – there exists this wacky concept called 'freedom of speech,' which many people feel is one of the paramount achievements in mankind's mental development," Bill wrote in one of the answering letters. "I myself am a strong supporter of the 'Right of free speech,' as I'm sure most people would be if they truly understood the concept. 'Freedom of speech' means you suppose the right of people to say exactly those ideas which you do *not* agree with otherwise you don't believe in 'freedom of speech,' but rather only those ideas which *you* believe to be acceptably stated."

Bill was back in West Palm Beach by the middle of the month for another string of shows at the Comedy Corner. At the first night's performance, Tuesday 15 June, he was visibly in pain when he walked off the stage. Colleen McGarr had already scheduled a doctor visit with Bill for that Thursday, but she looked at him and said, "We gotta get you in tomorrow."

Suspecting a gall bladder problem, the physician, Dr. William Donovan, had Bill sent for an ultrasound. Nothing. According to

McGarr the person doing the ultrasound said, "We have to get [Bill] over to the hospital. We have to do a biopsy because this isn't gall bladder."

Thursday Bill was sent for a biopsy. "He was really digging it," said McGarr of Bill's stay in the Good Samaritan Hospital. "He had been on the road non-stop and he was so happy to have no pandemonium, no suitcases . . . he could finally rest." In the early morning hours of Saturday 19 June, Dr. Donovan called McGarr at home. He asked her to come down to the hospital.

"This is the worst news I could give anybody," he said. At the hospital he explained that Bill had pancreatic cancer and that he had about three months to live. They let Bill sleep for a little while longer. At 7:30 that morning, Colleen and Dr. Donovan went to see Bill. Donovan told Bill that he had stage-four pancreatic cancer.

Prognosis negative. Survival rates for pancreatic cancer are the lowest. Of all people diagnosed with pancreatic cancer, only about 20 per cent are alive one year later. During the 1990s the five-year survival rate for men with pancreatic cancer was around 2 per cent; and for those diagnosed with advanced stages of the disease, as Bill had been, survival rates dipped to about 1 per cent.

It made no sense though, which is why Donovan had first thought to examine Bill for a gall bladder problem. People in their early thirties don't get pancreatic cancer. Bill was in two, maybe three, risk groups – male, smoker, and perhaps pancreatitis (if that's what he had been experiencing for the better part of a decade when he felt something in his side while tripping, but that's pure speculation) – but, no, people in their early thirties don't get pancreatic cancer.

Bill was calm as the news sank in. Then he looked at Dr. Donovan and asked, "What's the battle plan?"

Out of the hospital, Bill called his family to tell them. His brother Steve in Austin. His parents in Little Rock. He called Fallon Woodland. That night he tried calling Kevin, but hearing a party on the other end, he hung up and called Rob Fiorella, a comedian friend in Buffalo. For the longest time that was the list of people that knew: his family, Duncan Strauss and Colleen McGarr, Fallon, Rob, oh, and his AA sponsor. He had a standard joke he had started telling many of his other comedian friends: that he had a tumor the size of a baseball that had Pamela's name all over it. But nobody thought it was anything more than a joke.

Said his brother Steve in a radio interview after Bill's passing: "Essentially nobody knew. It's the way Bill wanted it because he didn't like to impose on people. This was his deal. And frankly he believed he was going to beat it. We all believed he was going to. For five and six months after he was diagnosed, it was life as usual."

Bill kept his booking at the Comedy Corner for Sunday night. Monday he started chemotherapy. Bill also decided to base his treatment out of West Palm Beach and, not wanting to stay in a hotel, he moved in with Colleen. Because an aggressive treatment would have almost completely debilitated Bill, a compromise treatment was designed so Bill could continue to work and perform.

He did. He pushed ahead with everything. One weekend after being diagnosed, he was on the road at the Funny Firm in Chicago. He had already recorded shows in Austin for his next record, and was scheduled to perform in San Francisco in a month's time to do more for the same album. He was pushing ahead with *Counts of the Netherworld*.

Chemo couldn't keep Bill down. It just wasn't having an enormous impact on him physically. He kept going; performing, writing. Bill was also fighting cancer with his mind and spirit. As part of his arsenal he got hold of *A Course in Miracles* – a text and a workbook with a set of daily lessons, as well as a manual for teachers, that trains people to create miracles. The book was "written" by Helen Schucman, a professor of Medical Psychology at Columbia University; Schucman actually experienced an inner voice which dictated all three books of the Course to her. The widely accepted claim is that the voice, the real author of the Course, speaking to Schucman is that of Jesus. But it's not necessary to accept that notion (or even accept Jesus) for the Course to work.

This wasn't something Bill had just picked up out of desperation. He had known about and performed the Course for years before this, dating back to his Houston House days. When he went into recovery it became particularly important for him; he did the entire Course over a year's time, faithfully executing each daily lesson. But he needed it now. He needed to create a miracle. And those who knew about the cancer thought it would happen. Bill thought it would happen. He was going to beat it. Somehow.

He discussed the Course with friends without specifying that current interest was heightened. One of those people was Linda Corke. Bill first met Corke in Montreal at the *Just For Laughs* festival in 1990. Corke, who was then working at Jimmy's Comedy Alley in Queens, had heard that Bill had had a UFO experience, and went over to ask him about it. Bill told her, "I tell you what, you hire me in the club and I'll tell you all about it."

She started booking him about three times a year and they got to be friends, particularly over the phone, but as Bill was living in New York they also did some hanging out. Bill turned Corke on to the Course and many of their conversations were about it.

Corke had a friend, Robin Chambers, who was Robert DeNiro's personal assistant. Bill had no formal management arrangement to push his projects. Corke asked him to give her the material for the *Counts of the Netherworld* pilot and *Arizona Bay* so she could pass it to Chambers and take it to DeNiro's production company, Tribeca Productions. Tribeca did film and TV and they were in the formative stages of putting together a record label.

Tribeca loved Bill. That summer they set up a meeting. But Bill was still loyal to the people at Tiger Aspects, with whom he had already been in discussions about *Counts*, so he got them involved. All three parties were participants at the meeting.

Channel 4 was then suffering the effects of advertising recession, so new shows were suddenly on a slower commissioning route than they would have been normally. Bill was getting frustrated that things with Tiger Aspects were proceeding at such a slow pace. But his vision for the show was further complicating things. For aesthetic reasons, he was insistent on shooting *Counts* on film; and film was far more expensive than video. So he wanted to do an expensive show precisely when budgets were shrinking.

On top of that, Bill was a comedian and that's how he was known to the network: that was the basis of his popularity in the UK. Certainly his ability to make people maybe think while laughing was part of what separated him from other comics, but *Counts* was shaping up to be something far more serious than the one-man stand-up performances that Channel 4 had previously aired, with potentially lower viewing figures.

Then with the inclusion of Tiger Aspects in the meeting with Tribeca, interest in the project from the side of DeNiro's people evaporated. They were suddenly going to be co-producers on a project they would be funding for a company across the pond. The message given to Tiger Aspects was: if you are looking for financing, why don't you go to a bank?

Bill's loyalty and desire to create one big happy family amongst all of the parties had created a situation where it was going to work for none of them. It even caused a rift between Bill and Linda Corke as she had got the ball rolling on the project, but once Bill had started using Strauss and McGarr to manage him, she found herself on the outside. Bill sent Corke flowers.

Tribeca was out, Tiger Aspects was still in. It was just that the project was still on a slow track. And the clock was ticking.

If Bill slowed down in the immediate aftermath of his diagnosis, it was only because of the time demands of his treatment and his desire to spend more time in West Palm Beach with McGarr. Bill was even spending time on the beach. He had never been a fan of the beach; he had never been a fan of direct sunlight.

It was an odd situation. Bill was sharing more about his life with Colleen, seemed to be developing feelings for her; but McGarr and Duncan Strauss weren't just business partners, and even though Strauss was based on the West Coast they had been maintaining a long-distance relationship the entire time that Bill and Colleen had been growing closer.

In August Bill went back out to California to clean out his apartment. It had never held that much stuff. A few items. Some clothes and his guitars. Six months before, Bill had told a girlfriend about how he was tired of the road, tired of traveling, and that he wanted to own nice furniture, wanted to have a couch, wanted to have a place that felt like a home. Now he was giving away the few possessions he still had, made easier by the fact he had never acted on the urge to furnish.

Steve Epstein recalls: "Bill came over to my house and gave me a bunch of this stuff, a bunch of his silk shirts, his microwave, his silverware. And I said, 'Bill, why are you giving me all of this shit?' And he goes, 'You know Eppy, every once in a while I think it's good to clear out all your possessions. Start over.'"

Maynard Keenan, the singer for Tool, had also invited Bill to introduce the band to the stage for its appearance at the LA area Lollapalooza show. As unsuccessfully as Bill was flowing into the mainstream, he was equally successful at catching on with rock 'n' rollers on the road. Many a band looking for something to listen to while touring had found Hicks, then would pass tapes of his shows to other bands, who quickly became fans and returned the favor. It's how Tool first found him.

"They became a staple of the road," Keenan said of the tapes in an interview after Bill's passing. "We're speaking the same message, but in a different language." Tool cited the comedian as inspiration in the liner notes of *Undertow*, the band's full-length debut. Keenan then mailed a copy of the record to Hicks and initiated a phone relationship.

Even though Keenan had only got to see Hicks do stand-up live once, Tool had almost worked out the plans for a co-headlining tour with Bill just before his death. Bill really was proceeding with life as if there were nothing wrong, or as if there was no temporary detour from which he wouldn't eventually be able to get back on track.

A couple of days later Bill was in the hospital receiving chemo treatment. He left the hospital, and went straight to LAX to pick up his brother, Steve, who had flown to Los Angeles to join Bill in a drive back across the country to home. Bill then proceeded to drive eight hours out into the desert. Steve marveled at his brother's strength, and, recounting the episode later, said to Austin's KUT deejay Larry Monroe, "It never affected him physically, the treatment didn't."

Bill once told a writer in Austin: "I wanna come out on TV one night with a straitjacket and a gag over my mouth, and just hop out, go, 'hurrur, urrur, hurr hurrur,' and hop away."

He almost got his wish.

It's the irony of ironies. Throughout his career Bill consistently did between 200 to 300 nights a year. He worked tirelessly, willing to perform anywhere and in front of any audience. He just wanted to be seen and heard. But the one thing Bill is most famous for on his home soil? It's for not appearing on TV.

Bill taped twelve episodes of David Letterman's late-night talk show. Eleven aired. The one that was never broadcast brought Bill – his words – "more attention than [his] other eleven appearances on Letterman times a hundred."

The morning of the show, Bill hopped on a flight to New York City. When his plane landed, he headed straight for the show's studio. Before Bill even left for New York the material for his set had already been "approved and re-approved" by *Letterman* segment producer Mary Connelly. Still, once at the show's offices, Bill sat down with Connelly and went over the set again. After a quick tour of the theater (courtesy of Connelly), Bill went back to his hotel. There he went over his set a couple more times. What he described as his "usual routine."

Late that afternoon Bill headed back to the Ed Sullivan Theater for the 5:30 taping of the show. He got his make-up done, then went to wait in his dressing room. Midway through the taping Connelly called Bill and his manager Colleen McGarr out into the hallway. Bad news. The show is running long. Bill is getting bumped. No appearance for Bill on *Letterman* tonight.

As Bill described the bumping after the fact, "[It] isn't as bad as it sounds. You still get paid, free hotel room, and your flight back to wherever you're going," He had been through the drill before. Connelly apologized and told Bill they would reschedule him for the show as soon as possible. Bill and Colleen went to dinner. The Palms. "Lobsters the size of canoes." Bill said that he felt fine about the whole situation. He flew back to Florida the next day.

A week later, Bill was back in New York to do a gig at Caroline's. He also had a handful of nights booked at the Comedy Corner in West Palm Beach, Florida, after the appearance in NYC. For press in advance of that engagement, Bill had an interview with a reporter in South Florida. He called. They did the interview. It was uneventful. But then something strange happened – the first of a few strange things to happen that day. At the end of the interview the journalist said, "Oh, by the way, congratulations."

Bill said, "Thanks. What for?"

He replied, "Well, you're doing *Letterman* tonight." Strange. A stringer for the local paper knew Bill was doing *Letterman* that night, but Bill didn't. He figured he should find out what, exactly, the fuck was going on.

He called McGarr's office and got her assistant: "Where have you been all day? The Letterman people have been trying to reach you. They want you on the show tonight."

The original guest, a former Mob informant who had written a cookbook and wanted to pimp it on the show, had been canceled from the show after *Letterman* staff started getting suspicious phone calls from heavily accented people, so Bill was in, provided they could find him. Bill hadn't made it easy by checking into his hotel under the alias Otis Blackwell. Blackwell was the author of Elvis' hits such as "Don't Be Cruel" and "Return to Sender." It was also a joke

343

Bill told to himself to have a laugh at Denis Leary, for whom Bill had written material.

Bill got off the phone with McGarr's office and called Mary Connelly at *The Late Show*. Could he do it? Yes, of course. A car would be by to pick him up at 4:15. That gave Bill forty-five minutes. He got dressed and went through his set – the one that had been approved and re-approved for the show one week earlier.

Backstage there was no bad news from Connelly. Bill was on. He waited by the side of the stage, taking a few last drags from a cigarette, just like the first time he ever did the show. But unlike every other time he did the show, he eschewed his Man in Black outfit. Bill was instead clad in bright fall colors – "an outfit bought just for the show and reflective of my bright and cheerful mood" – when he walked out to center stage to perform his set.

Lights. Camera. Hicks.

Afterwards Bill walks over to Letterman's desk and David joked: "Good set Bill! Always nice to have you drop by with an uplifting message." Sarcasm.

They go to a commercial break.

During the break, Letterman and Bill do some light catching up. David asks Bill how things are going and if he's lost weight. Bill: "I tell him, 'Yes, I've been drinking about a quart of grapefruit juice a day.'"

Both Mary Connelly and Robert Morton went over to Bill. Both were smiling and both told him the set was good. Bill asked again how they thought it went. Insecurity? Maybe a bit, but understandably so. This was not 200 drunk patrons in a club. It was eight million people in all fifty states. Morton and Connelly again reiterated that Bill killed: "Great. Didn't you hear the audience response?"

There was some more banter between Bill and David. Bill told David he's started enjoying a cigar every now and then, and David handed Bill a Cuban.

They came back from the commercial break. Letterman said, "Bill, enjoy answering your mail for the next few weeks." Thank you.

Goodnight. Blah blah. End of show. Bill headed back to the green room and got the same feedback from other people congregating backstage: "Great set." Graham Parker, another guest on the show that night and someone Bill was a big fan of, he came up to Bill with a big grin: "Great! Loved it, mate!"

Bill also ran into Bill Sheft. Sheft was a writer on the show and a comic who not only warmed up the audience before shows but also got them to applaud in and out of the breaks. To do this latter task he usually parked himself just to the left of Letterman's desk during the taping. Bill asked Sheft if he thought Letterman enjoyed Bill's performance. Sheft's response was unequivocal: "Are you kidding? Letterman was cracking up throughout the whole set."

Unanimous praise for Bill's set. By everyone. Period.

Bill went back to his hotel to take a bath and unwind. About 7:30 p.m. he was just getting out of the tub when his phone rang. It was *Late Show* producer Robert Morton. He told Bill he had some bad news: they had to edit his segment from the show. Cut it completely. "I don't understand. What's the problem, Robert? I thought the show went great." Morton agreed. It had. He proceeded to tell Bill that CBS Standards and Practices felt some of the material was, as Morton put it, "unsuitable for broadcast."

Bill wanted to know what, exactly, was thought objectionable in a set that had been checked off more than once by the show's producers (including Morton) ahead of time and lauded by the same after the performance. "Almost all of it," Morton replied. "If I had to edit everything they object to, there'll be nothing left to the set." They decided just to cut the entire set. Morton: "Bill, we fought tooth and nail to keep the set as is, but Standards and Practices won't back down. David is furious. We are all upset here, Bill, this has nothing to do with how we feel about you. We loved the set."

They hadn't been through anything like this with Standards and Practices before, but they weren't backing down. Still in shock, Bill protested: "Bob, they are so obviously jokes." He repeated this over and over throughout his conversation. Bill pointed out that he ran the set by his 63-year-old mother in Little Rock, Arkansas. A litmus test for acceptability if ever there was a thing. If she wasn't offended, how could anyone else be?

They'd try to get him back on on the next couple of weeks, that was Morton's offer to Bill to assuage the blow. Bill's immediate reaction was: "I don't think I can learn to juggle in that short a time." He managed not to say it. Discretion might be the better part of valor but, in reality, Bill was simply too stunned to get something this snide out of his mouth. Morton took some blame for not having spent more time editing out the "hot points."

"Bob, they're just jokes. I don't want to be edited by you or by anyone else. Why are people so afraid of jokes?"

"Bill, you've got to understand our audiences."

By this point, Bill had shaken off the shock, and he understood, maybe better than Morton. He retorted, "We taped at 5:30 and the audience had no problem with the material then." They didn't. They laughed. Hard and often. Bill continued, "Does the audience become overly sensitive between the hours of 11:30 p.m. and 12:30 a.m?

"By the way, Bob, when I'm not on the show, I'm a member of the audience for your show. Are you saying my material is not suitable for me? This doesn't make any sense, why do you underestimate the intelligence of your audience?" Bill might as well been talking to a wall. Nothing he said was going to get him cut back into the show. His segment was replaced by a canned set by Bill Sheft.

Bill went to Colleen's room. He told her and her mom that he'd been cut from Letterman's show that night. At first they thought he was joking. He kept repeating to himself, "They're just jokes." But Bill wasn't joking. McGarr called Letterman's people and talked to Mary Connelly. Connelly told McGarr exactly what Morton told Bill. McGarr asked for a tape of the segment. Connelly said she would get one off to her on Monday. Bill still had a show to do that night at Caroline's.

Bill got back to Florida. They continued to ask for a copy of the show. McGarr gave Letterman's producers her address and

FedEx number. They were assured a tape would be overnighted. One day. Two days. Nothing came. They asked again. It's in the mail. They waited again. Finally the show tells them that they don't think they are legally allowed to send a copy of a show that didn't air.

So without any tape to roll, Bill had no proof of exactly what he had said. But he knew the set in and out. And it had happened. Bill fired off a letter to John Lahr. A thirty-nine-page handwritten letter. Lahr's profile of Bill for the *New Yorker* had been languishing in editorial limbo. Now, with the episode of Bill being censored off *Letterman*, the magazine might be more interested in resurrecting the story and with some urgency. There was now an angle.

In the letter, Bill did his best to recount exactly what he had said in his set and the audience reaction. Some of the things that might have been "hot points" include:

> "You know I consider myself a fairly open-minded person, but speaking of homosexuality, something has come to my attention that has shocked even me. Have you heard about these new grade-school books for children they're trying to add to the curriculum to help children understand the gay lifestyle? One's called *Heather's Two Mommies*, the other one is called *Daddy's New Roommate*.
>
> [Here I make a shocked, disgusting face]
>
> "Folks, I gotta draw the line here and say this is absolutely disgusting. It is grotesque, and it is pure evil . . . "
> [Pause]
> "I'm talking of course about Daddy's New Roommate."
> [Audience laughs]
> "*Heather's Two Mommies* is quite fetching . . . "

Bill then moved on to some material on pro-lifers, joking:

"You know what bugs me about them? If you're so pro-life, do me a favor. Don't lock arms and block medical clinics. If you're so pro-life, lock arms and block cemeteries."
[Audience laughs]
"Let's see how committed you are to this idea."

Later in the set he mentions that he was in Australia during Easter and discovered, interestingly enough, that they celebrate the holiday the same way we do, specifically by telling their children that "a giant bunny rabbit left chocolate eggs in the night."

"Gee, I wonder why we are so messed up as a race? You know I've read the Bible – can't find the words 'bunny' or 'chocolate' in the whole book."
[Audience laughs]
"Where do we get this stuff from? And why those two things? Why not 'Goldfish left Lincoln Logs in our sock drawers?' I mean, as long as we're making stuff up, let's go hog wild."

There was more, but like Bill said, "They are just jokes." However, if he wanted to offend the religious right wing in America, he had pretty much hit a trifecta – abortion, homosexuality, and the death and resurrection of Jesus Christ.

That, of course, was to miss the whole point. Bill used to talk about it all the time. Does someone "get me"? If you got Bill, you understood the joke wasn't about homosexuality, it was about the double standard in people's perception. Two men. That's disgusting and unnatural. Two women. That's hot. But is it really a "hot point"? Again: they're just jokes.

While waiting for the tape from *The Late Show* to arrive, Bill was experiencing what he described as a "maelstrom." Phones were ringing incessantly. The media had picked up on the story. Bill couldn't have generated this much attention if he had sought it. There was some hesitancy in the Hicks camp about filling all of the interview requests. They had told Letterman's people about the media interest: show producer Morton was less than enthused about the prospect of any media attention. Bill noted to Lahr that Morton took a particularly "dim view" of any mention of the incident in the *New Yorker* profile.

Still, Morton reiterated to Bill how much the show loved him the previous night. It was out of their hands with Standards and Practices at CBS. And the show still wanted Bill back with a set that worked for everyone.

In the midst of the "maelstrom" Bill got a call from Jay Leno. After some general conversation ("Why do you hate me, Bill?" "I don't hate you, I hate what's become of you and *The Tonight Show*") Leno asked Bill if he wanted to come on *The Tonight Show* and do the set that had been cut from *Letterman*. Bill agreed to do it on the condition that he got to do the same set, unedited, without having to run it by the producers. For all Bill had said about Leno, it was a remarkable offer. Until Leno called back and asked McGarr for a tape of the set. It wasn't an unreasonable request, but it wasn't part of the deal. If Jay insisted on seeing the set beforehand, Bill wouldn't do it. Jay insisted. Bill reconsidered.

Bill decided to go ahead with the interviews. Interview after interview. Print, radio, TV. "All I have to do is tell the TRUTH over and over again. At least it's easy to remember," said Bill.

He appeared on Howard Stern, the top-rated FM radio show in America. Bill also appeared on a radio show in the San Francisco Bay area, the Alex Bennet show, which hit the air in front of a live studio audience. The audience laughed at many of the same jokes that got censored off CBS. And instead of getting offended by "hot points" and flying off the handle, one listener to the show was instead offended by the cowardice of CBS.

Of his own volition he fired off a letter to the network telling them how incensed he was by their decision to censor Bill's set from the show. The listener got an interesting letter back from CBS, which he promptly faxed to Hicks.

It is true that Bill Hicks was taped that evening and that his performance did not air. What is inaccurate is that the deletion of
his routine was required by CBS. In fact, although a CBS
Program Practices editor works on the show, the decision was
solely that of the producers of the program who decided to substitute his performance with that of another comedian.
Therefore, your criticism that CBS censored the program is
totally without foundation. Creative judgment must be made in
the course of producing and airing any program and, while we
regret that you disagreed with this one, the producers felt it
necessary and that is not a decision we would override.

This completely contradicted the party line of Connelly, Morton and
The Late Show. They didn't fight "tooth and nail" for Bill. According
to the network, the show producers were the ones who decided to
nix Bill from the show. Hicks couldn't get the tape. There were two
contradictory stories coming from CBS and *The Late Show*. Clearly,
someone was lying to him.

Despite everything that had happened, Bill maintained his
opinion that Letterman had the best talk show on television. Bill was
cut from a show on 1 October 1993, a Friday night. The following
Monday night, he was back in front of his TV at 11:30, watching *The
Late Show* with David Letterman.

Bill never rescheduled on *Letterman*.

[*   *   *]

Kevin Booth

Electric Ladies Man, my latest band was rehearsing. I was drunk and stoned when I heard the phone ring. Bill was on the other end, and I could hear he was crying. He told me he wanted to tell me something, but it was fucking loud with the rest of the band making a lot of noise – drinking, smoking, laughing, dicking around with their instruments – and I was slow-witted because my lucidity was impaired. He was probably trying to tell me about the diagnosis, but I ended up not hearing him and just going, "Huh? What?" into the phone.

Bill hung up and I thought our friendship was over because for the next two weeks he avoided me. He wouldn't answer my phone calls and wouldn't return when I left a message. I called Little Rock: Mary lied to me, telling me Bill just had a gall bladder problem, and that he was going to be fine. I asked if he was mad at me and she said he wasn't, and that everything was fine. Then just a couple of days after the last time I talked to Mary, Bill called me out of the blue and in a totally good mood said, "Hey, why don't you fly to San Francisco and let's start work on a new *Ninja Bachelor Party* film and a new album."

It was around 10 July when I met Bill at the hotel in San Francisco. Something was weird. He was smoking again. He had all these weird toiletries, shit you'd only see in hospitals. I'd spent so much time in hospitals with my brother that I could recognize the difference between over-the-counter supplies and critical care paraphernalia. The latter was spilling out of Bill's suitcase like he was an MD. He also had a huge bottle of Percocet. "Dude, what is this stuff?" He gave some bullshit answer – he was taking it for a stomachache – and brushed it off.

He also made some attempt to rationalize it as recreational. Bill had been clean for four years and I could tell he was a little intoxicated. I started looking for traces of alcohol. No, couldn't find any.

But things were not adding up. He was playing this brutal new-age healing music all the time. He had incense burning. He told me he was taking B-vitamin injections. Yet he was pushing himself harder than I had ever seen before. We were filming the next *Ninja Bachelor Party* instalment during the day, all day, every day. Then recording performances at night. He was doing two jobs all at the same time. And the performances were amazing. He had more energy and power in San Francisco than I had ever seen come out of him before.

It would have been silly to push the issue because he was functioning and getting things done, but he was different than the Bill I last saw. For example, when filming, we'd have a cab driver take us to some famous tourist spot in San Francisco where we'd jump out, set up the camera and start fighting until people asked us for a permit or asked us to leave. But when people told us we couldn't film, we didn't just leave. Bill would either ignore the person or continue shooting until the cops came up and almost physically removed us. In other instances he just started handing the irritant twenty-dollar bills until they shut up and went away. He wasn't going to let anyone tell him he couldn't do what he wanted to do. He wasn't going to let them waste his time.

The place we were recording in San Francisco was tiny. Held 125. And this was one of the cities where Bill had fans. He stopped caring if people laughed, if people cared: "Fuck it," he told me in the hotel. "If it's funny, it's funny. If not, then not. I don't care, I just want to get the message out."

That's the key phrase. It was something Bill and the Houston comics had talked about a lot – "getting the message out" – when they thought they were going to change the world with comedy. He hadn't bandied it around much lately, but he started saying it again, and seemingly with a sense of purpose.

However, that almost made it worse. Because he had made the decision to make the message the show, he was confusing new faces and, to some extent, disappointing the old. People who had shown up not knowing who Bill Hicks was, many of them were left with an impression that, well, it was interesting but wasn't like the kind of stand-up comedy they were used to seeing on TV. The people who came to the shows because they were Hicks fans would scream, "Do Elmer Dinky," or "Do the door is ajar," like Bill was a fucking jukebox. There's a surefire way to piss off a guy with literally six months to live.

Still, they were fucking great shows. Just listen to the record.

John Magnuson also joined us that week. Magnuson was a close friend of Lenny Bruce and had also directed *The Lenny Bruce Performance* film. Magnuson's appearance really meant a lot to Bill. The comparisons were overblown and even a bit inaccurate – Bill's standards were Woody Allen, Richard Pryor and Charlie Chaplin. It's also something Magnuson had probably heard a thousand times – he's the next Lenny Bruce – about a thousand other comedians, but when he saw Bill he was blown away.

19 September. That was the date. It was David Johndrow, Bill and myself out at the ranch.

Bill showed up with a couple of ounces of mushrooms. Very, very good ones. Very, very expensive ones. Golden Teachers they were called.

Electric Ladies Man had a song called "I'm Sick". The signature lyric was "I'm sick. I'm sick. I'm sick. I'm real, real sick." Not exactly Verlaine, but we were a rock band. It was a song we had rehearsed and recorded. For some reason both David and I had it stuck in our heads that day at the ranch. We kept singing it around Bill. He didn't say anything, but, God help us, the things you say when you just don't know.

A couple of hours before sunset we took the mushrooms. As always, the idea was to peak through the sunset. The sun goes down. The moon comes up. You get the color change, the transition of the day. The transition always had the most intense colors and sounds. Lotus positions facing the pond. That's where we were.

Bill spent his trip focusing on his upcoming *Letterman* appearance, meditating on it very intensely. He was mentally preparing for the show. He was putting so much into it, the feeling was almost palpable. He was also clearly more nervous. He had been on the show many times before, it just seemed like this time was going to be a bigger deal. In retrospect, he had to be thinking something like, "This might be the last time I'm ever on *Letterman*. Whatever I do this time is what I leave everyone with for ever."

Bill was smart to pay the hundreds of dollars he did for the mushrooms. We were swimming.

At one point during the trip I turned to Bill and told him: "Dude, I just figured out what cancer is." Complete coincidence.

"Really?" he asked.

"It's when you get darkness into your mind or in your spirit and you allow your positive side to be eaten by that darkness. Cancer is a spiritual thing," I told him.

Bill response was unequivocal. "Man, you're right. You are totally right," he said. It was just something I pulled out of my ass. It was weird. Just one of those things. After that Bill would occasionally turn to me and tell me, "Kevin there is so much we need to talk about. There is so much."

Later we were back at the house. We stood in the kitchen eating carrots, and David and I and Bill started talking about another *Ninja Bachelor Party* instalment. The joke was that the movie would stay exactly the same. Same actors, same plot, same dialogue. Everything. The only thing that would change would be what Clarence Mumford wanted to do for a living. "Mom, Dad, I think tennis would be a fine career for me." That would be the only difference. Everywhere it said "ninja" substitute "tennis."

It was such a great moment because of how we laughed. It was a hard, cleansing, uncontrollable laugh. We laughed and laughed and ate carrots. It was the kind of laugh that made you feel alive and it was the last time I remember hearing Bill laugh. The last time I laughed with him.

There was one other creepy thing of note that happened during that last trip. We had a pool put in at the ranch, and this was the first time Bill had seen it. We went for a dip while tripping. Bill dove in the pool and popped out of the water right in front me. And for a split second I saw not Bill's face, but the face of a skeleton.

Right before he died, Bill sent the rest of the mushrooms we had taken for that trip back with Colleen to give to David and me. I buried them in the yard. In the wake of Bill's death we had been doing so many interviews, and interviews that mentioned the use of mushrooms, that I had become paranoid. I thought I'd be safer if they were out of sight.

On the one-year anniversary of that last trip, David and I went back to the ranch to finish off what Bill had left us. The spirit of the thing was gone. We were each in our worlds, David and I; but we had a duty to honor the memory of our friend. We both took shitloads of the mushrooms and we went back down to the pond. We braced for it. But nothing happened.

About a week after the episode at the ranch with Bill and David, I got a call. It was late Friday afternoon in Austin, so it had to be right after the taping. *The Late Show with David Letterman*. Bill was stoked. He was clearly still riding the residual high of the adrenaline rush from performing. "Dude, it went great. It was fucking awesome. Everyone thought so. I really felt like the message got through tonight."

We talked for a minute about the jokes he did – we had already recorded the material for *Rant*, so I was familiar with most everything in the set – and not much else. He did mention that he got to sit next to David after the set. It was kind of a litmus test. Even though Dave loved him, it seemed like Bill would be on his last joke when the credits were rolling, like they couldn't get to the end of the show fast enough once Bill got on.

Certainly it was just a function of time. There are only forty-four minutes in the show. If they don't have time for a segment with Bill in the guest seat, they don't have time. But Bill had mentioned it enough to know that he took it personally. If only a little bit. If they truly liked him, they would make sure he had time to sit and chat with Dave. A little respect, that's all he asked.

The phone conversation was short. Just the facts. Went great. Felt great. Broke through. Got the message out. But the short conversation just meant that Bill had a list of people to call and wanted to make sure he got a chance to speak with everyone.

It's amazing. Those phone calls say more about Bill than almost anything else. It's not what he said in the call, but that he called. *Letterman* had just started on CBS and was wiping the floor with Leno. Bill does just about the hottest show on TV and everyone thinks it went great. What does Bill do? Does he go out and get knee-deep in hookers and blow? Okay he's sober, so maybe hookers and poundcake. But no. His first priority is to call his friends and family to tell them how it went. And he wants to make sure he gets to everyone. For all of the shitty things I can remember Bill doing every now and then, he really was a mensch.

A couple of hours later, Bill called again. This was unexpected. And this time he sounded like he was in tears. It was the complete opposite. He told me what had happened. "No, they're not going to use it. I don't understand. They are just jokes, people."

I was fucking confused. "Why? Why?" I kept asking Bill.

"I don't know. I don't know. Obviously, I don't understand who the audience is. They are telling me I don't know who the people are in their audience. I keep thinking that I am their audience because I watch the show, but obviously I'm not."

Calling Bill "stunned" would be an understatement. Something very deep inside of him had been shaken. The show's producers had told Bill he didn't understand the audience. Bill reminded him that he was their audience. He watched *Letterman*. It was like someone had told Bill he didn't understand himself.

A few days later we were talking. I remember Bill saying, "Well, they've asked me to come back on." We both agreed that it was ridiculous. "Fuck them," he said.

It's *The Late Show with David Letterman*. Not *The Late Show with Morton and Donnelly*. Not *The Late Show Partially Funded Tonight with Advertising Dollars to Promote a Pro-Life Agenda*. But it was a grim, sad, sorry reminder that everyone has a price. Bill wanted to believe that he didn't. I guess the cool thing is that Bill got to leave this planet without that ever happening. Maybe if he had lived long enough, he might have done a Jeep commercial.

That's not idle speculation. When Bill was sick with cancer he used to rave about how much he loved Aloe Vera gel. He was hanging out in Florida and felt like part of the reason he'd gotten cancer, was because he had lived his whole life actively avoiding the sun. So he started really making it a point to get outside, to go to the beach and get sun on his body. He was still so pale that the sun scorched his skin. Aloe gel helped soothe him. He was constantly buying bottles of it.

But we were talking about commercials, and Bill said, "You know what, I would do a commercial for Aloe Vera gel. I really like it. If people wanted to ask me about aloe gel, I would do something about it." It's not heresy, it happened. There's your patron saint of anti-marketing. Maybe he was hopped up on pain medication goofballs when he said it. I don't want to make excuses for Bill. Is it a "price" if it's something you believe in? It's just something he once said. He also turned down every endorsement opportunity he was ever offered.

It wasn't so much whether you did a commercial, it was whether you were peddling some bullshit product just for a buck. That's the point missed by a lot of the Hicks fans who worship him for his anti-advert doctrine. That's what took you off "the artistic honor roll."

Leno peddled Doritos, and it's the very fact that it was Doritos. Do people need Doritos? No. Do Doritos make your life better? It depends how you measure utility, but it's a bullshit product like McDonald's or something that's been made and marketed so you'll just get hooked on it even if it makes you fat. So the fact that Leno was up there pushing those things for money is what disgusted Bill so much. Maybe the reason Bill unleashed all the vitriol towards Jay was because maybe Bill, somewhere deep down inside, feared he might act the same way when the dumptrucks loaded with cash pulled up in his driveway. Maybe it's a good thing Bill never owned a house.

The Tonight Show was also something sacrosanct to Bill, and by becoming a spokesmodel, Leno had defiled something sacred. But I think it speaks highly of Jay that, despite all of the shitty things Bill said about him from the stage, that when CBS kept the shit from hitting the fans, Jay offered Bill a second chance. He offered him the chance to do the exact same set that had been cut from *Letterman* on *The Tonight Show*. Leno put one small condition on it – he wanted to see the material before the show – and Bill balked. (Bill also got called by the Arsenio Hall show with a similar offer. That made Bill laugh. "I'm blacker than Arsenio is," Bill said.)

It's something we never talked specifically about, but Bill didn't hold his hand too close to his chest. A few weeks later, when Bill was back in Austin, we went and ate at the Korea House and over dinner he told me about the profile in the *New Yorker* and the letter he had written to John Lahr. He also told me that Lahr had wanted to talk to me. Bill arranged for Lahr to call us both while they were hanging out in the studio together. From the tone of the conversation, it became apparent that Bill was playing up his victim-hood.

He was wronged, no doubt about it. He was censored and he was lied to. But Bill was also playing the part. He skirted back and forth over the line between righteous indignation to self-righteous indignation. He was spending equal time on both sides. It's a little bit of what the act is. It's like a gangster rapper going around talking about how he was shot at. Similarly for Bill, playing outlaw was much easier once you had done something to get outlawed.

Bill certainly could be angry. But he couldn't be that surprised. This was America and it was television. Having to adjust his set to appease the folks at *Letterman* was something he had had to deal with every time he had been on the show. It was almost just a matter of degree this time.

Even Bill himself made a point of pointing out that he was censored off the same stage as Elvis. Elvis got in trouble for what he was doing from the waist down, Bill, from the neck up. It's not a trivial distinction; censorship was nothing new in America.

Over dinner at Korea House that night Bill lamented, "The whole world has become this giant corporation. I can't even go on this little talk show and do a five-minute comedy routine. Maybe someone will lose some sales because I said this thing."

When Bill's set got censored off *Letterman*, he was at least able to take his story to radio stations across the US and tell people what happened. If it had happened a decade later, it's conceivable that Bill would have been shut out from even making appearances on the radio. A vast majority of the radio stations in the US are owned by just a few corporations. Say something at political odds with two or three of them, and you've got no place to go. It's like one of Bill's favorite social critics and political activists Noam Chomsky said: "If you're not cynical, you're not paying attention."

It's sad because it undermines the whole role of the comedian as Bill thought of it: "The comic is the guy who says, 'wait a minute' as the consensus is building."

I was calling Bill's house. It was like dialing into a *Twilight Zone* episode. Bill and his mom would pick up the phone at the same time. You'd hear two "Hellos" then Bill would hang up the phone and I'd ask Mary if Bill was there. "Uh, Bill can't come to the phone right now."

"What? Is he mad at me?"

"No, he's just really busy upstairs."

I'd press just to talk for a minute. What is going on? Is he still mad about Marble Head Johnson: "No no, Kevin. He's excited. He's excited about all the work you two are doing together. He has nothing but good things to say about you."

"That's great, but then can I talk to him?"

"Well, okay here he is."

"Kevin. Hey . . ." He sounded super-high. "So much is happening, dude. It's a miracle. I can't tell you everything right now, but you're not going to believe it, dude. We're the luckiest people in the world.

God loves us. He loves us." I knew he wasn't drunk, but it was the voice of Bill on ecstasy. It was narcotic.

He kept saying he had so much to tell me, and that there was so much going on with his life and his career. Bill told me. "The world is getting ready to open up to us, Kevin. It's finally going to happen, dude."

I'm thinking, "That's cool, but, shit, did I call the right house?" Is Bill okay? I asked him if he was off AA, if he was back to partying.

"No, dude, I just took a bunch of my White Martinis. Everyone should take these White Martinis, they make you feel so good."

Me: "Uh, that's cool, but you're just jamming out on that shit right in front of your mom and dad?"

"Kevin, my mom gets it. She finally gets it. We are having these huge breakthroughs. I showed her the Jimi Hendrix documentary and she gets it. I'm still not there with dad yet."

He told me about the bet. He bet Steve $500 that he could get his dad to take mushrooms with him.

"I'm gonna do it. It's going to be amazing."

"What's going to happen when you do it?"

"He's finally going to see the light. It's going to open up all of these channels. It's going to be amazing."

Bill's behavior on the phone was weird. Well, everything was weird. His moving out of LA to move back to live with his parents was weird. He was taking off in England, why did he move back in with his parents? And he had also been spending a lot of time in West Palm Beach, why was that? It all makes sense now – the answers being "cancer" and "Colleen" respectively – but we didn't know anything about the cancer, and we didn't know much about Colleen. It was just another one of the things Bill compartmentalized.

It was November when he came back into town. He had just got back to the States after he and Fallon had their meeting in London for *Counts of the Netherworld*, the meeting where everything fell apart. The story he told me was that he got frustrated and lost it. He had a temper tantrum, got up on the table in the middle of the meeting and started marching around – on the fucking table itself – yelling at everyone in the room like a crazy person. Everyone at the meeting just sat there giving him sad stares. The show went from, "Hey, let's greenlight this" to "What the fuck is going on?"

All that time in Los Angeles, the city he despised, all that time was to try to make something like *Counts* happen, to try to make TV that trusted people to be intelligent and speak up to them, not talk down to them. Bill had fought his whole life to get to that point. And that meeting was it. It didn't matter that it was in London and not LA. All the better. The British got him. He didn't have to worry about going over people's heads or how his show played with a test audience.

He had made it over all the hurdles and got to the point of his dreams, where he was going to get the TV show he wanted. He's pitching it. It's a little conceptual and it's not like other things on TV, but it looks like someone wants to make it. Everything in his life that he's worked for is in this moment. And he's got cancer. God had thrown Bill a curveball that he could have never ever hit.

I finally took Bill, somewhat against his will, to the critical care unit at the hospital where my brother was being treated for his seizures. Bill was telling me he was not really interested in hanging out in the hospital, but I took him, just not knowing. We went to the critical care unit at Seton Hospital. It was not a happy place. Car wrecks, heart attacks, strokes, cancer. People were on the verge of death. Families facing terror and loss. God, if only I had known. When we were walking around Bill told me that he could feel the "presence of angels" in the place.

Bill suddenly broke down crying. I asked him what was wrong. Fighting through the tears, he finally told me: "Kevin, I have cancer. I've had cancer all this time." I said, "God, I knew it. I knew you had cancer." I didn't "know" but I knew. It wasn't just the Percocet. Bill had morphine pills, and he had given me some. I showed Jere, and her being the drug expert she was, she knew it was what they gave cancer patients. A friend's mother had cancer and it was exactly what they gave her. Damn. That was the tell.

Bill started telling me he was going to be okay and that he was fighting it. "You know, it's gonna be okay. We're gonna make a miracle happen. It's very important you don't tell anybody, don't tell anybody about this."

Looking back, it was better that I hadn't known. I couldn't have designed the night he called my house when he first tried to tell me, but if I had known earlier, we wouldn't have been able to work.

I would not have been able to go to San Francisco and make those recordings for *Rant* or do any of the shit Bill and I did together in the intervening months. And not because of Bill, but because of me. I would have been the one sitting there going, "He's dying. He's dying," I would've been a basket case and *Rant* wouldn't exist. I needed not to "know" so that I could be in a state of denial. Bill wanted to create a miracle? That Bill was able to be there and keep it together and do work and go on stage and make people laugh, that was the fucking miracle.

After all these years of David and Bill getting on me like I'm a big baby because of all of the horrible stuff I'd been through with my brother – watching him shit himself while tubes filled with blood hang out of him – and telling me to get over it, Bill was suddenly compassionate. He was in the same place and had been going through horrors of his own.

One of the first things he told me about cancer was not about himself, but about how brave some of the other patients in the cancer ward were. The bravest he'd ever seen. He told me about sitting there with a tube in his arm for four hours while he would get his chemo, and he would see these kids ravaged by radiation and chemo, some so bad they had to wear a hood.

It was such an evil and sick twist of fate. Karma? No. Nobody – fucking NOBODY – deserves cancer. Bill had spent so many years telling the joke about his mom, how everyone she knew had a tumor, and how she had to tell everyone else that everyone she knew had a tumor; it's just the most miserable type of irony.

Bill did the extended bit about how he was stuck in the back of the car, the family is driving a fourteen-hour stretch without breaks, peeing in Dixie cups, the sun is shining through Bill's window the whole time, and he feels like "an ant under a magnifying glass," and is becoming a "sun-stroked mongoloid" because it's hot and his dad won't turn on the A/C so he can save two cents a mile. Meanwhile, his mom has spent the last ten hours talking about tumors before offering Bill a plum. "Plum – tumor. You get the similarity of it all?" he asked.

He also made jokes about using terminally ill people to do stunts in movies. I know the joke was more about shaming people who leave their loved ones to die alone in nursing homes, but fuck, there were so many jokes that it just added this horrible and shameful weight to the situation. I thought: wow, Bill is one of those. Bill is one of those relatives with tumors, like his mom was always talking about. You couldn't even turn back to Bill's own comedy and not get spooked.

Everybody fears and hates the things they know deep down inside are a reflection of themselves. Deep down inside, from the very earliest age, especially when tripping, maybe Bill knew he had cancer inside of him. He certainly knew he felt something.

We left the hospital and I found out he was staying at Steve's house, which was odd because he would usually have his own hotel room. The fact he was at his brother's house felt like a concession to how bad things really were and kind of made it feel like he was losing the fight.

I went home that night and I started crying. I knew he wasn't going to make it.

[*   *   *]

Robert Morton

He was the best. Bar none. Bill was as good as it gets. All those years we were constantly blown away by Bill Hicks – to the extent we put him on that much so that he wouldn't do other shows. And he did become pretty associated with the Letterman show.

What happened was that I got a call from Jay Leno, and he basically turned us on to Bill. He said, "This guy is unbelievable, he's ready for a shot. He's not right for *The Tonight Show*, you should use him." One look at the tape and we were totally bought. This guy was special. He had his own voice that had not been seen before. He was Bill Hicks.

I don't remember exactly how it unfolded from there. I think we made an appointment to see him at one of the clubs and we started booking him. I remember there was some issue with him early on, but I don't remember exactly what brought it on. And I don't remember what got him back. Ultimately he got back on the show because we thought he was right to be back on the show. And a lot of time we took breaks from people who had a lot of initial exposure, and it got to the point where it was, "Well, we don't want to have that person on too much. They need to refresh their material."

So, I remember there was some incident, but I also remember on that program that we never said, "we're not putting this person on again because they did this type of material." We would never do that. I know that we never did that. There might have been an incident – and I'm not sure this is the case, I'm just speaking hypothetically – if someone said to him, "Don't do this," and he went on the air and did it, chances are we wouldn't want to have that person on any more because they were not playing by the rules and they were not cooperating with us, and ultimately we are the end user. I think that might have been an issue, but I don't recall. I'm just saying these are reasons we might have had someone off the air for five years.

There have been acts over the years that we tried to put material on that we said, "Please don't do that," for whatever reason. To tell you the truth, Bill was a working comic. It wasn't like he was anyone special then or when he had that one shot. Bill was a very good stand-up comic, an exceptional stand-up comic, but something was not given license to him that other people weren't given.

You know, we are talking about one comic out of, well, I would venture to say we would put on at least one comic a week and I was there for fourteen years, so do the math: That's forty original weeks, times fourteen years, and we are talking about, what, one shot? It's interesting in that you have to look at the producers' side. We dealt with those things every single day. Even the incident where his entire act was cut, it wasn't the first time we dealt with stuff like that. That's an occurrence that happened before. I remember once it happened with Sam Kinison.

I think Bill always had a way of making the events in his life more extraordinary than they in fact were. And I think rightfully so. They were his words, and it was his act. But from a producing standpoint, these are the decisions we make. You know, we cut people's material, we told people to do things. That's what the job is. So in our doing our job, which we did forty weeks a year, to isolate one show or one experience is close to impossible, because these weren't things that made marks in our lives. It was par for the course. It was the job. Every night I would go to a club and tell a comic: you can't do this, you can't do that; please try and stay away from this, stay away from that; I don't think the timing is right for something like that.

And it was influenced by hundreds of different things, from what was going on in the news to what was sensitive in the media at the time. There was a time when religious material was very sensitive; and I remember at NBC, they were getting pressure from Jerry Falwell and other religious right groups. I remember Falwell coming up to NBC to have lunch – I forget who the chairman was at the time – but I remember Falwell in the building having lunch with the chairman of NBC. Seeing him in the building. And it was like, "Holy Jesus, that's pretty frightening."

And here's a guy in Bill that wanted to be Lenny Bruce, and idolized a guy like that. And a lot of the things he was right about. I'm not saying Bill was wrong for making a big deal over these things, especially the last incident, but I don't think he took into consideration that it's about commerce.

Look, we are advertiser-supported television. You have to be sensitive to the people that are paying the bills. We dealt with it every day. And we were at a point in our lives where we all had something to say. This was the 1980s when I was in my 30s. Everyone else was in their 20s and 30s and we had a lot to say; and every day we were told that we couldn't do things. I can't tell you arguments I had with Standards and Practices people over the years. Forget about somebody else's act, what we wanted to achieve on the program. The point I'm making is that it was an everyday occurrence for me representing our own material as well as the material we wanted to put on the air from other people. So it's the job.

It was never anything personal; it wasn't that we didn't like the material. This was with every comic. We were putting these people on, so obviously we liked what they were doing. We were network television with license holders across the line at some 200-odd stations, and we have to represent their interests, so what do you do?

What I recollect about that last show we taped with him, is that it was all pretty new. How long had we been at CBS? Five or six weeks? I think how much we could take material where it wouldn't have been given a second thought about at NBC, where we were on at 12:30 and we were considered the young upstarts, I think at CBS we were very sensitive about everything we did.

I don't think it's anything different between CBS and NBC. I think their broadcast standards in general are probably the same. I would venture to say that neither of them look forward to putting on controversial religious material, only because they don't want the switchboard to light up the next day. It's really that simple.

We had ultimate authority to put anything we wanted on the show, as any show does. Any show does. At least the shows I have done. You are given a rule of standards and practices, a Standards and Practices person might say to you, "We want you to lose that," for whatever reason. Ultimately the producer will put it on or not, then you deal with: is the network going to call us on the line for this, or are they going to let it go?

So as much as they would have called us and said we couldn't do certain things, we also had to watch, guard, and make our own interpretations on things. CBS didn't have any Standards and Practices people at a show. I remember the phrase. It was always, "Shared responsibility" they called it, where the producers used to patrol the shows for themselves.

Looking back now knowing he had cancer, the only thing it changes as far as looking at it from this perspective goes is that I think he had something to achieve. He had to make that mark knowing he was a dying man. I think he had something to achieve. It explains why he was so vehement about it. As I said, Sam Kinison had a set that was also taken out of the show, but you never read about it, you never heard about it. It's happened a few times, as it's happened on any show. I would venture to guess that if you asked *The Tonight Show* they would say that they have had incidents. Most shows do. Especially if you are doing live to tape.

At the time I was thinking, "Yeah, they are only jokes and, yes, it's only a stand-up act." But we weren't judging based on whether it was a funny joke or not. And I think Bill always made a case that: these are my words, these are my jokes. The judgment was never made on whether it was funny or not.

Towards the end Bill took himself very seriously. And I think there was a mission on Bill's part. I don't know what to say about it. And I've never given it that much thought. That's the odd part. It's nothing that I've ever thought about that much and I don't think anybody on the show thought about it that much. It was made a much bigger deal than in fact it was.

I think Bill always sensed we were censoring him, when in fact we were deciding on what to buy and what not to buy, it's that simple. And I always liken doing a show to being in the fashion business where somebody at a department buys a suit, if they decided to put the suit on sale, that's their call. It's a business and you are selling product. Somebody is buying that product and those buyers are often people who don't look at it like it's just a joke.

I think Bill was probably right in saying, "They're just jokes," because, you know something, we bought them as jokes. But you look at advertisers who are sensitive, you look at networks who are sensitive about offending not only viewers but people who are spending money. In all honesty the viewers are often the last consideration in these cases. I don't think it was ever about: your material will offend viewers. I think it was all about: your material will cause advertisers and the Wal-Marts of the world that are conservative companies to pull out of a new show on CBS.

[*   *   *]

CHAPTER 11

Dave Pruett hosted an Access Show in Austin called "CapzEyEz." Bill sat down with Pruett for an extended interview. When Pruett asked Bill where he was living, Bill slapped his hands down on his knees and said, "In these jeans." Pruett chuckled like it was a joke. It was and it wasn't. Bill had no home. He really was a nomad. He had given away most of his remaining possessions when he left LA, and, after *Letterman,* he had just a handful of performing obligations on his plate: the Comedy Corner in West Palm Beach, the Laff Stop in Austin, Igby's gig out in LA, and he was scheduled to play Caroline's in New York City the first week of January.

During the shows, Bill was doing the set that CBS cut. More or less. Usually more. He wasn't constrained by commercial breaks so he let it breathe, if only a little. But he did all the bits. Then he let the crowd know it had been cut from the boob tube. That someone or some-ones at the network didn't think it was appropriate for them to see.

Then Bill usually tore into the network. At the Comedy Corner show he called CBS the "Cunt Broadcasting Network" and railed: "You have standards? Isn't this the same network that shows *Full House*?" Actually, that was ABC, but point taken.

"It amazes me how afraid they are of one person, basically a joke blower. That's basically all I am is a joke blower, on the back of some Mexican blowing jokes all over the driveway. Fairly harmless guy that

369

I am, believer in love and anti-war and truth and the values of this country that it originally formed: freedom of fucking expression . . . I know their big fear is the pro-life movement because those people are terrorists. Okay? But they are a minority, they are not the majority. You know what? The majority of people are very reasonable, I find. And you know what? They don't write letters when something offends them on TV because reasonable people know, it's just television."

After the last shows in LA, Thanksgiving Day to be exact, Bill flew to London to do a pitch meeting for fucking television, for *Counts of the Netherworld* specifically.

After the meeting, the producers at Tiger Aspects felt the very best they would get would be a pilot, and that was on Bill's name alone. It was still a big enough name.

The truth is that, had the show been given a green light, it still faced a hurdle. Bigger. A wall, maybe. Bill would not have been able to keep his condition a secret before doing any show. As the main performer in a series, he would have to have been insured, and that would have required at least a very basic physical. There was no way.

Post-meeting, the group was meant to go to a play, followed by dinner. Bill said he couldn't make it, he was too tired. Then he hugged Brand and thanked him for his commitment to Bill and the project. "I love you for what you have done," he said.

When he returned to the US, Bill was back in Palm Beach with Colleen. They had an early Christmas tree-decorating party at her house. Bill drew a reindeer on a hand-made ornament and stuck it on the tree. When McGarr opened it she read what Bill had written inside: "Will you marry me?"

Bill returned to Little Rock for his 32nd birthday. He also wrote letters to David Letterman and Jay Leno. In his letter to the former he was still seeking understanding about what happened on the show back in October. He gloated mildly about contributing to *The Nation*, the left-leaning magazine; and enclosed a copy of his first submission to the same, as well as a Macanudo cigar. Returning the favor of the Cuban that David had given Bill on the ill-fated show.

He closed the letter: "P.S. I'm writing you on the eve of my 32nd birthday. Christmas is just around the corner. You know what I want, besides us clearing up the air? A copy of my last set on your show! My folks think I fucked up!"

To Leno he gloated mildly that he had his own show going in the UK, and once that "bug" was out of his system, he would be happy to talk about doing Jay's show. Also, the things he had said about Jay's show were also said by others and Bill hoped they weren't taken seriously.

He had been writing. Not just letters. He was getting more offers from publications to contribute, and off of the *Letterman* publicity there was interest by publishers in a book. He was being as prolific as could be, given his condition, but quality varied widely. The thoughtfulness in an essay on his love of smoking and the freedom to choose was averaged down with an outline for a banal TV show idea called *Free Press*. It was centered around an independent newspaper in a college town. The characters were amazingly archetypal. The paper started by the son of a wealthy but unethical industrialist and staffed by Rainbow, the free spirit; Dutch, the ex-athlete sports reporter; Tricia, the gung-ho journalist major. Etc. The mission of the paper (much like Bill's) was "to speak for the disenfranchised." It was not Bill at his creative best.

From Little Rock, Jim and Mary took Bill to Austin for Christmas at Steve's house. Then on the 29th he met Colleen in Las Vegas. The following night the couple went to see Frank Sinatra at the MGM Grand.

On New Year's Day, Bill and Colleen were back in Florida where Bill was taken to the hospital. His condition was deteriorating rapidly. Still, against McGarr's desires, Bill was determined to play his four nights of shows at Caroline's. He spent the next couple of days resting to regain strength. He was also half-whacked out from time-release morphine patches that Dr. Donovan had given him for pain.

They flew to New York. Colleen tried to get Bill not to perform, to get on a plane and go back to Florida. "I've gotta do this," he said to her. Trying to stop Bill from something he was determined to do had always been wasted energy. But the emotional toll was now becoming unbearable.

Bill got on stage. He did thirty-five minutes before he stopped and asked, "Colleen? Are you here?"

"Bill, I'm right here," she said from the back of the club.

"I can't do this any more," he said. Colleen went up, and pulled Bill down offstage. They left the club, grabbed a cab, headed back to the hotel, and McGarr booked the next flight to Florida. In Palm Beach Bill was admitted back into the hospital.

On January, Bill was taken back to Little Rock. To St. Vincent's Hospital, then two days later was moved into his parents' house for hospice care. Bill wanted to be alone with his family. Only then was a press release finally drafted, and still it only said that Hicks was "seriously ill." Two weeks later, Bill called the people close to him who still didn't know: Dwight, Pineapple, Laurie Mango. Then he stopped talking. He took a vow of silence two weeks before he died.

According to his brother, "The very last thing he ever said to me was, 'Steve, how are Marti and Ryan and Rachel?' – my wife and two kids. Not his problem, but how is my family doing? Because he knew that was important to me, and that's what was important to him. We did not dwell on his situation. He wouldn't let it happen that way."

Letters came flowing in. His family members read them to him. His mom read him the *Lord of the Rings* trilogy. She was unable to make it through *The Return of the King* before 11:20 p.m. on 26 February.

Bill fought to the end. Even after he stopped talking, he kept walking. Every day he was insistent on walking the house. Right up until the day he passed away.

[*　　*　　*]

Kevin Booth

After Bill left town, I went to every medical professional of any stripe or training I could find who would hear my questions. I wanted to know if there was anything he could do to improve his chances. Shark cartilage, that was one of the things I came across. Apparently sharks don't get cancer. At the time there was evidence to suggest that human consumption of shark cartilage might be effective in fighting cancer. I also advised Bill to get a juicer and start drinking fresh juices to boost his immunity system.

Mary was part of the fight. She didn't want to give in, but she was also the one telling me, "This is pancreatic cancer." And, of course, when I told every one of my doctors that he had pancreatic cancer they were: "Oooh, Kevin. I'm sorry to hear that." It wasn't just "Oooh," it was the kind of "Oooh," where they suddenly inhale through their pursed lips before speaking. It was the tell-tale sign, "Shit, that's bad."

                    KEVIN
        But they cure cancer all the time.

                    DOCTOR
        Yeah, but not pancreatic cancer.

                    KEVIN
        You don't know my friend. He's different.

Bill was different. And sometimes in ways – shit, you just had shake your head because it was so like Bill, not just to get cancer, but get the worst kind. The one you can't cure. It's hard to say that, but there was just something about him. There had to be something unusual about him even in his passing away.

He was getting tumor markers, where they would measure the size of the tumor; and he told me that, sure enough, it was shrinking. I would go to my doctors and tell them what Bill had said to me; and they would explain 'metastasizing' to me. The tumor in the pancreas could be tiny, but it was likely to spread to his liver, and it wasn't his pancreas that was going to kill him, it was his liver.

KEVIN

But you don't understand. You don't know my friend. It's
going away. It's going away.

DOCTOR

I hope it works and I'll pray for you and for him.

It was about four weeks from the time he finally told me he had pancreatic cancer until Bill was next in town. His brother Steve was having the family Christmas at his house in Austin. Steve's kids, his wife, Bill and Mary and Jim Hicks were there to celebrate the holidays.

Bill and I had a date that afternoon at Computize, a local computer store, where I was going to help get him set up with a computer to write on. I arrived early. I went inside, sat down at one of the machines, and started typing: "It was a cold December day when two friends met . . ." I had written a little dramatic scene. When Bill showed, he sat down to read it. And while he did, I just remember looking at him. It was the first time I had really looked at Bill. His arms were so frail. They were black and blue and riddled with holes where he had taken a needle. His stomach was distended. His face was boney. He looked bruised. It was like watching a ghost being born. It was intense.

Bill was trying to decide whether to get an Apple or a Wintel machine. Of all the stupid things to fret over. Maybe it seemed important at the time, but it shouldn't have been. He decided to get a Mac. Bill told the salesman: "Give it to me. Give me all of it. Top of the line." Just what a salesman working on commission wanted to hear. Bill gave the guy a credit card. The salesman came back and told Bill his card had been declined. He also came back with an attitude. While Bill got annoyed by shit like that, he was never the kind of guy to come out and say, "Listen, I just had an HBO special and

374

I got paid thousands and thousands of dollars." Instead Bill told him he needed to learn how to treat customers, and that he had just given him the wrong card.

It was another one of the ways Bill seemed to be aging rapidly. Like his tastes in music changed, it was John Hiatt and jazz. And now, the way he lectured the salesperson, talking about manners, it was very old-man "listen to me, sonny boy." He actually had given the salesman the wrong credit card and had to go back that night with the right one. He also got overcharged. I guess it didn't matter much. People with a couple of months to live, spending time bargain-shopping probably isn't a priority.

Later that afternoon into early evening, I was telling Bill he should let David Johndrow know. Several times I told Bill he should. I was politely persistent. He wasn't against it, he just wasn't sure if he was for it. Finally he said, "Yeah, you're right, let's tell David." So we did. We called David and told him he needed to come over to my house. David had a life and it was the holidays. Still he seemed unusually preoccupied.

The three of us decided to go have sushi. David met us at my place. He looked like he thought Bill was going to tell him something was wrong with him and that he was in trouble; maybe that Bill never wanted to speak with him again, or maybe even that Bill had a gay crush on him. Who knows? Bill's health was probably not on his mind. But when Bill broke the news to David, it looked like David's way of dealing with it was not to deal. It looked like he didn't even take it seriously; looked like Bill had told him that his favorite color was orange. David told Bill he was sorry, he might have even used the word, "Bummer."

Then he started talking around the subject. He had an aunt that had pancreatic cancer or something. His dad was going to be coming to town soon. He didn't really address Bill or his problem. Bill asked him, "Dude, did you hear what I told you? I just told you I have cancer, I have pancreatic cancer, it's really serious." David said that he heard him.

The whole energy between the three of us was completely ginsued. Back in the day, we had been like the Three Musketeers. When you are tripping with certain people, there's an unspoken understanding about what to say and what not to say. One of the things we all knew was not to talk about outside shit, like what was going on with your dad, or the kind of shoes you just bought. We were usually all mentally in sync. If we weren't all on the same wavelength we were at least in the same wave pool. That was gone. David seemed to be in a completely different place.

We went to Musashino, the restaurant, to eat. Bill kept talking about the cancer and *A Course in Miracles*, and creating a miracle, and that he was going back to England to do a TV show; but David was bringing in an outside energy – he had his sister coming into town, and a lot of other things going on. Again, maybe his way to deal was not to deal. We had long since stopped being Musketeers, about that we could no longer delude ourselves.

We ate sushi, a lot of really expensive sushi. Then Bill walked into the bathroom and threw it all up.

During this period when he was in town we would write little letters back and forth to each other. At the time they felt sincere. In retrospect they sound corny:

"Dear Bill, We've been through so much together. This is going to be the greatest test and the greatest adventure. We are going to come through this to the other side and be even stronger. There is no such thing as death. The season of healing is upon us."

I would take a little dime bag and fill it with pain pills, then tape candies around it. I'd include that with the letter, and turn it into a little care package. He opened one up when he was up at the hospital. Bill has this card with pills spilling out of it, and the doctors are looking at him saying, "What the hell is that? You can't take those." Bill took them anyway, then he came back and said to me: "Eh, those pills you gave me, Kevin, they weren't that strong. Next time can you give me more of them?"

We also bought each other lots of books, a lot of them about American Indian culture and healing, a lot on Shamanism. One of the meanings he got out of what he was reading was that his mission had changed. He was spreading his message into the cancer ward, to other people who were dying. It went from Bill needing to be on stage in front of people telling them what their government was doing to them or doing to others in their name, to something far more important. Now he had to be in a cancer ward to tell a kid dying of cancer to have hope.

At some point, Bill bought some blank Christmas cards – plain cards with no prewritten pap sentiments – to give to people who were in his inner circle: me, Jimmy Pineapple, Jere, Huggins, Fallon. It was a list of people. It was almost like his final, not goodbye, but his way of telling his friends where he felt they were in life. It was a really deliberate act. He made a list of these people that he wanted to do this for and systematically went through it to write each person a message.

Mine read: "Dear Kevin, May all of your Christmases be happy and free. Love, Your best friend Willy." It had this light, open, happy feeling to it.

Bill invited Jere and I to come spend Christmas Eve with his family. Of course, I was going to see Bill, but I also wanted to spend some time alone with my girlfriend. Jere and I went to Musashino (again) and had a nice quiet dinner together. But, God, did we just gorge ourselves on sushi. Oh, and we took a couple of pain pills as an aperitif.

After dinner, we drove up to Bill's brother's house up in Cedar Park, far north Austin. Bill wasn't there. He had been taken to the emergency room. They said it wasn't anything big. I suspected it was related to all of the bowel problems he was having from his medical treatments and the pain medication: abdominal cramping, constipation and diarrhoea.

We stayed and waited for Bill to get back. Bill's mom could not have been nicer. She offered us food. We were barely keeping down the piles of sushi we had devoured.

Ever since Bill had got sick his mom had been doing anything and everything for him. And it was something he started joking about: "Bill, can I get you something to eat? Can I cook you a turkey dinner?" It was his impression of her: "Bee-yull . . ." She would run into the kitchen at the drop of a hat to put together the most elaborate meal. She was trying so hard to be the best mom in the final hour. He was touched by it, but it was also so ridiculous that he would laugh about it. So when Mary Hicks offered us a turkey dinner, we couldn't say no.

We were bloated to the point of wanting to puke and Mary handed us enormous plates of food. We sat there and forced ourselves to push it down. In the midst of this painful charade, Bill finally came home. I told him we were trying to eat to humor his mom, but that we were about to throw up. He started laughing, then played good cop by taking control of the situation. He got his mom to stop feeding us. He took the plates away even though there was still food piled on them.

We spent some time getting his Mac set up. I was trying to get a word processor installed and running, he wanted to sit there and play video games. Then it was time for the Hicks family Christmas program. And it was a little program, written out and everything. They went around the room. Bible verses. Then religious Christmas Carols. "O Little Town of Bethlehem." Luke 2:11. "Away In a Manger." Jim was playing the songs on a little electronic handheld keyboard. It was really sweet.

Of course Bill had given Jere and me each a handful of Percocets. So everything was sweet.

It came time for Bill to do his scripture reading for the program. He started, then at Matthew 2:12 – "And being warned of God in a dream that they should not return to Herod, they departed into their own country another way" – he stopped and changed direction. "I want everyone to repeat after me," he said. "There is nothing to fear." I think one of Steve's kids might have repeated after Bill. "I am as God created me."

378

Bill began to recite a passage from *A Course in Miracles*.

When Bill did this, his father Jim spun around and turned away. He refused to participate. It was a crucial moment. It was just a few weeks before Bill stopped speaking; and here his father wouldn't participate because maybe he didn't believe it was a Christian doctrine. I don't know for sure. All I know is I watched Jim Hicks make a deliberate move to literally turn his back on his son.

It was heavy.

Thankfully things did lighten back up a bit. Bill played with his niece and nephew. He also ad-libbed some impromptu lyrics to an Elvisesque version of "Here Comes Santa Claus."

"Belchin' and a poppin' and a tootin' and a hootin', he's feeling great."

Even better, after things seemed more normal in the room Bill did his own visual commentary. He made a blow job pantomime. Seriously. He made the fist then waved back and forth in front of his mouth. The international hand signal for blow job. And he rolled his eyes. His was the everyfamily. And it was funny. It was hysterical. Timing. Facial expression. Everything.

Bill never lost his sense of humor. I want to say it was amazing, but he just stayed himself until the very end, and humor was how he dealt with most every conflict, problem, or uncomfortable situation. The joke was his out. But it wasn't just the joke. Like he did with "Crossover Rule," if Bill got in an argument with someone he would write a funny little song about it, and often leave it on their answering machine. That was his way of deflecting things and leaving everyone with a smile on their face. Bill had very few unhappy endings or bitter falling-outs, he was a guy that was able to maintain a positive link with most people he met.

He was just Bill . . . even in the heaviest of situations. That was his gift. And fortunately for his friends he never tired of giving it. Merry Christmas, from Bill.

It started after he went sober. It was an unspoken tradition that had developed. Every Christmas – usually either the night before or the night after – we would spend a night together at my house, just the two of us, hanging out and talking and playing music. It was a real Christmas celebration, with people you care about, talking about meaningful stuff: the past year, the coming year, and what you are looking forward to both experiencing and accomplishing.

We both loved Christmas and not just from the perspective of celebrating Jesus' birthday. Bill loved Christmas because he loved to give gifts to people. That last Christmas, he gave me a blue and gold tapestry with a big smiling sun on it. Bill's gifts were usually a little more thoughtful than socks and ties. I remember another year he gave me porn. The perfect thing for thinking of Bill.

Looking back, God, you would take things for granted. I would. I did. I remember some of those previous Christmas nights with Bill I was bummed, thinking I should be with my girlfriend. I feel ashamed of that now. I was being selfish. This year was obviously different. How could it not be? I can't remember ever looking forward to seeing my friend so much, but a lot about that night was unusual. He came over and he was in a weird mood.

BILL
I don't know if I have the energy to do this tonight.

KEVIN
Well, you know, we don't have to do it, Bill. We can blow it off.

BILL
No, no, no. I want to do it.

We were both being passive-aggressive, but Bill was also big on feeling it. He wanted to know that he was wanted, and that it didn't feel like it was being done out of obligation. I told him we didn't have to, but I didn't want to blow it off. We were hanging out and drinking tea. Bill couldn't even drink coffee. His stomach couldn't handle it.

We talked about all of these projects we had ideas for, the things we wanted to do next. Then Bill brought up the one argument we ever really had, the one over Marble Head Johnson. "Well, I guess you won't have to play with me any more." On one hand, Bill was certain we were going to create this miracle. Through prayer and positive thinking, everyone together, we were going help Bill kill the tumor in his body. On the other hand, Bill was giving indications that he was resigned to it. He said things to indicate he knew he was going to die.

"You won't have to play my stupid blues songs any more." It was also a personal dig, and a cheap ticket for a guilt trip. Self-pity maybe? What else? God, it was hard. It was so fucking hard. I am looking at my best friend, who I'm starting to realize really might be dying. He might not beat cancer. I had had little doubt all along, but now, I don't know. And he's the one planting those seeds.

I had also put all my proverbial eggs in Bill's basket. My entire career at that point was Bill. And that Christmas I was completely broke. I didn't have a dollar to my name. Zero in the bank. Zero in my pocket. Maybe some change in the couch cushions, but that was it. I had stopped pursuing all my other projects and working with other people just to concentrate on things with Bill. There were a handful of other things, and there was hope that we had this deal coming. But none of them did.

Bill said to me, "When I get back to England, I've got my office next door to Paul McCartney. I think I'm going to start using him as my new bass player."

Okay, Bill. He was feeling sorry for himself, but with a tear in his eye. I thought we had got over that, got beyond Marble Head Johnson. He was obviously still bummed out about it. He knew this was probably the last time we were going to be able to talk about it.

"Bill, I just couldn't do it at the time. I thought you understood by now. I thought you could see what people go through. What you and your family are going through is a lot like what me and my brother have been going through for a long time." My brother didn't have a deadline like Bill, but we had near-death experiences all the time. It's like a rollercoaster ride. Even when he was well, he still had to have someone take care of him. The combination of everything going on in my life, I didn't want to play the blues.

KEVIN

I just wasn't in the mood to play these wacky songs. I wasn't
into it. Plus what we are doing now is more serious. It's better.

BILL

I know. But I also know you don't like playing with me.

KEVIN

I do like playing with you.

BILL

No. Come on. Quit lying. You don't like playing with me.
You're going to be happy when I'm gone and you don't have
to play with me any more.

It's hard to admit, but maybe in some weird way he was right. There
did come a time when Bill came over to play music that I would
stress out because it wasn't exactly what I wanted to be doing. There
were other things I wanted to explore but he was kind of putting me
in a position of either, or. As it was, I felt like I was sneaking around
behind his back to do Electric Ladies Man. It was a combination of
things. And like I said, I thought it had cost me our friendship, the
night Bill first called to tell me about the diagnosis.

BILL

It's sad you felt this way, Kevin, because I thought we shared
this amazing communication. You always understood exactly
what I wanted to do without me having to explain it to you.

He mentioned Fallon and David Johndrow.

BILL

When I try to do stuff with other people, we spend so much
time talking about what we are going to do. We talk and talk
and talk about it. The cool thing with you is that we just shut
our mouths and do it.

KEVIN

Bill, I like doing this. You are my best friend. There is nobody else like you in my life nor will there ever be. I'm never going to know anybody else like you.

BILL

Well, then, why didn't you have faith in me?

KEVIN

You were trying to deceive me, Bill. You were trying to get me to quit playing music with other people that I wanted to play with, telling me we were going to be on Letterman. You knew we weren't going to be on Letterman playing music.

BILL

Yeah, but I wanted to.

KEVIN

But you knew it wasn't going to happen, and you weren't even pushing for it to happen. Don't lay the guilt on me. I have a life to lead, too.

BILL

I know you do. And I know you've dedicated a lot of life to our projects. I couldn't have done so much of this without you.

KEVIN

Bill, it's pretty amazing, that, one, we've only had one falling- out our entire lives together, and, two, we are sitting here talking about it.

BILL

Yeah, but I still think I'm going to start playing with Paul McCartney.

KEVIN

Okay, Bill. You know what? I think you should start playing with Paul McCartney.

It was with a grain of salt. It was one brother trying to prepare another one for the absence. And like I said to Bill, it was a small miracle that two people who spent as much time collaborating as we did only had one serious falling-out, and we could talk about it without it becoming another issue.

We hung out some more and talked about our life and our friendship. It wasn't quite a goodbye, but it felt like a precursor to a goodbye. He was real low on energy. We tossed back some Percocet and drank some more tea. Bill mentioned that if we were there with other people – David, or any of the Houston comics – that we wouldn't be playing music. We would just be spending the night talking. That was the difference.

We walked into the studio, he picked up his gold hollow-body Les Paul, and said, "Oh my God. It's so heavy." He had never said anything like that before. Watching him put it on was like watching a kid trying to lift an anvil. He didn't expect it to be heavy. It was a burden, but he got plugged in and I rolled tape.

I played drums. Bill played his guitar and sang. We did a song called "Goodbye Smokes." We first played it a little over a year before, when he had written it. We were going to put it on *Arizona Bay*, but there just wasn't a place for it. It was a jazz instrumental. A few chords. Not that complicated. It was obviously about his quitting smokes.

When we played "Goodbye Smokes" this time, it had a different meaning. Now it was: when I leave this world, I'm leaving all kinds of things I love behind. Bill talked about the things he was going to miss. The biggest was maybe guacamole; just sitting in a Mexican restaurant, drinking ice tea and eating chips and salsa and guac. That and smokes and women. Simple things. Except maybe women. They aren't that simple. But it wasn't like he was going to miss the spotlight and the stage. The things he wanted to take with him and the feelings he didn't want to leave behind, they had nothing to do with showbusiness.

All of this time he was fighting like a champ. No one could tell him, "No." Nobody could keep him from doing a show. If he was going to do it, he was going to do it. Not me. Not Colleen. Not his mom. There were times when Colleen would try to talk him out of performing because he would freeze up on stage, or need a pill or just go off on some weird tangent to where it was clear there was something wrong. But it had nothing to do with his ego and his need to be in front of an audience. It might have been to get the message to as many people as possible and to fight that fight until the end.

Bill's strength was incredible. He willed himself to do things he probably shouldn't have. This night, he totally let his guard down in front of me. He allowed me to see how weak he really was. How much pain he was in. Maybe it was part of what I needed to see to be able to start letting go. I was still, "No, no. Bill is going to beat this thing. We are working on a project for TV in Australia."

Bill had been looking forward to the afterlife. He had been talking about it his whole life, talking about the day the spaceships would come pick him up, or about the day of ascension to the pearly gates. But he was also starting to get scared, that this was a goodbye to everyone he was so close to. He may have been in some enlightened stage where he thought he or his spirit was still going to be around those people, to be in their lives somehow after his body was gone, but something about the relationships and the way it all worked in this world, something about that would change. No matter how much he tried to sit there and say, "There is no such thing as death," he knew it was going to be different. It was sad. But it was okay to be sad. It takes a man to admit he's sad. Bill admitted that he was going to miss the place – Mexican restaurants, his friends, Colleen, the way women smelled.

We played until Bill couldn't play any more. It was only about forty-five minutes. It was too much of a struggle for him. He wanted to sit down for a while. So we did. "You're definitely going to beat this," I told him. And I meant it. We also talked about some of the dreams we had that we thought were omens, things about our fates. And we talked about our UFO experience.

BILL

Why were you always so afraid to tell people about that? It was
like you were trying to make me look like an idiot.

KEVIN

I don't know. I was embarrassed by it. So many of our friends
tried to convince me that the UFO shit was just something
that happened in your mind.

BILL

But you know it was more than that.

KEVIN

I know.

BILL

So why did you leave me hanging with that?

KEVIN

After a while I tried to come around.

BILL

I know. And you have come a long way in the last
couple of months.

At the end of the night he told me he wanted me to overdub key-
boards, bass lines, percussion. He also wanted me to get Bob Riley,
the singer from Year Zero, to come in and add backing vocals, then
mix it and have a copy done in six hours so that he could take it back
with his parents to Little Rock. I wasn't sure if he was joking or not.

He took off about two in the a.m. About 8 o'clock that morning
he called, wanting to come by and show his mom and dad the studio.
Sure. The place was only half done with insulation and wires sticking out of the walls. His parents walked around the place like they
were on a museum tour.

He asked me to put on the tape, and play it for his parents. I said,
"Well, I gotta be honest with you. I only got as far as bass and key-
boards, and I mixed it." I only got two hours of sleep, but I got that far.

He cleared up any uncertainty I might have had when he replied, "I was just kidding, Kevin." I told him that, no, I wanted to give him something to drive home with. "That's too cool," Bill said.

I tried to grab a moment to talk with Mary. I wanted to know what Bill's situation really was. In any instance like that, there is always that shameful behind-the-back discussion: "Well, what did the doctor really say?" Bill was supposed to get a new tumor marker in a few days. And he knew it was going to be half the size. He prayed that. The miracle was going to happen over Christmas. This was going to be it. It was about ten days away. That's what he was focused on. That's when the miracle was going to happen.

I gave Bill some cassettes of the recording, and he left. It was like shop talk. "I'll talk to you later. We'll get back to work on this."

They walked out my front door. He had his mom on one side and his dad on the other and they all had their arms around each other. They were helping support him, helping him walk. I only realized then how much he had been struggling the night before. I knew he was weak, but shit he could barely walk. The amount of effort he put out the night before to hang out and give as much of an appearance that he was not completely debilitated, and that he just wanted to spend that night with me and have it seem as normal as possible, that was the greatest gift my friend Bill Hicks ever gave to me.

As Bill and his parents walked out my front door, I saw the three of them perfectly silhouetted against the sunlight. It was extraordinarily bright. And I watched them disappear into the light. That was the last time I ever saw Bill.

It was surprising that Bill had taken the route of chemotherapy to begin with. It was so unlike Bill, or so unlike what his friends would have predicted. It was almost like God was testing his faith, a test to see if he would submit straight to what western medicine prescribes. He never would have done anything like that before. Bill didn't believe in modern medicine. He thought it was horseshit, that had nothing to do with healing people, but was only for people to profit from.

After Bill told me he was already undergoing chemo, and that once you start, there is no going back, I had real difficulty with how the whole miracle was going to go down. If we really were going to have this whole miracle happen, why did he give in so fast?

Imagine a doctor comes out and tells you that you are really sick and that you only have three or four months to live, so the best course of action is to start on chemotherapy right away. The Bill that I always knew, he would have said: "Wait, you say I only have three months to live? Then fuck it. I'm not going your route. I'm going to fight this with my spirit. There is no such thing as death. We are all just energy condensed to matter." The miracle was about Bill being able to prove so many of the things he had been preaching for all of those years.

I feel like Bill had thrown in the towel when he agreed to start doing chemo. I could never have said that to him when he was alive or to any of his family without them just ridiculing me and laying into me, without telling me that they were doing everything they could. I know they were or they felt they were. That's not meant as a slight, but everybody was saying that they had the best doctors. It's just not possible with all of the moving around he was doing. But when anybody gets cancer those around him or her always say, "We've got the best doctors there are. And we are going to the best hospitals there are." Everybody wants to believe it.

Bill bought the whole package. Not to say I wouldn't either. But it was out of his character. The rubber hit the fucking road. He had to turn his beliefs into actions. And he didn't. Either that or his actions reflected his true beliefs and everything he had been saying his whole life was crap, or at least was suspect. He failed the most important test of his life. That's not a judgment of Bill's character. He was strong. Stronger than I think I would ever be. I know that. And I have no idea what goes through a man's head or his heart when a doctor tells him that he has pancreatic cancer and three months to live. What's to say that I or anyone else wouldn't have done the exact same as Bill? I bet I would. I bet most of us would.

I always thought Bill was different from "most of us." I still do, but when he had the greatest chance to prove it, he didn't.

Another uncharacteristic thing Bill did was that, right before he died, he said he wanted to be buried in the Hicks family plot in Mississippi. After almost every trip, it was one of the ideas he always came back to: "My body doesn't need to be lying in the ground rotting. Why take up that space? Let the living use that land. Burn me up. I won't need this body any more."

It was another very strong, strong belief of his that he changed his mind on. Why? Who knows. Maybe it was pressure from his parents. Maybe it was wanting to make his parents happy and accede to their wishes. Bill did a handful of things during the last months and days of his life that I will never fully understand.

[* * *]

CHAPTER 12

Rob Fiorella

Bill called me the day he was diagnosed.

I wasn't part of his cadre of other friends. I didn't know his other friends. The day he got diagnosed he called me, he told everybody else a lie. He even told me he was going to tell everyone else a lie. "I've got pancreatic cancer," he said. I almost dropped the phone. It was unbelievable.

If there was anybody who could have beaten it, it was Bill. That's the way I felt from the very beginning.

Bill had no idea what his prognosis was. That was the best part of those first few months that he was ill. As soon as he told me what was wrong with him, though, well, I knew what the statistics were for pancreatic cancer. I knew how dismal that particular prognosis was. Back then you're talking ninety-nine out of a hundred people died. It was awful. The statistics aren't a hell of a lot better now. Plus, Bill didn't even have health insurance.

He had everything possible going against him, including the fact that he was traveling all over the country. He wasn't located near one good hospital. He was getting a number of opinions.

When I was 23 or 24, I was on a hike with a bunch of kids and fell down. Six months later I was in the terminal ward with a very rare infection. I was there for four years.

I had four real death experiences. They weren't near death. I died and came back. The defibrillation paddles. Being resuscitated. I got in the habit of talking about them to a lot of people and really getting off on that. I enjoyed being the center of attention talking about death and dying. Then I had a near-death experience that scared the shit out of me and never talked about it the same way again. I never romanticized death again.

So I talked to Bill about that. And I talked to him about what the death thing was like. We got to talking about philosophy of life and the kinds of things he had been involved in.

We also spent a lot of time talking about drugs. When I met him he was relatively fresh in the 12-step program. He was off coke, still smoking heavily, and he was drinking on and off every once in a while. Not often. He was always conflicted about drugs. As long as I knew him he was conflicted about it.

I had a very different take on them from the 12-steppers. I thought drugs were great, but my involvement with them came as a result of need. I never saw drugs as an evil because they saved my life on a number of occasions. I always had a great attraction to them but I never got involved with them the same way that Bill did and the same way that a lot of addicts do. They cut down my sex drive. Bill was fascinated by that because he was hyper-sexual and he did let drugs get in the way of that for a period of time. We talked about that a lot.

There are times when I was dangerous for him and other times when it helped out, especially when he got sick, but for a while I don't think I was doing him a lot of good. We needed to stop talking about drugs, which we eventually did.

Bill started calling me with things he had written. Not comedy, it was never about comedy, but he wrote a lot of essays. He wrote about politics or smoking or business in America – all of his political itches.

He would scratch one and write the beginning of a really good article and call me and read it to me but never finish it. He did that all the time.

So he'd call me from wherever he was in the country and bitch and moan about where he was and how awful it was. He was getting closer and closer all along the time I knew him to becoming famous, to getting exactly what he wanted. Certainly at the end he was so fucking close.

I was screwing around doing past-life stuff on the weekends with a woman I was working with out in California, but I never knew if I believed in it or not. Bill loved all of the pseudo-science things. He wasn't much of a sceptic. He had a very fecund ontology. For instance, Bill had this real belief in aliens. He talked a lot about going out into the desert and having a close encounter of whatever kind. What happened to Bill on the Harmonic Convergence, he talked about it as if it were just as real as the last shit he took.

The conscious, the subconscious, the collective unconscious – he was very much into those particular areas of philosophy or psychology or whatever you want to call it. I was really undecided. The fact that past-life stuff works is a phenomenon, whether it's because reincarnation is real or not is a whole different story. But I talked to him about what I was doing on the weekends and the kinds of people I saw. And he kept wanting to do that.

It wasn't until he got sick that we finally got around to doing the past-life experiences. We did four, and we had a really good time with it. But Bill had some atypical experiences. In every one of them he had an experience that dealt with the ocean and the sea (he was constantly on a ship) and he always had short lives. In every one of them he died before he was 40. Generally speaking, when you do this, people go and bring things back that are all over the board. They don't usually come back with a single message every time. But he did.

And certainly the experiences he came back with were adventurous. Again, generally he died young. In a couple of the experiences they were violent deaths, in the others there was violence involved.

When people were under or down, I used to ask them a whole bunch of questions and then snap my fingers and have them come to. One of them was: "Figure out why you are there. I want you to fix on a word that will tell you what you are supposed to be learning in this life." Bill came back with: struggling, pain and patience.

He had a feeling about reincarnation. He believed in it to a certain extent.

He talked a lot about the Septuagint, about how they rewrote the Bible and they took out all of the stuff about reincarnation. That was something he found fascinating. He believed that the Bible initially talked about reincarnation. So I know that he had feelings about reincarnation. I don't know how strong.

But I know he was also annoyed – and maybe he thought it was just because I was being a hypocrite – that I was doing past-life work and I kept saying that I didn't know if it necessarily proved there was reincarnation. I also think there is something called genetic memory. You have biochemical links to your great-great-great-great-grandfather in genes.

Bill definitely thought there was something else. He definitely thought he would be going on somehow or other. And I think he was hoping that he was going to be coming back. Because he was impressed by the fact that in every one of those experiences that he had, he came back, and the life he led was short. He died before he was 40 in every one of the four different experiences he had.

Bill had mixed emotions about whether he would live or die. And he would call me and talk about this – talk and talk and talk about dying, what dying was like, and what he thought was going to happen to him. It was causing conflict in him. But he was also listening to a lot of people who were telling him what to do.

If the people looking out for him told him, "You gotta put on a cheerleading outfit today and you've got to do a big cheer, 'I'm gonna survive. I'm gonna live,'" he'd do it. In some ways, he was trying to talk himself into it. But when you are dealing with someone who is smart and astute, you get to a point where you can't say to them: "You look great. You look healthy." That's bullshit and he knew it. What happens is that you push that too hard and the person says, "My God, you are lying about everything."

He was jaundiced. It wasn't difficult. It didn't take a Rhodes Scholar to figure out that he was really, really sick.

When I talked to him he sounded more and more conflicted all the time. He was saying, "Yeah, I'm trying this and trying that." But he wasn't saying to me, "I'm gonna get well. I know I'm gonna get well." He was saying: "Do you think I'm going to die? I think I'm gonna die. I don't know if I am going to die." And obviously in the dark, alone at night, those were the things that were eating him alive.

I know that's not what he was doing when he hung up the phone. He was putting on a brave face and going along with what he was involved with. And he had a lot of people around him telling him all of this stuff. "You're going to get well. We're going to do this. This is going to work. You just gotta believe this. And if you only believe." I sometimes think that was a horrible disservice. I'm not saying they shouldn't do that, but it needed to be balanced and they should have been dealing with the other aspects.

The kind of chemotherapy he was getting was not good. He was getting very mild chemo. They didn't do anything aggressive with him. I think if he had had one really good oncologist – and Florida is not where you would go if you want treatment for cancer, but that's where he wound up because that's where he was diagnosed when he was there with Colleen – but if he had had a really good oncologist, things might have been different.

I'd listen to what Bill would say, and I'd call everyone I knew – and my son is a doctor – and they always had the same kind of advice: "Plant his ass in one hospital and let him go A to Z." He couldn't do it.

He would have run out of money in 15 minutes at one of those places. Money was a big deal for him towards the end because he just didn't have any. He didn't know how he was going to afford the next treatment. They were costing him $1000, $1500 a pop. If they told him he had to go into the hospital he didn't know where he was going to get the money to do it.

It was a situation where Bill was confronted with a choice: he could either quit the business and deal with the cancer or forget the cancer and stay with the business. Essentially he was somewhere in the middle, trying to deal with the cancer and trying real hard not to let anybody find out. And it was grueling. It just wound up sucking the energy out of him.

The whole thing was driving him nuts. He was running out of money. He had the thing with Tribeca going. He was scared to death that people in the industry were going to find out. The thing with Letterman happened. There were a lot of nasty things that occurred in the last six months.

I think he would have really liked it if he had got together with Colleen and they had got married and he had got some time to breathe. That never happened either. He stopped talking and locked himself in a bedroom. But it seemed to me that he was dancing as fast as he could that whole year. He was on a treadmill that whole time, running and not catching his breath. He was always in a different city, he was always involved in negotiations. There were all of these things going on so he was torn in a thousand different directions all the time.

The whole romantic thing about marrying Colleen became more and more of a draw in him. It would have been nice if he could have got married and stolen some time with her. They could have had a week together where he could have just forgotten everything else and just relaxed for a while. But he was never able to relax. There was always something going on. It was just a mess.

Was he going to be making movies? Or producing a new kind of television show? One of the things that seemed very much in the forefront of his mind was producing some new kind of television. He wanted to take the best pieces of the things that Letterman did and take it from there.

Bill wanted to make television sing. He wanted to make it reach out and grab mostly young people. He wanted to grab teens by the neck and show them things and give them humor on a visceral level. That's what he wanted to do, and the thing that pisses everybody off is that he probably could have done it. But he was so anxious to get a program that he was going to be able to put together himself and obviously have his friends as the guys to work with him. It was going to be their group, and they were going to do something bold and very unique.

And by the way, he loved those guys. That's one of the things I can tell you as an outsider. As a person who didn't know his friends from earlier in life, he loved those guys. Like nobody's business. Bill wanted brothers. And that's how he got them. He thought they were just the beginning, the middle and the end. It was a very, very different and very close relationship for him. And that's what is funny. I know that Steve has kind of rewritten his relationship with Bill, and they were best friends, but I didn't even know Bill had a brother until he went back home. But I sure knew about his friends, Kevin and Dwight and the other guys he worked with. He talked about them in glowing terms.

The funny thing is, the kind of things he was talking about doing were the kinds of things that were later on incorporated into the best shows in the first season of, believe it or not, *Ally McBeal*, where somebody would say something and they would show somebody who was wounded and a dozen arrows would appear going into a guy's chest or a cannon ball would blow his head off.

He had a lot of really far-out ideas about what he wanted to do. He was frustrated. He didn't want to work clubs any more. Even before he was first diagnosed, he was sick and tired of working small crowds. He was tired of the fact that in these smaller places people didn't appreciate him. He would go play Albany or a place that's even smaller and he would have trouble drawing a crowd. He just didn't want to do it any more.

He had to. He needed the money.

Everything that was going on with Bill was getting worse. He saw it too. He was saying, "We're going to create a miracle. We're going to make a miracle," but he knew he was getting worse. Part of that may very well have been Bill trying to make his friends think, and trying to make his friends believe that what they were talking about was going to come to fruition. But he knew he was getting worse. There is no question about that. He would tell me he was having trouble eating, or that his stomach was distended or that he was tender.

He always talked to me about how much pain he was in because he talked to me about drugs probably more than anyone. I had been there and done that.

He was telling me he was going to die three or four months before he was talking about it as actively to anybody else. Bill asked me a lot if I thought he was going to die. And for the longest time I told him that I didn't. Towards those last three or four months I started saying, "What do you think?" I started feeling like if I continued to say that "I didn't" to him, he would stop calling. I almost felt like he was testing to see if I was going to bullshit him. I asked him what he thought. And he said he thought he was going to die.

There were a lot of people around him telling him to try alternative medicine, eat these herbs, and try this doctor over here. It just confused him. And I don't think he knew how to die. That bothered him a lot, too, because he hadn't made his peace with anything. It was really frustrating watching him at the end.

And that was how he felt, extremely frustrated. He got paralyzed. I think he stopped doing everything. I didn't see him running to the microphone and trying to get his last breath out. At the end he was overpowered and overcome by all of it. He knew he was dying way before he admitted it. I think he didn't know what to do, and as a result he didn't do anything.

When Bill moved home, I couldn't believe it. It was like finding out that his worst nightmare was going to come true. He wound up living back in the house that was . . . I mean, his father told him he was going to burn in hell. Now he was in his weakest condition going right back into that, to somebody who was going to beat him over the head with his Bible.

Certainly Bill was never a big fan of Christianity or the Bible or any of that other bullshit. Bill was very much into the Bible, but not as a theologian. He loved reading the Bible for the inconsistencies he found in it. And the idea that somewhere or other he accepted Christ as his personal savior at the very end kind of made me retch. I don't believe it. It wasn't who he was. He may very well have believed in God and Jesus and all the rest of that stuff, but he certainly didn't believe it the way Christianity demanded.

Bill never believed in the heaven-hell dichotomy. From his background, I know it was something that haunted him. He talked about it with me and in his material; the two sides of every person – the good side and the bad side. He certainly gave vent to the evil part of himself and the person that was saying all of the negative stuff. He liked to give that guy a voice.

I know he was fascinated by religion. He was. He was interested in all of the feelings he was having and where they were coming from. But he was the antithesis, at least philosophically, of what his parents believed. It's almost like they said "white" so he said "black." He may have rebelled against their traditional beliefs just because they believed in it.

He didn't condemn his parents. It just bothered him that they were at such odds. He was diametrically opposite to his dad. It hurt him deeply, though, that his father condemned him and that his mother went along with his father. Although I know she cared about him and I knew that he knew that, too. He was always very close to his mother, closer to his mother, but it bothered him because I think part of him respected his father, respected parts of his father. Bill was trying his best to be this brilliant comedian and the one person he would have really liked to impress was telling him it was blasphemy. Maybe a part of him thought that, at some point or another, his father might have begrudgingly relented to tell him that he was smart or good or whatever. But he never got that, unless something happened at the very end that none of us knows about.

That Bill stopped talking says a whole lot in and of itself. I think he stopped talking because he gave up. It was days. People were around him, but he just closed down.

I talked to Bill the day before he stopped talking. We had one last conversation. I asked him, "Do you want me to come down?" He was having trouble with pain and he was on oral morphine, which has a lot of nasty side effects including depression. And I thought I could give him some pain-blocking hypnosis. But he didn't want me to come down, which is just as well.

It was a bizarre situation; the whole thing was very odd. I wouldn't have done anybody a service. Certainly not Bill. It was just the very end of his life was the saddest part of it. It was just awful. Everybody was walking on eggs. And I would frequently rant about his father, because I thought it was unforgivable that a parent would be like that. I told Bill how brilliant I thought he was, and I told him that his father was an idiot for not seeing that. A big piece of me had some paternal feelings about Bill and I think he knew that. He also knew what was going on down there would have made me really unhappy, and he also knew that I had a big mouth.

In that same conversation he said, "Please don't come to my funeral. Don't come down for that." I said, "Okay." Then he stopped talking. That was it.

He was a really fun guy to be around, aside from the fact that he was the darkest son of a bitch I ever met in my life. He was happy-go-lucky and easy-going. There was always that dichotomy with him. In all the time I knew him, the depressing periods with him where he was out of sorts were never the kinds of depression that a highly artistic person gets. He was never down on life. When he got sick, that's when he got truly depressed.

But during this period of time when he was well, he got angry. He didn't get depressed like, "I want to die." He would get depressed in the way that would make him upset and he'd get mad. And that's when he was funny. The angrier he got, the funnier he got. And anything

400

would set him off. That's where a lot of the comedy came from.

I remember when he saw the movie *Basic Instinct*. The thing that he did in his act with the lesbian sex scene, that is exactly what he said when he saw the movie. It wasn't like he wrote that. That was exactly what he said walking out of that movie.

The things he did on stage, I saw him develop a lot of those things. The thing I liked about it, I'd be at the bar talking about something bizarre with him, then the next night it was part of his act. And I loved him and hated him for it. I've never seen anybody with that particular ability before or since in my life.

There are comedians who are constantly finding lines: "Oh, I gotta write that down. And I gotta get that into my act." That never happened with Bill. He never thought of clever things that he was going to include in his act in the next night. What happened to him was something would occur to him that was interesting that he wanted to talk about. That was as far as it would go. The next day or the next week, it was ten minutes of comedy. It was amazing to watch that happen. You see it and you appreciate it, but you don't know how the fuck he did it.

Bill was a comedian. That's all he was. And that's what he was about. He was brilliant at it. He was one of those people that was self-taught and it was unbelievable to get to know him and realize he didn't go to college, didn't have a PhD, and had never gone through the academic rigor of taking a thesis and following it to the end. I've never been around anyone with the same kind of academic acumen that Bill had that didn't have the formal training.

I know he wanted to get out of stand-up, but that was what he was designed by the creator to do. And as much as he wanted to get out of it – and, my God, towards the end he hated it – he was just brilliant at it. It was what he was born to do. And as much as he liked working with other people, it's still what he belonged doing, he belonged working by himself. Bill was brilliant when he stood in front of the microphone and opened his mouth and just talked. Live, it was just electric.

[*   *   *]

Ron Shock

I talked to Bill the day before he died. He called me up and he goes, "I'm going to die tomorrow." And I asked him, "How do you know that?" He said, "Sam came to me in a dream."

And it was like Sam possessed me there for a moment. I go off into this rant and I'm doing Kinison talking to Hicks. "You're a pussy, Hicks. All you have to do is step through the veil and you're going to be okay." I'm doing Kinison perfectly, and I can't do other people. And when I get through he goes, "That's exactly what Sam said to me."

"There you go. I'll see you on the other side, Bill."

He said, "Okay. Goodbye."

I got back from the club in Lexington and I got the call. My wife called me and told me Bill died. I said, "Yeah, I know. He told me last night he was going to today. Bill always did what he said he was going to do."

I didn't go to the funeral. I don't do funerals.

[*   *   *]

Mark Wilks

I just happened to call. I called his mom to see how he was doing, and I said that I guess he's got big things going. "Yep, big things," she said.

Fifteen minutes later I get a call. "Wilkie I'm dying come see me." And I thought he was joking. Of course, I'm shaking. I don't believe this. He hadn't told me anything and he had been five years sober.

I get there and he's on the front porch, on one of the wrought-iron chairs. I came up the steps and he started crying, then I started crying. "I thought I'd cried all my tears, Wilkie. I didn't think I had any more left." I wanted to hug him, but his stomach was very swollen. I sat down and his mom left us alone. I had told her that if she let me come over I could make him laugh.

I said something about the pain. And he said it was like no other pain he had felt. It was a numbing, throbbing pain. I said, "Billy, it's so classic."

And he just looks at me and says, "Isn't it, though?"

I told him that I was getting out of LA because I was having problems with coke. In LA my dealer lived just around the corner. Bill asked, "Well, where are you getting this coke?" "Right under my nose," I told him. He thought that was funny. I was being serious.

I tried to quit, and the guy just started doubling the strength, then cut the price in half. So I just got in the car and went to Branson, Missouri. He said, "The next thing you are going to tell me is that you found Jesus."

We had a small hall closet in Houston House. It was his closet and it was so full of books that there wasn't a space where another single one could fit. You would have had to shove it in sideways and slam the door. That was the religious book closet. He had studied every religion known to man and probably some from other planets. He did the entire *Course in Miracles*.

And I'm glad this is all I could come up with at the time. I wanted to be more profound, but I made a mistake and tried to be funny. The only joke I could make was: "Well, you had three careers, you little fucker." And I was referring to his baseball career, his guitar-playing career and his comedy career. He knew what I meant.

I gave up on trying to make him laugh. And I said, "Well, I have found Jesus. That's our brand." He said, "Me too. Me too."

"There are different brands for different people. I think that's the category we fall into. When you're in the foxhole, you've got to name somebody that you're praying to."

He said, "I have, too." I tried to pray, he said, "Pray with me."

It was the only thing I could say to him: "Billy, you just don't know how many people you have touched." He had no idea, and I had no idea that a whole other generation would find him. And maybe that was the best thing we could have prayed because maybe he pondered on that.

He looked at me and he said: "Whoopi fucking Goldberg." And he was bitter.

He didn't have to explain it to me. What he was saying was that they would help her, but they wouldn't help him.

I went to Igby's when he was in town and all of the powerful people were there. He was telling me: "There's Billy Crystal's manager. There's Robin Williams' manager. There's William Morris." The entire room was all power. The room held about 120 and there's about 160 people there. And that's when he was with Jack Mondrus, and none of them would help him. They were all afraid of him because he wasn't for sale. That was his legacy. They were willing to help someone like Whoopi Goldberg, but not someone like Bill.

He sent me after cigarettes and Sprite. I had quit cigarettes for six days. So he sent me after cigarettes, and I came back. I just couldn't say goodbye.

"You know I hate long goodbyes, Wilkie." He said, "I'll always be watching over you." I don't know why he said that.

I asked him: "What about the Houston story?" And he said, "It'll happen, I just won't be there to see it."

And I said, "Yes you will, you just promised me you would be watching over me."

Bill agreed, "I did. I will." Then he told me: "Wilkie, if you don't do anything else, get to be friends with your family. Because at the end of it that's all you've got."

We had this big gathering at a motel in Little Rock. This guy, Steve Moore, was late. And Moore is a clothes hound. He always dressed well. Before he arrived somebody said, and who I can't recall, "Wouldn't it be funny if Bill had somehow arranged that Moore had to show up in his traveling clothes." Lo and behold, he finally shows up and he says, "Guys, I flew on Southwest. I had no connections and they somehow lost my luggage." He had to go to the memorial service in his khaki outback jacket. He kept apologizing for not having his clothes. But it was a premonition.

That night I told the story that Bill and I had prayed together and he had given his life to Jesus. Moore was incensed that I would say that. Huggins comes to my defense and says, "I don't see where that is a stretch."

Most of Bill's friends were still in the realm of thought of "Rebel," capital "R." With all of the religion Bill had studied and all of the comments he made about religion and Christians from the stage, it was disappointing to some. I just figured that there's no atheist in the foxhole. When you are facing it down, you have got to name your God. He had to talk to somebody personal.

He talked about his dream that he was being handed pages of prose to read. He kept having a dream. He didn't say he was on a spaceship. But I don't know if he even mentioned the word "beings." He didn't use the word "aliens." He said, "I have this dream where I'm being handed page after page of prose to read." Then he goes to a psychic and the psychic tells him it's aliens preparing him for a book he's going to write.

I was on a boat, working a cruiseship, and I was trying to get him to take a break. And he wouldn't do it. He wouldn't break work. And I understand now why he wouldn't do it. Maybe he had an internal clock and knew he had a short time.

[* * *]

Andy Huggins

I spoke at the service. I think it was a Tuesday. He died on a Saturday night. So I bet it was on a Tuesday. I don't remember what I said but I remember speaking. A lot of people spoke. It was very nice. I remember putting Bill's casket in the hearse. We went back to some restaurant and told stories for hours and hours and hours. It was nice, quiet, low-key.

But I got in an argument with Steve Moore who expressed himself in what I thought was rather presumptuous skepticism and anger. The minister said during the service that Bill accepted Jesus Christ as his personal savior. Moore's view was: "Well, of course Bill didn't. And the minister was making it up," as a recruitment tip or something. I don't know why but he thought the minister was making it up.

But I have no reason to disbelieve it. I know Bill was very spiritual. And I can't even imagine what you might go through under those circumstances. And what you were taught, what you learned, what made an impression on you when you were a child. You are there with your parents. Who knows how everything comes together. He said he did and I believe him.

I have no reason to doubt it. I find it, if not easy to believe, I can accept that it happened. I have no reason to call a minister a liar. He said it happened.

I think about Bill every day. Every day. For a lot of reasons. For a lot of us he was an important friend. I have a couple of important friends who have died recently and I think about them all. But you don't forget somebody that makes you laugh as much as Bill did.

He was a good friend to a lot of people. And I think a lot of people had the sense that Bill was special and part of me thinks he knew he didn't have very long. He knew he wasn't going to be around very long. But it was something you could silently brag about to yourself, that I was Bill Hicks' friend.

[*   *   *]

Steven Doster

I was in a theater in Telluride Colorado, doing a sound check. The only phone for the stage was an old phone from maybe the Fifties. It rings. Whoever answered it said it was for me. I thought it was my wife calling. "No, it's not your wife. It's a friend and they say it's an emergency." I am panicking because now I think something has happened to my wife or my son.

It was David Cotton. He told me that Bill was dying. "Bullshit." "No, it's true Steve." I did not see it coming. "Where is he?" I asked.

David told me that he was at his parents' house in Little Rock. "But I don't think you'll be able to talk to him. He's getting pretty near the end." I was just in a state of shock. I called the house and got his mom on the phone. She told me Bill was no longer speaking.

So I went and wrote a letter to him and Fed-Exed it there. I told him how much I loved him and respected his integrity. That I want my son to have integrity like that. That I hope Django grows up to be half the man Bill was.

I remember Bill's black leather jacket. He thought it was a terrible thing that a rock 'n' roll guitar player didn't have a black leather jacket. He wore his religiously. Even in the summer, he was the man in black. Bill left me his leather jacket. Some day I will give it to Django.

Steve and his sister would fight over who got to read Bill the letters. So he pointed at my letter, and Steve said after he read my letter, Bill put his thumb up.

Steve told me after Bill went home to Little Rock that he didn't have health insurance but had been used to being successful, but now he didn't have money any more. Bill said something like, "All this time, I spent my life trying to do something that had integrity, well, it looks like the joke was on me." Steve said, "No, you're wrong, Bill." And right at that time the letters started coming in. Shortly after that. Everybody.

When I went to the funeral, Bill's mother came up to me. I introduced myself and I told her my name. She said, "I know you, you're the one with the little boy." I said, "Yeah." His mom was holding herself together well at the funeral. But she said "You're the one with the little boy" and remembered the letter. Then she said, "Bill wanted to have a little boy, just like you [did]," and broke down. She lost it pretty bad.

A lot of these people – Bill's other friends – they were being really judgmental because the minister at the funeral said that Bill accepted Jesus as his personal savior. We had a wake and we split into two different groups. The parents went to one restaurant, Bill's friends, we went to another. It was quite a drag. A lot of these guys were all in this pissing contest and trying to insult each other. It was really annoying to me. We were here paying our respects to Bill, and they were playing this little game. It was pretty nasty.

Most of the people there were going, "That was all bullshit." As if finding Jesus and giving himself to a higher power meant Bill had been weak. Well, who is not going to be thinking that if they are sick and they are dying? Not knowing what's around the corner. Who's not going to want to be risen to the light? And these assholes are going, "That's a bunch of bullshit, he would have never caved in, man."

I found it offensive that they thought it was weakness that would tarnish their image of a strong Bill, a Bill who would stand up to anything. The guy is just a regular person, and I'm sure he was scared to fucking death.

What do you do? You muster up all of the courage you can. Steve Hicks said he thought it was really wonderful how much dignity he had because he got worse and worse and at the very end he deteriorated rapidly. He said that Bill would hold a handkerchief and he would just want to walk. Walk and wipe his mouth because he couldn't really control his mouth and couldn't keep it clean. He wanted to walk. He wanted to be strong.

But I thought it didn't really matter. If they were words said simply to comfort the parents: big deal. I didn't personally take offense to the friends – and a lot of those guys are really great guys – but they were bitching that it was just a bunch of bullshit and putting words into Bill's mouth. I thought, "Well, how do you know? And what does it matter?"

I found that more offensive than what the preacher said.

[*   *   *]

Laurie Mango

He left me till late. He did one of those things with me where he met me while he knew, and didn't say anything. I guess I understand. I was living in New York and we had lunch. He was in town to do *Letterman*, and he had a stand-up performance as well. He just said, I'm in New York, let's get together.

I think a lot about that lunch now, because it's so strange to think retrospectively about it, when you knew someone knew something like that and couldn't tell you. It was very funny, because I had just met the man I ended up marrying, and Bill asked me if I was seeing anyone. And I told him – I'll never forget – I told him that I had met this guy, and I wasn't sure yet, but that he seemed to love me in a very genuine way. And Bill said, "Oh yeah, me too." He was talking about Colleen.

I was very open with him. For some reason, I just completely opened up with Bill. I said, "I'm not sure, I'm not sure if I'm attracted to him," because I was having all these doubts. And he said, "Oh, it's the same with me with this woman. But there's something so wonderful about being loved that way, it's so special."

I hadn't seen him for a while, so it wasn't completely out of context, but they were strangely dramatic questions. Things like: so, what do you think about life now? What's important to you now? Are you happy? What is happiness? It was not completely out of character for Bill, but for having a lunch in New York, it was a little strange. Now it makes sense. We talked about all these big questions. I don't remember how I answered. It's clear in retrospect that it was a goodbye lunch.

I heard that he wasn't telling people about the cancer because he wanted his last months on the planet to be as normal as possible. If he told people, it would just have them acting weird towards him. He didn't want that. Especially because he wanted to be able to perform, too, from what I had heard. And he didn't think he'd be able to in the right way if people knew. I do think that's odd not to tell his friends because it would have given him a much better support network. That's classic Bill to be weird about something like that. I really wish he had told us.

He called my house over Christmas, but he still didn't say anything. He called and left a message saying. "Hey, it's Bill. I can't believe I still remember this phone number." My parents had the same phone number in the same house for over forty years now. He added, "I just wanted to say 'Hi' and wish all the Mangos a Merry Christmas." That was it. That was all he said.

I should have called him then, but I didn't. I just remember thinking, "That's weird that he called." Then he didn't call again and tell us what was going on until mid-February. I called him immediately when I found out.

It was Valentine's Day when we actually connected the first time since that lunch. We talked, and I wanted to come and see him. He discouraged that. He just said he didn't think it would be a good idea, that he would prefer not. He didn't tell me absolutely "No," but I was going to follow whatever his wishes were. I got the sense that it was about privacy and that he was far enough towards the end that he preferred to be by himself.

We were very sentimental with each other. I told him a lot that I loved him and always would. He said the same, and how amazing it was that we had known each other through so many parts of our lives. That really was amazing. Usually you say, "Wow, the person I loved at 15, I would never consider at 25 or 35." You change so much and mature, you change and your interests change. While it was true that our paths diverged in terms of being able to have a relationship together in some ways, in other ways there was a really deep bond that never ever went away. And no matter how much we changed, it never left.

He also talked about getting close to his mother, and how wonderful that was. I thought that was wonderful, too, because he had never been close to his mother. But he talked about how he had bonded with her totally, and she opened up, almost like she was a different person. He got to know her in a way he never ever had before. They talked a lot about God and his views on the book, *A Course in Miracles*.

There was a rumor that after he and I talked, he didn't talk to anyone else. I heard that rumor, but I don't believe that. Maybe he didn't talk to anyone else externally, but not his mother. I'm sure he talked to her.

I really did think we would end up together somehow, Bill and I. When my father told me that Bill had pancreatic cancer – of course, having a medical background, I knew immediately that he was going to die. There was no question in my mind. It was a lethal cancer. It's horrible. No one survives. And even when I heard that his tumor had shrunk and he was going for treatments, I still thought, "No way. He's dying. He's gone. He's just going to die." Anyway, one of the first things I thought after that was, "Oh my God. We won't get married." I had some part of me that had thought eventually we would, that somehow our paths would reconnect again. I saw some of that in New York, we talked and he talked about Coleen – and I don't even know if he used her name – but that he was in a serious relationship with this woman and she was important to him. He might have even told me he was engaged. I don't remember. I think I found out at the funeral. That was something that struck me. "Wow, we won't be together." And "This is a weird ending to the story."

Although as much as it was weird, and it sounds contradictory, in the same way my next thought was, "Yeah, but this is totally like Bill. This is just so like him to completely surprise everyone." Obviously he didn't do it on purpose, but it was just fitting, fitting of his character, fitting of his life. Who would think coming out of suburban Houston in a family like his you would have such a remarkable and creative genius, from a housewife and an automobile executive? It's: "Where did this come from?" In the same way it's: "Where the hell did this death come from?" It just didn't fit. So much of Bill was unique. He broke all molds, all of what is typical in people. He was just constantly surprising.

Of all the people I met in my life, he came the closest to making me believe in reincarnation, because he was so much like some soul that has lived before in different times, and seen other things, and learned, and had different and interesting perspectives. Then it was implanted in this body as a kid in suburban Houston.

It seemed almost alien, just how differently he saw things. And it was inexplicable by what he read or who he grew up with. None of those things could come close to explaining what a special, intellective soul he had. And not all special for the good, it had its real torturous side to it. But I never met anyone like that. He has lived in other worlds and other lives, and it was what drew people to him. "Wow, this is somebody really unique. This is an interesting and different perspective," and it was the source of his comedy. No doubt about it.

It's a tragedy. I think he had a lot more to say. But it's like what my father said. He said that Bill lived more intensely and had a richer life than the vast majority of people ever have on this planet.

[*   *   *]

James Ladmirault (Jimmy Pineapple)

I can only speculate why he kept it a secret, and mainly because, like I said before, Bill and I were soul mates in a lot of ways when it came to comedy and we thought on the same plane. I know for my part I would never want to be known as the cancer comic. And I don't think he didn't trust any of us with it not to get out. I would have never told if he had said not to tell, but once something is out there . . .

A good comic wants to be known by his work, not by anything else, any personal stuff. That was never flatly said, but for some reason I either assumed that or I picked that up.

In any case, I thought he would be okay. You know how it is with cancer now? A lot of people beat it when you catch it early enough. So the tone of the thing was: we're going to beat this. But I had no idea what pancreatic cancer involved. Then it started sinking in when we started talking more.

He was up and down. Some days things were getting better, or there was a new treatment, or there was a recession. Then the next day he would be very down. They say the friends and the family go through the same stages. There was denial. I was in denial for quite a while. I haven't even got over the anger yet, to this day. It was a while before it really stuck to me. Of course I knew when he went back home and didn't want to see anybody that it was serious, that it was grave.

Steve called me. I guess it was about 11 o'clock at night. It wasn't a surprise. I guess it had gotten to be kind of a death-watch and we knew it was coming soon.

Andy and I rode in together, I went through Houston to pick him up. I had met Bill's parents before, and when we got to Little Rock, we went to his parents' home. Mary was extremely, extremely nice to me. She pulled me aside from the rest of the group I was with – I came with a group of comics–and she and I had a nice long talk. It was really pleasant.

We just started talking about Bill. I guess when she pulled me aside, my friends thought, "Oh, this is probably going to start getting heavy," but all they heard was a lot of laughter coming out of the room. I was telling her stories and she would laugh; and she would tell me things about Bill. That I really remember as the most special moment for me: going over memories with his mom.

She told me a story about the Possum Queen. Because Bill used to do this story about her being the Possum Queen in her little hometown parade or festival. A lot of the stuff that Bill was doing about her on stage, Bill didn't realize she knew. And I don't want to get it wrong, but paraphrasing what happened, she just took him by surprise one day and said something like: "Bill, you know I really wasn't the Possum Queen." He was blown away because he didn't even know that she knew about that bit.

When Bill did his mom, it really slayed me. And it was my own personal thing, but I always suspected that Dana Carvey stole Bill's mom when he did the Church Lady because they had the same facial expressions. Not as funny as when Bill did his mom. If it wasn't a rip-off, he must have been channeling Bill.

It's one of the things, when you do a good character like that, even when you know the material, you can watch it over again. Every time I was in the green room when Bill was doing a set, I always made sure I came out to watch Bill when he did his mom.

I was extremely honored that Steve said Bill asked me to be one of the pallbearers and to speak. I kind of choked on the speech. There was so much I wanted to say and do, and all of that. Especially for a comic, it should have been glib and free-flowing. I've never been very good at getting emotions out without punchlines attached to them. If I speak for more than a minute and I don't hear at least two laughs in that time, then I think I'm bombing.

I remember what I wanted to say. There was a quote, but I couldn't find it in time. It ticked me off because it kind of summed up, not my whole life with Bill, but the last couple of years.

The quote was from Thornton Wilder:

"Without your wounds where would your power be? The very angels themselves cannot persuade the wretched and blundering children on Earth as can one human being broken in the wheels of living. In love's service, only the wounded can serve."

When the minister said that Bill had accepted Jesus Christ as his savior, I didn't blink. I remember one of the comics, Steve Moore, he just couldn't get over that. Everybody kind of summed Bill up in their head, especially with all of the shows that he did about religion. Bill had nothing against Christ, Bill had something against the hypocrites who used Christ as the rationale to legislate their morality. We talked about that. He never put it in words, "I accept Christ as my savior." But Bill believed in Jesus Christ.

It was in his comedy also. He wasn't against Christ, he was against hypocrites who use Christianity or any other religion for war, for money, to control people. That's what his problem with religion was. Not Christ or Buddha or anyone who was trying to bring wisdom and peace into the world. Look back at even Bill's earliest stand-up. The questioning was always there. Like any good artist, all of Bill's interests showed up in his work.

The next day they, the family, were taking Bill to Mississippi, or they were leaving for Mississippi. Leakesville. Where the family has a burial plot. Mrs. Hicks invited me along and I told her no, that I wanted to stay with the guys.

This was really vivid to me. The day of the services we went to our motel – and everybody was staying at the same motel, which was kind of fun – and it was a blast. It's kind of hard to imagine everybody being floored like that, then people having so much fun. It was a rollercoaster. Very emotional at the service, then the big release of everybody laughing and having a good time. We had a Bill party at the hotel room.

Andy and I shared a room, and all the guys came by and we just sat around and told stories for I don't know how long. It was a blast.

We just laughed and laughed and laughed. And you could just feel Bill's presence in that room because there was nothing Bill liked more than listening to stories. He'd get mad – not "mad" mad, but a playful-type mad – if there was a story out and he didn't know about it.

[*   *   *]

Kevin Booth

We were driving home – and this was back in our high school days – when we turned down Bill's street and saw a dog squirming in the middle of the road. It was Sam, Bill's dog. We ran out to the dog with Bill saying, "I don't know what to do. I don't know what to do." Dwight and Bill then ran over to Bill's house to get his parents. I tried to pick up the dog. Sam bit my hand. Somehow we got him wrapped in a towel, then put him in the back of my car.

I quickly went to Bill's house, because my wrist was cut open and bleeding profusely from the dog bite. Mary handed me this tiny little Band-aid. And after we rushed him to the vet, Jim lectured me about speeding. To this day I still have the scar right across my wrist from where Sam bit me.

Eventually we got Sam to the vet, but it was too late. They had to put Sam to sleep.

Afterwards, Bill, Dwight and I went to La Hacienda, a Mexican food restaurant. It was the first time the three of us had a conversation about death. Bill was saying, "I should be really sad right now. I feel like there's something wrong with me that I am not sad by this. God, Sam my dog just died this horrible death. I can't tell if I am supposed to be sad or angry, I don't really feel anything. It's just really weird."

It might be the one thing about Bill that never changed that much: not knowing how to feel about death. Maybe that's why he had always adhered to some variant of the notion that there was no such thing as death. It wasn't just convenient, it kept him from having to deal with all of the negative aspects of death and dying. And now looking at his own death, instead of feeling nothing, I think he felt everything: sadness, anger, fear, frustration. But that guy put on the bravest of faces, just about every time I saw him in the last few months of his life.

Not long after Christmas Bill was getting another tumor marker. This was it. This was going to be the miracle. We were all hopeful, and looking back maybe naively so. We wanted to believe so badly, but even at Christmas Bill looked so frail and his stomach was distending. The day of the marker, I never heard from anybody. No news was bad news. If it had come back smaller, the word would have spread to everyone quickly.

The next time Bill and I talked was in mid-January. The subject of the marker never came up. There was a planetary alignment that month, another Harmonic Convergence, he was telling me, and that he wanted to do something together for it, but was too sick.

I stayed in Austin and took mushrooms with my girlfriend Jere. We went for a hike along the Barton Creek greenbelt. No spaceships. No cosmic revelations. It was largely uneventful. The only thing out of the ordinary to happen was that a large owl landed next to me and starting hooting. Looking right at me. Hooting. I came back and talked to Bill later that night. I told him about the owl. He sighed. Very resigned. Like it was bad news. I didn't get it. I talked to David Johndrow later that night and I told him the whole thing. He told me that to many cultures – some Native American and African – the owl was an bad omen, a harbinger of death.

A few days later I was walking on the creekside trail behind my house and another one, a giant barnyard owl, started screeching at me. Then I had another owl incident at the ranch. Bizarre. It kept happening. I didn't tell Bill, but I told David and he kept telling me, "Whoa, dude. That's heavy."

Every February I took a ski trip. In 1994 I was thinking of canceling the plans to go to Red River, New Mexico, and go to Little Rock to see Bill instead. He said no and told me he would much rather me go out and have some kind of adventure than have me visit him. I wasn't going to be doing him any kind of favor seeing him in that condition. He didn't want me to mourn, he wanted me to live.

We had one last phone call right before I left to go skiing. We talked about how we would meet up again. Bill told me that for me it was going to seem like an eternity, but for him it would seem like mere moments had passed. He said, "You are going to be a rich man some day, Kevin." I didn't know how to take it. I didn't question him on it.

He started to cry. He told me that I had been the best friend he ever had. I told him that he was my best friend. Then he said that after he died nothing was going to change. I just know that Bill wanted everybody in his life to continue doing what they were doing. For everyone he had brought together to continue on like a family.

One of the last things he said was, "You know what? I'm probably not going to die. I am just going to sit on my parents' porch and drink spring water for a few years. I will be fine." I laughed. We both cried. That was it. We said our final goodbye.

At Red River, I went on a long climb up in the mountains where I had a vision of a crystal that appeared in front of me. It was an hallucination, but it seemed real. It communicated to me that Bill was going to die, but that nothing was going to change.

I did talk to Bill once more, but he was completely out of it. I don't think anything really registered. And thank God. Colleen and Duncan were in Austin. We called Bill from their hotel. I had been sending Bill anything I could to maybe cheer him up, to make him laugh. So, I sent him a tape of *Joe Arab and the Nazis*, just this horrible music we had done as kids. I said, "Dude you have to listen to it. It's going to kill you." Choking on my heel.

Colleen and Duncan were looking at me like I was this horrible monster. Like I meant to be mean. I don't even consider that our last phone call. He was so sick and so gone. He could barely talk. In fact he soon stopped altogether. Two weeks before he died, Bill went silent. He stopped talking. I think he just didn't want to try any more. He was ready for the transition, it was just going to happen at someone else's choosing.

Jere and I got to Little Rock for the funeral the night before the services. When I got there I looked Mary Hicks in the eyes and said, "Oh my God, I can't believe he is gone." And Mary told me that I needed to accept it, because they, the family, already had. I was kind of taken aback by how dispassionate they seemed. It made me feel like a whiny baby, but I was hurting.

A number of people came by the house that night: his mom and dad, his brother and sister. It was the first time I met his sister Lynn. Several of Bill's aunts and uncles. Dwight was there, a few other friends. Mary offered me some pineapple. I couldn't help but notice the symmetry. The first words she ever said to me were, "Do you want some pineapple, Kevin?"

Several of us were speaking at the services. I was nervous about what to say. I wanted to find the perfect words, but I couldn't write anything down. I literally had a hard time writing. It was comical. I would get a pen from the front desk of the hotel and it wouldn't work. Then I would grab a piece of paper, but set it down on the table right in the middle of a small spill of water. It was one thing after another. I wanted to write the perfect words to say, but something was thwarting my efforts. Something? Bill.

So I did what Bill would do. I closed my eyes, walked up, and let whatever was going to come out of my mouth, come out. I said something like "Mission accomplished." He had done everything he wanted to here on Earth and had moved on somewhere else to do more work.

The big moment of the service, the thing that hit most everyone was the Baptist minister saying that Bill had accepted Jesus as his only savior. You could feel half the crowd turn their heads and coughed in disbelief. I actually went up to the minister afterwards and questioned him about it. He admitted to me that Bill didn't say that he accepted Jesus as his only savior – "only" being the operative word – and that he put that in to comfort the family. Bill did accept Jesus as a savior. He had always accepted Jesus, but he didn't think he needed Jesus as a middle man to God. And Bill wasn't exclusive in offering himself up to a higher power. He accepted Buddha, he accepted Krishna. He accepted everything. He accepted all deities at once.

Personally, I do believe that Bill chose to take the route of his family. It was something to make amends with them before he died, and it was a wound left from his childhood that he needed to heal before he died. And I don't think it was simply to patronize his parents, but to really be a part of something very important to them. I know that Bill was getting incredibly close with his mother during that time. Who knows? We were all in a state of shock, Bill's closest friends were. I'm sure everyone has their own account of what and why. Other people I talk to about the funeral, they tell me that they remember Mary being hysterical and crying. I remember her being amazingly calm.

Steve asked us to be pallbearers, me, Jimmy Pineapple, Andy Huggins and Dwight. I can't recall if Steve himself was one. I just remember picking up the coffin and Jimmy and I looking at each other. We were staring at each other, our fixed gaze saying, "We are carrying the dead body of Bill." There is nothing so real in the world. But at the same time it was like a dream. How did this happen? How come Bill is dead? He was fucking 32. Thirty-fucking-two! The strangest, most beautiful person I ever knew or ever will. And he's dead at 32.

I got back to Austin from the funeral. I was still taking care of Curt. He needed to be taken care of. That didn't stop. That didn't change. It sounds stupid – why wouldn't he still need care? – but it was hard to comprehend. I thought the whole world was going to come to a stop. When someone who changes your life so much passes you expect the whole world to change, or at least everyone to stop and acknowledge that the world is now a completely different place. But no. People just go about their lives like nothing happened. People shop and drive and eat and jog and fill out forms and do whatever it is they always do with their days.

I was driving the old brown Blazer by Seton Hospital near my house. I caught something out of my periphery. I looked over and Bill had appeared, sitting shotgun in my car. He told me that he had done it, that he had pulled off the world's biggest joke. Like it was all a magic trick. He popped into the world, this guy who never really fit in – he didn't even look like he came from his parents – he delivered his message, then, poof! He was gone.

At one point, Colleen went to a psychic who told her that Bill was happy where he was at, even though it wasn't what he had been anticipating it to be. And that the final chapter hadn't been written yet. I also had dreams that he wasn't yet at his final resting place. He was still struggling to get the message of love and hope across. It was just happening in a different place, time and dimension. So when Colleen told me about her reading, it really rang true.

Bill was always moving, always changing. And if things weren't moving and changing around him, he would go nuts. So he wouldn't want to die to go sit somewhere and relax, to sit surrounded by goddesses, fulfilling his every desire, he always had to be moving and working. I just think at 32 he had done everything he needed to say and do here. He's moved on to do it somewhere else. As bad as things seem here sometimes, I just know there's another place that needs him more. And he is doing his work there.

Bill told me he wanted things to stay the same, but to say that the people once closest to Bill, in his absence have not all honored that wish, is putting it mildly. Without getting into detail, things haven't always been friendly. Mary Hicks and I often speak through lawyers and other third-parties to negotiate (although we do sometimes speak personally). The bridge mightn't be that long, but more water has flowed under it than I am proud of. People have said to me: "Bill would be upset to see what was going on with you and his mom." Maybe. Probably. I think he is up somewhere looking at us and screaming at us, "No, you are doing it wrong. This isn't what I wanted." And we all shoulder the responsibility. But Steve once told me that he thought Bill was up there rooting for everyone, and this was even after things had gotten very sour. He intimated that Bill would get a kick out the fact that everyone is still so emotional about it, that everybody cares so much. And that he was up there just rooting for a happy ending, even though the happy ending could take years.

Bill's last Christmas, he gave David Johndrow and me some socks with little mushrooms on them. And he told us that we would always be able to meet in our dreams out at the pond. It wasn't about the corporeal world. It was more about a place in time to focus on, an idea that existed in our head. Our own private Arizona Bay.

[*   *   *]

EPILOGUE

Kevin Booth

Bill talked about going to college a number of times. It was something that was always there – the idea of it at least. For a while he was thinking he would go to Rice University, although honestly he didn't have the grades. Rice was the Harvard of the South (or, as the kids at Rice joked, Harvard was the Rice of the East). He tried going to the University of Houston, but lasted just a few weeks. In December of 1993, just a couple of months before Bill passed away, we went to see a movie that was showing at the Dobie Theater next to the University of Texas. We were walking around campus, and he took a deep inhale: "You smell that smell? That's the smell of academia." He was right. College campuses have their own scent – part-ivy, part-cafeteria food, part-stale beer-stained carpet. We walked quietly for a couple more minutes. Bill broke the silence, "You know, I didn't miss anything by not going to college. I'm really glad. I spent my whole life thinking I needed to regret the fact that I didn't go to college, but I didn't miss anything. To tell you the truth, I feel like I've learned a lot more than most people that come through here; the books I've read, the experiences I've had."

The world was Bill's classroom. When I was with Bill, I felt like he was a teacher in that classroom. He taught me what a joyful place the world can be. Inevitably people find a way to fuck it up, but there are moments where the world is almost too beautiful to take. Most of those moments in my life were moments I shared with Bill. Maybe I didn't even realize it while they were happening, but they are memories I will treasure like nothing else. People say that it was a tragedy for someone so talented to go so young. No. That's wrong. Bill's life wasn't a tragedy, it was a celebration. People spend two or three times as long on this island earth as Bill did and they don't live a fraction of what Bill lived.

I've been accused of riding on Bill's coat tails. That I'm somehow only trying to profit from the memory of my friend. "Get over it, Kevin. Get on with your life." Well, I have got on with my life. I have my own projects. I've produced work for bands and other comedians.

As for profiting from the memory of my friend, put it this way: You spend seventeen years working with someone, and for the first fifteen there's hardly a dime in it. Then the guy dies and people are coming out of the woodwork going, "Can I borrow a recording of such and such. I'm not in it for the money. I just want to spread the word of Bill." The truth of the matter is, I was in this for the money right from the start. We – both Bill and I – we were in it for the money from the start. I mean, yes, more than anything, we did the work we did together for its own sake. We are creative people, and we like making things. But, shit, I wanted to make some money, too. And so did Bill. There's his whole "Those of you in advertising, kill yourselves" bit that Bill did, but it's a slippery slope.

Bill had to eat and drink and drive a car and fly and buy products and pay bills just like anybody else did. He drank Cokes and drove a Jeep. And to think he didn't want his CDs or his videos or anything to be sold is just fucking ridiculous. It's a fine line. It's cool that people want to play prophet for Bill, but entertainment is a fucking vicious industry. And I don't think Bill ever thought, "Hey, I'll be a comedian so that I can be dead fucking broke my whole life. I'll go on the road and do 250 to 300 nights a year so that nobody will ever know who I am." Let's not be naive. Or stupid.

Bill was my best friend. And I am sure there are many other people that make the same claim, who say Bill was their best friend. That's one of the most beautiful things about Bill – that he meant so much to so many of the people he let into his life. Just like friends, we would spend time together doing stuff. Only that stuff often ended in the form of "product." Some guys spend their time sitting on the couch with their friends drinking beer, watching football, and making fart jokes. We told fart jokes too, but most our fucking around and having fun together usually ended up in the form of movies and records and things that people can sell and buy.

When he died, God, Bill was on the cusp. I swear he was. There is no way of knowing what was going to happen. He was on his way in Britain. Things were only going to get bigger and better for him there. At home, he might never have broken through in America, a place that rewards mediocrity, enjoys TV sitcoms, and thinks controversy is a rap record. But the albums Bill made in the last year and a half of his life, *Arizona Bay* and *Rant in E Minor*, shit, a decade after Bill left us, they still sound as if they could have been made yesterday. Even history has conspired – Bush, Iraq – to keep the material headline-fresh. In ten more years, there will be different politicians and different wars, but the jokes, the principles and observations they were based on, they will still play and still make people laugh.

What a gift to leave. Decades after you are gone, you can make people laugh who weren't even born when you left the world. It almost makes me cry to think that he still lives in people's lives that way.

One of the things that Bill said he was going to miss the most after he died was him and me sitting in a place like El Azteca and eating guacamole. Just that feeling of being in a dark and cold, cheap Mexican restaurant, and seeing each other for the first time in a while and catching up on stories. It'd be a way for me to get away from my girlfriend, talk to Bill about her, and him to get away from the rigors and frustrations of comedy and showbiz, and the women in his life. It was just always like this secret meeting place, the nondescript little harmless Mexican restaurant.

Me? I just miss my friend.

INDEX